P9-AFF-327

Windows
XP Networking

Windows
XP Networking

Kackie Cohen

Andrew Daniels

♦♦Addison-Wesley

Boston • San Francisco • New York • Toronto • Montreal
London • Munich • Paris • Madrid
Capetown • Sydney • Tokyo • Singapore • Mexico City

L.C.C. SOUTH CAMPUS LIBRARY

Many of the designations used by manufacturers and sellers to distinguish their products are claimed as trademarks. Where those designations appear in this book, and Addison-Wesley was aware of a trademark claim, the designations have been printed with initial capital letters or in all capitals.

The author and publisher have taken care in the preparation of this book, but make no expressed or implied warranty of any kind and assume no responsibility for errors or omissions. No liability is assumed for incidental or consequential damages in connection with or arising out of the use of the information or programs contained herein.

The publisher offers discounts on this book when ordered in quantity for bulk purchases and special sales. For more information, please contact:

> U.S. Corporate and Government Sales
> (800) 382-3419
> corpsales@pearsontechgroup.com

For sales outside of the U.S., please contact:

> International Sales
> (317) 581-3793
> international@pearsontechgroup.com

Visit Addison-Wesley on the Web: www.awprofessional.com

Library of Congress Cataloging-in-Publication Data

Cohen, Kackie.
  Windows XP networking / Kackie Cohen and Andrew Daniels.
    p. cm.
  Includes index.
  ISBN 0-321-20563-4 (pbk. : alk. paper)
  1. Microsoft Windows (Computer file)   2. Operating systems (Computers)
  3. Computer networks.   I. Daniels, Andrew.   II. Title.

  QA76.76.O63C6416 2004
  005.4'46--dc22

                                                2004012579

Copyright © 2005 by Pearson Education, Inc.

All rights reserved. No part of this publication may be reproduced, stored in a retrieval system, or transmitted, in any form, or by any means, electronic, mechanical, photocopying, recording, or otherwise, without the prior consent of the publisher. Printed in the United States of America. Published simultaneously in Canada.

For information on obtaining permission for use of material from this work, please submit a written request to:

> Pearson Education, Inc.
> Rights and Contracts Department
> 75 Arlington Street, Suite 300
> Boston, MA 02116
> Fax: (617) 848-7047

ISBN: 0321205634
Text printed on recycled paper
1 2 3 4 5 6 7 8 9 10—CRS—0807060504
First printing, July 2004

QA
76.76
.O63
C6416
2005

JAN 1 2 2006

Kackie Cohen's Dedications

In memory of Warren Knight, my friend and telecom collaborator.
His advice, ideas, and opinions on every topic
from technology to BBQ were priceless.
And for Cory, my favorite, who hung on so long,
but finally had to leave me shortly after I finished writing this book.
She was the best dog in the world.

Andrew Daniels' Dedications

Let me begin by saying without my close friends,
my sanity would have been lost long ago,
but would have been especially at risk through the writing of this book.
I would like to thank some including John Watson,
Paige Mandera, Matt and Patty Brailey,
Ramon Poblet, and Evelyn Freeland.

Contents

Preface

Welcome to *Windows XP Networking.* This book was written to help you understand and configure Windows XP networking in a variety of environments—from the home office to larger networks with stringent security requirements. Windows XP has many exciting new features that can be easily integrated into new or existing networks. After you have discovered what those features are and what they do, this book will guide you in the configuration of those features.

Who This Book Is For

Windows XP Networking is for administrators of small, medium, and large networks who will find this book to be helpful in the planning and implementation of Windows XP networking. The reader is assumed to have some knowledge of TCP/IP, Windows NT domains, and the Active Directory, but the authors have made every effort to ensure that the information that is presented is of value to both newer administrators as well as the more experienced administrator.

What's In This Book

Windows XP Networking covers a range of topics. The first few chapters in the book introduce local area network protocol configuration, with a special emphasis on TCP/IP configuration, the default Windows XP protocol. Heterogeneous networking, including services for UNIX, are covered in this section as well. Network bridging is also discussed. The next section expands the TCP/IP networking concepts of the LAN to the Internet. The Internet Connection Firewall and Internet Connection Sharing are discussed in great detail, from operation details and best practices to step-by-step configuration instructions.

In addition, this book provides information on wireless networking, including new features in Windows XP, such as Universal Plug and Play support and the configuration of wireless networking.

Later chapters cover security, from general information and a basic overview of network security to specific recommendations and best practices for networks with Windows XP computers. Chapters on system hardening, access control, authentication, authorization, and virtual private networking are included.

While access to the Internet is widely available, not every user has 24/7 high-speed access. This book presents information about other networking services available to mobile or remote users, including dial-up networking and remote access services. In addition, coverage of IP telephony and Quality of Service is provided to assist the administrator when making decisions about how to take advantage of the built-in capabilities of Windows XP in these areas. And last but not least the appendix presents information about network diagnostics, remote assistance, utilities, service packs, and command line tools to help the administrator troubleshoot networking problems and quickly restore service to their end users.

How To Use This Book

Administrators with less experience will find it helpful to read the chapters in sequential order. Each chapter builds on the information in the preceding chapter to provide a total picture. More experienced administrators might prefer to use the table of contents and index to target the specific topics that interest them. Alternatively, administrators may want to approach this book by scanning the chapters to get an overview of what each one covers and then go back to chapters of interest for a more detailed look. The appendix is designed as a reference tool, and is meant to be scanned in exactly this manner.

Acknowledgments

Hey Drew—this was a fun project. I'm glad you were willing to work on it with me. Now it's Maui time!

Thanks to the technical reviewers whose advice and comments made this a better book: Sean Grimaldi, Jeffrey Hicks, Cristof Falk, James Edelen, Doug Ellis, and Chris Crane.

The biggest thanks of all go to Connie Leavitt and her team at Bookwrights, who took our manuscript and turned it into a work of art.

To my fantastic family and marvelous friends. You are all fabulous and quite deserving of awards and cash prizes. I'm sure you are very proud of me (and now the rest of the world knows why you are deserving of such loot). So no one's feelings are hurt, I've listed you in no particular order, but believe me, you are all tied for number one in my book. Kregg, Scott, Melissa, Mom and Dad, Tim, Cory, Dillon, Grammie and Bumpaw, Bob and Joan, Karen W., Tyler W., Mari W., Terri W, Raquel G., Betty N., Tricia T., Jerry H., John A., Lynn and Martin, Greg C., Gary and Harriette C., Melissa's Mom and Dad and Brother, Kenny R., Mike "Mr. Wall Street" E., Tony B., Yang C., Turbo, Ruckus, Wailea, Cary, Audrey, Doris, Kregg's Mom and Brother, Aunt Linda and Uncle Dennis, Dr. Salzman, Chuck A., Norm and Susan, John M., Matt S., Dave T., Beth H., Albert V., Marc W., Ran L., Steve B., Steve M., Rob T., Hans A., Tim B., Dori and Stephen and Baby Usner, Tim K., Cousin Chris, Brian N., Bob T. and Family, Jim W., The Whole CXN Gang, Woosh_good_friends, NSIPS Buddies, Judith D., the great folks at the AOC, and everyone else in my world—past, present, and future. You are all magnificence personified—thank you thank you thank you!

—*Kackie Cohen*

I feel I have a lot of good friends, all of whom were helpful to me during this effort. The ones who were aware of the stress I was under and who either intentionally or unintentionally helped me include Shelby Burt, Duane Nascimento, Vince Hoang, Jeff Graham, Karl Mueller, Melody Yoon, Jill Luster, Karin Anderson, and everyone else who was there to support and in some cases defend me. Thanks to all those folks on IRC and on Mirkwood who also were supportive. I would also like to thank my friends and co-workers at Oracle.

I'd also like to thank Kackie, with whom I wrote this book. While my sanity was challenged throughout the project, you know it wasn't because of you, Kackie. Without you, this project would have never survived, and because of you this project will have good memories.

I also would like to thank our reviewers (I refer you to Kackie's acknowledgments for the names), all of whom had a lot of work on their hands. Without them this book couldn't have been possible. I also would like to thank Elizabeth Zdunich, one of our editors, for putting up with my frayed nerves.

—Andrew Daniels

Chapter

1

Overview of XP Networking Enhancements

This chapter provides an overview of the enhancements made in Windows networking with the release of Windows XP. These new features, as well as handling of existing network functionality, are covered in greater detail in the remainder of the book. For now, let's start with a look at what's new in Windows XP.

Network Setup Wizard

Microsoft has made ease of use, which leads to higher user productivity, a priority in its products and many of the enhancements in networking are a result of this philosophy. One such user-friendly update is Windows XP's Network Setup Wizard, shown in Figure 1.1. This Wizard makes it easy to configure networking on computers running Windows 98, Windows 98 Second Edition, Windows Millennium Edition, and Windows XP. The Network Setup Wizard can be run from the local hard drive or a CD or floppy disk. This Wizard enables the user to quickly and easily configure a shared Internet connection and enable the Internet Connection Firewall (ICF) on the network "master" host, configure the network adapters, and combine multiple network connections via Network Bridging if so desired. The Wizard does not work on computers running Windows 95, Windows NT, or Windows 2000, but these operating systems can be manually configured to participate in a multiprotocol network with Windows XP.

Figure 1.1 The Network Setup Wizard

Network Diagnostics Features

Windows XP provides Network Diagnostics Tools to assist with diagnosis and repair of networking problems. Network Diagnostics runs a variety of tests that can be divided into Test, Ping, and Show categories. These tests utilize built-in command-line tools you may already be familiar with, and automates them so that you do not have to determine which utility to use and which addresses, adapters, switches, and so on to type in at a command line. This is also a boon to users who are not experienced administrators and are neither aware of what utilities are available nor how to use them. The results output can be saved and printed.

The following items are included in the tool.

Network Diagnostics Web Page and NetSh Helper

The Network Diagnostics Web Page makes it possible to quickly discover useful information relating to the network. The information presented by these automated tests includes computer and operating system information and hardware and network configuration information gathered from the registry. The Web page also provides solutions for different network troubleshooting problems. The information can also be gathered manually, but this Web page automates that process, combines all the data, and then presents it to the user as a single integrated report. This is much easier both for users calling in for remote support and the help desk or administrative staff providing assistance. The process is quicker and easier for the user to understand and information can be communicated back to the help desk more clearly. The reports can even be saved, printed, or e-mailed for support, eliminating transposed characters or skipped details. Note that some screens, such as Help and Support, might be different from the screen shots shown here. Some OEMs (original equipment manufacturers), like Dell, have highly customized versions of Windows XP, including a customized Help and Support screen within the Network Diagnostics Web page. Note the OEM logo in Figure 1.2.

The Network Diagnostics Web page can be started from the Network Connections folder, the Tools section of Help and Support, or the Help and

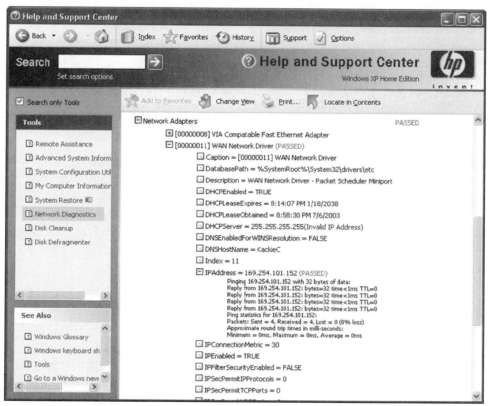

Figure 1.2 Network Diagnostics features output

Support detailed information section. A NetSh command line tool can be used to conduct more extensive tests than the Web page, but the tests are not as easy for the average user to perform. The NetSh helper is accessed from the "diag" context of NetSh and has a wide range of parameters used to gather networking information.

Network Connections Support Tab

A Support tab is now included in the Status page for each network connection in the Network Connections folder, shown in Figure 1.3. This addition to the network connection status page is very helpful in solving network-related issues. The same information can also be gleaned from the command-line utility

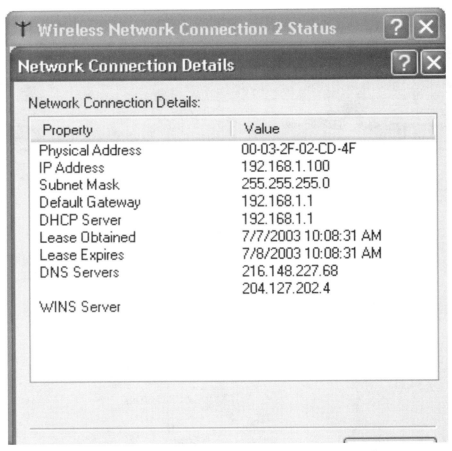

Figure 1.3   IP configuration information provided by the
Network Connections Support tab

ipconfig, but again, for ease of use by the average user, the speed with which the detail is presented, and the compact presentation, this is really a positive feature.

Information provided by the Network Connections Support tab includes the following configuration details:

- **Address Type:** In any of the configurations below:
  - Assigned by DHCP (Dynamic Host Configuration Protocol)
  - Manually Configured
    - Automatic Private IP Addressing (APIPA) (169.255.x.x)
  - Invalid IP Address (0.0.0.0) because of:
    - IP address conflict
    - DHCP unavailable and APIPA disabled
- **IP Address:** Manual or assigned by DHCP
- **Subnet Mask:** Manual or assigned by DHCP
- **Default Gateway:** Manual or assigned by DHCP

By clicking the Details tab, shown in Figure 1.4, you can view more detailed information about the network adapter information, including

- Physical Address
- IP Address
- Subnet Mask
- Default Gateways
- DHCP Server. DHCP Servers assign, or lease, an IP address assignment to computers configured as DHCP clients.
- DHCP Lease Obtained
- DHCP Lease Expires
- DNS (Domain Name Service) Servers. DNS is used for domain name-to-IP address name resolution.
- WINS (Windows Internet Naming Service) Servers. Some Windows networks, especially those networks using Windows NT 4.0 domains, utilize this name resolution mechanism for NetBIOS name-to-IP address name resolution.

Network Connection Repair Link

The Network Connection Repair tool runs a series of six configuration repair steps that are typically used when initially identifying and isolating a networking

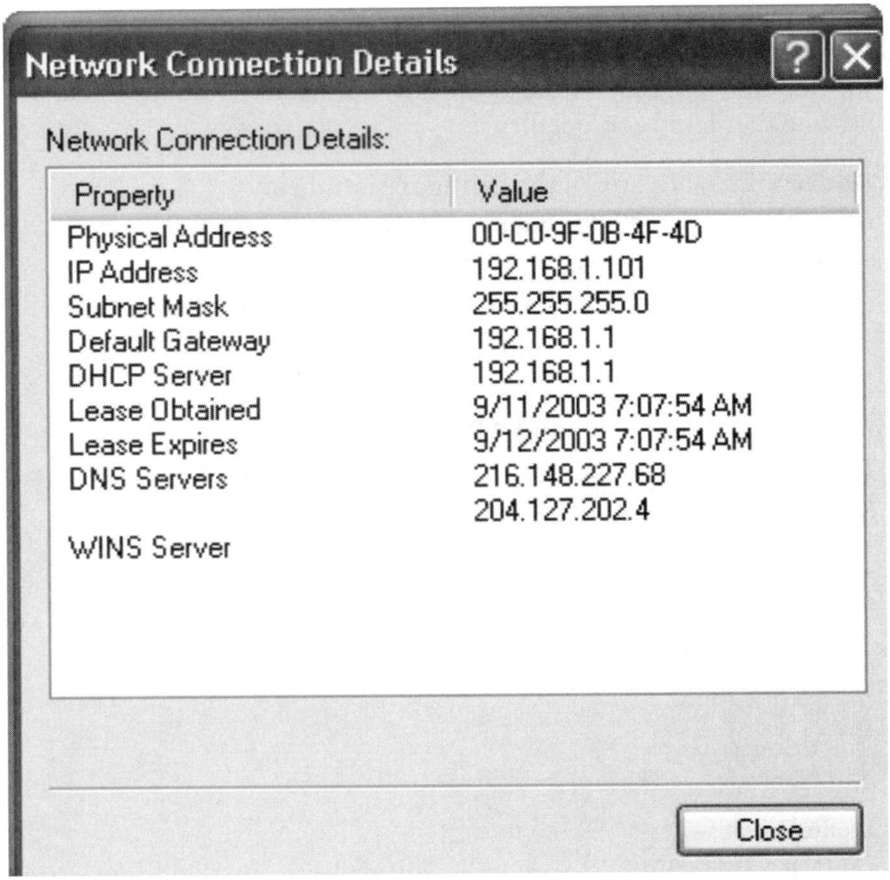

Figure 1.4   Advanced configuration information is available on the Details tab.

problem. All these steps have been automated in a single task, which makes troubleshooting networking problems easier and less time consuming. This tool is extremely helpful when the network configuration gets into a critical situation that does not allow network communication and when a quick resolution is required. The troubleshooting steps performed by the Repair Link are:

- Broadcast DHCP Lease Renew
- Flush ARP cache
- Nbtstat –R
- Nbtstat –RR
- Flush DNS cache
- Register DNS name

Task Manager Network Tab

Another great feature is the Task Manager Networking tab shown in Figure 1.5. This tab is similar to the Performance tab you may already be familiar with. It displays each network adapter installed on the machine and the fraction of network utilization by each NIC (Network Interface Card).

The Networking tab provides a wide range of information to the user. This information includes how the data gathered should be presented to the user and

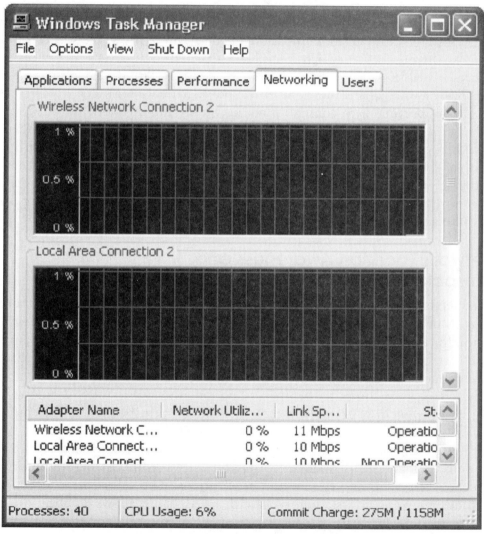

Figure 1.5   The Networking tab in Task Manager shows utilization by each NIC in a computer.

what information should be gathered. The Networking tab can display 26 different types of networking information, which is very helpful for trouble-shooting network slowdowns.

Universal Plug and Play Client Support

Universal Plug and Play (UPnP) brings the ease of plug-and-play hardware installation to the world of networking. However, UPnP goes far beyond just making installing a network a simple process. UPnP is a standard that applies to all types of network devices to make them work "automatically" when connected to a network. This means that when a UPnP device is connected to a network through any UPnP-compatible media, wired or wireless, the device searches the network to which it has been attached to discover the services and devices available. As these discoveries are made, the UPnP device self-configures to provide a totally hands-free out-of-the-box experience for users.

By supporting zero-configuration networks and network autodiscovery, UPnP enables data communication between any two UPnP-compliant devices regardless of operating system, development platform, or hardware. UPnP devices can enter and leave a network with no configuration on the part of the user or the network administrator. This makes services like wireless network access in airports and coffee shops and downloading digital photos from a FireWire digital camera possible.

Network Location Awareness and Winsock API Enhancements

The Network Location Awareness feature in Windows XP is a treat for mobile users. Moving a laptop between networks, and subsequently reconfiguring the laptop for each location, is not everyone's favorite task. Previously, if your laptop used a static IP address at your home office and your corporate headquarters used dynamically assigned addresses, you had to manually reconfigure and possibly reboot your computer before settling down to work. With Windows XP you simply plug in your network cable and the operating system will attempt to detect and reconfigure the laptop for the correct current environment.

The Network Location Awareness service handles the system-level tasks of detecting and subsequently conveying network infrastructure information between operating system and applications. The information it collects includes network connection type and speed. This allows applications to swiftly become aware of changes in the network environment and to respond dynamically. Network-aware applications can detect network connections on a given host and adapt to that host's connectivity. This service supports Internet

Connection Sharing and the Internet Connection Firewall that are part of Windows XP.

Wireless LAN Enhancements

One of the most exciting features for mobile users of Windows XP is enhanced support for 802.11b wireless networking. Zero-configuration and roaming enhancements in Windows XP make Wi-Fi (IEEE 802.11b) more secure and super easy to use. The most valuable enhancement in Windows XP is the way that it instinctively handles 802.11b wireless LAN connectivity. This is very helpful when using public wireless networks such as those in airports, hotels, and cafés. It is possible to seamlessly move from network to network without any user intervention, except where the Wi-Fi network operator has required manual credential presentation.

Windows XP automatically recognizes most wireless NICs, although some vendors' hardware will require installation and configuration via the vendor's software. Once the NIC is installed, it will attempt to self-configure and subsequently detects and presents a list of available wireless networks to join (see Figure 1.6). Some wireless NICs behave better than others in this regard, so be sure to buy Windows XP–certified hardware to get the best performance and ease of use.

In the absence of a wireless hub in the network, Windows XP can configure the wireless adapter to use ad-hoc networking. Ad-hoc networking is also known as peer-to-peer networking.

Wireless Roaming Support

This feature of Windows XP allows you move between wireless networks by detecting the availability of a network and self-configuring accordingly. Wireless Local Area Networks or WLANs use radio frequencies to send and receive data, rather than traditional cables. Media sense capability is generally used to control the configuration of the network card and informs the user when the network is available or if it becomes unavailable. Media sense refers to the ability of the card to detect the presence of a network conduit, such as a CAT5 cable or a wireless network infrastructure. Forced authentication when moving to a new wireless access point adds another level of security to wireless networks. If you are in an area with several wireless LANs, you may be particularly pleased to find that you can configure a list of preferred WLANs to join. All installed wireless NICs automatically connect to those in the order specified, preventing you from wasting time hooking up to WLANs where you do not have an account, such as in an airport where two or more wireless service providers have set up service.

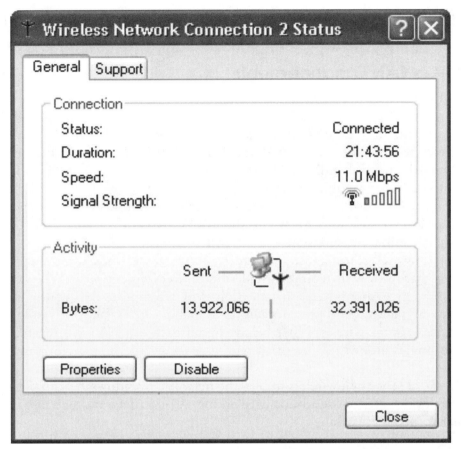

Figure 1.6   A wireless NIC's status sheet

Internet Connection Firewall

Windows XP also includes a firewall: the Internet Connection Firewall. The Network Setup Wizard can be used to set up ICF. This enables users who are security conscious, but are unfamiliar with firewalls, to easily protect their network resources. While it is not a substitute for more advanced firewalls that run on dedicated hardware or powerful multipurpose servers, it is ideal for small or home offices. No extra hardware or software is required beyond just what is required to run Windows XP. It is possible to configure advanced settings on the Internet Connection Firewall if so desired. Users who want to configure specific filters or other settings can do so this way.

ICF supports logging of dropped packets and successful connections. In the case of dropped packets, all denied packets would be logged. This will create a record of all packets that are denied transit from either side of the firewall. Administrators can use ICF's ability to log successful connections to track any connections permitted through the firewall, including in- and outbound connections, as shown in Figure 1.7. These logs maybe helpful to skilled administrator-types for troubleshooting connectivity problems as well as determining if a security incident has happened or is under way.

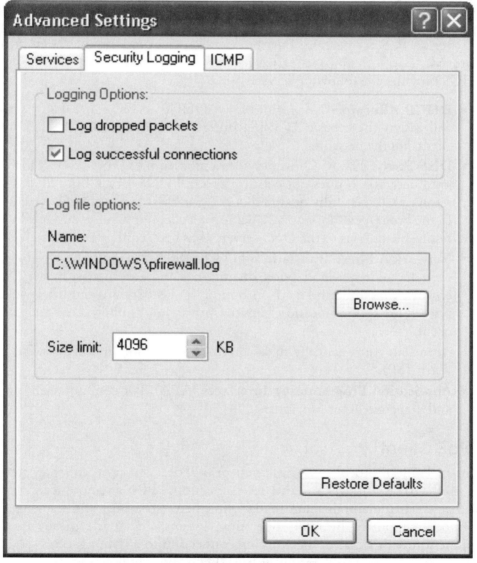

Figure 1.7   Logging within Internet Connection Firewall

Internet Connection Sharing Enhancements

Internet Connection Sharing (ICS) is not new to Windows. ICS has allowed users to share a single Internet connection since Windows 98. However, it has been enhanced with Universal Plug and Play support. This upgrade eliminates some of the issues related to network address translation (NAT) and specific applications that were not successfully NAT'ed out of a network using ICS. NAT is used to translate private IP addresses assigned within some LANS to public IP addresses used on the Internet. There are still a number of applications, particularly Internet gaming applications, that do not function well over an ICS connection, but the overall user experience has been greatly improved.

ICS provides the following services:

- **DHCP Allocator:** Not a full-blown DHCP server, this DHCP service will assign these basic TCP/IP configuration parameters to all DHCP clients on the network.
- **DNS Proxy:** The ICS host provides a modicum of DNS services for your local network. It does not perform as a full DNS server, but rather it will resolve FQDNs (fully qualified domain names) for local network clients. In the event it cannot resolve a name for a client, it will forward locally unresolvable queries to the DNS server it has been configured to use.
- **Network Address Translation:** NAT provides a mapping service to associate IP addresses and ports on internal and external addresses. NAT ensures that inbound and outbound IP headers are modified appropriately so communication between private and public IP addresses can occur.
- **Autodial:** Automatically dials connections to your Internet Service Provider (ISP).
- **Application Programming Interfaces (APIs):** For configuration, status, and dial control for programs.

PPPoE Client

Point-to-Point Protocol over Ethernet, or PPPoE, is a protocol that permits PPP traffic to be sent over an Ethernet connection. PPP is a remote access protocol that creates, maintains, and ends a link between a host and a client. It is a protocol supported by many operating systems, and it is typically used in conjunction with a dial-up networking connection to a remote access server or to an ISP. With the proliferation of broadband Internet access, however, many

ISPs were scrambling to find a way to integrate Ethernet traffic from broadband customers into their dial-up-service-based authentication infrastructure. PPPoE addresses this problem by combining the two protocols. It is a win-win solution for users and ISPs. Users only need to know how to set up a standard dial-up networking connection to their ISP from their PC or their Internet connection sharing device, and ISPs can continue using existing RADIUS (Remote Authentication Dial In User Service) servers for authentication of all types of customers. RADIUS servers are used by ISPs to handle authentication, authorization, and accounting for user accounts.

PPPoE connections are configured with the New Connection Wizard in Windows XP. The user simply selects PPPoE from the list of options presented, as shown in Figure 1.8.

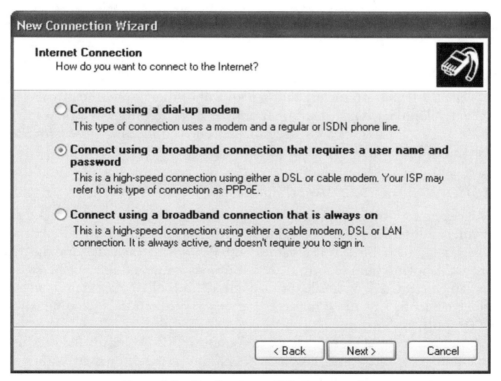

Figure 1.8 Configuring a PPPoE connection

IPv6 Development Stack

Internet Protocol version 6, or IPv6, is the next version of the Internet Protocol. It is intended to eventually replace the current version of IP in use (IPv4). It is sometimes referred to as IPng, for Internet Protocol Next Generation. IPv4 is over 20 years old and has performed well, but it was not designed or initially deployed to support such widespread use as it does today. The most important problem associated with IPv4 is the lack of extensibility of addressing. The dearth of unique IP addresses stands in sharp contrast to the ever-growing number of devices that require unique IP address to access the Internet or other network resources. A number of private addressing schemes and sub-netting methods are available to alleviate some of these problems, but it is truly a matter of time before a completely new version of IP is needed to address all problems associated with IPv4, including routing issues and network auto-configuration.

Windows XP supports IPv6 by providing an IPv6 stack. IPv6 will not become the dominant IP protocol in the near future. Indeed, IPv4 and IPv6 are expected to coexist for a number of years, and as a result IPv6 must interoperate with IPv4 successfully. Microsoft has provided the IPv6 stack in Windows XP to assist with application development and testing so that when IPv6 does become the principal IP version the migration path will be much smoother. In addition to the development stack, three IPv6 utilities have been included in Windows XP: Ipv6.exe, Ping6.exe, and Tracert6.exe. These utilities are used for troubleshooting and connection verification.

Credential Management

Credentials are the username and password combinations used to access network or Internet resources. Windows XP provides an advanced credential management tool: Stored Usernames and Passwords reached from the User Account's applet within Control Panel or from a command line. These credentials can be created dynamically or manually. This tool, or "key ring," can store various credentials required for accessing network resources, including Microsoft Passport, as shown in Figure 1.9.

In addition to Microsoft Passport, Windows XP Professional stores username and password pairs as well as the X.509 certificates used with smart cards. Windows XP Home only stores dial-up networking, Virtual Private Network (VPN), and Passport credentials.

When a user attempts to access a resource that requires a credential set for authentication and authorization, such as a file on a server in an untrusted

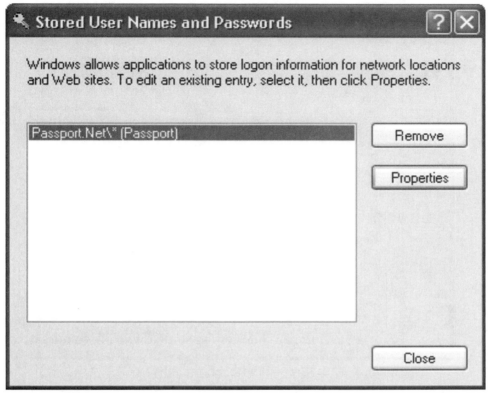

Figure 1.9   Storing a Passport within a user account on Windows XP

domain, a dialog box will pop up prompting for the correct credential pair. Figure 1.10 shows a prompt for a credential pair for an Internet resource.

If the credentials for this particular resource have been stored with the user account, however, this information will be transparently provided to the remote server, requiring no intervention from the user.

Connection Manager

Connection Manager is a preconfigurable client dialer included in Windows XP Professional that contains all parameters and settings required to connect a computer to a particular remote service. Connection Manager provides these preconfigured connections for remote users to access an ISP, a Virtual Private Network, a private remote access server, or some other remote resource. Its features and benefits are much more advanced than the basic Windows XP dial-up networking options. Connection Manager dialers cannot be configured within

Figure 1.10   Credentials for an Internet resource

Windows XP, however. This requires the Connection Manager Administration Kit, part of Windows 2000 Server, which allows the administrator to preconfigure and distribute remote connection information for these remote services to users easily. Windows 2000 uses Connection Manager 1.2, while Windows XP ships with Connection Manager 1.3 components. Unless you specifically configure a Connection Manager profile to use version 1.2 components, however, Windows XP will use version 1.3

A number of improvements and enhancements have been made in version 1.3, including

- Support for multiple simultaneous instances of Connection Manager service profiles
- Connection logging
- User selection of VPN servers
- Support for terminal windows
- Better support for ISDN (Integrated Services Digital Network)
- Automatic route addition

- Split tunneling
- Connection settings favorites list
- Automatic callback for dropped connections

Network Bridging Support

Another feature of Windows XP is its ability to join multiple network segments without a separate hardware device. Network bridging provides this functionality. Only one network bridge can be configured on a given computer, but there is no limit on the number of bridges that can be installed in any given network. The number of segments that can be joined by a single bridge is only constrained by the number of network connections a computer can accommodate. The Windows XP Network Bridge uses both Layer 2 and Layer 3 bridging.

In Ethernet networks, only one device may transmit data over the network media in a given network segment or collision domain. A computer that wants to transmit data "listens" to verify the network is not in use before sending its data. It is possible for two or more devices to transmit simultaneously because they detected no activity on the network at that time. The data that is transmitted collides and is usually corrupted. This results in a need to retransmit the data. The more devices there are on the network, the greater the potential for collisions.

Bridges isolate each network segment, thereby isolating collision domains, while treating the network as a single logical network at the same time. This is accomplished by forwarding and filtering traffic based on source and destination networks. Layer 2 bridging is based on MAC (Media Access Control) or physical computer addresses, while Layer 3 bridging uses IP address for forwarding and filtering. Bridges can also be used to connect networks of different media types, such as FireWire and CAT5 Ethernet

An example of a bridge being used in a network is shown in Figure 1.11.

IEEE 1394

IEEE 1394 is a standard for connecting various devices to a PC. The connection will transmit data at 400Mb/s! It is true plug and play—IEEE does not require a driver to be installed. The standard goes by a number of monikers, including FireWire (Apple's term) and I.Link (Sony's term). It is typically used to connect digital cameras or external storage devices to a PC via a cable. Once installed, the device will typically appear as a drive on the local computer, and data can be dragged and dropped between PC and device.

Figure 1.11 A Network Bridge joins two or more physical networks into a single logical network.

In addition to connecting audio and video equipment, you can use IEEE 1394 to network computers together. Simply join two IEEE 1394–capable PCs running Windows XP via an IEEE 1394 cable and you are all set. Windows XP will assign an IP address to the IEEE 1394 interface on both computers, which can then be reached just like any other network resource (browsing, UNC name, etc.). By setting up a Network Bridge on one of the two computers, the other computer is reachable by all other computers in the network as well. Figure 1.11 demonstrates this type of configuration.

Quality of Service Enhancements in Windows XP

Under normal circumstances, network traffic is sent on a best-effort delivery basis. This is not a problem for many applications, but for some applications it spells big trouble. For example, when real-time audio or video transmissions suffer from latency and packet loss, the result is sound that cuts out or a jittery picture. Quality of Service (QoS) is used to prioritize network traffic to avoid this type of problem. It is analogous to an emergency vehicle having the right-of-way on a congested highway during rush hour: Everyone else must allow the ambulance/police car/fire truck to pass them by.

QoS is not a single mechanism, but rather a bundle of techniques for ensuring that the higher-priority applications get the appropriate amount of bandwidth. One method is to modify the size of the adjustment of TCP/IP parameters. Another is using a round-robin scheme to allocate and service data flows for application data. The QoS Packet Schedule service handles these functions. The packet scheduler marks each packet with a priority, and then schedules delivery based on the priority of the packets. QoS within Windows XP also provides the necessary objects required for performance monitoring.

HomePNA

Microsoft has designed Windows XP to be the best Windows platform for home networking. In addition to the ease of use and zero-configuration features, it also supports many alternative networking systems, including Home PNA. HomePNA uses existing telephone cabling to provide the network infrastructure for a network. All that a user needs is a HomePNA-compatible NIC and a phone jack. The jack serves as the network port for up to 50 devices within 500 feet of each other, at speeds of up to 10Mb/s. The phone line can simultaneously carry HomePNA Ethernet traffic and voice/fax services with no degradation of either service.

HomePNA has been around since 1998. It is an industrial collaborative effort, with 150 companies such as Microsoft, Xilinx, Linksys, and Hewlett-Packard developing the standards and specifications for the technology. HomePNA-certified products must adhere to the standards developed by this group.

IP Telephony

IP telephony is the integration of voice, video, and data into a single network and application or suite of applications. These applications replace conventional mechanisms for communication, such as telephones or television broadcasts, with computers and the appropriate communication device for that application. Data from the applications is packeted and the resulting data stream is sent over an IP connection to another computer. The receiving computer reconstructs the data stream and the user is able to collaborate in real time with the other user. Media types include audio, video, and conferencing applications.

Windows XP supports three IP telephony methods:

- Session Initiation Protocol (SIP)
- H.323 protocol
- IP multicast conferencing

IrDA Provides an IrCOMM Modem Driver

IrDA is an industry standard for using infrared waves to transmit data. The acronym itself is taken from the name of the group that brought about the standard: the Infrared Data Association. IrDA sends data wirelessly between devices, such as printers and computers or between PDAs, at speeds between 9,600b/s up to 4Mb/s. The devices must typically be within one meter of each other and a clear line of sight available between them.

IrDA has been supported in various versions of Windows, going back to Windows 95. Windows XP offers even better support for IrDA (except for 64-bit Windows XP, which does not support IrDA) than Windows 2000. You may experience a few glitches with IrDA applications written for Windows 95, Windows 98, or Windows Me, but upgrading a driver or other software to an XP-supported version (if the manufacturer has made one available) should correct any problems.

A number of protocols exist within IrDA, and Windows XP supports four of them, including

- **IrComm:** Enables you to use your IrDA cellular phone for dial-up networking.
- **IrNet:** Provides peer-to-peer networking capabilities between two or more IrDA-enabled computers.
- **IrTran-P:** Enables you to transfer digital images, such as photos, from camera to PC.
- **IrLPT:** Allows you to send print jobs directly to your printer without any cables.

With IrComm modem support now native to Windows XP, you can use your IrDA mobile phone with an IrDA-enabled PC to create a dial-up networking connection. Simply create a dial-up connection with the IrDA port on the computer, place the phone near the IrDA port on the PC, and tell Windows XP to dial that connection.

TAPI 3.1 and TAPI Service Providers

Telephony Application Programming Interface (TAPI) is a set of APIs that allows Windows applications to share telephony devices with each other. APIs provide access points for developers to create custom software that utilize various features of another piece of software or operating system. Windows XP uses TAPI version 3.1 and TAPI 2.1 to provide backward compatibility with older versions of Windows.

TAPI provides the telephony infrastructure for all communications and connection-related functions between a computer and telephony network. This includes Public Switched Telephone Network (PSTN) call control functions such as managing the interface between the computer and the phone line to ensure that calls are dialed or answered, conducted, and ended in the appropriate manner. TAPI also provides the same types of communications management services for ISDN, PBX, and IP telephony.

TAPI uses service providers to enable communication between TAPI-compliant applications and TAPI hardware. A TAPI service provider can be thought of as essentially a driver. There are two TAPI service providers in TAPI 3.1: Telephony and Media. Telephony service providers (TSPs) handle the interaction between the telephone network and the modem or other hardware device that connects a computer to the telephone network. Media stream providers (MSPs) provide the link to the actual content a connection is sending.

Real-Time Communication Client APIs

Windows XP also includes Real-Time Communication (RTC) Client APIs, providing a strong platform for SIP-enabled services, including a familiar contact list interface, PC-to-PC voice and video calls, instant messaging, collaborative whiteboarding, and application sharing. Session Initiation Protocol, provides a means for deploying advanced telephony and real time media services across the Internet. SIP is an ASCII-based signaling protocol for setting up connections for various types of telephony applications, such as conferencing, that require real-time connections. SIP protocol simplifies communication by enabling an individual to be located by a variety of methods, including desktop phone, cell phone, PDA, and e-mail, with a single SIP URL. This is analogous to having a single phone number for home, work, cell phone, and pager, even though there are unique devices at each site. There are a number of third-party vendors that support RTC applications, and one is actually built into Windows XP: Windows Messenger.

Conclusion

As the preceding discussion of new and enhanced features for Microsoft Networking shows, Microsoft has made great advancements in the way of networking ease of use and functionality. From here the book moves into a discussion of the basic components of a Microsoft network, including name-resolution services and account management, as well as configuration and implementation of the networking features of Windows XP. We also discuss networking protocols and heterogeneous networks or networking with non-Microsoft specific networks. Security is an important part of every network, and we cover the foundation of security policies, authentication, authorization, and Windows XP–specific security features.

Other topics included in this book are remote access and dial-up networking and computer-based telephony. We wrap things up with appendices covering troubleshooting and utilities that can help you figure out what needs to be done when your network is not functioning as intended.

2

TCP/IP Overview

In this chapter, we cover six things that are essential information for your in-depth understanding of the purposes and uses of TCP/IP in this book. The first area we discuss is a brief history of TCP/IP as well as a primer that will hopefully bring you up to speed. If you are not already familiar with the necessary information you need to read this chapter carefully.

Next, we spend some time explaining the differences and purposes of IPv4 and IPv6, which are the two versions of IP available on the Internet today. We discuss IEEE 1394, which is a recent, fast IP transportation method, and talk as well about IP filtering.

History and a Primer

Networking, as we all know, is essentially a set of protocols, standards, and "agreements" that computer personnel have made on how one computer will exchange data with another computer. There are two protocols that are in wide use currently. TCP/IP is the one that is the essence of the Internet as we know it today.

TCP/IP stands for Transmission Control Protocol/Internet Protocol which, as the name suggests, are two protocols bound tightly together to form one authoritative communication suite that is used by everything from FTP to Telenet, HTTP to SSH/SCP, and beyond. Without TCP/IP most of the computer industry that we know, would not exist, and most of us, since we are focusing this book on the administrators of larger networks, would be without jobs.

First let's talk about TCP/IP in general. The reason TCP/IP is written the way you see it is that we are dealing with two separate protocols that work in correlation to provide a service. TCP operates at Layer 4 and IP works at Layer 3 (we discuss both shortly). Because they are two separate protocols they are written as TCP "/" IP to avoid confusion.

There are four primary concepts that you need to know to get the most out of this book, and this chapter will be a refresher course for those who have lost some of the fundamentals that are the building blocks of our point-and-click world.

The four building blocks that we discuss in this chapter are the OSI model, encapsulation, windowing, and the TCP/IP handshake.

Let's start with a brief history lesson, and describe where the fundamentals of the protocols came from and essentially who or what brought about their creation. It is very important to note that we have condensed the history, the purpose, and the founding visions into a few short paragraphs and that there will be varying opinions on whether or not our rendition is an accurate account. Therefore, we strongly recommend that you read the related RFCs, seek other accounts of these statements, and understand that there is some level of confusion and overlap present in this era of networking development.

The Internet, and therefore TCP/IP as a protocol family (or a group of protocols)/hybrid, came into being sometime in the very late 1960s and early 1970s, as a project sponsored by the Defense Advanced Research Project Agency (DARPA). While this network, referred to as ARPANET, was probably the first recorded use of technologies that would later become the Internet, the concepts employed here were first envisioned in the early 1960s and were published around 1964–1965. MIT, BBN, Stanford Research Institute (SRI), and RAND Corporation played a huge role in developing the technology behind the networking concepts that were first installed.

Depending on whom you ask, you may get many answers to the question as to what and why DARPA became interested in the Internet. It is commonly held that one of the major project goals was to help ensure a command and control authority in the event of a catastrophic attack against said authority. At the time, the cold war was building up and there was concern that an attack against our military would be against our communications, thereby damaging our ability to respond. The Internet also helped a great deal in emergencies and times of large-scale disasters where not only the military, but also government agencies, were able to communicate with each other.

This command and control was achieved through communication. One hard and fast rule for winning is readily available communication throughout an organization (such as an army or government). The concern of the day, however, was with intercontinental ballistic missiles being able to knock out primary control locations. Orders had to continue to be issued, received, and processed so that in the event that some location was knocked out, the remaining locations could continue to function as one heterogeneous entity. Up until this point it meant picking up a phone and trying to call these diverse locations to authenticate and deliver the necessary orders. Around this time, however, computers were replacing some of the functionality and needed a way to do this much faster and with "fewer moving parts" than existed at the time.

As we said earlier, this is just one brief recap of hundreds of stories and thousands of documents that are available on the subject. There are several great books that you might spend time and money on if you want to know more.

OSI Model

The first concept that we discuss is the Open Systems Interconnection (OSI) Model. The OSI Model was developed in the early 1980s, primarily as a common way for multiple computers to communicate based on a structure they were to follow in packaging information. The OSI Model consists of seven layers, and just like standards in your kitchen (measurements) or your garage (tool diameters), it is a simple way that connectivity can be built into a computer system and taught much like a language.

The OSI Model also makes it easier for us to diagnose problems, and vendors can "bind" their products to a specific layer or set of layers of the model, thus taking advantage of other vendors' work at lower or higher layers without affecting their competitive stance significantly.

Now let's take a quick look at the OSI Model. From there we move on to describe what should happen at each layer, and then give some examples of applications, services, or functionality that occur in each of these layers.

- Application (Layer 7)
- Presentation (Layer 6)
- Session (Layer 5)
- Transport (Layer 4)
- Network (Layer 3)
- Data Link (Layer 2)
- Physical (Layer 1)

Application layer (Layer 7): This layer consists of programs that the user interfaces with and is where the most useful information communication between a user and his or her programs occurs. You find such programs as Telnet, FTP and HTTP at the application layer.

Presentation layer (Layer 6): This layer helps to define how data is presented. By that we mean what basic language the data displays in so it can be "presented" to the application layer. Within the presentation layer, you are likely to find common formats that we all know well, such as ASCII, JPEG, GIF, MPEG, and MIME.

Session layer (Layer 5): At this layer, sessions are established and torn down; the concept of end-to-end communication between two nodes on the network is handled here. Protocols or APIs that you might find here include the SQL Language, NetBIOS, and RPC.

Transport layer (Layer 4): This layer is responsible for sequencing the data and helping to guarantee that it is delivered in the same order in which it is received. It can also do error checking and flow control. This layer also includes Same Order Delivery, that is, it gives each piece of data a number and makes sure that they arrive in the numbered order. This is very important with some applications, such as voice transmissions. Protocols that operate here include TCP, UDP, and NetBEUI.

Network layer (Layer 3): This layer is responsible for quality of service, most routing functionality, and most switching and routing in modern networking. This functionality has become increasingly important in congested networks. The network layer is also responsible for translating logical addresses into physical ones so that the lower layers can interpret the data.

Data link layer (Layer 2): This layer is responsible for providing functional means to transfer data between networks, and to detect and correct errors that may occur on the physical layer. Most hubs and dumb switches operate at this layer, because it provides connectivity among locally attached devices.

Physical layer (Layer 1): All the layers are important, but this layer, just like Layers 3, 4, and 7, has the most visible impact on users because it exists in part to provide the communications medium, and allows communication resources to be shared among multiple users. This layer is also responsible for modulation. In case you are not familiar with modulation, it is encoding the data onto a carrier signal (like playing your CD and getting music).

You now have some information on the layers and how they interrelate. This information is important in our overall discussion of TCP/IP, as well as networking within Windows XP. Layers not only relate to one another, but each layer is also dependant on the next, as you will see in the following information on encapsulation.

Encapsulation

Encapsulation is essentially one layer taking what it has done and then handing it to the next layer, which then "wraps" its efforts around the previous layer's work. This is how the layers can interoperate with each other; yet they never really interact because a specific layer can only know what happens at its own layer and not that of the one above or below it.

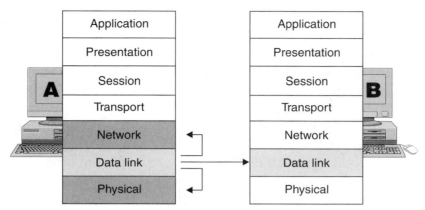

Figure 2.1   An illustration of the OSI Model

As you can see in Figure 2.1, Host A's OSI Model (or Stack) talks only to the layer that matches on Host B's OSI Model (or Stack), thereby not requiring that the layer know what needs to happen above and below, which would make it more challenging and bloated. The data link (Layer 2) from Host A only needs to talk to the data link (Layer 2) from Host B. That is the essence of encapsulation and how the OSI Model works.

TCP Windowing

TCP Windowing is a lot like the regular windows you are familiar with; you have bedroom, living room, kitchen, and bathroom windows. Each window has a different size and each has different uses. In TCP Windowing, the same kind of thing happens. You have different-sized windows for different computers talking to each other. One set of computers may end up being on a slower network and therefore cannot have really large windows, whereas another set of computers can be on a faster network and therefore can handle more data and process it faster.

The reason TCP Windowing is important is not so simple, but let's spend a few minutes trying to appreciate its functionality.

There are two types of size delimiters commonly found in TCP. The first is the Maximum Transmission Unit, or MTU, which is a packet limit that is determined during the setup of the connection-oriented session that is the essence of TCP. The second is the TCP Windowing size, which is typically much larger than the MTU and is meant to be a way for two hosts to communicate how long each should wait before it receives an acknowledgment or ACK (we find out what ACK is in the TCP Handshake discussion that follows).

Typical TCP Window sizes are 8,192 bytes and 24,000 bytes, which means that if you have an MTU of 1,500 and a window size of 8,192 bytes, then you are going to send about 43 packets before you have to see an ACK to the data. This is figured by converting the window size to bits and dividing it by the MTU. Please note that the TCP Window size is advertised in every packet. This allows a computer to intelligently determine if it is receiving too much or not enough data and it can reduce or enlarge the window thus allowing it to process data more slowly or quickly.

The MTU is an agreement. Both computers will agree on a maximum transmission size; but in regard to windowing they do not necessarily have to agree, though they usually do (because it is typically only one of two values). It is very important to realize that this is a simplified explanation of how this whole process works. There are books written specifically on TCP and how it functions and we refer you to those works for a more detailed explanation. For the more scientific reader, this is similar to the sliding window principle.

The next subject we need to spend some time on is the handshake, which is required for the connection-oriented functionality of TCP. Before we can get into that, however, we have to talk about packet makeup and about the separation of TCP from IP. As we mentioned in the beginning of this chapter, TCP and IP are two separate protocols that function together to provide the basis of the Internet. While both protocols are separate and independent, neither can effectively provide the service they do without the unity of the two protocols.

To recognize the value of the unity of two separate, versatile protocols, we need to understand and appreciate their differences. However, we limit our overview of both protocols to IP version 4, also referred to as IPv4. The other version, IP version 6, also referred to as IPv6, is yet to make its mark.

TCP Headers

As previously discussed, TCP/IP is the pairing of two protocols and there are two headers—one for TCP and one for IP. We talk about both, but not to the level of detail that will make you an expert on either, as this chapter is an overview.

TCP headers are probably the less complex of the two, because just as with TCP/IP, the IP protocol works with several other protocols to provide seamless services including ICMP (most ping and trace-route functionality), AH and ESP, and also GRE and L2TP for encryption and authentication. Therefore, we focus on TCP headers first.

The TCP header has five key components. The first four key components are the offset, the reserved bits, the flags (probably the most important), and options. We cover each briefly and then go on to the fifth component, the connection state, which we cover more extensively.

Offset Bits

The offset describes where the data begins in the packet. Packets can be somewhat dynamic, based on the amount of data that can be sent and received, so the receiver needs to know when to stop looking for header information and when to start interpreting the remainder of the packet as data to be pieced back together to be handed up the information chain.

Reserved Bits

The reserved bits are just that, six bits reserved for future use.

Flags

The flags are important and we need to understand them to appreciate the TCP Handshake. The flags are basically like traffic lights: green for go, red for stop, left arrow for turning, and so on. These can sometimes be referred to as control flags because they indicate what should be done with the packet. There are six in total and they are described here.

- **URG:** Urgency of the packet. It indicates that the urgent pointer field is significant.
- **ACK:** Acknowledgment. Essential to a connection-oriented session as well as any TCP Handshake.
- **PSH:** Push. Somewhat like pass in a game where you have nothing to do that turn.
- **RST:** Reset. Another important flag for the handshake, indicating the session is over. This is the flag sent to reset the talker and receiver and lets them both know that the connection has ended and that they should reset, which can be normal or abnormal.
- **SYN:** Synchronize sequence numbers. Each TCP/IP packet has a sequence number, which is based on many factors, including the operating system type, and is random. Therefore, both the sender and receiver need to know this value, because a connection-oriented session needs to be aware of the packet received before the current one and the one that follows it.

- **FIN:** Finish. There will be no more data from the sender. This is somewhat like the RST flag, but is more gradual, and allows the connection to close slowly and more gracefully. You typically see things such as FIN-WAIT-1 and FIN-WAIT-2 in your Netstat output that is related to this flag.

Options

This is where you find information about padding and timestamps, and not a whole lot more.

Connection State

There are a number of states that a connection can be in. To understand the next bit about handshaking, you need to know these states and what they mean. Technically speaking, there are ten states that a session can be in.

- **LISTENING:** This state represents a connection that is waiting for a request from any remote Transmission Control Block (TCB) or port.
- **SYN-SENT:** This state represents a talker waiting for the matching connection request to arrive from the receiver.
- **SYN-RECEIVED:** Just the opposite of SYN-SENT, in which the receiver is waiting for the talker to acknowledge the receipt of the connection request.
- **ESTABLISHED:** This is an open connection in which data is presumably being sent and received. The normal state of the connection is established.
- **FIN-WAIT-1:** As described above in the FIN flag, this is a representation of a connection termination request from the remote host. It could also be an acknowledgment of the request previously sent.
- **FIN-WAIT-2:** Same as above; just another opportunistic delay, in case the first WAIT failed to produce the result requested or required.
- **CLOSE-WAIT:** Represents waiting for the connection termination request acknowledgment from the remote host.
- **LAST-ACK:** Not normally seen, this represents waiting for an acknowledgment of the connection termination request that was previously sent to the remote host. This would include an acknowledgment of its own termination request.
- **TIME-WAIT:** This is an attempt to wait long enough to be sure that the remote host has had enough time to pass on any final information including the acknowledgment of the termination request.

- **CLOSED:** Represents no connection state at all. This is a theoretical state, in that this should never be represented anywhere but on paper since the lack of a state means there is no connection and no connection means there is not any need to represent.

States progress from one to another in response to events that are initiated by the user. This is similar to FTP. When you want to FTP to somewhere you OPEN a connection, then you SEND your login data, then you RECEIVE a response, and finally after transferring data you CLOSE the session. You can have an abnormal ABORT, and you can also request STATUS.

Let's talk about the Netstat command, and then we'll show you the state of several connection states.

```
C:\Documents and Settings\Andrew Daniels>netstat/?
Displays protocol statistics and current TCP/IP network
connections.

NETSTAT [-a] [-e] [-n] [-o] [-p proto] [-r] [-s] [interval]

  -a            Displays all connections and listening ports.
  -e            Displays Ethernet statistics. This may be combined
                with the -s option.
  -n            Displays addresses and port numbers in numerical
                form.
  -o            Displays the owning process ID associated with
                each connection.
  -p proto      Shows connections for the protocol specified by
                proto; proto may be any of: TCP, UDP, TCPv6, or
                UDPv6. If used with the -s option to display
                per-protocol statistics, proto may be any of: IP,
                IPv6, ICMP, ICMPv6, TCP, TCPv6, UDP, or UDPv6.
  -r            Displays the routing table.
  -s            Displays per-protocol statistics. By default,
                statistics are shown for IP, IPv6, ICMP, ICMPv6,
                TCP, TCPv6, UDP, and UDPv6; the -p option may be
                used to specify a subset of the default.
  interval      Redisplays selected statistics, pausing interval
                seconds between each display. Press CTRL+C to stop
                redisplaying statistics. If omitted, netstat will
                print the current configuration information once.
```

Here are those examples for the connection states: there are several not displayed here, but some are very difficult to capture because they do not last very long in the output window.

```
C:\Documents and Settings\Andrew Daniels>netstat -an

Active Connections

Proto  Local Address          Foreign Address        State
TCP    0.0.0.0:135            0.0.0.0:0              LISTENING
TCP    0.0.0.0:445            0.0.0.0:0              LISTENING
TCP    0.0.0.0:5000           0.0.0.0:0              LISTENING
TCP    0.0.0.0:5679           0.0.0.0:0              LISTENING
TCP    0.0.0.0:6331           0.0.0.0:0              LISTENING
TCP    0.0.0.0:8755           0.0.0.0:0              LISTENING
TCP    0.0.0.0:8765           0.0.0.0:0              LISTENING
TCP    127.0.0.1:3003         0.0.0.0:0              LISTENING
TCP    127.0.0.1:3013         0.0.0.0:0              LISTENING
TCP    127.0.0.1:3066         127.0.0.1:8755         TIME_WAIT
TCP    127.0.0.1:3192         127.0.0.1:8755         CLOSE_WAIT
TCP    127.0.0.1:3200         127.0.0.1:8755         CLOSE_WAIT
TCP    192.168.100.210:139    0.0.0.0:0              LISTENING
TCP    192.168.100.210:3010   204.149.130.71:6346    TIME_WAIT
TCP    192.168.100.210:3014   193.49.161.205:80      CLOSE_WAIT
TCP    192.168.100.210:3032   220.49.43.191:6346     TIME_WAIT
TCP    192.168.100.210:3033   63.166.98.176:6346     TIME_WAIT
TCP    192.168.100.210:3047   24.136.148.225:24417   FIN_WAIT_2
TCP    192.168.100.210:3052   68.18.12.247:6346      TIME_WAIT
TCP    192.168.100.210:3056   24.233.119.184:6346    TIME_WAIT
TCP    192.168.100.210:3069   208.119.195.25:6346    SYN_SENT
TCP    192.168.100.210:3071   68.18.108.93:6346      SYN_SENT
TCP    192.168.100.210:3073   69.12.103.21:6346      TIME_WAIT
TCP    192.168.100.210:3074   65.166.159.179:6346    SYN_SENT
TCP    192.168.100.210:3075   24.42.188.224:6346     TIME_WAIT
TCP    192.168.100.210:3076   67.17.24.36:6346       SYN_SENT
TCP    192.168.100.210:3077   206.68.172.136:6346    TIME_WAIT
TCP    192.168.100.210:3078   64.58.27.10:20490      ESTABLISHED
TCP    192.168.100.210:3079   63.78.35.75:6346       SYN_SENT
TCP    192.168.100.210:3080   192.168.100.209:445    ESTABLISHED
TCP    192.168.100.210:3081   12.213.73.153:9427     ESTABLISHED
TCP    192.168.100.210:3082   68.114.241.244:6346    SYN_SENT
TCP    192.168.100.210:3083   61.63.159.179:6346     SYN_SENT
TCP    192.168.100.210:3418   192.168.101.101:445    ESTABLISHED
TCP    192.168.100.210:3619   226.116.233.138:5050   ESTABLISHED
TCP    192.168.100.210:3621   204.146.106.57:1863    ESTABLISHED
TCP    192.168.100.210:3622   164.112.31.24:5190     ESTABLISHED
TCP    192.168.100.210:3625   164.112.201.2:5190     ESTABLISHED
TCP    192.168.100.210:3824   166.20.2.164:80        ESTABLISHED
TCP    192.168.100.210:4525   168.115.158.85:6346    ESTABLISHED
TCP    192.168.100.210:4638   192.168.100.209:5631   ESTABLISHED
TCP    192.168.100.210:4728   63.102.146.133:6346    ESTABLISHED
TCP    192.168.100.210:4831   62.205.146.53:6346     TIME_WAIT
```

```
TCP    192.168.100.210:4859    21.116.148.225:24417    TIME_WAIT
TCP    192.168.100.210:4906    21.116.148.225:24417    TIME_WAIT
TCP    192.168.100.210:4928    211.214.59.192:22       ESTABLISHED
TCP    192.168.100.210:4938    63.152.198.16:80        CLOSE_WAIT
TCP    192.168.100.210:4947    212.146.186.10:6346     TIME_WAIT
TCP    192.168.100.210:4950    163.132.139.17:6346     TIME_WAIT
TCP    192.168.100.210:4951    124.16.148.225:24417    TIME_WAIT
TCP    192.168.100.210:4954    167.110.89.153:4874     ESTABLISHED
TCP    192.168.100.210:4962    110.149.43.191:6346     TIME_WAIT
TCP    192.168.100.210:4963    168.33.26.249:6346      TIME_WAIT
TCP    192.168.100.210:4966    124.19.67.5:6346        TIME_WAIT
TCP    192.168.100.210:4969    107.37.51.40:6346       TIME_WAIT
TCP    192.168.100.210:4996    124.26.148.225:24417    FIN_WAIT_2
UDP    0.0.0.0:135             *:*
UDP    0.0.0.0:445             *:*
UDP    0.0.0.0:500             *:*
UDP    0.0.0.0:1028            *:*
UDP    0.0.0.0:3007            *:*
UDP    0.0.0.0:3020            *:*
UDP    0.0.0.0:3617            *:*
UDP    0.0.0.0:4621            *:*
UDP    0.0.0.0:4637            *:*
UDP    0.0.0.0:5467            *:*
UDP    127.0.0.1:123           *:*
UDP    127.0.0.1:1900          *:*
UDP    127.0.0.1:3686          *:*
UDP    127.0.0.1:4537          *:*
UDP    127.0.0.1:4902          *:*
UDP    192.168.100.210:123     *:*
UDP    192.168.100.210:137     *:*
UDP    192.168.100.210:138     *:*
UDP    192.168.100.210:1900    *:*
```

TCP/IP Handshake

As we described earlier, TCP being connection-oriented requires that the talker and the receiver know a lot about what is being said. This includes some initial introductory messages.

The typical TCP Handshake begins with a SYN packet. Once received, the receiver copies the original SYN packet and includes an ACK packet; and finally, when the sender receives the SYN-ACK, it sends an ACK of the SYN-ACK. When this is done data begins to flow, and based on the window size ACK packets come about fairly often in a predetermined fashion. When the data portion is finally done (the web page has loaded, you have transferred the file), then the connection is closed with a FIN-ACK or a RST-ACK, which informs the receiver that the sender is finished and wants to close the connection. All of this

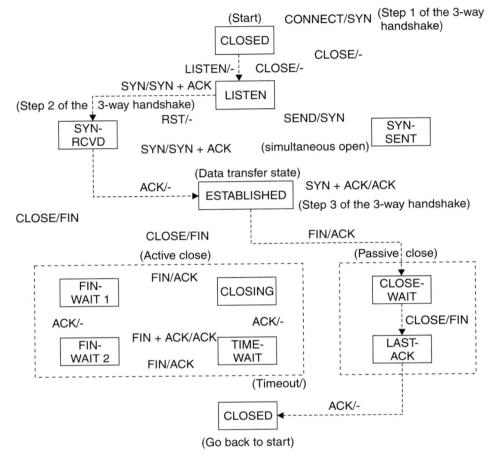

Figure 2.2 Flowchart diagram of TCP connection including handshake

can happen in a fraction of a second, or if the data is overwhelming, can take days under certain circumstances. Figure 2.2 is a flowchart diagram of TCP connection including handshake.

IPv6

As mentioned in the history and primer of the OSI Model, and subsequently in the TCP/IP protocol suite as a whole, one part of this process is addressing. When originally devised, addresses were plentiful and no one imagined that additional addresses would be necessary.

A quick history lesson might be useful here. IP addressing, as we know it now (IPv4), first came about 20 years ago. IPv4 addressing is based on a 32-bit value and will allow for roughly four billion addresses. Because every device on the planet that wants to talk to another device will probably need an IP address, four billion is unlikely to be enough in the long run.

There has also been substantial misuse in organizations where IP addresses are wasted unnecessarily. Many organizations have started to realize this waste and are using features in the original protocol like nonroutable addressing (RFC 1918). However, as more devices become enabled and more individuals become connected, obviously these tactics alone will eventually fail to meet growing needs.

IPv6, like IPv4, is based on a value. In IPv4 the value was 32 and in IPv6 the value is 128 bits, which takes the possible addresses available from about four billion to 340 trillion.

Both IPv4 and IPv6 are available within Windows XP, as they were in Windows 2000. This book cannot really provide you with reasoning, or help you to make your case for using either form of addressing. Whichever best meets the needs of your organization and your upstream providers should be determined outside of this reading.

Installing IPv6 is extremely simple in Windows XP, but before doing so, you should make sure that IPv6 is not already installed. From our information and testing, it appears that it may be, by default. To check or test from a command prompt, type `ipv6` and if you receive information about parameters in return, it is already installed.

If you do not get a response that provides options, then you may need to install it, which you can do from the same command prompt. Do this by simply typing `ipv6 install`. If you would like to do it from within the Windows XP GUI, the process is a bit more complicated, but still very quick to implement.

For the IPv6 protocol for the Windows XP with SP1, you can also do the following:

- Log on to the computer with a user account that has privileges to change network configuration.
- Click **Start**, click **Control Panel**, and then double-click **Network Connections**.
- Right-click any local area connection, and then click **Properties**.
- Click **Install**.
- In the Select Network Component Type dialog box, click **Protocol**, and then click **Add**.
- In the Select Network Protocol dialog box, click **Microsoft IPv6 Developer Edition**, and then click **OK**.
- Click **Close** to save changes to your network connection.

- To use Remote Procedure Call (RPC) applications over IPv6, you must first restart the computer.

Some additional reasons to consider the use of IPv6 include better support for QoS and the fact that IPv6 has built-in support for security.

To help with debugging, Microsoft has updated Ping for IPv6 addressing, and we have included a brief summary provided by Microsoft to help use this tool.

The IPv6 Protocol for Windows XP includes the Ping6.exe tool, an equivalent to the Ping.exe tool supplied with TCP/IP in Windows XP. Ping6.exe sends ICMPv6 Echo Request messages to the specified destination and displays round trip time statistics on the corresponding Echo Reply messages. Here is the Ping6.exe syntax:

```
ping6 [-t] [-a] [-n count] [-l size] [-w timeout] [-s
srcaddr] -r {name| dest[%scopeID]}
```

The **-t** option pings the specified host until interrupted.

The **-a** option resolves addresses to host names.

The **-n** *count* option specifies the number of echo requests to send.

The **-l** *size* option specifies the send buffer size.

The **-w** *timeout* option specifies the time-out, in milliseconds, to wait for each reply.

The **-s** *srcaddr* option specifies the source address for the Echo Requests. The -s option can be used for pinging a multicast address.

The **-r** option specifies that a routing header be used to test the reverse route.

The **name** option specifies the destination name.

The **dest** option specifies the destination address.

The **scopeID** option specifies the scope or zone of the destination for Echo Request messages.

For link-local addresses, the scope identifier (ID) is typically equal to the interface index, as displayed in the output of the ipv6 if command. For site-local addresses, the scope ID is equal to the site number, as displayed in the output of the ipv6 if command. If multiple sites are not being used, a scope ID for site-local addresses is not required. The scope ID is not required when the destination is a global address.

For example, to send Echo Request messages to the link-local address fe80::260:97ff: fe02:6ea5 using scope ID 4 (the interface index of an installed Ethernet adapter), use the following command:

```
ping6 fe80::260:97ff:fe02:6ea5%4
```

IEEE 1394

IEEE 1394, first known as *FireWire,* is a serial technology that in a local area network has proved to be an inexpensive, fast alternative to Ethernet. Prior to FireWire, choices in the consumer mainstream market were 10Mb and 100Mb Ethernet with 100Mb being the most expensive. However, because IEEE 1394 was designed for high-speed data transfer, it performs as a cheap alternative at nearly 400Mb/s. The original benefit of this technology was its high bandwidth and low cost. Today it is still a good small office alternative to Ethernet even though the cost associated with faster than 100Mb has come down significantly.

IP Filtering

TCP/IP filtering is the practice of specifying exactly what types of incoming traffic will be processed for the destination interface (yours). This feature is designed to isolate traffic that is being processed from Internet and Intranet clients in the absence of better protections, or as additional protections beyond your firewall or other filtering services such as proxies.

This filtering can occur on any interface that is receiving nontransit TCP/IP traffic (that means traffic that is destined for the local host). Some rules for processing include

- The destination TCP port matches the list of TCP ports. By default, all TCP ports are permitted.
- The destination UDP port matches the list of UDP ports. By default, all UDP ports are permitted.
- The IP protocol matches the list of IP protocols. By default, all IP protocols are permitted.
- It is an ICMP packet.

To configure TCP/IP filtering:

- In Control Panel (default view), click **Network and Internet Connections**.
- Click **Network Connections**.
- In Network Connections, right-click the local area connection you want to modify, and then click **Properties**.
- On the **General** tab, click **Internet Protocol (TCP/IP)** in the list of components, and then click **Properties**.
- Click **Advanced**.
- Click the **Options** tab, click **TCP/IP Filtering**, and then click **Properties**.

- In the **TCP/IP Filtering** dialog box, select the **Enable TCP/IP Filtering** check box and then add the numbers of all TCP and UDP ports and all IP protocols for which you want filtering enabled.
- Click **OK**.

TCP/IP filtering can be enabled and disabled for all adapters by selecting a single check box. This helps troubleshoot connectivity problems that might be related to filtering. Filters that are too restrictive might unnecessarily limit connectivity options. For example, if you decide to allow only specific types of UDP traffic and do not include RIP (UDP port 520), then the RIP Listener service does not function.

Chapter

3

WINS, DNS, and DHCP

In this chapter, we talk briefly about auxiliary services around Windows networking. These services have been around for a long time and have not changed a great deal in Windows XP; therefore, this chapter briefly covers basic configuration, troubleshooting, and any tips and tricks that we believe will help you gain better control over your enterprise.

We first talk about the history of each service. Then we cover installation and configuration, including screenshots, to walk you through the process step-by-step. And finally, we help you troubleshoot problems with the installation or configuration and provide you the tips that we have found most useful to us.

All of these technologies are important because at some level they are the glue that provides a common "word based" naming convention for workstations and servers on your network.

WINS Basics

Windows Internet Naming Service (WINS) is essentially the same thing as DNS. It just provides a different naming functionality. In DNS you are mapping an IP address that is sometimes harder to remember to a more familiar hostname, whereas with WINS you are mapping NetBIOS names to IP addresses so you need to remember just the more familiar "short name."

With the release of Windows 2000, Microsoft made significant enhancements to WINS. These improvements were suggested in some part by network managers, like you, who were using the product.

With the release of Windows XP, however, Microsoft decided to depreciate WINS. There are many reasons why Microsoft might have made this decision, but we think the primary reasons center around their concentration on Active Directory and the framework previously known as .NET. Between these two technologies and the fact that WINS is always used by Microsoft exclusively, depreciating it made some sense. Regardless of the depreciation, there are a lot of environments that will still use and depend on WINS; therefore, we go through how to configure it on the client.

WINS Configuration

To begin the WINS configuration on the client you need to open the Network Property tab where your interfaces are listed. You can do this in many different ways, but the two easiest ways (in our opinion, of course) are either through the Start menu or by right-clicking on **My Network Places** on your desktop, if you have enabled it to appear on your desktop. We do it from the Start menu, as shown in Figure 3.1, so that there are not any missing steps.

Now we to need to select the **Local Area Connection**, at which point we should see the graphic appear on our screen as shown in Figure 3.2.

From here we need to click on **Properties** and the image displayed is shown in Figure 3.3.

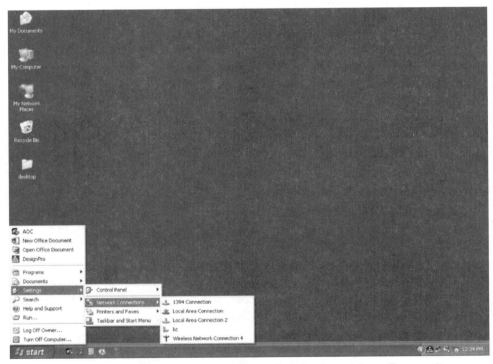

Figure 3.1   Locating the Network Property tab - Local Area Connection

Figure 3.2   Local Area Connection Status

Figure 3.3   Local Area Connection Properties

We need to highlight the **Internet Protocol (TCP/IP)** as shown in Figure 3.4, which is where the properties are found. Now we want to click on **Properties** directly under and to the right of Internet Protocol (TCP/IP).

We now need to click on the **Advanced...** button in the lower right corner, as indicated in Figure 3.5.

From here we need to click on the **WINS** tab in the upper menu bar between DNS and Options, which will present the dialog as it appears in Figure 3.6.

Now here is where the real configuration can be found. The first section deals with identifying your WINS servers, so be careful to put them in the order in which you want them queried. It is not recommended that you have more than two or three WINS servers unless the network connection in front of the WINS server (not in front of your client) is unstable and unreliable.

The second area deals with the LMHOSTS file shown in Figure 3.7. This is the file that defines local machine hosts that you know statically. You can speed up access to it without the computer having to look them up. This also saves the penalty in memory from not having to cache these lookups.

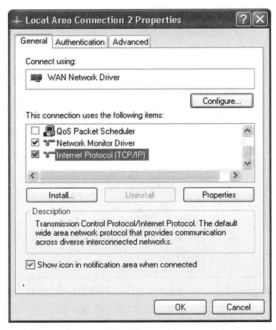

Figure 3.4 Local Area Connection Properties—selecting TCP/IP Properties

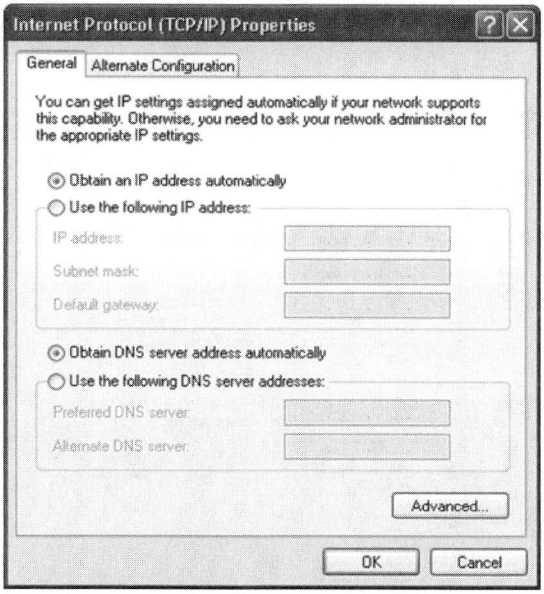

Figure 3.5   General Properties—TCP/IP settings

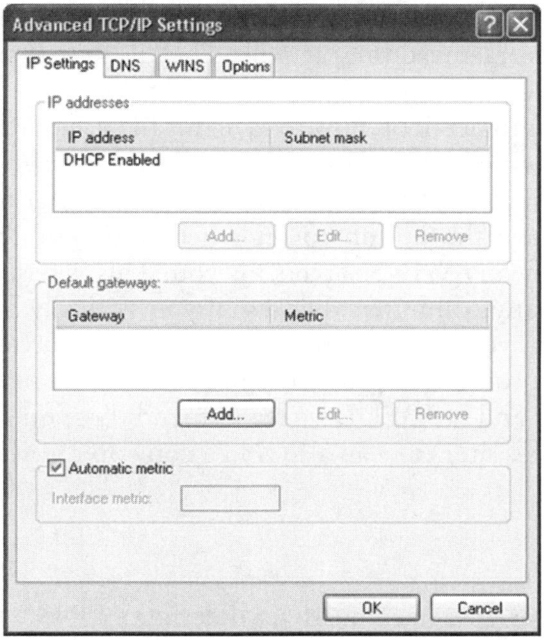

Figure 3.6   Local Area Connection Properties—Advanced settings

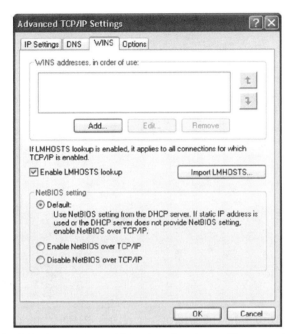

Figure 3.7   Windows Internet Naming Service settings and properties

With Windows 2000 and beyond this file is read dynamically, therefore you should have no problem adding at will. The file has example properties, is located in C:\<ROOT>\System32\Drivers\etc, and is called LMHOSTS.

We do not go into detail on how to save this file using notepad, but typically when storing files with a .txt extension in notepad you just need to "quote" your filename when saving with the proper extension or association.

Finally, you have the option to set whether or not the DHCP retrieval process can identify any WINS servers for you. This is best in an environment where you have many computers, because if you statically assign this value and then change it later, you will need to manually modify each and every machine.

That is about it for WINS properties in XP. For more information about the future of NetBIOS and NetBEUI, we recommend that you search for those keywords on Microsoft's site. You can also find a copy on the Windows XP installation CD-ROM.

DNS

The history of DNS goes back nearly two decades. DNS was the first of many "friendly" name-to-computer logical naming programs that came about, widely used in both Windows products as well as UNIX and even some other environments. It has become the de facto standard for friendly name-to-IP address mapping.

Unlike WINS, DNS is a long way from going away, because not only does it have a basis in making the naming of machines much easier, it is also necessary for domain infrastructure that we are all familiar with, such as .com, .net and .org.

There are many popular DNS servers out there, from free GNU/Public Domain versions to proprietary versions such as Microsoft and others. All the servers work in a similar fashion, but because this is a Windows book, we go over how to configure it on a Windows client. Since we are talking exclusively about Windows XP Professional and not Windows 2003 Server, we do not go over the server configuration bits because they are not available in XP Professional or Home editions, and both can only be clients to existing servers.

Once you have configured the server side and have it working to your satisfaction, you need to configure the client. You have two options in identifying your DNS servers: the first is to manually specify, the second is to have the DHCP server provide them. Obviously in a large environment it is highly recommended that you obtain your DNS servers from the DHCP server, but there are reasons why you might want to manually configure, including limiting the amount of work the DNS server has to do.

With Windows XP configuring, DNS is very similar to the images shown earlier in this chapter. Specifically we follow the steps we used from Figure 3.1 through Figure 3.6 and then we differ from the WINS discussion. However, we also have an opportunity to discuss DNS on Figure 3.5 duplicated now as Figure 3.8. As shown in Figure 3.8, you can set your two DNS servers and choose whether or not to use DHCP instead of manually configuring. As you probably already know, you cannot do both; therefore if you choose DHCP assigned, the actual manual configuration area will gray out and be unavailable to you.

You also have an option to do much more configuration by clicking on the **Advanced. . .** tab. You will see the same image we saw in Figure 3.6, which is reproduced in Figure 3.9. Along the same tab line (near the top) where you found the WINS configuration you find the **DNS** tab, so let's click there now.

You can set your DNS search order and add more than two DNS servers if you set it manually. You can also decide how DNS is used on this workstation, including determining what suffix will be applied to each request for DNS information. Toward the bottom of Figure 3.10 you see that you also have the ability to tie this information back into the DNS server if it supports dynamic updates. This is useful if your workstation has a fairly dynamic address and services that others may try and connect to. A static address does not need to use the dynamic features; just enter the static entry in your DNS table.

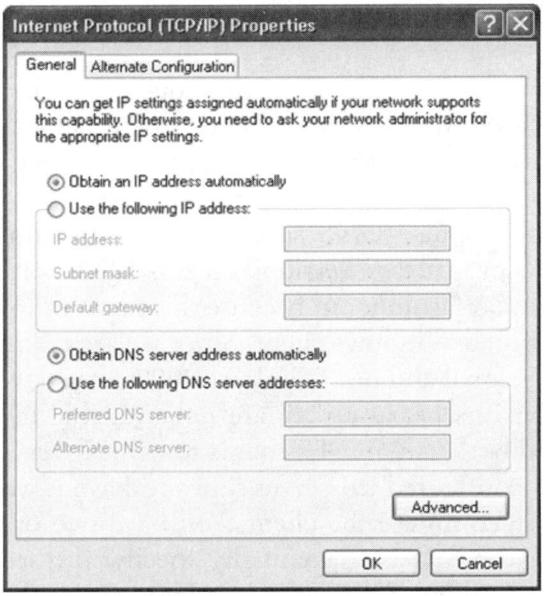

Figure 3.8   Local Area Connection Properties—TCP/IP Properties

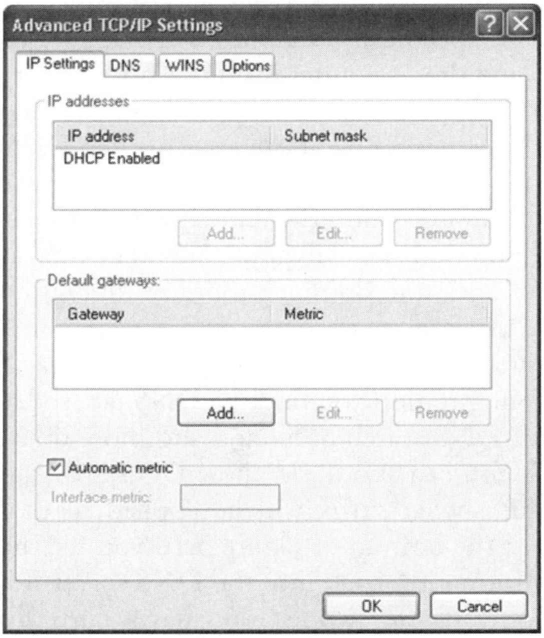

Figure 3.9   Advanced TCP/IP Settings

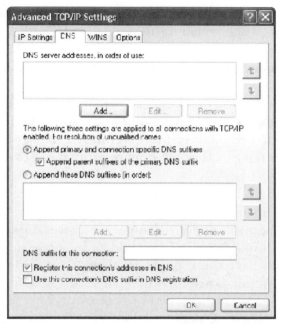

Figure 3.10 Domain Name Service settings properties

DHCP

Dynamic Host Configuration Protocol (DHCP) has existed for about ten years and has primarily involved assigning an IP address dynamically to a host. Over the past few years, however, we have seen DHCP doing more for a host computer through the use of providing additional variables like WINS, DNS, and Dynamic host updates.

DHCP configuration on a client is fairly simple, but it is defined on a per interface basis; therefore, if you have multiple interfaces in your workstation, you need to configure it on the interfaces that you want changed.

All these changes can be found on Figure 3.5 referenced earlier in the chapter. There are very few parameters; you can set the IP address to be DHCP selected, as well as the DNS records. As you remember from our discussion on WINS you can also set the WINS address through DHCP.

Troubleshooting

Troubleshooting WINS, DNS, and DHCP issues can be challenging in a Windows environment because typically there is not a lot of information that is displayed. The three areas that will be of most use to you is the Event Log found in Start Menu/Control Panel and then selecting **Administrative Tools**. Under this folder you find **Event Viewer**, which lets you view any of your events. This is where stop errors, such as failure to obtain an IP address from the DHCP server, are listed.

Typically, though, if you obtain a DHCP address or you have a static address and the failures are around DNS or WINS, the best thing you can do is make sure you can interact with the server providing that service. Testing this is a simple matter of pinging and tracerouting to the server in question (your destination server). Some sites limit or prohibit pinging and tracerouting to various servers so if you get failures, it does not necessarily mean that you have a server-side problem.

Other common problems include mistyping the server name that provides the service. In an environment such as yours where there should be multiple workstations, it is best to test your changes on a second workstation and see if you encounter the problem again. If you do and you are sure you have typed it in properly, you may have a server-side problem.

Finally, there is the possibility to enable an alterative configuration if your primary configuration has failed or is not working correctly. This is done by configuring the alternate configuration on the Properties tab as shown in Figure 3.11.

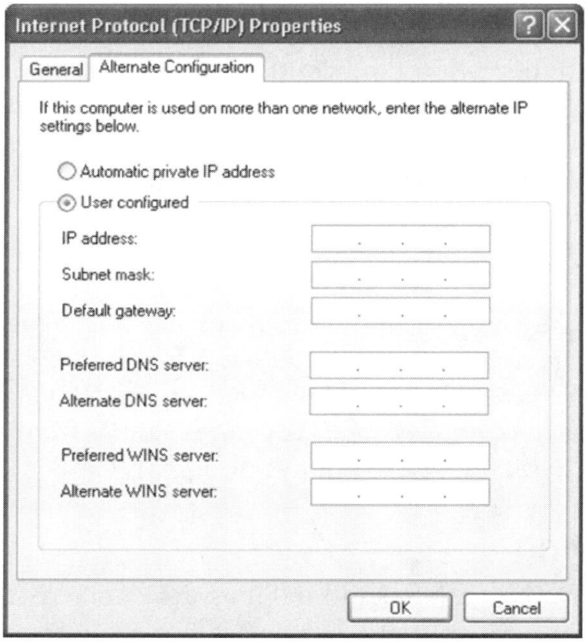

Figure 3.11   Internet Protocol TCP/IP Properties—Alternate Configuration

4

Active Directory

In this chapter we talk about Active Directory and the tools and support functionality that depend on Active Directory. We discuss the history of directory services, ITU (International Telecommunications Union), and ISO (International Standards Organization) standards, including X.500 and subsequent standards that have developed from that original committee. We discuss how directory services are similar and not so similar to databases, and include a brief discussion on hierarchical and relational data structures.

We also talk about where Active Directory can be found in the infrastructure, and how Active Directory assists you administratively versus previously available resources and tools. We briefly discuss concepts surrounding deployment as well as roaming and backups that might help make your administrative experiences more effective.

History

The evolution of the computer industry has led over time to volumes and volumes of information. Computers have become networked objects, not just the computer as a whole, but also its peripherals—printers, storage, scanners, and other connected devices. These objects, combined with the number of systems and the amount of data stored on those systems, have required changes.

These changes, as a normal evolution of computing, have brought about databases and directory services that help store the additional volumes of information, organize and make available the resources that have come into being and, above all, make the most of all of this data and resources.

A directory service is a lot like a database, but with better standards and a typical layout that is represented consistently in most directory services. A typical directory structure is accessed more than it is written to, whereas a database can be either or both. A directory service has a clearly defined set of objects and structure that was defined as part of the specification, whereas a database has a schema that can be made to function however the designer feels best suits the application in question.

A directory service is essentially a network interface to data that can be accessed by multiple users in different ways at the same time. It is a very cool concept that at the end of the day should improve your company's level of security, will hopefully improve your company's privacy, and will certainly help to enable your company to do more with less.

Directory services grew from the X.500 standard and as part of that began its most effective life as Lightweight Directory Application Protocol (LDAP). LDAP brought forward the concept not only of a hierarchical view of various objects, but also its permissions and security structure, which is important when contemplating network availability of sensitive, private, and confidential information.

In the context of a computer network, a directory (also called a data store) is a hierarchical structure that stores information about objects on the network. Objects include shared resources such as servers, shared volumes, and printers; network user and computer accounts; as well as domains, applications, services, security policies, and just about everything else in your network.

One example of the specific kinds of information a network directory might store about a particular type of object is that a directory typically stores a user's name, password, e-mail address, phone number, and so on, for a user account.

A directory service differs from a directory in that it is both the directory information source and the services making the information available and usable to administrators, users, network services, and applications. Ideally, a directory service makes the physical network topology and protocols (formats for transmitting data between two devices) transparent, so that a user can access any resource without knowing where or how it is physically connected.

To continue the user account example, it is the directory service that lets other authorized users on the same network access stored directory information (such as an e-mail address) about the user account object. Directory services can support a wide variety of capabilities. Some directory services are integrated with an operating system, and others are applications such as e-mail directories.

There are products released from many companies that have envisioned part of the lightweight directory protocol. The products with the most knowledge and information, and by far the most robust, come from four primary areas. These products, each in its own right worth examination, will unfortunately not be covered in this book. However, we felt that they were significant enough to mention each product. These products are not listed in any specific order.

- **Novell:** Novell Directory Service (NDS)
- **Oracle:** Oracle Internet Directory (OID)

- **Sun Microsystems:** Iplanet Internet Directory Service
- **Microsoft:** Active Directory

Active Directory is one of the later entries into the directory services arena and has been linked at the lowest levels of the Microsoft family of operating systems since Windows 2000. With Active Directory many things are now possible, and in this chapter we discuss many of these things as they relate to Windows XP specifically and Microsoft products as a whole generically.

In Figure 4.1, we show an example of a simple LDAP/X.500 directory structure, which will become important later when you see an Active Directory structure. We also include a diagram that shows how multiple users can use access in a lightweight directory and be given only specific rights and access.

As you work with directories you will find that over time these new tools will be very useful in your administration of systems, devices, users, and resources, and also in centralizing your logging, your administrative activities, and any number of other areas that will inevitably make your administrative experiences more functional and useful.

Figure 4.2 is an example of a directory permission structure. It should help you understand how a directory generically, and Active Directory specifically, will be able to assist you. An accurate policy, an accurate deployment guide, and certainly a detailed understanding of how directories work and permissions are required to implement a useful Active Directory structure.

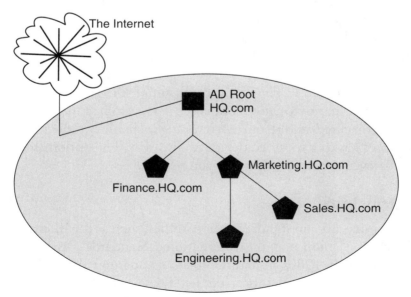

Figure 4.1   An example of a simple hierarchal LDAP/X.500 data structure

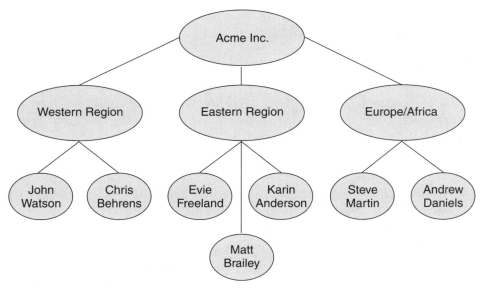

Figure 4.2   An example of simple directory permissions, logically applied

While the diagram in Figure 4.2 is somewhat simple, it gets the point across. In the diagram, John Watson and Andrew Daniels are in the development group and need large amounts of storage so they have access to the networked storage. All the users have access to the black-and-white printers. Karin Anderson and Steve Martin have access to the color printers because they are in marketing and need to print out graphs and spiffy color presentations. Finally, Chris Beherns and Matt Brailey have access to the scanners because they work in sales and need to scan in signed sales orders to be attached to customer accounts to eliminate a physical paper trail.

Despite the diagram in Figure 4.2 being simplistic, you can easily come up with a hundred scenarios for your company's usage: from granting specific access rights to directory trees and resources to setting availability times and what levels of access a user has to a specified device or directory. The options are nearly unlimited; whatever you need, whenever you need it.

X.500 Standard

Many of the international standardization bodies, such as the International Telecommunications Union and the International Standards Organization, came together in the early 1980s in an attempt to standardize things such as e-mail protocols and domain name infrastructure. They created the early X.400 standardization, which helped to create the need for, and interest in, directory data structures.

The X.500 standardization was created to handle and support pretty much any electronic data storage in a hierarchical data directory. The X.500 standard is actually multiple standards including, but not limited to, the X.500 standard, which defines the objects, and the X.509 standard, which talks about certificates commonly found in directory structures.

Think about how Domain Name Service (DNS) works and you will understand the hierarchical nature of the directory structure. When you make a query, it will, for example, first ask your domain, say acme.com. If for whatever reason acme.com does not know, then it will ask .com, and if .com does not know, then it can ask the root name servers sometimes referred to as ".".

Active Directory 101

Active Directory is a lot like the DNS or an organizational chart in which you have a CEO at the top and various levels of management below the CEO. A directory service (Active Directory included) is a structured directory. It bases a lot of how it works on the hierarchy, which is essentially like a tree with a few large branches that have many smaller ones, which then have leaves. In Figure 4.3, we have created a very basic diagram that compares the Active Directory hierarchy to a DNS tree structure.

This directory combines with your infrastructure much like your use of a domain in previous versions of the Windows operating system. With it you have greater flexibility and will be able to accomplish a lot more, much faster than you could before.

So at this point, we need to determine what Active Directory means to you. This begins with a planning stage. The planning stage determines what, where, and how many of the various infrastructure components need to be in place to support your infrastructure.

Active Directory in a Windows environment is a good choice—more expensive than some, but with Active Directory you can have a central point of administrative management for user accounts, workstations/servers, and applications.

Active Directory has several characteristics that are important from a historical as well as a practical perspective that you as the implementer need to understand to take better advantage of the available resources.

Active Directory is a unified directory, which means that just like other directory services, it is based upon the LDAP/X.500 loose standardization

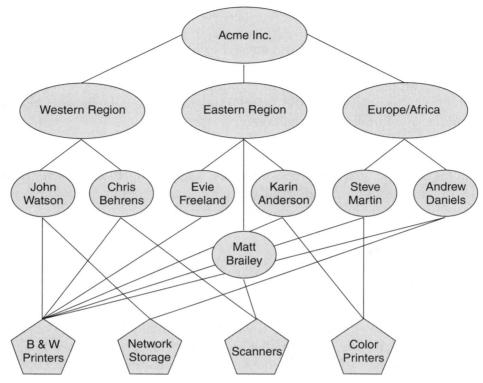

Figure 4.3 An example of how Active Directory and DNS are similar

and designates each object independently. It offers a standard name space for all the resources; it was designed to manage the operating systems resources including printers, storage, and other peripherals. Active Directory was also designed to play a crucial role in working with specific application management requirements including helping to manage your telephone directory, your e-mail, and e-commerce subsystems (assuming you are using Microsoft products throughout).

Active Directory, as we have previously mentioned, also acts as a centralized management structure to manage access to files and peripherals, and can also structure access to the network connections, users, and other miscellaneous resources. In a hierarchical organization, accessing the data in a way that can be searched and browsed is important and useful.

Active Directory, much like Oracle's Internet Directory, is based, on a central storage engine and database. This database is based upon Microsoft Exchange 4.0 and provides for large data stores.

Much like other directory services, which are based upon the LDAP/X.500, Active Directory works with three primary concepts, which are attributes, classes, and objects. Here is a brief description of each for your reference.

1. **Attribute:** An attribute (in the schema of the directory) is an area of the directory characterized by properties such as the type of value it can contain; for example, a character string. It can be simply compared to a database table that has rows and columns (we talk about this shortly).

2. **Class:** A class is a description of a record in the directory. It can consist of multiple attributes and can contain its own characteristics, including identifying how many occurrences that class can have. The X.500 standard and more specifically the Lightweight Directory Application Protocol have standardized classes including people, group, and organization.

3. **Object:** An object is an instance of a class, which in a database would be described as a record in a table. Each object in the directory must be associated to a class that describes its attributes.

Some important concepts not yet mentioned include the possibility of integrating with Public Key Infrastructure (PKI) and single-sign-on products. Another concept that we demonstrate in Figure 4.4 is the possibility that an object can belong to more than one class. This is important to note because this is where some of the real success can be had with the structure.

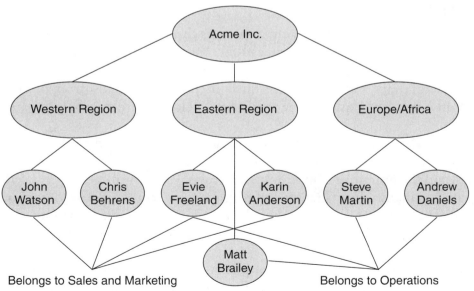

Figure 4.4   An example of objects belonging to more than one class

Active Directory, XP, and You

As with many of the things we have talked about in this book, XP Professional is very limited in its server-side functionality. Microsoft has therefore decided to make XP Professional and Home the workstation/client software while keeping alive Windows 2000 and pushing Windows 2003 Server as its replacement.

Because of this, our discussion about Active Directory and XP naturally has to be limited; there is be very little you can do to configure Active Directory on XP. However, we can talk at length about how Active Directory in your organization, either on Windows 2000 Server or Windows 2003 Server, will effect positive changes and enhanced functionality in your organization.

In this section, we talk about three key areas where XP has the most impact in your Windows XP environment. We discuss the area and the tools surrounding that area, as well as provide some food for thought on why these areas should be important to you. Hopefully, your environment is one that is mostly non-heterogeneous and can benefit from tools that work on a global scale.

We hope that these three areas we examine will assist your organization's profitability through streamlining your team's workload, as well as reduce the repetitive nature that an IT job can sometimes have. These include tools such as IntelliMirror that deal with such issues as roaming and user experience, and the Group Policy Object (GPO) that deals with security and overall functionality.

IntelliMirror

Deploying similar workstation environments throughout your environment is a goal of choice for most IT organizations; for you to effectively support your users they must have environments you can duplicate. This similarity can be achieved in ways not really envisioned in previous Microsoft environments without extensive consulting or some sort of cloning process for your desktop images.

IntelliMirror is a group of tools and functionality that, through Active Directory, lets you centrally manage permissions, privileges, the capabilities of your users, and the respective computing resources of your organization. This centralization has many advantages, including giving you the ability to work with and for your users wherever they may be. It also allows your users the ability to roam and have their desktops and many of their personalization options available to them wherever they may be.

IntelliMirror is composed of four pieces, but we need to reiterate that IntelliMirror relies (through one of those four components) very heavily on Active

Directory. While there are technologies available to do much of the work that IntelliMirror can do for you without Active Directory, that is not what this chapter is about. Also, Microsoft has put a lot of work into Active Directory and it is a technology that is easier, a lot more integrated, and certainly aligns with not only the large enterprise/technological goals of this chapter, but the book as a whole.

Some of the components we talk about exist outside of IntelliMirror and as you learn and utilize these tools, you will find that the functionality can enhance more than the roaming and data availability of your users. As mentioned earlier, it can also enhance the privacy, data security, and confidentiality of your environment. Specifically, we are talking about the Group Policy Object, which will require Active Directory.

It is important to remember that the GPO is not related, at least in our discussion, to the Local Group Policy Object (LGPO), which is specific to the local computer and therefore has nothing really to do with the global architecture.

The IntelliMirror components can help you to:

- Centrally create and manage user desktop configurations.
- Create roaming user profiles and folder redirection (including offline files) so that your users can access files from anywhere.
- Deploy software in an automatic fashion to ensure that all users have the software that they need to do their jobs.
- Create, manage, and enforce centralized data storage that helps you keep important files backed up on that central data storage.
- Build new systems to replace older ones using the Remote Installation Service (RIS). Through this service you can also install, maintain, and even replace applications across your network as required.

Group Policy Object

Group Policy Object is exactly what it sounds like, a group of objects that have a policy or set of rules that allow that group to be accessed and utilized. With GPO, you target a specific portion of the tree/directory or hierarchy and apply those roles and rules. These rules allow you to set up various roles for not only your resources but also for your users, much like what has been demonstrated in Figures 4.2 and 4.4.

With Group Policy Object, security templates, and Active Directory you can set up a number of functional restrictions, protections, security, and privacy elements.

How Group Policy Object Affects Startup and Logon

The following sequence shows the order in which computer configuration and user configuration settings are applied when a computer starts and a user logs on. With this list you can understand how the restrictions that you set up will be applied.

- The network subsystems are loaded and started. Remote Procedure Call System Service (RPCSS) and Multiple Universal Naming Convention Provider (MUP.exe) are started after the network components load.
- An ordered list of GPOs is obtained for the computer. The list contents may depend on these factors:
  - Whether the computer is part of a Windows 2000 domain and is therefore subject to a domain Group Policy using Active Directory.
  - The location of the computer in the hierarchial structure of Active Directory.
- If the list of GPOs has not changed, then no additional processing is done. You can use a Group Policy setting to change this behavior, and we do so in the Windows domain. We process folder redirection, registry, scripts, and security policy, even if the policies are unchanged.
- Next, computer configuration settings are then processed. This occurs serially by default and in the following order: the local GPO, any site GPOs, domain GPOs, organizational unit (OU) GPOs, and so on. The user interface is not displayed while the computer is processing these settings. If there are any startup scripts, they run at this time. This is hidden away from the user, and runs serially by default; each script must complete or time out before the next one starts. You can use several Group Policy settings to modify this behavior.
- Once all of these activities are completed, the user presses Ctrl+Alt+Delete to log on.
- After the user is authenticated, the user profile is loaded, governed by the Group Policy settings in effect.
- An ordered list of GPOs is then obtained for this specific user. The list contents may depend on these factors:
  - Whether the user account is part of a Windows 2000 domain and is therefore subject to Group Policies through Active Directory.
  - Whether loopback is enabled, and the state (Merge or Replace) of the loopback policy setting.
  - The location of the user in Active Directory hierarchy.

- If the list of GPOs to be applied has not changed, then no additional processing is done. As we listed in the previous section, you can use a policy setting to change this behavior.
- User configuration settings are then processed. This occurs serially by default and, just as before, in the following order: local GPOs, site GPOs, domain GPOs, OU GPOs, and so on. The user interface is not displayed while the computer is processing these settings. Any available logon scripts run next. Unlike Windows NT 4.0 scripts, Group Policy–based logon scripts are run hidden and asynchronously by default. Finally, the user object script runs last.
- The operating system user interface prescribed by Group Policy appears.

How Group Policy Objects Are Processed

Group Policy Object settings are processed in the following order:

1. **Local GPO:** In Windows 2000, each computer has only one GPO stored locally, referred to as the local GPO.
2. **Site GPOs:** Any GPOs that have been linked to the site are processed next. Processing is synchronous; the administrator has the ability to specify the order in which GPOs are linked to a site. We do not use this in the WIN domain.
3. **Domain GPOs:** Multiple domain-linked GPOs are processed synchronously; the administrator also specifies the order in which these GPOs are listed.
4. **OU GPOs:** GPOs linked to the OU highest in the Active Directory hierarchy are processed first, followed by GPOs linked to its child OU, and so on. Finally, the GPOs linked to the OU that contains the user or the computer are processed. At the level of each OU in the Active Directory hierarchy, one, many, or no GPOs can be linked. If several group policies are linked to an OU, then they are processed synchronously in an order specified by the administrator.

This order means that the local GPO is processed first, and GPOs linked to the OU, of which the computer or user is a direct member, are processed last (being at the highest level of the domain structure), overwriting the earlier GPOs as needed. For example, you set up a domain GPO to allow anyone to log on interactively. However, an OU GPO, set up for the domain controller, prevents everyone from logging on except for certain administrative groups. Basically, conflicts are resolved by the GPO that loads last, so OU GPOs can override previously defined functions and variables.

Exceptions to the Processing Order

The default order of processing Group Policy settings is subject to a few exceptions:

- **A computer that is a member of a workgroup (and not a domain) will only process the local GPO,** because no sites or domains are involved, and Active Directory and the organizational units are not present.

- **No Override:** Any GPO linked to a site, domain, or OU (not the local GPO) can be set to No Override with respect to that site, domain, or OU, so that none of its policy settings can be overridden. Naturally, this could cause a conflict if two GPOs have "No Override" set. In those cases, the highest one in the hierarchy that can be partially specified by the administrator takes precedence.

- **Block Policy Inheritance:** At any site, domain, or OU, Group Policy inheritance can be selectively marked as Block Policy Inheritance. However, GPO links set to No Override are always applied and cannot be blocked. Block Policy Inheritance is applied directly. It is not applied to GPOs, nor is it applied to GPO links. The Block Policy Inheritance deflects *all* Group Policy settings that reach out to the site, domain, or OU from above. It does not matter from which GPOs these settings originate.

- **Loopback setting:** Loopback is an advanced Group Policy setting that is useful on computers in certain closely managed environments such as kiosks, laboratories, classrooms, and reception areas. The ordered list goes from site-linked to domain-linked to OU-linked GPOs, with inheritance determined by the location of the user in Active Directory and in an order specified by the administrator at each level.

- **Replace:** In this case, the GPO list for the user is replaced in its entirety by the local GPO list.

- **Merge:** In this case, the GPO lists are concatenated. The GPO list obtained for the computer at computer startup is appended to the GPO list obtained for the user at logon. Because the GPO list obtained for the computer is applied later, it has precedence if it conflicts with settings in the user's list.

Group Policy Inheritance

Generally speaking, the Group Policy is passed down from the parent to any child containers; this is an anticipated behavior in a hierarchical data structure. Any Group Policies assigned to a parent apply to any containers below that parent. This includes any user and computer objects that are found.

However, if you specify a Group Policy setting for a child container, the child container's Group Policy setting overrides the setting inherited from the parent container.

If a parent OU has policy settings that are not configured or defined, then the child OU does not inherit them because nothing has changed. However, if you explicitly disable a policy, these are inherited in the disabled state, because this is an explicit action. Also, that child inherits any policies that are configured for a parent, but are not explicitly configured for a child.

If a parent policy and a child policy are compatible, the child inherits the parent policy, and the child's setting is also applied. Policies are inherited as long as they are compatible. There are cases where this can get confusing, such as if the parent's policy causes a certain folder to be placed on the desktop and the child's setting calls for an additional folder, the user sees both folders even though that may not have been the original intent.

If a policy configured for a parent OU is incompatible with the same policy configured for a child OU, the child does not inherit the policy setting from the parent because this will generate a conflict.

Using Security Groups to Filter Group Policy

Because you can link more than one GPO to a site, domain, or OU, you may need to link GPOs associated with other directory objects. By setting the appropriate permissions for security groups, you can cause any Group Policies to affect only the computers and users specified by the administrative user.

Using IntelliMirror

With Active Directory and Group Policy you can use IntelliMirror. Without Active Directory, you can still use some of the components of IntelliMirror, but you will not be able to take full advantage of it. (See Table 4.1.)

The key to understanding Active Directory beyond its core components is to realize that information stored within the directory is logical. This information is automatically replicated to other domain controllers across the network to simplify finding and managing data, no matter where the data is located in the organization. The Active Directory structure you create determines how you apply Group Policy settings. Group Policy allows you to define and control the state of computers and users in an organization. Group Policy allows you to control more than 500 customizable settings that you can use to centrally configure and manage users and computers.

Depending on the size of your organization, managing desktops, users, and their permissions can be a very complex task, especially because changes

Table 4.1   Management Tasks That Use IntelliMirror

Management Task	IntelliMirror Feature
Configure a registry-based Group Policy setting for specific computers and/or users.	This is done through the use of Administrative Templates.
Manage any local, domain, or network security.	This is done through the configuration of Security Settings.
Centrally install, update, and remove software.	Group Policy–based software distribution (the old way was to use SMS or some other complicated scheme).
Change or modify Internet Explorer settings after a computer has been deployed.	Accomplished using the Internet Explorer Maintenance feature.
Apply scripts during user logon/logoff and computer startup/shutdown—much the same way it has always been.	Scripts
Centrally manage users' folders and files on the network and make shared files and folders available offline.	Folder Redirection Offline Files and Folders
Centrally manage user profiles—much the same way it has always been.	Roaming User Profiles

constantly happen. For example, users join and leave organizations, get promoted and transferred, and regularly change offices. Similarly, printers, computers, and network file shares are frequently added, removed, and relocated.

You can associate or link a particular Group Policy Object to one or more sites, domains, or OUs in an Active Directory structure. When multiple GPOs are linked to a particular site, domain, or OU, you can prioritize the order in which the GPOs are applied by determining when in the processing order particular settings are processed.

By linking together all the GPOs that are available in sites, domains, and OUs, you can create settings that can affect your organization in different ways; basically, you can use a wide brush or a very narrow one, you can have specific, tightly integrated goals or broader less specific needs.

Just remember that a GPO linked to a specific site applies to all users and computers in that site (after local and domain GPOs are applied, unless there is a conflict). So take care in applying your policies and make sure that what you want to do is not complicated, overridden, or exempted by other policy objects defined at higher levels.

User Data Management

Files that a user creates and uses are considered user data. Some examples include word processing files and spreadsheets. User data belongs to the user and is located on the user's computer or on a network share to which the user has rights.

Less obvious forms of user data include Microsoft Internet Explorer Cookies, Favorites, and customized templates. User data is usually hard to recreate—for example, a template that has undergone extensive design work and customization. With IntelliMirror, users can transparently access their data from any Windows XP Professional–based computer on the network, regardless of whether or not that computer is their primary computer.

IntelliMirror technologies that support user data management include

- Folder Redirection
- Offline Files and Synchronization Manager
- Roaming User Profiles

Protecting User Data by Using Folder Redirection

You can redirect user data to a network share, where it can be backed up as part of routine system maintenance. This can be done so that the process is transparent to the user. It is recommended that users be trained to store all user data in My Documents (in the built-in subfolders My Pictures, My Music, and My Videos, and in any subfolders they create to organize their data).

There are two primary ways to implement folder redirection. The first is with the use of Group Policy and the other is using the Registry Policy Editor. Most of the folders you will want to redirect are already redirected in the templates provided. We instruct you on how to redirect additional folders later in this chapter.

The My Documents folder is then redirected to a network share. This capability helps to enforce corporate directives such as storing business-critical data on servers that are centrally managed by the IT staff. If users are in the habit of storing files on their desktops, you should also consider redirecting the desktop.

Although the Application Data folder can be redirected using Folder Redirection, this is generally only recommended in the following cases:

- To reduce the size of the profile, thereby decreasing logon time on multi-user computers where you have enabled a Group Policy setting to delete cached profiles. This gives users access to their application data, but without the need to download possibly large files every time they log on.

- To reduce the size of the profile in situations where keeping initial logon time short is a top priority, such as on terminals.
- For Terminal Services clients.

Accessing Data When Disconnected from the Network

By using Offline Files and Synchronization Manager, administrators can ensure that the most up-to-date versions of a user's data reside on both the local computer and on the server. You can use Offline Files in conjunction with Folder Redirection to make available offline those folders that have been redirected to a server.

Users can manually configure which files and folders are available offline, or administrators can configure them through Group Policy. The file is stored on a server, and the file on the local computer is synchronized with the network copy. Changes made while offline are synchronized with the server when the user reconnects to the network. Offline Files now supports Distributed File System (DFS) and Encrypting File System (EFS).

Enabling Roaming User Profiles

Although profiles are commonly used as a method of managing user settings (such as a user's shortcuts and other customizations of their environment), the profile also contains user data, including Favorites and Cookies. When roaming user profiles are enabled, users can access this data when they log on to any computer on the network. Windows XP Professional Group Policy settings allow the profile to roam correctly and free up system memory.

User Settings Management

With the user settings management tools in Windows XP Professional, you can centrally define computing environments for groups of users, and grant or deny users the ability to further customize their environments.

By managing user settings, you can

- Reduce support calls by providing a preconfigured desktop environment and help users be more efficient by making available their profiles, including their documents and environments, regardless of the computers they are using to log in.
- The primary IntelliMirror technologies that support user settings management are Roaming User Profiles and Administrative Templates. The settings in Administrative Templates can control the desktop with predefined configurations; for more information, see the section titled Administrative Templates later in this chapter.

A user profile contains

- The portion of the registry that stores settings such as Windows Explorer settings, persistent network connections, taskbar settings, network printer connections, and user-defined settings made from Control Panel, Accessories, and application settings.
- A set of profile folders that store information such as shortcut links, desktop icons, and startup applications.

User profiles are located by default on the local computer; one profile is created for each user that has logged on to that computer. By configuring user profiles to roam, you can ensure that the settings in a user's profile are copied to a network server when the user logs off from the computer and are available to the user no matter where he or she next logs on to the network.

While useful for roaming users, roaming user profiles are also beneficial for users that always use the same computer. For these users, roaming user profiles provide a transparent way to back up their profiles to a network server, protecting the information from individual system failure. If a user's primary workstation needs to be replaced, the new computer receives the user's profile from the server as soon as the user logs on.

Some folders in a user profile cannot be configured to roam; these are found in the Local Settings folder, and include the subfolders Application Data (not to be confused with the "other" Application Data folder that is a peer of Local Settings, which *does* roam), History, Temp, and Temporary Internet Files. These folders contain application data that is not required to roam with the user, such as temporary files, noncritical settings, and data too large to roam effectively.

As an illustration of using roaming and nonroaming folders, you might configure Internet Explorer to store a user's Favorites in the roaming portion of the user profile and store the temporary Internet files in the local, nonroaming portion of the user profile. By default, the History, Local Settings, Temp, and Temporary Internet Files folders are excluded from the roaming user profile.

Computer Settings Management

Group Policy settings also allow you to define how desktop computers are customized and restricted on your network. For optimal control of workstations, use Group Policy objects in an Active Directory network to centralize computer management.

The Computer Configuration tree in the Group Policy Microsoft Management Console (MMC) snap-in includes the local computer-related Group Policy settings that specify operating system behavior, desktop behavior, application settings, security settings, computer-assigned application options, and computer startup and shutdown scripts. Computer-related Group Policy settings are applied when the operating system starts up, and during periodic refresh cycles.

You can also customize computer configuration settings by using the Group Policy MMC snap-in, thus simplifying individual computer setup.

Group Policy–Based Software Distribution

Group Policy provides some ability to deploy software to workstations and servers running on Windows XP Professional. With Group Policy–based software deployment, you can target groups of users and computers based on their location in the Active Directory. Group Policy–based software deployment uses Windows Installer as the installation engine on the local computer.

This Software Installation and Maintenance component allows you to deploy, patch, upgrade, and remove software applications without visiting each desktop. This gives your users reliable access to the applications that they need to perform their jobs, no matter which computer they are using.

Group Policy–based software distribution enables you to:

- Centrally deploy new software, upgrade applications, deploy patches and operating system upgrades, and remove previously deployed applications that are no longer required.
- Create a standard desktop operating environment that results in uninterrupted user productivity and straightforward administration.
- Maintain version control of software for all desktop computers in the organization.
- Identify and diagnose Group Policy setting failures by using Resultant Set of Policy (RSoP) in logging mode.
- Deploy, in combination with Windows Installer, 64-bit applications as well as 32-bit applications.

Using the Software Installation extension of the Group Policy MMC snap-in, you can centrally manage the installation of software on a client computer, either by assigning applications to users or computers, or by publishing applications for users. (See Table 4.2.) You can

- **Assign software to users**. As an administrator, you can install applications assigned to users the first time they log on after deployment, or you can have the application and its components install on demand as the user invokes that functionality.

Table 4.2 Approaches to Assigning and Publishing Software

Situation or Condition:	Publish	Assign to User (Install on Demand)	Assign to User (Full Install)	Assign to Computer
Once the administrator deploys the software, it is available for installation:	The next time the user, to whom this application's Group Policy setting applies, logs on. It is also immediately visible in Add or Remove Programs.	The next time the user, to whom this application's Group Policy setting applies, logs on. It is also immediately visible in Add or Remove Programs.	The next time the user logs on. It is also immediately visible in Add or Remove Programs.	The next time the computer is started.
The software is installed:	By the user from Add or Remove Programs or, optionally, by opening an associated document (for applications deployed to auto-install).	By the user from the Start menu or a desktop shortcut or by opening an associated document.	Automatically when the user logs on.	Automatically when the computer is started.
The software is not installed and the user opens a file associated with the software:	The software installs only if Auto-Install is selected.	The software installs.	Does not apply. The software is already installed.	Does not apply. The software is already installed.
The user wants to remove the software by using Add or Remove Programs:	The user can uninstall the software, and subsequently choose to install it again by using Add or Remove Programs.	The user can uninstall the software, but it is re-assigned the next time the user logs on. It is available for installation again from the typical software distribution points.	The user can uninstall the software, but it is re-assigned the next time the user logs on. It is available for installation again from the typical installation points.	Only the local administrator and the network administrator can remove the software.

- **Assign software to computers**. When you assign an application to a computer, the installation occurs the next time the computer starts up, and the application is available for all the users on that computer.
- **Publish software for users**. You can publish applications for users only. Those users can choose to install the software from a list of published applications located in Add or Remove Programs in Control Panel.

Using Group Policy to Manage Desktops

Group Policy is the primary tool for defining and controlling how programs, network resources, and Windows XP Professional behave for users and computers in an organization.

Using Active Directory and Group Policy, an administrator can configure a computer once and then rely on Windows to enforce the configuration so that the computer remains in a healthy, functioning state. Quite a few of us have experienced user "tweaks" and found that in many cases, as the tweaking increases, so do the support calls. This not only increases our workload, it also decreases employee productivity.

You can define configurations by implementing Group Policy settings to several computers or users at the same time from a central location. Some possible examples include:

- Installing Microsoft Excel on all computers used by the sales department (because they do forecasting and calculation).
- Prevent contractors, vendors, or guests from accessing Control Panel and making modifications to the system.

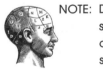 NOTE: Do not confuse Group Policy settings with preferences. Group Policy settings are created by an administrator and enforced automatically. Preferences are system settings and configuration options, such as a screen saver or the view in My Documents, that users set and alter without an administrator's intervention. Group Policy settings take precedence over preferences.

Group Policy Objects

Each combination of Group Policy settings that you configure is called a *Group Policy Object*. You can link GPOs to computers and users based on their location in an Active Directory hierarchy. That is, you can link a GPO to a site, domain, or organizational unit. Each GPO is applied as part of the startup process or when a user logs on to a workstation. The settings within the GPOs are evaluated by the affected clients, using the hierarchical nature of Active Directory, as described in "GPO Processing Order" later in this section.

NOTE: Every computer receives one LGPO, which is stored on the local computer itself. Because LGPOs must be set and modified individually on every client computer, it is recommended that you use LGPOs to manage clients only if Active Directory is not deployed in your environment, and only if you are not using Windows XP Professional.

Additionally, the use of LGPOs allows the enforcement of corporate policy even when the computer is not connected to the internal network.

To create, edit, and manage a GPO, use the Group Policy MMC snap-in, either as a stand-alone tool or as an extension to an Active Directory snap-in (such as the Active Directory Users and Computers snap-in or the Active Directory Sites and Services snap-in). When working in an Active Directory environment, the preferred method is to use the Group Policy snap-in as an extension to an Active Directory snap-in. This allows you to browse Active Directory for the correct Active Directory container and then define Group Policy based on the selected scope. To access Group Policy from either the Active Directory Users and Computers snap-in or in the Active Directory Sites and Services snap-in, select the **Group Policy** tab from the **Properties** page of a site, domain, or organizational unit.

When you create a GPO, start with a template that contains all of the Group Policy settings available for you to configure. Because Group Policy settings apply to either computers or users, GPOs contain trees for each:

- **Computer Configuration:** All computer-related Group Policy settings that specify operating system behavior, desktop behavior, security settings, computer startup and shutdown scripts, computer-assigned applications, and any settings provided by applications.

- **User Configuration:** All user-related Group Policy settings that specify operating system behavior, desktop settings, security settings, user-assigned and user-published application options, folder redirection options, user logon and logoff scripts, and any Group Policy settings provided by applications.

IMPORTANT: If an Active Directory domain contains both Windows 2000– and Windows XP Professional–based clients, any new Group Policy settings specific to Windows XP Professional that you configure do not apply to the Windows 2000–based clients. See Group Policy Help or the Extended view in the Group Policy snap-in for the desktop operating system required for each setting to apply.

Resultant Set of Policy

The biggest change in Group Policy for Windows XP Professional is the introduction of the Resultant Set of Policy MMC snap-in. RSoP gives administrators a powerful and flexible tool for Group Policy and for troubleshooting Group Policy. RSoP allows you to see the aggregate effect of Group Policy on a target user or computer, including which settings take precedence over others.

RSoP is enabled by Windows Management Instrumentation (WMI) by leveraging the capability of WMI to extract data from the registry, drivers, the file system, Active Directory, Simple Network Management Protocol (SNMP), Windows Installer, and many Windows programs, including SQL Server and Exchange Server.

Use Logging mode to determine which GPO settings are actually applied to a target user or computer. You can also use Logging mode on a stand-alone computer.

For example, a help desk worker can connect to any Windows XP Professional–based computer on the network and run Logging mode if he or she has local administrator access on the target computer.

Managing Users and Desktops by Using Group Policy Extensions

Group Policy provides several extensions that you can use to configure GPOs that enable IntelliMirror features and manage users. These extensions include

- Administrative Templates
- Security Settings
- Software Installation and Maintenance
- Scripts (computer startup and shutdown scripts and user logon and logoff scripts)
- Folder Redirection
- Internet Explorer Maintenance
- Remote Installation Services

 NOTE: Folder Redirection, Software Installation and Maintenance, and Remote Installation Services (RIS) require Active Directory; they are not present on the local Group Policy Object and cannot be managed by using the local Group Policy Object. If Active Directory is not deployed on your network, use System Policy instead.

You can use any of these extensions to apply Group Policy to users or computers, although settings are different for users and computers. Use the Group Policy snap-in to access the extensions. By default, all the available extensions are loaded when you start the Group Policy snap-in. Different extensions are available depending on whether you are viewing the local Group Policy Object or Active Directory domain-based Group Policy.

Administrative Templates

Administrative templates (.adm files) are *Unicode* files that you can use to configure the registry-based settings that govern the behavior of many services, applications, and operating system components, such as the Start menu. By default, the Group Policy snap-in contains four .adm files that cumulatively contain more than 600 settings. You can also access three additional .adm files that can be used with the Windows NT 4.0 System Policy Editor. The .adm files are described in Table 4.3.

An .adm file specifies a hierarchy of categories and subcategories that together define how the Group Policy snap-in displays the options. The file also indicates the registry locations where the settings are stored if a particular selection is made, specifies any options or restrictions in values that are associated with the selection, and might specify a default value if a selection is activated

In Windows 2000 and Windows XP Professional, all Group Policy settings set registry entries in either the \Software\Policies tree (the preferred location for all new policies) or the \Software\Microsoft\Windows\CurrentVersion\Policies tree, in either the HKEY_CURRENT_USER subtree or the HKEY_LOCAL_ MACHINE subtree.

Policy settings that are stored in these registry subkeys are known as *true policy settings*. Storing settings here has the following advantages:

- These subkeys are secure and cannot be modified by a nonadministrator.
- When Group Policy changes for any reason, these subkeys are cleaned, and then the new Group Policy–related registry entries are rewritten.

Table 4.3   Administrative Template Files

.Adm File	Use With	Description
System.adm	Windows XP Professional	Contains many settings that you can use to customize the user's operating environment.
Inetres.adm	Windows XP Professional	Contains settings for Internet Explorer.
Conf.adm	Windows XP Professional	Contains settings you can use to configure Microsoft NetMeeting.
Wmplayer.adm	Windows XP Professional	Contains settings you can use to configure Windows Media Player.

This prevents Windows NT 4.0 behavior, where System Policy settings result in persistent settings in the registry. A policy remains in effect until the value of its corresponding registry entry is reversed, either by a counteracting policy or by editing the registry. These settings are stored outside the approved registry locations and are known as *preferences.*

By default, only true policy settings are displayed in the Group Policy snap-in. Because they use registry entries in the Policies subkeys of the registry, they will *not* cause persistent settings in the registry when the GPO that applies them is no longer in effect. The following .adm files are displayed by default:

- **System.adm**, which contains operating system settings.
- **Inetres.adm**, which contains Internet Explorer restrictions.
- **Conf.adm**, which contains NetMeeting settings.
- **Wmplayer.adm**, which contains Windows Media Player settings.

Administrators can add additional .adm files to the Group Policy snap-in that set registry values outside of the Group Policy subkeys. These settings are referred to as *preferences* because the user, application, or other parts of the system can also change the settings. By creating non–Group Policy .adm files, the administrator ensures that certain registry entries are set to specified values.

One useful feature of the Windows XP Professional Group Policy snap-in is view filtering. For example, you can hide settings that are not configured or view-only settings supported on a particular operating-system platform.

To filter the view of the Group Policy snap-in:

- Click **View**, and then click **Filtering**.
- Select the **Filter by requirements information** check box, and then select the check boxes in the list box for the categories that you want to make visible.
- If you want to hide settings that are not configured, select the **Only show configured policy settings** check box. If you do this, only enabled or disabled settings will be visible.
- If you want to hide Windows NT 4.0–style system policy settings, make sure that the **Only show policy settings that can be fully managed** check box is selected. This option is recommended, and it is enabled by default.

You can also prevent administrators from viewing or using nonpolicy settings by enabling the **Enforce Show Policies Only** Group Policy setting in **User Configuration\Administrative Templates\System\Group Policy**.

The icon for nonpolicy or preference settings is red. True policy settings have a blue icon.

Extended View for the Group Policy snap-in now provides Explain text for the selected Group Policy setting without having to open a separate Help window. It also clearly shows which operating system client platform is required for the selected setting to apply. You can now more easily determine which settings will function depending on the existing desktop operating systems on your network.

Security Settings

Use the Security Settings extension to set the security options for computers and users within the scope of a GPO. The Security Settings extension of the Group Policy snap-in complements existing system security management features such as Local Security Policy snap-in. You can continue to change specific settings as needed.

You can configure security for computers to include

- **Account policies**, such as computer security settings for password policy, lockout policy, and Kerberos authentication protocol policy in Active Directory domains.

- **Important security settings** are applied only at the domain level. If configured at the OU level, they are neither processed nor applied.

- **Local policies**, including security settings for auditing, assigning user rights (such as who has network access to the computer), and security options (such as determining who can connect to a computer anonymously).

- **Event logging**, which controls settings such as the size and retention method for the Application, Security, and System event logs.

- **Restricted groups**, which allows administrators to control individual and group membership in security-sensitive groups. You can enforce a membership policy regarding sensitive groups, such as Enterprise Administrators or Payroll. For more information about using security, see "Security Settings" later in this chapter.

- **System services**, including services that control startup mode and access permissions for system services, such as who is allowed to stop and start the fax service.

- **Registry security**, which allows you to configure security settings for registry containers including access control, audit, and ownership.

- **File system**, which configures security settings for file-system objects including access control, audit, and ownership.

- **Public Key policies**, which controls and manages certificate settings.

- **IP Security policies**, which propagates Internet Protocol security (IPSec) policy to any computer accounts affected by the GPO. For users, you can define IPSec security. This propagates IPSec policy to any user accounts affected by the GPO.

Default Security Templates

The following security templates are installed when Windows XP Professional is installed on an NTFS (NT file system) partition:

- **Basicwk.inf:** Applies default settings for Windows XP Professional–based computers for all areas except User Rights and Group memberships.
- **Basicsv.inf:** Applies default settings for Windows 2000 Server–based computers for all areas except User Rights and Group memberships.
- **Basicdc.inf:** Applies default settings for domain controllers for all areas except User Rights and Group memberships.

User Rights and Group memberships are not modified by the basic templates because these templates are most often used for undoing file system or registry access control list (ACL) changes, or to apply the default Windows XP Professional ACLs to computers that have been upgraded from Windows NT 4.0. In these cases, administrators typically want to maintain existing User Rights and Group memberships.

Typically, you do not need to define the default security templates because they are installed by default on an NTFS partition. However, they can be useful if you have converted a drive from file allocation table (FAT) to NTFS, or if you have made customizations and want to restore the system to the default ACLs.

Do not deploy these templates by using Group Policy, because it can take a long time to reapply these basic templates. They are applied during setup. Incremental templates, on the other hand, are useful to deploy using Group Policy.

Incremental Security Templates

Windows XP Professional includes several incremental security templates. By default, these templates are stored in *systemroot*\Security\Templates. You can customize these predefined templates by using the Security Templates MMC snap-in or by importing them into the Security Settings extension of the Group Policy snap-in. These templates include

- **Compatible:** The Compatible template (Compatws.inf) relaxes the default permissions for the Users group so that older applications written to less stringent security standards are more likely to run.

- **Secure:** Two templates, Securews.inf and Securedc.inf, work on work-stations, servers, and domain controllers. These provide increased security compared to the access control permissions set by default when Windows XP Professional is installed. The Secure configuration includes increased security settings for Account Policy, Auditing, and some common security-related registry subkeys and entries.
- **High Secure:** The High Secure templates are Hisecws.inf and Hisecdc.inf. These provide increased security over the secure configuration and work on workstations, servers, and domain controllers. This configuration requires that all network communications be digitally signed and encrypted.

Software Installation

Use the Software Installation extension of the Group Policy snap-in to centrally manage software in your organization. You can assign (make mandatory) or publish (make optionally available) software to users, and assign (but not publish) software to computers. For more information about using the Software Installation extension, see the section Using IntelliMirror to Manage Desktops earlier in this chapter.

Folder Redirection

Use Folder Redirection to redirect certain Windows XP Professional folders from their default location in the user profile to an alternate location on an Active Directory network where you can centrally manage them and keep them secure. The Windows XP Professional folders that can be redirected include My Documents (and its subfolders My Pictures, My Music, and My Videos), Application Data, Desktop, and the Start menu.

Refreshing Group Policy from the Command Line

A new command-line tool, GPUpdate.exe, replaces the Secedit.exe tool to give administrators better control and flexibility in refreshing policy. Normally, Group Policy refreshes every 90 minutes for the computer and user. However, after you revise a GPO, you can use GPUpdate to refresh the GPO so that it takes effect immediately. GPUpdate replaces the Windows 2000 tool Secedit.exe and provides increased control and flexibility. The command-line parameters for this tool are described in Table 4.4.

Managing New Users

IntelliMirror, Group Policy, Windows Installer, and RIS greatly streamline adding new users and their computers to your network. You might use these technologies as follows to add a new managed user.

Table 4.4 Command-Line Parameters for GPUpdate.exe

Command-Line Parameter	Behavior
	With no parameters specified, GPUpdate behaves identically to the background refresh that occurs by default every 90 minutes. This includes optimizations for slow network connections and for not processing GPOs, unless you have changed the defaults.
/e	Enforce. This causes the refresh to ignore all processing optimizations, except slow network connections, and reapply all possible settings.
/i	Ignore slow network optimizations. This causes the refresh to ignore all processing optimizations, including slow network connections, and re-apply all possible settings. This enforces Group Policy processing as if on a fast link, even when on a slow link.
/l	Triggers a logoff after the refresh is complete. This is required for Group Policy client-side extensions that do not process on a background refresh cycle—but do process at user logon—such as user software installation, logon scripts, and Folder Redirection. This parameter has no effect if there are no extensions called that require a logoff.
/t	Targets Group Policy refresh for either the computer or the current user. By default, both will be processed and displayed.

A new user logs on to a new computer and finds shortcuts to documents on the desktop. These shortcuts link to common files, data, and URLs such as the employee handbook, the company intranet, and appropriate departmental guidelines and procedures. Desktop options, application configurations, Internet settings, and so on are configured to the corporate standard. As the user customizes his or her environment (within boundaries defined by the administrator), these changes are added to the initial environment. For example, the user might change the screen resolution for better visibility, and might add shortcuts to the desktop.

In this situation, a default domain profile and Group Policy are used to configure the new user's environment based on job requirements. The advantage of using a default domain profile is that all new users start from a common, administrator-defined configuration in an existing domain structure. You create a customized domain profile that applies to all new domain users the first time they log on, and they receive the customized settings from this profile. Then, as the user personalizes desktop settings and items, these settings are saved in the user's profile that is stored locally, or in the case of a roaming user profile, in a predetermined location on the network.

By implementing a default domain profile in conjunction with Roaming User Profiles, the administrator provides users with the necessary business information as a starting point, and allows them to access their settings whenever and wherever needed. Finally, the administrator uses Folder Redirection to redirect the user's My Documents folder to a network location, so that the user's documents are safely stored on a network server and can be backed up regularly.

The administrator uses the Software Installation and Maintenance extension of Group Policy to assign Microsoft Word to a user or a specific group of users. The new user logs on for the first time and sees that the software required to do his or her job is listed in the Start menu. When the user selects Microsoft Word from the Start menu, or double-clicks on a Word document, Windows Installer checks to see whether the application is installed on the local computer. If it is not, Windows Installer downloads and installs the necessary files for Word to run and sets up the necessary local user and computer settings for an on-demand installation.

Managing Multi-User Desktops

A multi-user desktop is managed, but it allows users to configure parts of their own desktops. The multi-user desktop is ideal for public shared-access computers, such as those in a library, university laboratory, or public computing center. The multi-user desktop experiences high traffic and must be reliable and unbreakable while being flexible enough to allow some customization.

Users can change their desktop wallpaper and color scheme. Because many different people use the computers and security must be maintained, they cannot control or configure hardware or connection settings. The computers often require certain tools, such as word processing software, spreadsheet software, or a development studio. Students might need access to customized applications for instructional purposes and need to be able to install applications that the network administrator has published.

With the multi-user desktop configuration, users can

- Modify Internet Explorer and the desktop.
- Run assigned or published applications.
- Configure some Control Panel options.

However, users cannot

- Use the Run command in the Start menu or at a command prompt.
- Add, remove, or modify hardware devices.

In the multi-user environment, turnover is high and a user is unlikely to return to the same computer. Therefore, local copies of roaming user profiles that are cached on the computer are removed after the user logs off, if the roaming user profile settings were successfully synchronized back to the server. Roaming user profiles use the My Documents and Application Data folders that are redirected to a network folder. However, users can log on even if their network profile is not available. In this case, the user receives a new profile based on the default profile.

The multi-user computer is assigned a set of core applications that is available to all users who log on to that particular computer. In addition, a wide variety of applications are available by publishing for user or assigning to users. Due to security risks, users cannot install from a disk, CD-ROM, or Internet location.

To conserve disk space on the workstation, most applications must be configured to run from a network server. Start menu shortcuts and registry-based settings are configured when the user selects an application to install, but most of the application's files remain on the server. The shares that store the applications can be configured for automatic caching for programs so that application files are cached at the workstation on first use.

Replacing Computers

When a user receives a new or different computer, it can cause a time-consuming interruption in productivity. It is extremely important that such users regain productivity in the shortest possible time and with a minimum of support. This can be accomplished by storing user data and settings independently of any specific computer. By using the Group Policy features Roaming User Profiles and Folder Redirection, you can assure that the user's data, settings, and applications are available wherever the user logs on to the network.

To further simplify setting up a new managed computer on your network, use Remote Installation Services to create standardized operating-system configurations. RIS allows you to create a customized image of a Windows XP Professional or Windows 2000 Professional desktop from a source computer. Then you can save that desktop image to the RIS server. The image can include the operating system alone or a preconfigured desktop image, including the operating system and a standard, locally installed desktop application.

You can use that preconfigured image to set up multiple desktops, saving valuable time. Create as many standard desktop images as you need to meet the needs of all types of users in your organization. For more information about using RIS, see "Automating and Customizing Installations" in this book.

The following scenario shows how these technologies might work together.

A user's computer suddenly undergoes a complete hardware failure. The user calls the internal support line. Shortly, a new computer, loaded only with the Windows XP Professional operating system, arrives. Without waiting for technical assistance, the user plugs in the new computer, connects it to the network, starts it, and can immediately log on.

The user finds that the desktop takes on the same configuration as the computer it replaced because roaming user profiles are enabled: the same color scheme, screen saver, and all the application icons, shortcuts, and favorites are present. The user can seamlessly access data files on the server using the necessary productivity applications once they automatically install, because Folder Redirection and Software Installation are enabled.

Windows XP TCP/IP Configuration

TCP/IP installation and configuration are fairly straightforward. The main steps are simply the installation of the TCP/IP stack, configuring an IP address and a method of name resolution, and testing to verify that it is installed and working correctly. TCP/IP is installed by default on a "new" installation of Windows XP. If your Windows XP installation was performed as an upgrade to a previously installed operating system, however, the original settings are kept. Only those upgrades necessary to support Windows XP are installed. Proceed with caution if you are using a third-party TCP/IP stack, however. Windows XP removes these stacks and replaces them with the Microsoft Windows XP implementation of TCP/IP. If you have a third-party stack installed and you want to run Windows XP as an upgrade on that computer and do not want to run Microsoft's TCP/IP stack, be sure to have the installation media available to reinstall that third-party stack when your XP upgrade is complete.

TCP/IP is the most widely used networking protocol at this time. It is robust and, assuming that the user knows the specific information that is to be used, easy to configure. If DHCP is in use on the network where the computer you are configuring is to be installed, no configuration is required at all! Windows XP TCP/IP provides additional functionality and performance over previous versions of Windows TCP/IP. Built on the Windows 2000 TCP/IP base, the Windows XP TCP/IP stack provides all the standards-compliant features for interoperability that users have come to expect. Windows XP TCP/IP is interoperable with versions of TCP/IP released by other vendors.

Windows XP TCP/IP features

- Multiple IP addresses may be configured on a single interface.
- Multiple network interfaces may be installed, each of which can have multiple IP addresses.

- Configuration of multiple gateways, which allows a computer to use alternate network exit points in the event that the primary gateway is not available.

- Internetwork routing between installed interfaces means a Windows XP computer can take the place of expensive routing equipment in smaller networks, such as homes or home offices.

- Easily configured virtual private networking capabilities means even the smallest network can provide cost-effective and secure remote access to users.

- Printing to TCP/IP printers on non-Microsoft TCP/IP devices, such as Linux workstations.

- A wide range of command-line tools for testing, troubleshooting, and configuration, including ping, tracert, pathping, route, nslookup, and arp.

- Inclusion of a Simple Network Management Protocol (SNMP) agent enables monitoring and management of systems.

- Support for NetBIOS provides ease of connectivity between Microsoft hosts on the same network.

- Support for WinSock 2 means support for a wide range of network-aware applications using this widely used API.

Configuring IP Properties

The principal parameters to be configured for a Windows XP TCP/IP-based host are IP addresses and method of name resolution. A number of configuration method options for these parameters are available. This section discusses these parameters and their configuration.

Windows XP Professional provides four ways to assign an IP address to a computer. They are as follows:

1. **Dynamic Host Configuration Protocol (DHCP):** The default method, and the easiest to use. In a network with a DHCP server, a client configured to use DHCP requests and receives an IP address automatically. A DHCP server responds and provides this address.

2. **Automatic Private IP Addressing (APIPA):** Provides a "poor man's" DHCP capability. Essentially Windows XP TCP/IP automatically assigns itself an IP address and subnet mask (no gateway or name server addresses are provided) if a DHCP server is not available on the network. This applies whether there is no DHCP server at all, or if the server is simply not responding. The range of private IP addresses Windows XP TCP/IP uses for APIPA are from the range of 169.254.0.1 through 169.254.255.254 and the subnet mask is set to 255.255.0.0. These

addresses are reserved by Internet Assigned Numbers Authority (IANA), the organization responsible for coordinating IP addresses and domain names. These private IP addresses are not used on the Internet.

3. **Static IP Addresses:** The administrator or user must manually input the specific static, or manually assigned, IP address, subnet mask, and default gateway to be used by that computer.

4. **Alternate Configuration:** This is a hybrid of DHCP and static IP assignment. Using this method, the computer trys DHCP first. If the DHCP server does not respond, the workstation then falls back to a manually configured static IP. This is a more robust assignment method than APIPA, as the administrator can manually configure a name server and a gateway, permitting the user to continue accessing resources off the network regardless of the primary IP address assignment method of a given network. It is particularly useful with mobile users.

The standard methods of name resolution supported by other versions of Microsoft Windows hosts are also supported in Windows XP Professional. Name resolution is the manner in which a host name such as www.msn.com or ScottS is matched up with an IP address, in much the same way a phone directory is used to match up names with phone numbers. These name resolution methods are listed below in the order in which they are queried by a system using the default name resolution mode:

- **Cache:** The local name cache (use nbtstat to view, purge, or reload the local cache) is queried for the NetBIOS name of a resource. The NetBIOS name is the local computer name, such as MyComputer or DillonC.

- **Broadcast:** Hosts broadcast on the local subnet for services or applications on the local subnet. Broadcasts are announcements or requests sent out to every host on a given network. Broadcasts are used for NetBIOS names.

- **Windows Internet Name Service (WINS):** This provides name resolution for NetBIOS names and ensures continued communication with older applications or versions of Windows.

- **Hosts and LMHosts files:** These files are located on the host computer and provide name resolution for the specific resources listed within. These files are manually configured and maintained, and are not used as commonly as DNS or WINS.

- **Domain Name System (DNS):** Provides name resolution for fully qualified domain names (FQDNs) such as www.microsoft.com, and enables support for applications and services that utilize FQDNs. Examples of these are Internet Explorer and Active Directory.

If the name is not resolved by any of these methods, a "network name not found" message appears. The specific message is dependent on the application that is unable to find the resource.

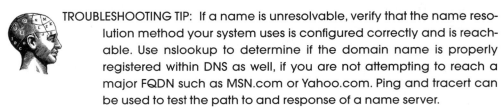 TROUBLESHOOTING TIP: If a name is unresolvable, verify that the name resolution method your system uses is configured correctly and is reachable. Use nslookup to determine if the domain name is properly registered within DNS as well, if you are not attempting to reach a major FQDN such as MSN.com or Yahoo.com. Ping and tracert can be used to test the path to and response of a name server.

Basic Installation and Manual Configuration of Windows XP TCP/IP

Before you can configure TCP/IP, it must be installed. TCP/IP is installed by default, so if you have done a fresh installation of Windows XP using all the default settings, it is already installed. If you have purchased a computer with Windows XP installed, it probably has TCP/IP installed as well. In the event that TCP/IP is not installed, or it has been removed at some point, this section provides instructions for installing TCP/IP.

1. Open the **Start** menu, then click **Control Panel**.
2. Select **Network and Internet Connections**, followed by **Network Connections**, as shown in Figure 5.1.
3. Right-click the **Local Area Connection** icon from **LAN** or **High-Speed Internet**. Select **Properties** from the context menu, as shown in Figure 5.2.
4. Examine the list of components to see if **Internet Protocol (TCP/IP)** is listed, as shown in Figure 5.3).
5. If **TCP/IP** appears, it is already installed. Skip to Step 10 if this is the case. If you do not see **Internet Protocol (TCP/IP)**, click the **Install** button.
6. Double-click **Protocol**, shown in Figure 5.4.
7. Double-click **Internet Protocol (TCP/IP)**.
8. At this point, you may be prompted for your Windows XP Installation CD. If you are, follow the on-screen instructions to complete the installation.
9. Click **Internet Protocol (TCP/IP)** and then click **Properties**, as shown in Figure 5.5.

Provide the IP address, the subnet mask, and the DNS servers (Preferred for the primary, Alternate for an optional backup DNS server) for your network,

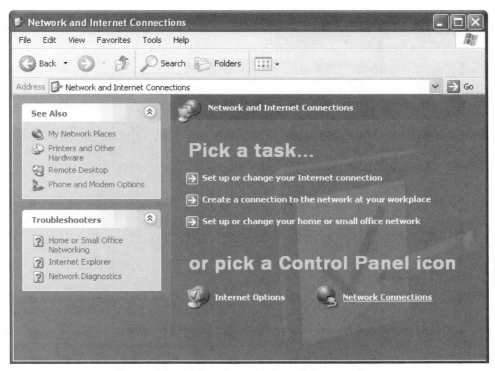

Figure 5.1   Network and Internet Connections

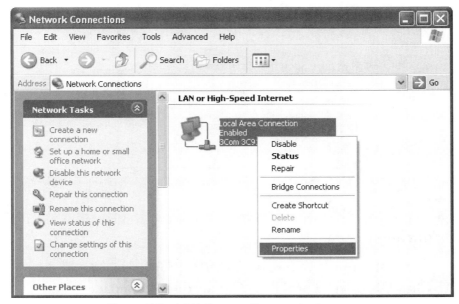

Figure 5.2   LAN Connection context menu

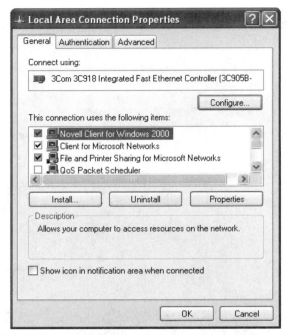

Figure 5.3 Networking components available for configuration

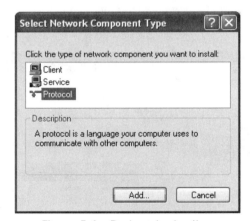

Figure 5.4 Protocol selection

as shown in Figure 5.6. Refer to your own network configuration documentation for this information.

10. Click **OK** button to close the **TCP/IP Properties** sheet.
11. Click **OK** on the **Local Area Connection Properties**.
12. Click **Close** on the **Local Area Connection Status** screen.

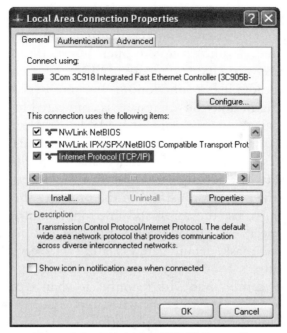

Figure 5.5   Displaying TCP/IP Properties

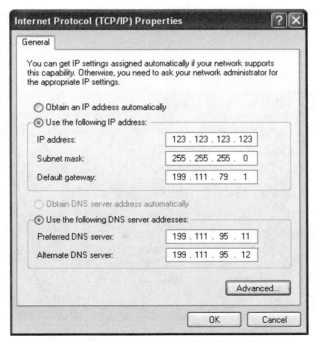

Figure 5.6   TCP/IP Properties dialog box

Testing TCP/IP Configuration

Now that that TCP/IP is installed and configured, you need to verify that it is functioning as desired. A quick test is to open Internet Explorer and type in a URL. If the Web site is reachable, you are in business. If you cannot reach the Web site (and you know it is a functioning Web site), verify that the network adapter for the configuration you are testing is connected to the network (cable attached, or that a wireless access point is available). If the network is attached, you need to verify your settings are correct. You can use the network status page of the network card's property sheet to verify this. Click **Start**, **Settings**, **Control Panel**, then **Network Settings**. Double-click the desired network card and view the details of the connection status in the property sheet. However, many administrators prefer to use the command-line tool ipconfig because it is quick and easy to use. Type `ipconfig` at a command line and press **Enter**. Examine the IP address, subnet mask, default gateway, and DNS server address to be sure they are correct. Figure 5.7 shows the output of ipconfig.

Various switches can be used with ipconfig, to change or view specific configuration parameters. To view these switches, type `ipconfig/help` at a command line for a complete listing and explanations.

- If ipconfig shows that TCP/IP is correctly configured, you need to determine where the problem is. It could be the local host, the local subnet, the gateway, or anywhere in between. Use the following list to isolate the problem.

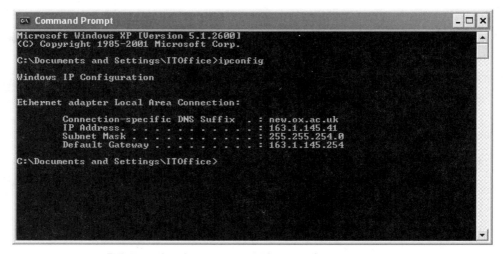

Figure 5.7 TCP/IP settings as displayed by ipconfig

- Ping the **loopback adapter** by typing `ping 127.0.0.1` at a command line. Ping is a tool that sends a message to a remote host to determine if it is responding or not. If ping fails, uninstall and reinstall **TCP/IP**.
- Ping the IP address of the local host. If ping fails, verify that there is not a duplicate IP address on the network. If there is no duplicate, uninstall and reinstall **TCP/IP**.
- Ping the IP address of the default gateway. If ping fails, verify that the gateway is operational.
- Ping the IP address of a host on the other side of the gateway. If your DNS server is maintained by a third party, such as your ISP or UltraDNS, try pinging those IP addresses.
- If pinging the remote host fails, verify that the remote host IP address is correct and that it is operational and reachable. Type `tracert x.x.x.x` at the command line (where `x.x.x.x` is the IP address of the remote host).

TIP: Once you have isolated the problem, you can begin solving it. Typically, the initial problems with connectivity are a result of a DHCP server being unavailable and an APIPA address (with no gateway or name server) is configured. Problems can also result from a wireless LAN connection that has not had time to "settle." It can take up to 30 seconds for a wireless connection to discover and join the local wireless network. If, after waiting 30 seconds, you still have not connected, ensure that any devices that can cause interference, such as cordless phones, are not in use. If that fails, verify that the wireless connection point for the network is operational.

Advanced Configuration
Automatic Configuration for Multiple Networks

The Network Location Awareness feature in Windows XP is a boon for mobile users. Moving a laptop between networks and subsequently reconfiguring the laptop for each location is not everyone's favorite task. Let's say that your laptop uses a static IP address at your home office, but when you visit your corporate headquarters, you must use a dynamically assigned address. Previously, you would have to manually reconfigure and possibly reboot your computer before settling down to work. With Windows XP, however, after a simple one-time configuration change, you simply plug in your network cable and the laptop detects the network and reconfigures itself for the correct environment. The only catches are that one of the networks has to use DHCP, and it is configured as your primary connection.

This functionality is provided by the Network Location Awareness Service. This service is also used to support Internet Connection Sharing and the Internet Connection Firewall. The Network Location Awareness Service handles the back-end tasks of detecting and subsequently conveying network infrastructure information between operating system and applications. The information it collects includes network connection type and speed. This service can collect this information independently or it can facilitate direct, nonadministrative access to the kernel by applications. This allows applications to swiftly become aware of and respond to changes in the network environment dynamically. Network-aware applications can detect network connections on a given host and adapt to that host's connectivity. Additionally, these applications can enumerate network connections, obtain information about the connections, and request notification when the connections change.

Enabling Automatic Configuration for Multiple Networks

As stated previously, DHCP is the default IP address assignment method in Windows XP TCP/IP, and at least one of the two networks you wish to move between must use DHCP. If a DHCP server is unavailable, whether because it is offline or there is no DHCP server on the current network, Windows XP TCP/IP automatically tries an alternate configuration. If an alternate configuration has not been manually configured by the user or administrator, APIPA is used to assign a private IP address to the host. However, if an alternate configuration has been provided, TCP/IP utilizes those settings for the network connection.

To set up an alternate configuration:

1. Launch **Network Connections**, either from within **Control Panel** or from the **Settings** group on the **Start** menu if you have configured it to expand **Network Connections**.

2. Locate the connection to be configured and right-click on it. Select **Properties** from the context menu.

3. If you are configuring a local area network connection, select the **General** tab. For any other type of connection, such as a network interface to an ISP, select the **Networking** tab. Then select **Internet Protocol (TCP/IP)**, and then click the **Properties** button.

4. On the **General** tab of the **Internet Protocol TCP/IP Properties** dialog box that appears, ensure that the **Obtain an IP address automatically** radio button has been selected.

5. Next, click the **Alternate Configuration** tab and select the **User configured** radio button, as shown in Figure 5.8.

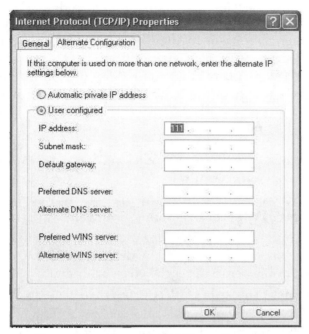

Figure 5.8 Alternate TCP/IP configuration

6. Provide the appropriate values for the following items:

   - **IP address**
   - **Subnet mask**
   - **Default gateway**
   - **Preferred** (primary) and **Alternate** (backup) **DNS server**
   - **Preferred** (primary) and **Alternate** (backup)**WINS server**

7. Click **OK** to close the **Internet Protocol (TCP/IP) Properties** dialog box.
8. Click **Close** to close the **Connection Properties** dialog box.

TIP: If you are not able to successfully set an alternate configuration, it may be because you are not logged in as an administrator, or it could be due to policies that have been configured for the network. Verify that you are logged in with an account that has root access and that network policies have not prohibited this action.

Configuring DNS for Name Resolution

As described earlier, DNS is a method of resolving Fully Qualified Domain Names to IP addresses. Windows XP workstation DNS configuration can be handled by DHCP or manually assigned by a user or administrator. This section reviews how to configure basic and advanced options for Windows XP TCP/IP DNS.

To perform basic DNS configuration:

1. Open **Network Connections** by clicking **Start**, then **Control Panel**, and then **Network Connections**.
2. Right-click the network connection that you want to configure for DNS, and then select **Properties** from the context menu.
3. If you are configuring a Local Area Network connection, select the **General** tab. If you are configuring a wide area network connection, such as to your ISP, you want to select the **Networking** tab.
4. Select **Internet Protocol (TCP/IP)**, and then click the **Properties** button.
5. To have DNS server addresses assigned by a DHCP server, select the **Obtain DNS server address automatically** radio button as shown in Figure 5.9.

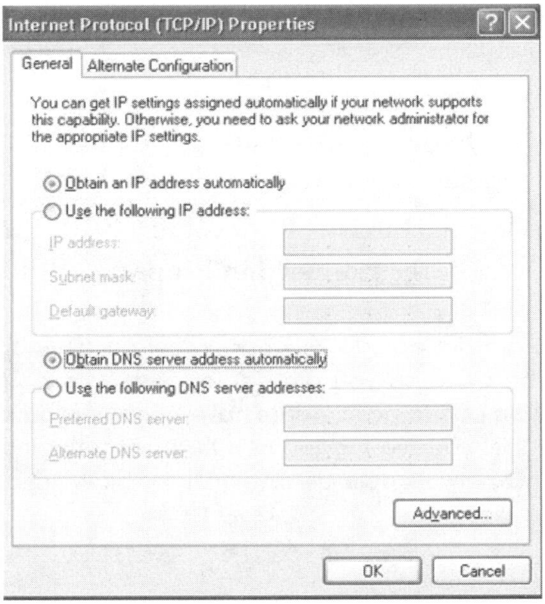

Figure 5.9   Using DHCP to obtain DNS server addresses

6. If you prefer to manually configure DNS server addresses, select the **Use the following DNS server addresses** radio button, and supply the **Preferred DNS server** (your primary DNS server) and **Alternate DNS server** (your backup DNS server) addresses.

Advanced DNS Properties

A number of advanced DNS features are supported by Windows XP TCP/IP. You find additional details about those features in Chapter 3—WINS, DNS, and DHCP. This section deals with the configuration of those features.

To configure any of the advanced options, you need to access the **Advanced TCP/IP Settings** dialog box by performing the following steps.

- Open **Network Connections** by clicking **Start**, then **Control Panel**, and then **Network Connections**.
- Right-click the network connection that you want to configure for DNS, and then select **Properties** from the context menu.
- If you are configuring a Local Area Network connection, select the **General** tab. If you are configuring a wide area network connection, such as to your ISP, you want to select the **Networking** tab.
- Select **Internet Protocol (TCP/IP)**, and then click the **Properties** button.
- Click the **Advanced** button.

Configure an Additional DNS Server IP Address

You can specify additional DNS servers to be queried, and the order in which they are to be queried. To do so:

1. Click the **Add** button in the top part of the **Advanced TCP/IP Settings** dialog box. This is located under the **DNS server addresses, in order of use** box.
2. In the **TCP/IP DNS Server** dialog box that pops up, type the IP address of the DNS server, and then click **Add**, as shown in Figure 5.10.
3. Use the up and down arrows to move selected DNS servers to new locations in the list.

Modifying the Resolution Behavior for Unqualified DNS Names

A number of options exist for resolving unqualified DNS names or a name that is not associated with a top-level domain. For example, "www.microsoft.com" is a fully qualified domain name, while "microsoft" is not. How Windows XP TCP/IP deals with unqualified names is dependent on the choices made on the

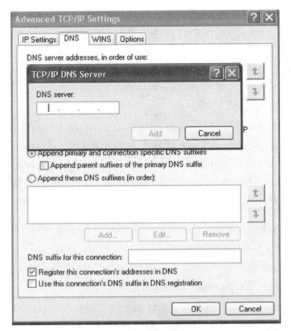

Figure 5.10 Configuring additional DNS server addresses

Advanced TCP/IP Settings DNS tab. Windows resolves FQDN domain names by a process called devolution, whereby it gradually removes the leftmost qualifier until it is able to resolve a name. For more information, see Chapter 3—WINS, DNS, and DHCP. To configure these settings simply check the radio buttons as appropriate for the desired setting.

Network Setup Wizard

Many of the features in Windows XP have Wizards to assist with setup and configuration. Networking is no exception. While not every feature of Windows XP has been included in the Wizard, a few of the more tricky tasks have been and, as a result, setting up a small office or home network has been simplified. The Network Setup Wizard automates the installation and configuration of a variety of networking components including

- Internet Connection Sharing server.
- Internet Connection Sharing client.
- Network Bridging.
- Creating a floppy disk that contains the Wizard files that can be used on another computer, including workstations that run Windows 98 and Windows Millennium Edition.

This section walks through running and using the Network Setup Wizard to set up a basic home or small office network, while Network Bridging is discussed in the next section. This section assumes that you have already installed the networking infrastructure, such as network cards, modems, cables, and routers, as required by the network you are creating, and that you have selected the computer that you plan to use as the Internet Connection Sharing host. This connection to the Internet is shared by all computers on your network, so ideally this is a computer that is always on, always reachable on the network, and has an "always on" Internet connection such as a cable modem or a DSL connection. If it does not, the other computers on the network will not enjoy uninterrupted Internet access. This computer also serves as the Internet Connection Firewall (specifics on Internet Connection Firewall and Internet Connection Sharing are covered in Chapters 7 and 8 in this book).

Once this principal system is set up, you can run the Wizard on Windows XP, Windows Millennium, and Windows 98 computers on your network. Sorry, but the Wizard does not run on Windows 95, Windows NT, or Windows 2000. You have to manually configure the network parameters on those systems to match the settings you have selected for your network. Once you have run the Wizard on all the systems in your network (or have configured the nonsupported systems), you have successfully set up file and print sharing and network names for all the hosts on your network.

 TIP: Do be sure that Internet Connection Sharing is not enabled on any other device on your network besides the designated host. Otherwise, clients may not be able to access the Internet reliably due to conflicting ICS servers.

The instructions given to launch Network Setup Wizard can be used for all versions of Windows that are supported by the Network Setup Wizard. Differences in setup are noted where appropriate for down-level operating systems.

Launching the Network Setup Wizard

There are three ways to start the Network Setup Wizard—by running the application from the local hard drive, from a CD, or from a floppy disk containing the setup files (created by running Wizard from the local hard drive of a Windows XP machine). Windows XP workstations support all three choices, while Windows 98 and Windows Millennium only support CD and floppy installations.

To run the Network Setup Wizard from your Windows XP hard drive, you can perform either of the following steps:

- Open the **Network Connections** folder from within **Control Panel**. Select **Set up a home or small office network** from under **Network Tasks**, as shown in Figure 5.11.
- Alternatively, you may select **Start**, then **All Programs** (or **Programs** if you are using the classic menu style). From there you select **Accessories**, then **Communications**, and then finally **Network Setup Wizard**, shown in Figure 5.12.

To run the Wizard from a CD on Windows XP, Windows 98, and Windows Millennium:

1. Place the Windows XP Installation CD in the computer's CD-ROM drive.
2. If autorun does not launch the Welcome screen automatically, navigate to the **Run** dialog box on the **Start** menu.

SHORTCUT: To launch the **Run** dialog box from the keyboard, press the **Windows** key + **R**.

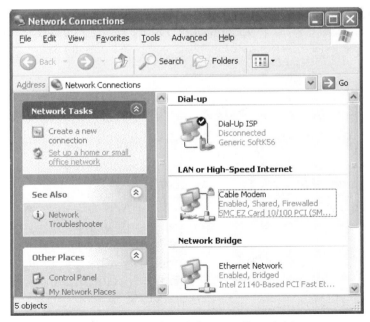

Figure 5.11   Network Connections folder

Figure 5.12   Accessing the Network Setup Wizard from the Start menu

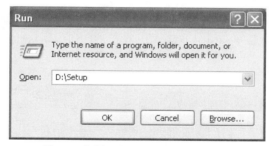

Figure 5.13   The Run dialog box

3. Type D:\Setup in the **Run** dialog box, substituting the appropriate letter for your CD drive, as shown in Figure 5.13.
4. Select **Perform additional tasks** from the **Welcome to Microsoft Windows XP** screen, then select **Set up a home or small office network** as shown in Figure 5.14.

To run the Network Setup Wizard from a floppy that contains the Wizard's setup files on Windows XP, Windows 98, and Windows Millennium, put the floppy disk containing the Wizard's files in the target computer. In the **Run** dialog box or at a **command line**, type A:\Netsetup, and press **Enter**, as shown in Figure 5.15.

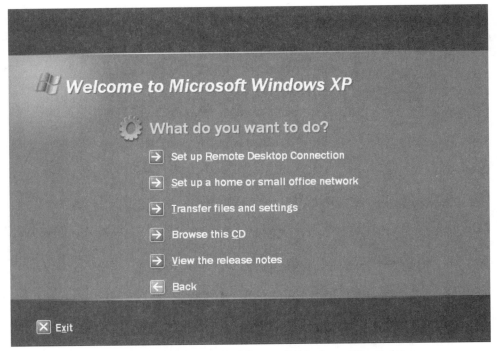

Figure 5.14   Welcome to Microsoft Windows XP window

Figure 5.15   Running the Netsetup command from the Run dialog box

Running the Network Setup Wizard

Now that the Wizard has started, you may continue with the configuration of the network.

1. If the Network Setup Wizard is launched from CD-ROM or floppy disk, the screen in Figure 5.16 appears. Click **Yes** to continue.

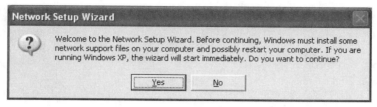

Figure 5.16   Network Setup Wizard dialog box

2. If you are running the Wizard on Windows 98 or Windows Millennium, you must restart your computer at this point, as shown in Figure 5.17. Remove the CD or floppy and click **OK**.

3. The Wizard's Welcome screen, shown in Figure 5.18, appears. Click **Next** to continue.

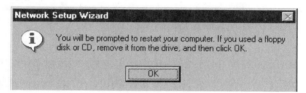

Figure 5.17   Prompt for restart

Figure 5.18   Welcome to the Network Setup Wizard

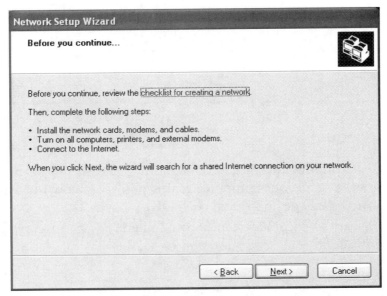

Figure 5.19   Steps to perform

4. The Wizard displays the list of preliminary steps shown in Figure 5.19.

5. Windows XP prompts you to review the **Preliminary Checklist**, shown in Figure 5.20. If you have completed all items on the checklist, click **Next**. If after reviewing them you discover you have not completed all the items on the list, click **Cancel** to exit the Wizard. When you have completed the checklist, restart the Wizard.

6. Select a connection method, shown in Figure 5.21.

7. You are prompted to answer several scenario-based networking questions. Continue the Wizard, providing responses as fitting for your network. When you have answered all the questions, you are prompted to review the configuration options that you have selected before agreeing to actually perform those configuration changes.

8. When the configuration changes have been made, the Wizard reminds you that you need to run the Wizard on all other computers in your network. If running Windows 2000 or later, you are presented with the following choices:

   • **Use the Network Setup Disk.**
   • **Use my Windows XP CD.**
   • **Just finish the Wizard.**
   • **I do not need to run the Wizard on other computers**.

   Select the option that is appropriate for you and then click **Next**.

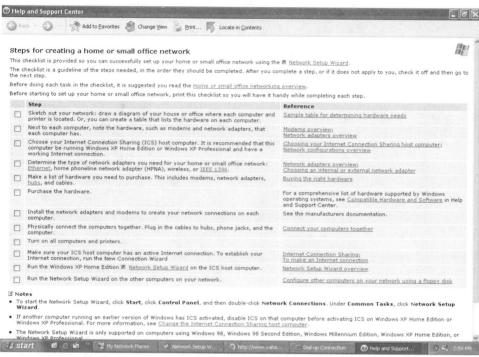

Figure 5.20   Preliminary Checklist

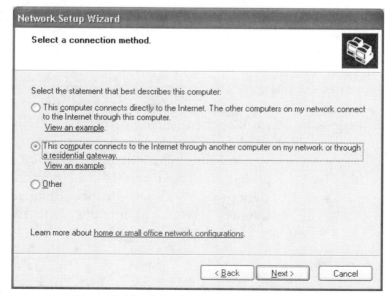

Figure 5.21   Select a connection method.

9. Follow the on-screen instructions as appropriate for your choice. Click **Close** on the final screen of the Wizard when prompted.

Network Bridging Support

Another great feature of Windows XP TCP/IP is its ability to bridge multiple network segments together without requiring a separate hardware purchase. The Network Bridge can join any number of Ethernet-based network segments into a single network segment. Although only one Network Bridge is permitted per computer, there is no limit on the number of bridges that can be installed in any given network.

The number of segments that can be joined by a single bridge is only constrained by the number of different network connections a computer can accommodate, because each segment to be bridged must be served by a different network connection. Put another way, if a given computer can only support two network connections—one wireless connection and one LAN connection, for example—then it can only bridge two network segments. Think of the Network Bridge segment capacity in the same way that you think of hub, switch, or router capacity: You can only connect as many devices as you have physical ports available. If you need more ports, you either have to add another connective device with more ports, or you have to add more ports to the connective device.

In Ethernet networks, only one device may transmit data over the network media in a given network segment or collision domain. A computer that wants to transmit data "listens" to verify the network is not in use before sending its data. It is possible for two or more devices to transmit simultaneously because they detected no activity on the network at that time. The data that is transmitted collides and is usually corrupted. This results in a need to retransmit the data. The more devices there are on the network, the greater the potential for collisions.

Bridges isolate each network segment, thereby isolating collision domains, while treating the network as a single logical network at the same time. This is accomplished by forwarding and filtering traffic based on source and destination networks. Layer 2 bridging is based on MAC or physical computer addresses, while Layer 3 bridging uses IP address for forwarding and filtering. Bridges can also be used to connect networks of different media types, such as FireWire and CAT5 Ethernet.

How Bridging Works

The Windows XP Network Bridge uses both Layer 2 and Layer 3 bridging. Each of these types of bridging functions at a different networking layer and, as such, works in a different way. This section provides an overview of both types of bridging and provides Windows XP–specific implementation details where applicable.

Layer 2 Bridging

The function of a bridge is to join two or more network segments and merge them into a single network segment. There are certain benefits afforded by a bridge that are not available with a simple hub. Primary among these benefits is the ability to maintain each network segment as a separate collision domain, while simultaneously treating the network as a single logical network. Conversely, you can also think of a bridge as a way to break up a single large collision domain into smaller segments, although the typical small Windows XP–based network does not have a large enough number of computers on a single segment that data collisions can cause performance issues.

The bridge's ability to divide a network into separate collision domains is due to its ability to forward and filter traffic based on source and destination networks. Hubs forward all traffic to all ports, while a bridge can forward destination-specific data to the port where that host is located, based on the MAC address. MAC addresses are found at Layer 2, or the data link layer. Layer 2 bridging is also known as transparent bridging, and requires that all network adapters support promiscuous mode.

Because a Layer 2 bridge is an intelligent network device, it is actually more appropriate to compare it to a switch than a hub. Effectively, a switch and a bridge provide much of the same functionality, but the switch's logic is built in at the hardware level, while bridging logic is implemented in software. A switch typically provides much faster performance than a bridge in a large network, but if you are looking for a budget-conscious solution for joining disparate networks in your home or small office, the Network Bridge is a reasonable option to consider.

As traffic flows through the bridge, it learns which MAC addresses are located on which ports or interfaces. It does this by examining the source MAC address and storing that information in a bridging table that maps the relationships between ports and MAC addresses. The bridge consults the bridging table to determine how to forward packets intelligently, rather than flooding the entire network for every request. Let's look at an example of how this works.

Computer A and Computer B are located on Interface 1, while Computer C and Computer D are located on Interface 2. When data is sent from Computer A to Computer B, the bridge consults the bridging table and discovers that the source and destination MAC addresses are on the same interface. As a result, it does not pass that traffic to Interface 2. However, when Computer A sends data to Computer C, the bridge forwards that traffic to Interface 2 because the bridging table indicates that Computer C is reached through Interface 2.

If a packet is received for a destination that is not in the bridging table, it is forwarded to all ports except the source port. This is known as flooding. In addition to unknown packet flooding, broadcast and multicast traffic is also flooded.

Because all unknown, broadcast, and multicast traffic is flooded to all network segments, it is possible for a packet storm to result if multiple bridges are used in a single network. These packet storms erupt when loops between bridges are formed, and flooded traffic is bounced incessantly between bridges. A loop is shown in Figure 5.22.

The Spanning Tree Algorithm (STA) is used in the Network Bridge to help alleviate this possibility. STA prevents loops from forming, regardless of the physical architecture of the bridge connections. Microsoft's STA is IEEE 802.1C–compliant, self-configuring, and enabled by default. It can, however, be disabled. To do so you need to edit the registry. It is worth mentioning that any modification of the registry can be detrimental to the health of your computer. Do not make any registry changes without a good backup to revert to and use the utmost caution when making changes.

To disable Spanning Tree Algorithm:

- Launch **regedit.exe** from a **command line** or the **Run** dialog box.
- Select **HKEY_LOCAL_MACHINE\SYSTEM\CurrentControlSet\ Services\BridgeMP**.

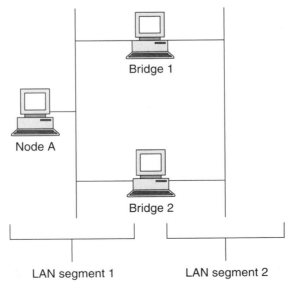

Figure 5.22 A looped bridge configuration

- Click the **Edit** menu and select **New**, then **DWORD Value**.
- Type `DisableSTA`; then press **Enter**.
- Double-click the new value. Change the value to **1**, then click **OK**.

The change takes effect after the next reboot.

Layer 3 Bridging

Layer 2 bridging requires network adapters on the bridging computer be placed in promiscuous mode. Because not all adapters offer this functionality, the Network Bridge also operates as a Layer 3 bridge. Instead of using MAC addresses to determine the source and destination ports for traffic, IP addresses are used. Naturally, this means Layer 3 bridging is limited to TCP/IP. Layer 3 bridging also differs from Layer 2 bridging in that the data frame is changed when it is forwarded by the bridge. An additional feature of the Microsoft Windows XP Network Bridge is that it supports DHCP packet forwarding. Many third-party network bridges do not proxy DHCP packets.

The bridging table for Layer 3 bridging is built using Address Resolution Protocol (ARP). ARP actually examines a data packet for the IP addresses of the source and destination, and matches it to a MAC address of the port that is the next hop in the path to its final destination. A device such as a bridge that uses, sends, and receives packets on behalf of network devices on different network segments is called an ARP proxy. This is illustrated in Figure 5.23.

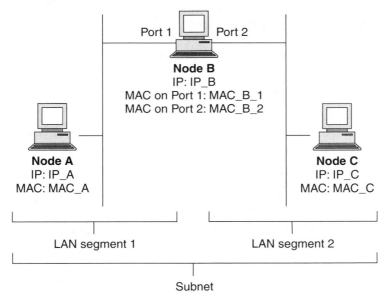

Figure 5.23 ARP proxying on a bridged network

This process is similar to the process used in routing, but the packets are actually forwarded based on information in a forwarding table, as opposed to a routing table.

Windows XP TCP/IP enables Layer 3 bridging by default when the Network Bridge is enabled. However, this behavior may be problematic in some networks, and can result in packet storms. If you are aware of such problems occurring in the past in your network, you may wish to disable packet forwarding. Use caution when performing this procedure—any time registry changes are made, it is possible to make typing mistakes that can result in an incorrectly (or even non-) functioning operating system.

To disable Layer 3 bridging:

- Launch **regedit.exe** from a **command line** or the **Run** dialog box.
- Select **HKEY_LOCAL_MACHINE\SYSTEM\CurrentControlSet\ Services\BridgeMP**.
- Click the **Edit** menu and select **New**, then **DWORD Value**.
- Type `DisableForwarding`; then press **Enter**.
- Double-click the new value. Change the value to **1**, then click **OK**.

The change takes effect after the next reboot.

Creating a Network Bridge

Creating a Network Bridge is a very simple operation. The instructions below assume that all adapters have been previously installed and configured and that the connections they support are working correctly.

1. Open **Network Connections**, either from **Control Panel** or the **Settings** group on the **Start** menu.
2. Press and hold the **Ctrl** key and select all the connections you wish to bridge together.
3. Right-click one of the selected connections and select **Bridge Connections** from the context menu, as shown in Figure 5.24.
4. Alternatively you can right-click each connection to be bridged and select **Add to bridge** from the context menu. This is a great way to add an additional connection to an existing bridge.
5. The message **Please wait while Windows bridges the connections** is displayed. After the bridge configuration is complete, the connections that were selected now appear under the Network Bridge group, as shown in Figure 5.25.

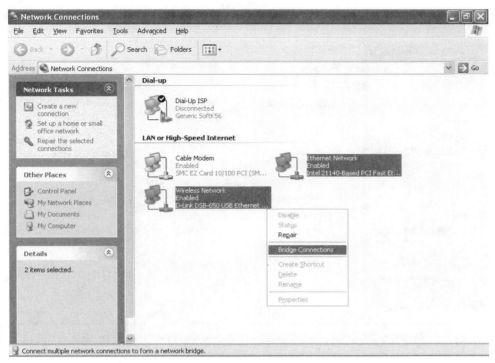

Figure 5.24   Creating a Network Bridge

Once a bridge is created, it takes on the properties of a regular network connection, and can be configured as such. Simply right-click the bridge and select **Properties** from the context menu to bring up the properties sheet. This is where you manage the bridge and its specific networking attributes, as shown in Figure 5.26.

While the Network Bridge has become manageable like a standard network connection, the connections that it is bridging lose their individual characteristics, as shown in Figure 5.27.

In fact, the bridged connections are no longer treated as network connections, but as ports on the bridge. Using the ipconfig command reveals that the bridged connections do not appear individually, but rather a single MAC Bridge miniport entry appears in the list of TCP/IP-configured adapters.

To remove a connection from the bridge, right-click the desired connection in the **Network Bridge** group, and then click **Remove from Bridge**. To disable a bridge, right-click the **Network Bridge** icon and select **Disable** from the context menu.

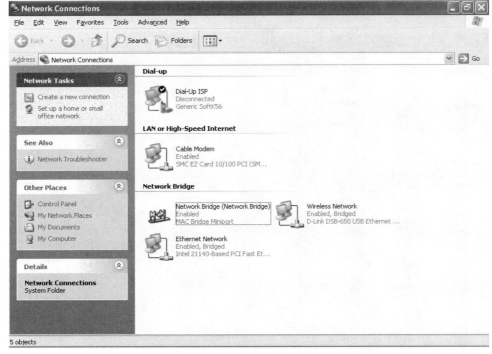

Figure 5.25 A Network Bridge has been successfully created.

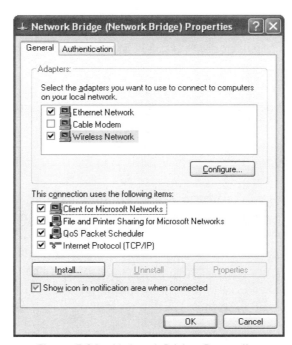

Figure 5.26 Network Bridge Properties

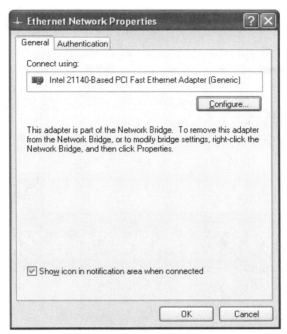

Figure 5.27 Properties of a bridged network connection

 TIP: Although no reboot is required when removing connections from, or disabling, the Network Bridge, experience has shown that a reboot can alleviate the inconsistent network connectivity that appears occasionally after making these types of changes.

Sliding Windows

Transmission Control Protocol offers guaranteed packet delivery, unlike Internet Protocol, which does not guarantee delivery of datagrams. This guaranteed delivery requires a connection to be opened between hosts before any packets are sent. TCP negotiates the connection between two hosts with a three-way handshake. All data that is sent must be acknowledged by the recipient. How much data TCP can send before it must wait for an acknowledgment is dictated by a flow control technique called *windowing,* or *sliding windows.* The size of the window sets the amount of data that can be sent, and is negotiated as part of the three-way TCP handshake that initiates the connection. TCP uses a window size of four times the size of the maximum TCP segment size negotiated during connection setup, up to a maximum size of 64K. The receiving computer sets the size for the transaction.

This window acts as a buffer for both the send and receive sides of the transaction. For example, Host A wants to send data to Host B via TCP. During their handshake, they agree to use a 64K window. Host A sends 64K of data to Host B and then waits for an acknowledgment from Host B that it has received some or all of the data. Host A then sends more data that matches the amount of acknowledged data. If all the data has been acknowledged, another 64K is sent. If 32K has been acknowledged, then that amount is sent. This continues until all data has been acknowledged as received.

The sliding window not only acts as a buffer on the receiving end of the connection, it also provides a means of traffic control on the network. By establishing the maximum amount of data a host can receive up front, the network is not overwhelmed by traffic being sent and resent to an overloaded host.

Larger receive windows can yield better performance in networks with high levels of delay. Sliding window size is adjusted in the registry. Please use care when changing the registry—it is possible for a simple error to result in the need to reinstall your operating system. Only change registry settings when absolutely necessary.

To adjust the size of the sliding window:

- Launch **regedit.exe** from a **command line** or the **Run** dialog box.
- Double-click **HKEY_Local_Machine\SYSTEM\CurrentControlSet\ Services\Tcpip\Parameters\Interfaces\<interface-name>**
- Enter a new Value. Suggested value is the larger of either four times the maximum TCP data size on the network or 8,192 rounded up to an even multiple of the network TCP data size.

TCP/IP Tools

The following list provides information about some of the TCP/IP diagnostic tools that are included with Windows XP. Unless otherwise stated, these tools are available from the command line.

Basic tools include

- **Network Diagnostics** in **Help and Support:** Provides diagnostic tests and configuration information.
- **Network Connections Folder:** Located in Control Panel, under Network and Internet Connections, it contains data about all network connections on the computer.
- **IPConfig:** Displays current TCP/IP network configuration values; updates or releases Dynamic Host Configuration Protocol–allocated

leases; and displays, registers, or flushes Domain Name System (DNS) names.

- **Ping:** Sends ICMP Echo Request messages to verify that TCP/IP is configured correctly and that the specified TCP/IP host is available.

Advanced tools include

- **Hostname:** Displays the host name of the local computer.
- **Nbtstat:** Displays current NetBIOS over TCP/IP connections; can be used to update the NetBIOS name cache.
- **PathPing:** Displays the network path to a TCP/IP host and reports packet losses at each router or hop along the way.
- **Route:** Displays the host's IP routing table and can be used to add or delete IP routes.
- **Tracert:** Displays the network path to a TCP/IP host.
- **Arp:** Displays the IP-to-MAC address resolution tables and can be used to modify the arp cache.
- **Netstat:** Displays status, protocols, and local and foreign addresses of current connections.

In addition to the TCP/IP-specific tools, you can also use Windows XP Professional tools.

- **Event Viewer:** Reports system errors and events in log format.
- **Computer Management:** Can be used to change network card drivers.
- **Registry editor (regedit.exe)**

TCP/IP parameters are stored in and read from the registry. If you so desire, you can make changes to those settings directly in the registry. However, do not arbitrarily make changes to the registry. Doing so can have disastrous results—your computer may never be the same again, and not in a good way! Only use the registry editor for making changes to parameters that you do not have a direct configuration dialog box for in the User Interface. The following items are the default TCP/IP settings in the registry for parameters that are not configurable from within Network Connections. All are located in \HKEY_Local_Machine\System\CurrentControlSet\Services\Tcpip\Parameters.

DatabasePath
Key: Tcpip\Parameters
Value Type: REG_EXPAND_SZ - Character string

Valid Range: A valid Windows NT file path

Default: %SystemRoot%\System32\Drivers\Etc

Description: This parameter specifies the path to the basic TCP/IP config files: HOSTS, LMHOSTS, NETWORKS, and PROTOCOLS. If you move your files from the standard location, you need to modify this registry entry to ensure your WinSock applications can find them.

ForwardBroadcasts

Key: Tcpip\Parameters

Value Type: REG_DWORD - Boolean

Valid Range: 0 or 1 (False or True)

Default: 0 (False)

Description: Forwarding of broadcasts is not supported in Windows XP TCP/IP. This parameter has been supplied for use by developers for future enhancements.

UseZeroBroadcast

Key: Tcpip\Parameters\Interfaces\ID for Adapter

Value Type: REG_DWORD - Boolean

Valid Range: 0 or 1 (False or True)

Default: 0 (False)

Description: A majority of TCP/IP implementations use ones-broadcasts, but some do not. Interoperability problems can result from using both ones- and zeros-broadcasts on the same network. Setting this value to 1 (True) uses zeros-broadcasts (0.0.0.0) instead of ones-broadcasts (255.255.255.255).

Conclusion

As you have seen in this chapter, configuration of TCP/IP in Windows XP is straightforward and simple. TCP/IP is installed by default when you install Windows XP, and beyond that, the only configurations necessary are adjustments that must be made to reflect the requirements of your own network. If you use DHCP on your network, no additional configuration is needed, because Windows XP TCP/IP detects and configures for this automatically.

This chapter also discussed the Network Bridge, which allows you to join networks of different media types or separate networks into a single logical network very simply. The computer acting as the Network Bridge uses a single Properties sheet to control all bridged connections, and as a result, is very simple to install, configure, and support.

The Network Wizard was also presented as an alternative to manual configuration of the various components involved in TCP/IP networking, including the Internet Connection Firewall and Internet Connection Sharing. This tool can be used for setting up networking on a single computer or it can be used to lay down the basic framework for a Microsoft network using a variety of down-level operating systems in a small office or home network.

TCP/IP is the most popular and prevalent network protocol in use today. However, it is not the only protocol. The next chapter discusses other networking protocols and heterogeneous networks. Heterogeneous networks are those that use more than one network systems, such as Novell and Microsoft networking or Unix and Microsoft networking. Novell and Unix interoperability with Windows XP networking and configuration are covered in Chapter 6.

Chapter

6

Other LAN Protocols and Heterogeneous Networks

This chapter covers NetBEUI (NetBIOS Extended User Interface) and interoperability with Novell NetWare and UNIX and Linux, as well as the LAN protocols and configuration options associated with each.

NetBEUI

Back in the latter half of the 1990s, NetBEUI was the favorite LAN protocol for small networks. It is fast and does not require any special configuration. Its only real drawback is that it is not routable, but since it is a rather "chatty" protocol due to its broadcast nature, that is not such a bad thing. TCP/IP has taken the place of NetBEUI as the protocol of choice. As a result, Microsoft has discontinued support for the NetBEUI network protocol in Windows XP. However, the NetBEUI protocol can be found on the Windows XP CD-ROM under the VALUEADD directory, in the event that you need to install it for backwards compatibility reasons.

To install NetBEUI:

1. Insert your Windows XP CD-ROM into the CD-ROM drive and browse to the **Valueadd\MSFT\Net\NetBEUI** folder.
2. Copy **Nbf.sys** to the **%SYSTEMROOT%\System32\Drivers** directory.
3. Copy **Netnbf.inf** to the **%SYSTEMROOT%\Inf** directory.
4. Click **Start**, click **Control Panel**.
5. Then double-click **Network Connections**.
6. Right-click the adapter you want to add NetBEUI to, and then click **Properties**.

7. On the **General** tab, click **Install**.

8. Click **Protocol**.

9. Click **Add**.

10. Click to select **NetBEUI Protocol** from the list.

11. Click **OK**.

12. Restart your computer if you receive a prompt to complete the installation.

The NetBEUI protocol should now be installed and working.

Interoperating with NetWare

Windows XP provides a suite of tools to let you connect to network resources that are members of a Novell NetWare network. This section provides a general overview of NetWare and its protocols, as well as the tools within Windows XP for connectivity to and management of NetWare resources. The configuration of NetWare services and protocols are discussed as well.

Overview

Unlike Windows XP, Novell's NetWare is not an operating system for a computer. Rather, it is a network operating system (NOS) that places a networking infrastructure on top of the operating system running on a computer. NetWare provides all the networking functions that are included in Windows, from file and printer sharing to support for applications that run over a network, such as e-mail. Novell developed NetWare in the early 1980s, and it is based on Xerox Network Systems.

NetWare is a client-server NOS that specifies networking functionality for the top five levels of the Open System Interconnection (OSI Model): Application, Presentation, Session, Transport, and Network. It uses standard media access methods for the lower layers, including

- Ethernet/IEEE 802.3
- Token Ring/IEEE 802.5
- Fiber Distributed Data Interface (FDDI)
- ARCnet
- PPP

Figure 6.1 maps the NetWare NOS to the OSI networking model.

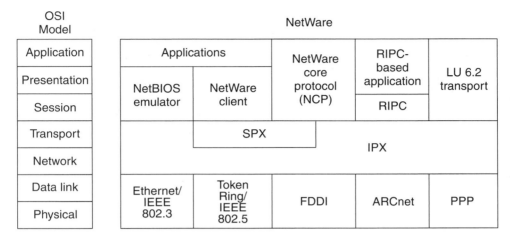

Figure 6.1   NetWare-to-OSI mappings

The IPX/SPX Protocol Stack

The IPX/SPX protocol stack is similar to TCP/IP in that it includes a number of protocols within the stack. These transport- and network-layer protocols provide a variety of functions and are covered in this section, within the context of NWLink, Microsoft's implementation of the IPX/SPX stack.

Since NetWare 5.0, Novell has implemented TCP/IP as the native protocol used within NetWare. However, prior to this shift, IPX/SPX was the native protocol used by NetWare. IPX/SPX is still supported and widely used within NetWare networks.

Even within the Windows family IPX/SPX was, and still is, widely used in many networks. IPX/SPX can be used within a Windows network to connect a wide range of operating systems, from DOS to Windows NT to Windows XP. Until the Windows 2000 release made TCP/IP the default protocol and made it simple to use, many network administrators utilized IPX/SPX for their LANs because it was easy to deploy. No special knowledge was required to implement a LAN of almost any size with IPX/SPX. Moreover, unlike NetBEUI, another simple-to-implement protocol provided with Windows, it is also routable.

IPX/SPX is officially called NWLink IPX/SPX/NetBIOS-Compatible Transport Protocol, but it is often referred to simply as NWLink, because the whole title can be quite a mouthful. NWLink includes the following protocols:

- IPX
- SPX
- SPXII

- RIP
- SAP
- NetBIOS

Each of these protocols are explored in the following pages.

IPX

IPX, or Internet Packet Exchange, is a Layer 3 protocol used for addressing and routing of packets through a network. IPX is a best-effort delivery protocol. Delivery of IPX datagrams is not guaranteed, nor is the order in which they are received guaranteed, much like Internet Protocol.

IPX is connectionless, which means that a session with a remote computer is not established before packets are sent. The overhead associated with session-establishment is avoided, but at the expense of flow control or receipt acknowledgment. Packets are sent from host to host, but no acknowledgment of these packets is ever sent. While this is not suitable for some applications, such as real-time audio or video, this works just fine for applications that are not dependent on guaranteed packet delivery. Additionally, smaller LANs tend to have fewer packet losses than larger internetworks, so the trade-off of the reduction of reliability in favor of the reduction of media overhead is acceptable in those environments.

Addressing

Each node on an IPX/SPX network must have a unique identity, just as it would on a TCP/IP network. This identification is based on a combination of network node ID and network ID. It is represented as a hexadecimal number, and contains a 32-bit network number and a 48-bit node number.

IPX uses the Media Access Control (MAC) address of a network device as the basis for its network node identification mechanism. Because each NIC already has a universally unique MAC address, no additional addressing scheme is required for node identification. Also, the network node identifier is the same as its MAC address natively, so there is no need for an IPX version of ARP, which you recall is used to map IP addresses to a MAC address for IP address resolution. The network ID is assigned by the LAN administrator.

IPX Packet Structure

An IPX packet is made up of 11 fields. Each of these fields provides a specific function, as described in Figure 6.2.

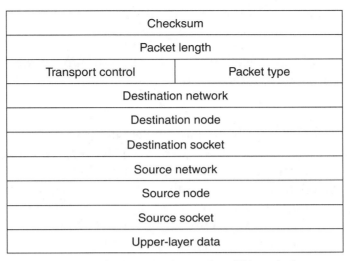

Checksum	
Packet length	
Transport control	Packet type
Destination network	
Destination node	
Destination socket	
Source network	
Source node	
Source socket	
Upper-layer data	

Figure 6.2   The structure of an IPX packet

- **Checksum:** If a checksum is to be used, it is indicated in this 16-bit field. If no checksum is to be used, this field is set to all 1s (FFFF in hexadecimal format).
- **Packet length:** The packet length is described here in bytes. The packet length includes the entire packet, not just the headers. It can be any length up to the MTU (maximum transmission unit) of the physical media in use.
- **Transport control:** The number of routers, or hops, through which a packet has passed. The maximum value of this field is 16. Once 16 is reached, the packet is discarded as a means of eliminating traffic that is occurring as a result of a loop somewhere on the network.
- **Packet type:** This field states which upper-layer protocol should receive the packet's data. Typically, the field is set to 5 for SPX (Sequenced Packet Exchange), or 17 for NCP (NetWare Control Protocol).
- **Destination network:** The network to which the packet is destined.
- **Destination node:** The node that is to receive delivery of the packet.
- **Destination socket:** The specific socket that takes delivery of the packet on the receiving node.
- **Source network:** The network from which the packet originated.
- **Source node:** The node that sent the packet.
- **Source socket:** The socket on the source node from which the packet was sent.

- **Upper-layer data:** Information required by processes running at higher layers in the IPX/SPX stack.

When NWLink is installed on a workstation running Windows XP, IPX is implemented with the Nwlnkipx.sys driver.

SPX

Sequenced Packet Exchange is the most widely used NetWare transport protocol. It offers connection-oriented, guaranteed delivery of packets over IPX. Because it is a connection-oriented protocol, a session must be set up, maintained, and torn down. This means additional overhead for session-related functions on the two hosts that are communicating, but the actual transmission carries less overhead on the wire. This type of connection is most appropriate for applications that require a continuous connection, in much the same way as TCP does.

SPX tracks the transmission of packets sent and the order in which they are sent. As each packet is successfully received by a remote host, an acknowledgment notice is sent to the sender. The sender compares the acknowledgments received against packets sent. If no acknowledgment is received, SPX retransmits the packet in question. This process can be repeated up to a maximum of eight times. At that point, SPX considers this to be a failed connection and halts further transmission.

Another similarity between SPX and TCP is the packet burst mechanism. Comparable to TCP sliding windows, packet burst (also called burst mode) permits a host to send a number of packets to a remote host in a connection-oriented session, without requiring an acknowledgment to be sent for each packet. The group of packets sent are acknowledged all at once. The sender compares the acknowledgments to the packets sent and retransmits any packets that were sent but not acknowledged. Only one packet may be outstanding at any time with SPX. SPX permits packet sizes up to a maximum of 576 bytes.

SPXII

SPXII enhances the connection-oriented services provided by SPX. SPXII permits more outstanding packets than SPX, allowing a sender to transmit more first-time data while waiting for acknowledgment of previously sent data. The exact number permitted is negotiated between sender and receiver at the time the session is established. It also increases the maximum packet size to 1,518 bytes, an increase of over 260 percent! Both SPX and SPXII are implemented in the Nwlnkspx.sys driver.

RIP

IPX/SPX supports two routing protocols: Routing Information Protocol (RIP) and NetWare Link-State Protocol (NLSP). Only RIP is supported natively in Windows XP. RIP is a distance-vector routing protocol. IPX RIP sends regular updates—every 60 seconds—to make the most effective routing decisions possible. In addition to allowing the sending node to determine the fastest route to a specific network, the data sent in these RIP broadcasts also allows RIP routers to share information with each other. Routers use RIP broadcasts to update their own internal routing tables, respond to route requests from other network nodes, or to alert other nodes of a change in network configuration.

To make routing path decisions, a measurement of delay called a *tick* is used. A tick is equal to an eighteenth of a second. The path to the destination network with the lowest tick count is used. In the event of a tie, the hop count is used to determine the best route. The path with the fewest hops (routers to cross) is declared the best route. The Nwlnkipx.sys driver provides RIP functionality.

SAP

Service Advertising Protocol is the means by which network resources are announced or advertised on a network. SAP was much more widely used in NetWare prior to NetWare 4.0. NetWare Directory Services (NDS) have largely replaced many of the functions provided by SAP in the past. In networks using NDS, workstations locate services by searching the list of available services in the NDS server. SAP is still required in NetWare 4.0 however, as SAP is used by workstations to locate the NDS server upon boot.

SAP announcements include the address of a resource, as well as the services provided by that resource. Resources in this context refer to file or print servers, while services being advertised refers to the shared files, applications, printers, and so on available on these servers. A workstation queries a router for a specific resource, such as a printer. The router responds to the query with the network address. The client then uses this information to contact the resource directly.

SAP advertisements are sent every 60 seconds by the resources with services available to the rest of the network. Routers include this information in their routing tables. Both the services and network addresses are included in these tables. These tables are also sent out as a broadcast every 60 seconds. The Nwlnkipx.sys driver provides SAP functionality.

NetBIOS

NetBIOS services are provided with NWLink. NetBIOS is a session-layer interface industry specification from both IBM and Microsoft. NetWare provides NetBIOS emulation software to allow NetBIOS-compliant programs to run within the NetWare environment. Microsoft provides IPX NetBIOS natively.

NetBIOS provides a programming interface for sharing services and data across a variety of network protocols, including IPX/SPX. There are three divisions of NetBIOS services:

- **Name service:** Allows an application to determine that its NetBIOS name is unique, via a broadcast query. Also enables an application to delete an unneeded NetBIOS application, and to use a server's NetBIOS name to determine the server's network address via a broadcast query.
- **Session service:** Allows a connection-oriented session to be set up between two hosts to transmit data in a reliable manner, and an acknowledgment to be sent to the sender upon receipt.
- **Datagram service:** Allows data to be sent as datagrams, without requiring acknowledgment. This enables applications to send broadcast queries.

NetBIOS is implemented in IPX via the NWLinkNB.sys driver.

Configuration

Now that we have covered the basics of IPX/SPX and its components, we cover how to set up and configure IPX/SPX. You need three pieces of information to completely configure the protocol:

- Internal network number
- Frame type
- Network number

Notice that there are two different entries for network numbers in the listing above. This is because NWLink actually uses two different types of network numbers. These two network numbers serve two distinctly different functions and are covered in detail.

Internal Network Number

The internal network number is used by a computer that is serving files, printers, or other network resources (called services in the NetWare world) and using SAP to advertise them. It is used for internal routing purposes, and although it is not exactly analogous, you can think of it as being similar to the TCP/IP loopback address. This number is used to further define a route from an external network to a virtual network running inside a server. This makes specific route definition possible when multiple equivalent routes exist from client to server. The internal network number corresponds to the internal IPX number found on a server running NetWare. The internal IPX network on a NetWare server uniquely identifies a server on multiple networks. The internal network number is expressed as an eight-digit hexadecimal number ranging from 1 to FFFFFFFE, and is unique across the network. This number is selected automatically by Windows XP by default, but you can change it by entering it in as directed in the instructions.

Frame Type

Frame type refers to the format or encapsulation scheme of a packet to be sent over the network. The frame type corresponds to the type of network in use. Multiple adapters in the same computer may be connected to different types of networks, and as such may need a different frame type for each connection. The default setting is Auto Detect, but the option is also provided for manual configuration.

The supported frame types for Windows XP NWLink are as follows:

- **802.2:** The IEEE logical link control (LLC) protocol used for communication over a token ring or Ethernet network.
- **802.3:** IEEE protocol offers carrier sense multiple access with collision detection (CSMA/CD). Also called Novell_802.2.
- **Ethernet II:** Also called Ethernet version 2 or ARPA. Ethernet version 2 includes the standard Ethernet header, consisting of a Destination and Source address field and an EtherType field.
- **SNAP:** This frame type extends the 802.2 header by providing a type field similar to the Ethernet II specification.

Network Number

The network number is used on the external network for routing purposes. Each frame type configured must have a corresponding network number, and each adapter connected to an IPX/SPX network must be configured for this information. Every computer on a given network segment must use the same network number, but each network number must be unique within that segment, in much the same way that all hosts on a given TCP/IP network must use the same subnet mask to define the specific network to which they all belong.

If you are not sure which network number to use, you can run IPXROUTE config on another previously configured Windows computer (on the same network) to locate this information, as shown in Figure 6.3.

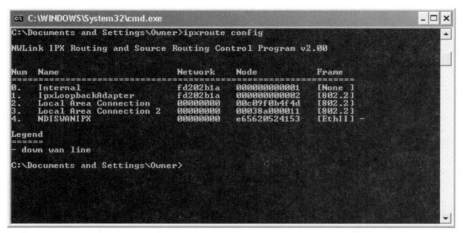

Figure 6.3   Using IPXROUTE to locate the network number

Protocol Configuration

To configure NWLink IPX/SPX/NetBIOS Compatible Transport Protocol you follow these instructions.

1. Click **Start**, then **Settings**, then **Network Connections**.
2. Right-click the LAN for which you want to configure NWLink and select **Properties** from the context menu. The connection's properties sheet appears, as shown in Figure 6.4.
3. On the General tab, click **NWLink IPX/SPX/NetBIOS Compatible Transport Protocol**, then click the **Properties** button. The connection's IPX/SPX configured properties appears, as shown in Figure 6.5.
4. On the General tab, enter a value for Internal Network Number
5. In Frame type, click a frame type, and supply a network number if requested, and then click **OK**.
6. Click **OK** to save your settings.

Installing SAP

Service Advertising Protocol is not installed by default. To install SAP:

1. Open **Network Connections** in Control Panel.
2. Right-click the local area connection for which you want to install SAP, and then click **Properties**.
3. On the General tab, click **Install**.

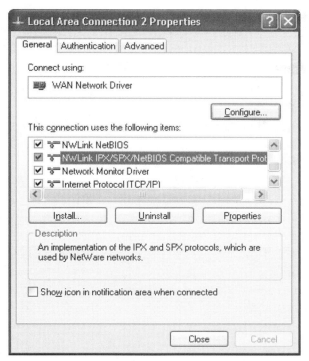

Figure 6.4 Opening the Connection Properties sheet

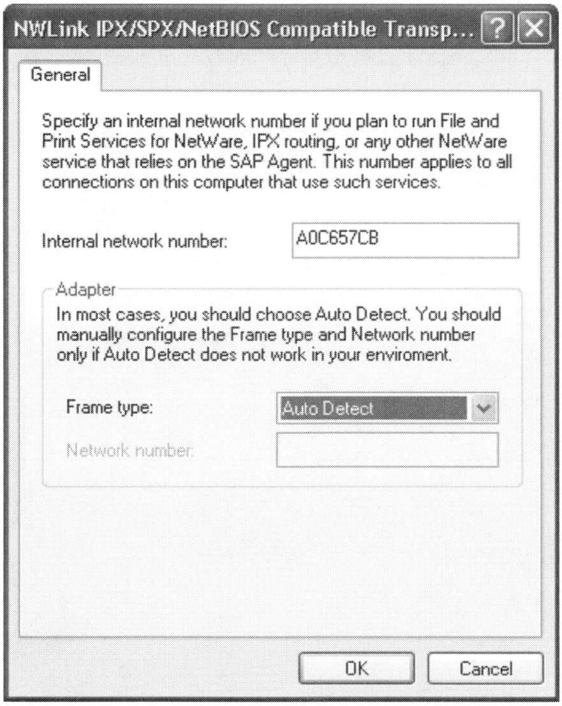

Figure 6.5 The Connection's IPX/SPX Properties sheet

4. In the Select Network Component Type dialog box, click **Service**, and then click **Add**, as shown in Figure 6.6.

5. In the Select Network Service dialog box, click **Service Advertising Protocol**, as shown in Figure 6.7.

6. Click **OK**, then click **OK** to close the network properties sheet.

Client Configuration

It is important to be aware of the distinction between the IPX/SPX protocol and the Client Services provided with Windows XP. NWLink is a protocol. It is only intended to transport data from one computer to another. In order to connect and actually log on to a remote computer containing the resources you want to access, you must install the proper client for the operating system that you are trying to reach. For Windows, this is the Client for Microsoft Networks, and in Windows XP, it is installed by default. In down-level versions of Windows you may need to install this manually to ensure that file and print services are available.

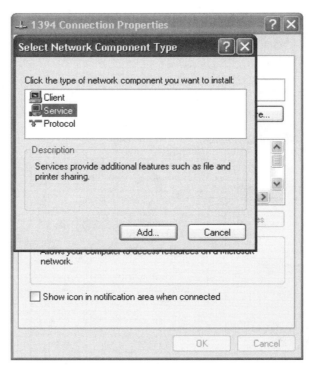

Figure 6.6   Select Service from the Network Component Type dialog box

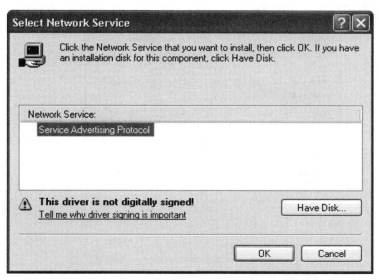

Figure 6.7 Select Service Advertising Protocol

To log on to a NetWare server, you also need to install a client. These clients provide what is called a redirector. The redirector allows packet forwarding between two systems with differing types of file and print services. Windows XP uses Common Interface File System (CIFS) for file and print services, while NetWare relies on the NetWare Core Protocol (NCP) for file and print services. Microsoft provides Client Services for NetWare for just such a purpose. *Note:* Windows XP 64-bit Edition does not support Client Services for NetWare. You may also use the Novell-provided Novell Client for Windows XP.

Each of these clients has specific features and benefits. Naturally, the Novell client provides more functionality within the NetWare environment, but it does require a separate installation of files not included with the Windows XP media as it was with Windows 2000. Further, it is important to know that if you install the Novell client, you still need to have the Client for Microsoft Networks installed if you wish to communicate with any other Windows XP workstation.

To install Client Service for NetWare:

1. Open **Network Connections** in Control Panel.
2. Right-click the local area connection for which you want to install Client Service for NetWare, and then click **Properties**.
3. On the General tab, click **Install**.
4. In the Select Network Component Type dialog box, click **Client**, and then click **Add**, as shown in Figure 6.8.

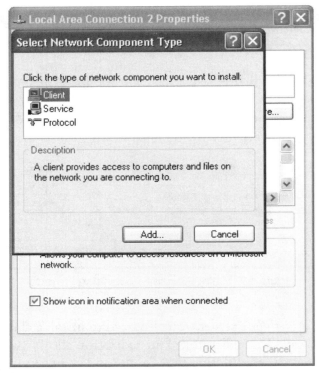

Figure 6.8 Select Client from the Network Component Type dialog box

5. In the Select Network Client dialog box, click **Client Service for Net-Ware**, as shown in Figure 6.9.

6. Click **OK**, then click **OK** to close the network properties sheet.

Administering NetWare from Windows XP

You can use a computer running Windows XP Professional and Client Service for NetWare to perform a wide range of NetWare administrative functions. The NetWare administrative tools that can be run from Windows XP include the following list. Multiple simultaneous instances of each of these tools is possible, to enable management of multiple NetWare servers concurrently from a single Windows XP workstation.

- **Chkvol:** Display information about any volume on a NetWare server.
- **Colorpal:** Modify NetWare's default color scheme.
- **Dspace:** Limits the disk space for a user on a given volume.
- **Fconsole:** Broadcast messages, view current user connections, and alter the status of file server.

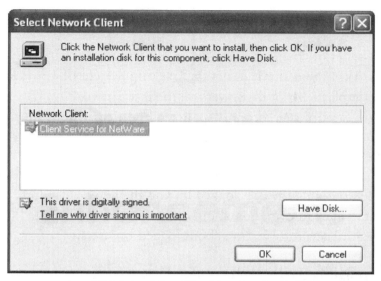

Figure 6.9   Select the Client Service for NetWare

- **Filer:** Change a directory's owner, creation date, and timestamps.
- **Flag:** View and change attributes of files in a specified directory.
- **Flagdir:** View and change attributes of subdirectories in a specified directory.
- **Grant:** Grants trustee rights to users or groups in a specified file or directory.
- **Help:** Get system help about NetWare.
- **Listdir:** View directories and subdirectories and their inherited rights mask, effective rights, and creation dates.
- **Ncopy:** Copy one or more files from one network directory to another.
- **Ndir:** View information about file names and sizes and their modification, access, creation, and archive dates.
- **Pconsole:** Manage print servers.
- **Psc:** View status of and control print servers and network printers.
- **Rconsole:** The remote console functions can be performed on the NetWare system console.
- **Remove:** Delete a user or group from the trustee list of a file or directory.
- **Revoke:** Revoke trustee rights from a user or group in a file or directory.
- **Rights:** View the effective rights in a file or directory.
- **Send:** Transmit a message between workstations.

- **Session:** Perform temporary drive mappings; create, change, and delete search drives.
- **Setpass:** Set or change passwords.
- **Settts:** Verify that the Transaction Tracking System (TTS) is functioning.
- **Slist:** Display a list of file servers on the internetwork.
- **Syscon:** Set up user accounts, policies, and permissions on the NetWare network.
- **Tlist:** View the trustee list of a directory or file.
- **Userlist:** View list of current users for a file server, each user's connection number, the time the user logged in, and the network address.
- **Volinfo:** View information about each volume on NetWare file servers.
- **Whoami:** View information about logged-on users.

Interoperability with UNIX and Linux
Overview

Windows Services for UNIX 3.0 (SFU) is an additional software component for Windows XP, Windows 2000, and Windows NT 4.0 (SP6a or higher) that allows nearly seamless integration between Windows and UNIX environments. Services for UNIX provides utilities and services that allow you to leverage your existing UNIX and Linux assets and expertise while consolidating Windows, UNIX, and Linux administration and management tasks. Windows Services for UNIX 3.0 supports a wide range of UNIX and Linux platforms. It has been tested with some of the most commonly used flavors of UNIX and Linux, but it is possible that it will provide similar levels of interoperability and functionality with other UNIX and Linux variants as well. At the time this was written, the UNIX and Linux platforms that SFU has been specifically tested with are

- Solaris 7
- Solaris 8
- HP-UX 10.2
- HP-UX 11.0
- AIX 4.3.3
- Red Hat Linux 7.0
- Red Hat Linux 7.2

Microsoft released the first version of Windows Services for UNIX in 1999. Each release has been successively stronger, easier to use, and more features-rich. Version 3 provides many enhancements and additions, including

- **NFS Client:** Now supports sticky/setuid/setgid bits and symbolic links. Performance has been improved as well. Additional language options have been provided for internationalized versions.

- **NFS Server:** Has been given client-matching support for sticky/setuid/setgid bits, and can be configured to provide active-active clustering of NFS shares. Root and anonymous access handling is on a per share basis, and Windows NT–to–UNIX permissions mappings have been greatly improved. The same internationalization enhancements made in the client are available in the server, and the significant improvement in performance is also provided.

- **NFS Gateway:** Several improvements in internationalized versions have been made.

- **Mapping Server:** Significant improvements in performance have been made. Security and scalability have been enhanced. A cluster-enabled mapping server is now possible, and redundant mapping servers are available for scalability and reliability. Internationalization improvements have been made in this area as well.

- **Server for NIS:** Security improvements have been made, including support for MD5 encryption. Significant improvements in performance, administration and usability have also been made.

- **Password Sync:** Support for Pluggable Authentication Model on UNIX has been added.

- **Telnet Server:** Support for dumb terminals and IPv6 has been added. Various security and scalability improvements have also been made.

- **Telnet Client:** Improvements in internationalization have been made. IPv6 support has been added.

- **Interix:** Although Interix 2.2 has been available for some time, the version that is incorporated in Windows Services for UNIX 3.0 offers many enhancements for migrating UNIX applications to Windows, including a new native POSIX-compliant subsystem and 400-plus utilities.

- **Interix SDK:** The Interix Software Development Kit (SDK) supports over 1,900 UNIX APIs.

In this section we discuss the components of Windows Services for UNIX and their installation, and provide an overview of some commonly used utilities included in SFU. We start with the components of this service.

Components

A number of diverse components make up Windows Services for UNIX. It is not required that you install all options if you do not need them. Besides, not all of these options are supported in Windows XP Professional. This section focuses only on the components that are supported in Windows XP. Disk space requirements for each of these options are covered in "System Requirements" immediately following this section, and the selection of components to be installed is covered in the Installation section after we have covered the system requirements.

Interix Subsytem

Interix is a UNIX environment that runs on the Windows kernel. The Interix subsystem is a true UNIX environment, not an emulated UNIX environment. It provides over 400 UNIX utilities and two shells—Korn and C—and provides genuine UNIX functionality. It is even possible for UNIX applications and scripts to be ported to Interix and run as if they were residing on a UNIX-based server.

This UNIX subsystem does not displace or eliminate in any way the Windows subsystem. Instead, computers running Windows Services for UNIX actually run Windows and UNIX simultaneously. Windows applications still run in the Windows environment, and UNIX applications, scripts, and commands all run in the Interix subsystem. The characteristics unique to each environment, such as UNIX's case-sensitive file and path names and Windows' case-insensitive file and path names, are intact.

Interix Software Development Kit

The Interix SDK provides the tools you need to port your UNIX applications to run on Windows computers through the Interix subsystem. These tools include utilities, command and script libraries, and 1,900 APIs. This allows you to continue leveraging your UNIX application investments and skill sets, even while migrating to a Windows environment.

User Name Mapping

User Name Mapping provides a way to map Windows and UNIX user accounts to each other. This permits users of Client for NFS, Server for NFS, Gateway for NFS, and Interix to access resources on other computers without requiring multiple sets of credentials for each resource being accessed.

Maps can be created between Windows and UNIX user and group accounts even if the user and group names in Windows and UNIX may not be identical. User Name Mapping permits the creation and maintenance of a single mapping database for an entire network. This provides easier administration of user accounts in environments with multiple computers running Windows Services for UNIX. User Name Mapping permits one-to-one and one-to-many mappings between Windows and UNIX user and group accounts. User Name Mapping obtains UNIX user, password, and group information from a Network Information Service (NIS) server or from password and group files located on a local hard drive.

Client for NFS

Client for NFS enables Windows users to map a drive to an NFS share. This method of access effectively sets up the UNIX share in the same way as a mapped drive to another Windows share point. Windows users can access NFS shares with Universal Naming Convention (UNC) names, just as with Windows share points. Authentication is provided by User Name Mapping or a Windows or UNIX-based PCNFS server.

Client for NFS enables users to access NFS resources without logging on to the NFS server. Client for NFS sends a user's Windows username to User Name Mapping, which verifies that the username has been mapped to a UNIX account. If a match is located, User Name Mapping returns the user identifier (UID) and group identifier (GID) to Client for NFS, which in turn sends those identifiers with the file-access request to the NFS server.

Server for NFS

Server for NFS allows an administrator to share Windows directories as NFS exported file systems. UNIX users can then mount these shares in the same way they would a share on another UNIX server. Again, this is a secured share, and authentication is provided by the Server for NFS service. User Name Mapping also matches UNIX accounts to Windows accounts to ensure that the correct level of access is provided to the UNIX users.

Server for PCNFS

Server for PCNFS facilitates access to NFS shares to Windows users by ensuring that the proper username and password credential set is provided before NFS file access is granted. UNIX authentication consists of providing a UID and GID to a user who presents a valid username and password, not unlike a Windows NT or Windows 2000 token. When the user logs on, the user's name and password are compared to those in a password file. If they match a credential set in the file, the server returns a corresponding UID and GID that identifies the user for NFS browsing and mounting operations.

Password Synchronization

Password Synchronization automatically changes a user's UNIX password at the time the user changes a Windows password. It also provides for the reverse option—a user changing a UNIX password has his or her Windows password automatically changed. This effectively creates and maintains a single password system for the entire network, and greatly simplifies the process of maintaining secure passwords in both environments. Password synchronization supports both domain and local Windows account password changes.

It is also easy to administer and provides a great deal of granularity in application of this feature—administrators can exclude specific users from being synchronized. Password synchronization is conducted by the transmission of encrypted passwords and occurs in real time, rather than on a delayed propagation basis.

Telnet Client

Telnet Client software allows a computer to connect to a remote Telnet server and run console/command-line applications on that host. Windows Services for UNIX includes a new and improved Telnet client. NTLM authentication is used for clients for Telnet connections between computers running Windows NT with Telnet Server or Windows 2000 or Windows XP, and passwords are sent in encrypted form. New in SFU version 3.0 is support for IPv6.

The Windows-based Remote Shell Service

Remote Windows users can use the Windows-based Remote Shell service to carry out commands on a server running the Remote Shell service.

The Windows-based Cron Service

The Windows-based Cron service runs scheduled commands using the crontab utility. It is very similar to the Windows AT command or Schedule Service, in that you can schedule actions to be performed at specific times.

ActiveState ActivePerl

This component allows you to run Perl scripts on your Windows XP computer. Complete documentation for this feature is available when you install ActivePerl.

Installation

This section deals with obtaining and then installing Services for UNIX on Windows XP. The only version of Windows XP on which Services for UNIX can be installed is Windows XP Professional; it is not supported on Windows XP Home.

Obtaining the Software

Services for UNIX is not included on the Windows XP media. It must be purchased separately from Microsoft. At the time of this writing, it was available for $99 from shop.microsoft.com.

System Requirements

In addition to running Windows XP Professional, you also need to have Internet Explorer 5 (or a later version) running on the system on which you are installing Services for UNIX.

Microsoft recommends at least 16MB of RAM over and above the minimum required for the OS. To save you checking the box your software shipped in, we remind you what that is: 64MB is the absolute minimum, and 128MB is the recommended amount. Anything less than 128MB is subject to some serious performance issues, which we can attest to from testing in our labs (constant paging to disk, slow response to keyboard and mouse input, and so on). This means at a recommended base point, you want to have 144MB minimum to run Services for UNIX. You get the best value for your money with at least 256MB.

The disk space requirements really depend on the specific components you are installing: 19MB on the low end, 186MB on the high end. For security and compatibility reasons, NTFS (NT file system) is the preferred file system for the partition where SFU is installed, not to mention the fact that for large partitions (over 500MB), you get much more efficient use of storage space with NTFS over FAT. The following list itemizes the disk space requirements for each component.

- Base utilities: 62MB
- UNIX Perl: 38MB, plus base utilities
- Interix GNU utilities: 1MB, plus base utilities
- Interix GNU SDK: 1MB, plus GNU utilities and Interix SDK
- Client for NFS: 1MB
- Server for NFS: 1MB
- Password Synchronization: 1MB
- Windows-based Remote Shell service: 1MB
- User Name Mapping: 1MB
- Server for NFS Authentication: 1MB
- Server for PCNFS: 1MB
- Interix SDK: 41MB, plus base utilities
- ActiveState Perl: 36MB

If you are planning to synchronize domain account passwords, you need to make sure the domain controllers are correctly configured with Services for UNIX. This means SFU must be installed on the primary domain controller of a Windows NT domain, not a backup domain controller. You need to be sure that your PDC can tolerate the additional load of this service before installing it. For a Windows 2000 domain, *all* domain controllers need to have SFU installed, and you need to ensure that they can also support the additional load.

While NFS (network file system) can use domain or local accounts for authentication, you must be sure that domain controllers are configured properly for NFS users if you plan to make this service available to domain users. This means that Server for NFS Authentication must be installed on all domain controllers in your domain.

Installation

Place the Windows Services for UNIX CD into the CD-ROM drive. The CD should auto-run. If it does not, navigate to the Start, then Run, and enter in `D:\setup.exe`, where D is the CD-ROM drive. The Windows Services for UNIX Setup Wizard launches, as shown in Figure 6.10.

Figure 6.10 The Windows Services for UNIX Setup Wizard

1. In the Windows Services for UNIX Setup Wizard dialog box, click **Next**.

2. In the User name box, type your name. If the name of your organization does not appear in the Organization box, type the name of your organization there.

3. In the CD Key boxes, type the product key found on the back of the CD-ROM case, and then click **Next**.

4. The End User License Agreement appears. If you accept the terms of the agreement, click **I accept the terms in the License Agreement**, and then click **Next** to continue installation. You cannot proceed if you do not accept the agreement.

5. To complete installation of default Windows Services for UNIX components in the default directory, click **Standard installation**.

6. If you want to specify a different set of components or a different installation location, click **Custom installation**.

7. If you selected Custom Installation, click the icon next to each component that you want to install and click the appropriate option, as shown in Figure 6.11. If you do not want to install a component, click the icon

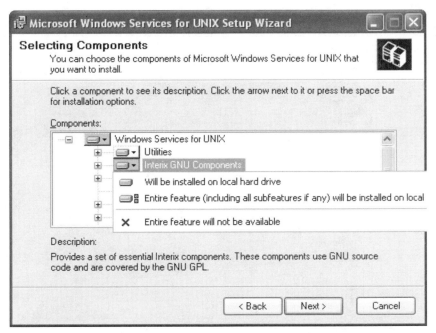

Figure 6.11   Customizing your services for UNIX installation

next to the component and click **Entire feature will not be available**. When you are finished specifying the components to install, click **Next**.

8. If you are installing the GNU Software Development Kit, the GNU Library General Public License appears, as shown in Figure 6.12. Click **Next** to continue installation.

9. If you are installing ActiveState Perl, the ActiveState Perl End-User License Agreement appears as shown in Figure 6.13. If you accept the terms of the agreement, click **I accept the agreement**, and then click **Next**.

10. The Security Settings screen appears, as shown in Figure 6.14. Select the behavior that you wish to enable, as appropriate for your environment, and click **Next**.

11. If you are installing base utilities, the Windows-based Remote Shell service, Client for NFS, Gateway for NFS, or Server for NFS, you are prompted for the name of your organization's User Name Mapping server, as shown in Figure 6.15. If you do not know the name of the User Name Mapping server, click **Next** without entering a name; you can specify the name of the server later using Services for UNIX

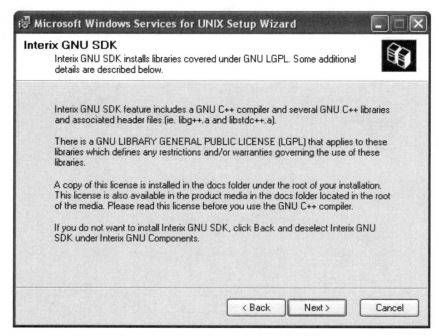

Figure 6.12   The GNU Library General Public License

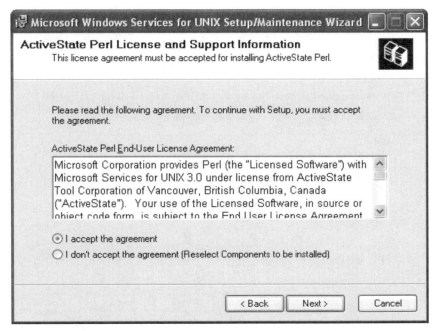

Figure 6.13   The ActiveState Perl End-User License Agreement

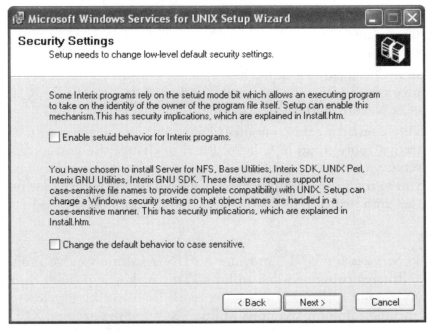

Figure 6.14   Select Security Settings as appropriate for your environment

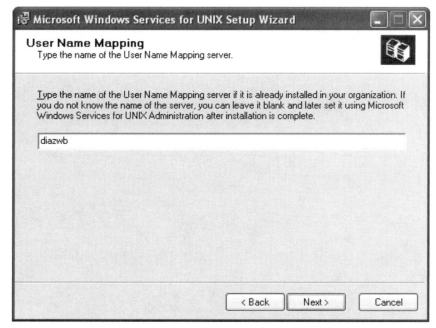

Figure 6.15   Specifying the User Name Mapping server

Administration. However, these components will not work properly until you specify the name of the User Name Mapping server.

12. If you are also installing User Name Mapping, type the name of the server on which you are installing Windows Services for UNIX.

13. In the Installation location box, type the fully qualified path of the directory where you want to install Windows Services for UNIX, and then click **Next** to complete installation.

14. Before restarting the computer (if required), use Services in the Administrative Tools group in Control Panel to change the startup type of the service to automatic and then start the service if Setup does not require you to restart the computer. To enable an Interix service (daemon), edit the /etc/inted.conf file before restarting the computer.

Utilities

Windows Services for UNIX provides 83 UNIX administrative utilities, and over 400 Interix command-line utilities. This makes it possible to perform nearly any type of UNIX administrative work from within Windows XP. The utilities include common Windows utilities, X-Windows utilities, X11R5 windows managers, terminal emulators, editors, and compilers. For environments with experienced UNIX administrators, this is a huge bonus. Most scripts and applications can be migrated to Windows with very few, if any, changes, allowing you to continue leveraging your UNIX skill base and script libraries. Some commonly used utilities provided with Windows Services for UNIX 3.0:

- **alias:** View or create command aliases.
- **autodfs:** Reads automount mappings, creates distributed file system links.
- **basename:** Displays file name component of path name.
- **bgjob:** Executes programs in the background through Telnet Server.
- **break:** Exits from loop in shell script.
- **cat:** Concatenates and displays text files.
- **cd:** Changes working directory.
- **chmod:** Changes access permissions of a file.
- **chown:** Changes the ownership of files or directories.
- **continue:** Skips to next iteration of loop in shell script.
- **cp:** Copies files.
- **cron:** Executes commands at specified dates and times.
- **crontab:** Schedules periodic background work.
- **cut:** Cuts out bytes, character, or character-delimited fields from each line in one or more files, concatenates them, and writes them to standard output.
- **date:** Gets or sets the date and time.
- **diff:** Compares two files and displays line-by-line differences.
- **dirname:** Displays the directory components of a path name. See *basename*.
- **dos2unix:** Converts text files with DOS-specific end-of-line characters to files with UNIX-specific end-of-line characters.
- **du:** Displays the disk usage of a file or directory.
- **echo:** Displays arguments.
- **environ:** Displays standard environment variables.
- **eval:** Evaluates arguments in a shell.
- **exec:** Executes a command in place of the current shell.
- **exit:** Exits from the shell.
- **export:** Marks names for export.
- **false:** Returns an exit status of 1 (failure).

- **fc, hist:** Displays, fixes, edits, and re-enters previous commands.
- **find:** Recursively searches a directory hierarchy, looking for files that match a specified Boolean expression.
- **getopts:** Parses options from shell script command line.
- **grep:** Searches files for a pattern and prints all lines containing that pattern.
- **gwshare:** Manages Gateway for NFS shares.
- **head:** Copies first *n* lines of specified file names to standard output.
- **iconv:** Converts a file from one code page to another.
- **jobs:** Displays the status of jobs in the current session.
- **kill:** Terminates or signals the specified processes.
- **let:** Evaluates arithmetic expressions.
- **ln:** Creates a hard link to a file. Links a file name to a target by creating a directory entry that refers to the target.
- **ls:** Lists file and directory names and attributes.
- **mapadmin:** Manages NIS maps.
- **mkdir:** Creates a named directory with read, write, and execute permission for every type of user.
- **more:** Filters and displays the contents of a text file, one screen at a time.
- **mount:** Mounts NFS network shares.
- **mv:** Renames and moves files and directories.
- **nfsadmin:** Administers Client for NFS, Server for NFS, and Gateway for NFS.
- **nfsshare:** Provides access to NFS shares.
- **nfsstat:** Resets counters.
- **nice:** Invokes a command with a specified scheduling priority.
- **nis2ad:** Migrates maps from NIS to Active Directory.
- **nisadmin:** Administers Server for NIS.
- **nismap:** Manages NIS maps.
- **od:** Displays files in specified formats.
- **paste:** Concatenates corresponding or subsequent lines of files.
- **perl:** Runs Perl programs.
- **print:** Displays arguments from the shell.
- **printenv:** Prints environment variables that are set.
- **printf:** Formats and prints data to the standard output.

- **ps:** Lists processes and their status.
- **pwd:** Displays the current working directory.
- **rcmd:** Runs commands on a remote server.
- **read:** Inputs a line to the shell.
- **readonly:** Marks variable as read-only.
- **renice:** Reprioritizes a running process.
- **return:** Returns from shell function or script.
- **rm:** Removes files.
- **rmdir:** Removes a directory.
- **rpcinfo:** Lists programs on remote computers.
- **rshsvc:** Provides a command-line shell or single command execution service for remote users.
- **sdiff:** Prints differences between two files and shows them side-by-side.
- **sed:** Copies named file names to a standard output; edits according to a script of commands (a stream editor).
- **set:** Sets shell flags and positional parameters.
- **sh:** Invokes POSIX-compliant (Korn) shell and command interpreter.
- **shift:** Shifts positional parameters.
- **showmount:** Displays mounted directories.
- **shpc:** Shows Windows 2000 Server– or Windows XP Professional–specific features of the Korn shell.
- **sleep:** Suspends execution for a specified interval.
- **sort:** Sorts the lines of all named files, groups them, and writes the result to standard output.
- **split:** Reads an input file and writes it to one or more output files.
- **strings:** Finds printable strings in files and prints to the standard output.
- **su:** Allows a user to become another user or the superuser without logging off.
- **tail:** Copies a named file to standard output, beginning at a designated place.
- **tee:** Transcribes standard input to standard output and makes copies in a file name.
- **telnet:** Starts the Telnet client.
- **test:** Tests for condition.
- **time:** Displays CPU and elapsed times for commands.
- **times:** Displays user and system times used by the shell and its children.

- **tnadmin:** Administers Telnet Server.
- **top:** Shows top processes sorted by CPU usage.
- **touch:** Updates the access time or the modification time of a file.
- **tr:** Writes the translated input characters from the standard input to the standard output.
- **trap:** Intercepts abnormal conditions and interrupts.
- **true:** Yields an exit status of zero, ignoring any arguments on the command line.
- **typeset:** Assigns attributes and values to variables.
- **umask:** Gets or sets the file mode creation mask.
- **umount:** Deletes all or specified NFS mounted drives.
- **unalias:** Removes alias definitions.
- **uname:** Prints information about the system on which the command is running.
- **uniq:** View unique lines of a sorted file.
- **unix2dos:** Converts text files with UNIX-specific end-of-line characters to files with DOS-specific end-of-line characters.
- **unset:** Removes shell variable or function.
- **uudecode:** Converts a text file to a binary file.
- **uuencode:** Encodes a binary file.
- **vi:** ASCII text editor.
- **wait:** Wait for process to complete.
- **wc:** View a count of lines, words, or characters in a file.
- **whence:** View how a shell interprets a command name.
- **which:** Finds a command and print pathname/alias.
- **xargs:** Constructs argument lists and invoke a tool.
- **ypcat:** Prints keys values in an NIS database.
- **ypclear:** Clears the NIS server cache for an NIS map.
- **ypmatch:** Prints the values of one or more keys from an NIS map.
- **yppush:** Propagates a changed NIS map.

For a complete list and descriptions of all utilities included with Windows Services for UNIX, refer to the Services for UNIX 3.0 online help.

Conclusion

Although the default protocol for Windows XP is TCP/IP, support for other protocols is included with the applications. Furthermore, tools for interoperability with other networking frameworks are provided to afford a broad base for leveraging existing applications and hardware that is deployed in your network. A suite of tools for connecting to and managing Novell NetWare resources is part of Windows XP. Together with Novell's tools for interoperating with Microsoft networking, it is possible to seamlessly integrate Novell and Windows XP. UNIX and Linux are also supported via Services for UNIX. Hundreds of tools and utilities are included to help Windows XP administrators and users connect to and manage resources on UNIX and Linux hosts.

Now that you have a foundation for the protocols used within Windows XP, let us start examining the functionality of Windows XP networking features. The first stop is the Internet Connection Firewall, covered in the next chapter.

7

Internet Connection Firewall

This chapter describes some key principles and the history of firewalls. We talk about what a firewall is and about different types of firewalls. We also discuss why firewalls are important, and what risks there are, if any, to running one in typical Microsoft environments.

The term *firewall* originated from the firewall that is in place in many building materials, such as doors and drywall, and in other applications, such as an engine firewall. These firewalls are designed to be a barrier to fire, though they can only delay the inevitable. They are not designed to completely stop a fire, but to allow escape by slowing its progress. The same is true of your network and host firewalls. You may have seen firewalls depicted on drawings as a brick wall, maybe with flames on it. These firewalls are not designed to be the final safety solution, but they do keep most bad things out. You still need security software to prevent viruses, Trojans, and other malicious activity on your network and systems.

Firewall Types

While there have been a few deviations from the given list in the past, there are essentially only three types of firewalls in common usage. Each type is described along with its most common name. There are several books that are excellent sources of information about firewalls in general and the networking components of the OSI Model, and we recommend that you review these for further detailed information.

Packet Filter

A packet filter sits at Layer 3 of the OSI Model and determines to which port a particular packet is heading. If that port is not permitted to be accessed at all or to be accessed from that IP address, then the packet is dropped on the floor and not permitted to pass. Packet-filtering firewalls are the oldest and easiest to set up, but will not adequately protect you in some cases. Specifically, since a packet-filtering firewall does not really know about state (for example, the TCP handshake), it is possible to take advantage of the firewall's lack of knowledge. A packet filter also has to briefly examine every packet because it does not care what came before or after the current packet. Packet filters are quite effective, but can be difficult to configure and IP addresses can be spoofed to get around the rules.

Stateful Inspection

Stateful inspection was first coined by the vendor, Checkpoint, a little more than a decade ago. Stateful inspection implies that the firewall is aware of, and cares about, the state of a connection. As discussed in other chapters, most of the traffic on the Internet today is TCP based and therefore connection oriented, but even User Datagram Protocol (UDP) traffic can be tracked in a pseudostate by hardware and services in the middle of the talkers. This state is then tracked by the firewall.

Stateful inspection firewalls are commonplace and are made by almost every vendor currently offering firewalls. A stateful inspection firewall is easier to configure and support than a packet filter and typically is not as resource intensive as an application gateway or proxy. It is also easier to prevent spoofing and "man-in-the-middle" attacks, both very common and a cause of great concern to computer managers.

Application Gateway (Proxy)

This firewall is sometimes also referred to as an Application Proxy Firewall or proxy service (think about the man-in-the-middle concept, in a good way). A proxy firewall operates at Layer 7 of the OSI Model and is the most scrutinizing firewall available, because it looks at application traffic and can determine the proper IP and the proper communication at that application layer. With an application proxy, the firewall becomes the source on one side of the channel and the destination on the other side. It sits in the middle of a communication between a client and server and it is a great way to hide a computer or even an entire network.

The Internet Connection Firewall (ICF) is a stateful inspection firewall and works in many of the same ways as a gateway (which is why you have to be very careful) or network-based stateful inspection firewall. As we talk about how this firewall works, some of the things that can go wrong with this type of firewall, and its level of security, it becomes clear why we need to configure it properly.

Other terms we discuss briefly include Network Address Translation (NAT), Encapsulation, Packet Forwarding, and Peer-to-Peer.

Network Address Translation

Network Address Translation is somewhat ambiguous as a term and those who do not work with networking may not be familiar with it. Basically NAT occurs when a device in your network takes the traffic from your workstation or server, opens up each packet, "strips out" the existing IP address of your workstation, and puts a different address in its place. This is a simplified explanation of NAT. Some NAT is also done through encapsulation.

Encapsulation

We spoke briefly about this in the TCP/IP Overview chapter and for more information you should refer to it. Encapsulation is exactly what you would think it means. It is taking something and wrapping it up with something else. In the networking world this usually occurs when referencing packets. With encapsulation, a device receives information from another source, "encapsulates" it, and then communicates to another device. The second device will either interpret and strip off that additional layer, or add its own encapsulation on top of the previous layer.

Packet Forwarding

Packet Forwarding is also an easy-to-understand term. It is essentially a packet that is transmitted to one device and then forwarded to another device for processing. This is sometimes done because the intermediary device is only a bridge or router that does not really change the information found within the packet, but is aware of another device that does change the information found in that packet.

Peer-to-Peer

Peer-to-Peer is essentially when two like computers want to talk to each other; typically, they are hosts found on the same network. This communication is simple and is usually from a workstation to another workstation for sharing purposes. However, this can also be referenced when one server wants to talk to another server on the same network. For example, a DNS server and a DHCP server might be considered peers.

Internet Connection Sharing

If you use Internet Connection Sharing (ICS) to provide Internet access to multiple computers, you should be careful about how the Internet Connection Firewall impacts your use of ICS. If for any reason you are not going to use Internet Connection Sharing, then you will find that enabling Internet Connection Firewall comes with very few penalties. Therefore, we recommend that if this condition exists and you do not have any Virtual Private Networking (VPN) enabled (that has not been compensated by opening the appropriate ports), then using ICF comes with few penalties and is very important to enable.

 NOTE: You should not enable the firewall on any connection that does not directly connect to the Internet. ICF is not needed if you already have a firewall or proxy server on your network, but it can be used to provide an additional layer of protection.

 NOTE: You must be logged on to your computer with an administrator account in order to enable the firewall.

You should not enable Internet Connection Firewall on VPN connections that are typically used to securely log in to a corporate network. You should not enable ICF on client computers that are part of a large company or school network with a server-client structure. ICF interferes with file and printer sharing in these scenarios.

If you are sharing an Internet connection, enable the firewall only on the host computer that is connected to the Internet. The host computer appears to the Internet as the only computer on the Internet, hiding the computers in your home network. The host computer with ICF enabled provides a single point of security for your host computer and home network computers. In such home networks, computers running earlier versions of Windows are protected without the need for additional firewalls.

In some rare instances, some Internet Service Providers (ISPs) do not allow the use of the Windows XP ICF. If this is the case, you should contact your ISP for their recommended security measures.

Internet Connection Firewall Considerations

There are a couple of reasons why you might not want to enable the Internet Connection Firewall in your environment. It is important to note that if you are unable to enable the protection provided by the ICF, you should make sure that you have enabled some firewall product at the edge of your network. Even if you enable ICF, a layered defense is better, therefore having an edge network firewall still provides significant benefits.

If you use your computer to communicate with a remote VPN, such as your corporate headquarters or the data center where your e-commerce applications are hosted, then enabling the ICF can disrupt your connection. The most effective way to deal with this is to enable or open the ports that allow your VPN to continue to function properly. These are:

UDP/50 – UDP Encapsulation
TCP/500 – ISAKMP (IKE) Handshake and Control channel

If you use Internet Connection Sharing and are considering enabling Internet Connection Firewall, the host computer needs very careful configuration or you might cause computers sharing your connection to become unavailable. Once you understand ports and how to enable additional ports, you should be able to work around this problem. Be careful when enabling ports to make sure you are enabling those ports for *specific* networks and not for the Internet as a whole. The narrower you make the "pinhole" you punch through your firewall, the better.

Enabling Internet Connection Firewall

To open Network Connections: Click **Start**, click **Control Panel**, and then double-click **Network Connections** as shown in Figure 7.1.

NOTE: If your Control Panel is set to Category View, click **Network** and **Internet Connections** as shown in Figure 7.2. Then click **Network Connections** as shown in Figure 7.3.

Click to select the Dial-up, LAN, or High-Speed Internet connection that you want to protect as shown in Figure 7.4.

In the task panel on the left, under Network Tasks, click **Change settings of this connection** as shown in Figure 7.5.

(Or, within the Network Connections folder, right-click on the connection that you want to protect and then click **Properties** as shown in Figure 7.6.)

On the **Advanced** tab as shown in Figure 7.7, under **Internet Connection Firewall**, do one of the following:

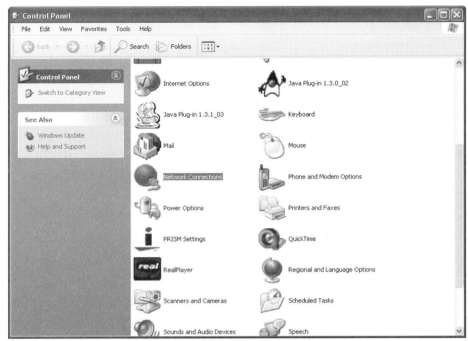

Figure 7.1 Open Control Panel and then open Network Connections.

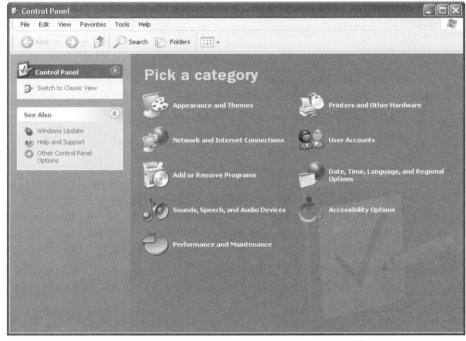

Figure 7.2 In Category View, click Network and Internet Connections.

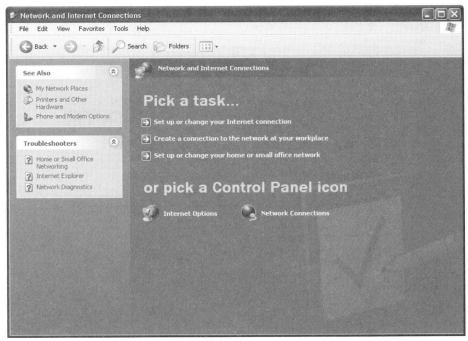

Figure 7.3   In Category View, click Network Connections.

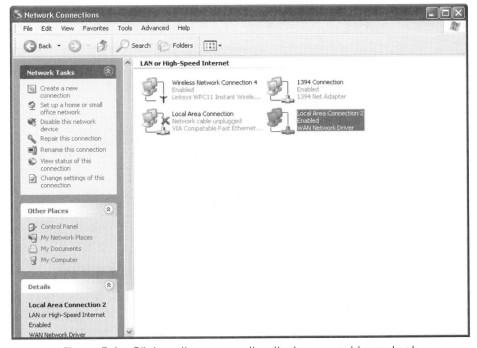

Figure 7.4   Click on the connection that you want to protect.

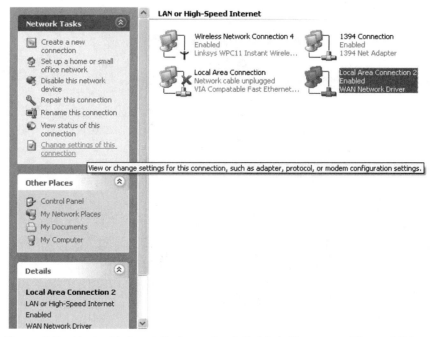

Figure 7.5 Under Network Tasks on the left, click Change settings of this connection.

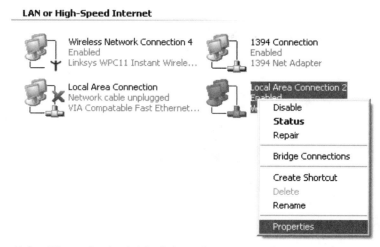

Figure 7.6 Alternatively, right-click on the connection and click Properties.

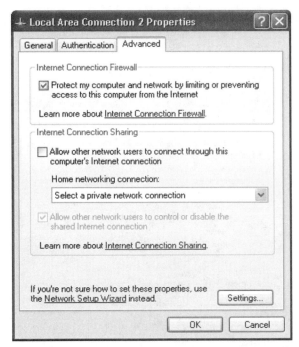

Figure 7.7   Check the box to enable the firewall.

To enable Internet Connection Firewall, select the **Protect my computer and network by limiting or preventing access to this computer from the Internet** check box.

To disable Internet Connection Firewall, clear the **Protect my computer and network by limiting or preventing access to this computer from the Internet** check box. This disables the firewall, and your computer and network are then vulnerable to intrusions.

Once you have enabled Internet Connection Firewall you need to configure your services. Typically on Windows XP this is not very difficult, but you may be running third-party applications such as an FTP server or a Web server for one or more of your applications. However, remember the best way to protect your workstations is to make them invisible, and configuring any of these services negates that approach. Additionally, any of these services can also be attacked.

Figure 7.8 shows a screenshot of the screen in question, which is fairly self-explanatory.

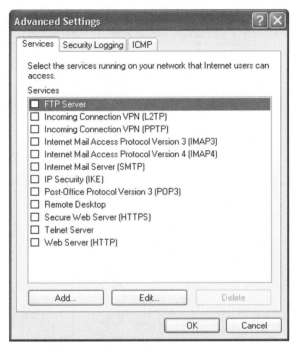

Figure 7.8 Select the services to be accessible from the Internet.

Internet Connection Firewall—Log File Monitoring

One of the first things a consulting organization looks for is backup. Are the proper data storage requirements occurring frequently; have they been tested? Second, is there a firewall? The third thing that requires as much attention is: "Anyone paying attention to the firewall logs?" The first question usually gets a positive response, with a mumble and a worried look for the next two questions.

Firewall logs are absolutely critical to your organization. A firewall is just a tool that slows down the fire, and with Internet/computer firewalls the same rule is in place. Your firewall should log attacks and you should review these logs frequently. The Internet Connection Firewall has a pretty good interface for reviewing the logs. A brief explanation of the program and its switches follows.

With Internet Connection Firewall, you have some options with logging, too. Typically, if you have a good security policy you do not really care about successful connections, but you can log all dropped, or successful, or everything (by checking both boxes). The security log has two major areas: the header information (source and destination information, ports, flags, and so on) shown in Table 7.1, and the body data that contains the date, time, and whether or not the packet was accepted, as shown in Table 7.2.

Table 7.1   Header Information

Item	Description	Example
#Version:	Displays which edition of the Internet Connection Firewall security log is installed.	1.0
#Software:	Provides the name of the security log.	Microsoft Internet Connection Firewall
#Time:	Indicates that all of the timestamps in the log are in local time.	Local
#Fields:	Displays a static list of fields that are available for security log entries.	date, time, action, protocol, src-ip, dst-ip, src-port, dst-port, size, tcpflags, tcpsyn, tcpack, tcpwin, icmptype, icmpcode, and info

Table 7.2   Body Data

Field	Description	Example
Date	Date, in the format **YY-MM-DD**, where YY is the year, MM is the month, and DD is the day.	04-01-12
Time	Same as above, very common format for time. **HH:MM:SS**, where HH is the hour in 24-hour format, MM is minutes, and SS is seconds.	21:36:59
Action	Specifies the operation that was performed on the packet, some of the possibilities are not descriptive enough. But you will get the idea after reading and watching the log for a bit.	OPEN, CLOSE, DROP, and INFO-EVENTS-LOST
Protocol	You normally see one of three protocols in here, but you may, however, see protocols surrounding VPN technologies.	TCP, UDP, ICMP
src-ip	IP address of the source (talker) in four octets three characters wide up to 255.255.255.254 (number).(number).(number).(number).	192.168.100.1
dst-ip	IP address of the destination (listener) in four octets three characters wide up to 255.255.255.254 (number).(number).(number).(number).	192.168.101.199
src-port	Specifies the source port number of the sending computer. An src-port entry is recorded in the form of a whole number, ranging from 1 to 65,535. This port info will only be displayed for TCP and UDP connections; all others will list a "–" for unknown or not found.	12434

continues

Table 7.2   Body Data   *(continued)*

Field	Description	Example
dst-port	Specifies the port of the destination computer. A dst-port entry is recorded in the form of a whole number, ranging from 1 to 65,535. The port info will only be displayed for TCP and UDP connections; all others will list a "–" for unknown or not found.	53 or 25
Size	Specifies the packet size in bytes.	60
Tcpflags	TCP Control Flags: **A**ck Acknowledgment field significant **F**in No more data from sender **P**sh Push Function **R**st Reset the connection **S**yn Synchronize sequence numbers **U**rg Urgent Pointer field significant **L**ook in RFC 793 for more information.	AFU
Tcpsyn	Specifies the TCP sequence number in the packet. This is very important because it relates to the stateful nature of connections.	1315819770
Tcpack	Specifies the TCP acknowledgment number in the packet.	0
icmptype	Specifies a number that represents the Type field of the ICMP message.	8
icmpcode	Specifies a number that represents the Code field of the ICMP message.	0
Info	Specifies an information entry that depends on the type of action that occurred. For example, an `INFO-EVENTS-LOST` action will cause an entry of the number of events that happened, but were not placed in the log from the time of the last occurrence of this event type.	`INFO-EVENTS-LOST`

Enabling Logging

To enable logging you need to follow a few easy steps and they are:

- Open **Network Connections**.
- Click the connection on which ICF is enabled, and then, under **Network Tasks**, click **Change settings of this connection**.
- On the **Advanced** tab, click **Settings**.

- On the **Security Logging** tab, under **Logging Options**, select one or both of the following options:
  - To enable logging of unsuccessful inbound connection attempts, select the **Log dropped packets** check box.
  - To enable logging of successful outbound connections, select the **Log successful connections** check box.

Internet Connection Firewall—Troubleshooting

Browsing Issues

Problem: After enabling Internet Connection Firewall, your ability to browse your local or remote networks, access your printers, or share files with others does not work (and it did before enabling it).

Microsoft's Web sites for the most part will tell you that the only way to get around this problem is to disable the Internet Connection Firewall. Doing so, however, reduces your security position. Therefore, we document how to manually allow for browsing.

To do this you need to know two things: first, the list of ports that need to be allowed, and second, how to manually enable a port with the Internet Connection Firewall. They can be found in Table 7.3 and Table 7.4. The list of ports

Table 7.3   List of Ports

Port	Application/Protocol
20/tcp	File Transfer [Default Data]
21/tcp	File Transfer [Control]
22/tcp	SSH Remote Login Protocol
23/tcp	Telnet
25/tcp	Simple Mail Transfer Protocol (SMTP)
37/tcp	Time
49/tcp	Login Host Protocol (TACACS)
53/tcp	Domain Name Server
66/tcp	Oracle SQL*NET
69/tcp	Trivial File Transfer
79/tcp	Finger

continues

Table 7.3 List of Ports (*continued*)

Port	Application/Protocol
80/tcp	World Wide Web HTTP
88/tcp	Kerberos
109/tcp	Post Office Protocol - Version 2
110/tcp	Post Office Protocol - Version 3
118/tcp	SQL Services
123/tcp	Network Time Protocol
143/tcp	Internet Message Access Protocol
156/tcp	SQL Service
161/tcp	SNMP
162/tcp	SNMPTRAP
174/tcp	MAILQ
179/tcp	Border Gateway Protocol
217/tcp	dBASE UNIX
220/tcp	Interactive Mail Access Protocol v3
389/tcp	Lightweight Directory Access Protocol
396/tcp	Novell NetWare over IP
401/tcp	Uninterruptible Power Supply
445/tcp	Microsoft-DS
481/tcp	Ph service
500/tcp	isakmp
689/tcp	NMAP
989/tcp	FTP protocol, data, over TLS/SSL
990/tcp	FTP protocol, control, over TLS/SSL
992/tcp	Telnet protocol over TLS/SSL
993/tcp	imap4 protocol over TLS/SSL
995/tcp	pop3 protocol over TLS/SSL (was spop3)

Table 7.4 Windows-Specific Applications

Applications	Ports
File and print sharing	TCP 139, 445; UDP 137, 138, 445
AOL Instant Messenger	TCP 443, 563
Backup Exec	UDP 137; TCP 3032, 3033
Exceed 7 and 8	Usually 6000 to 6039
LapLink	TCP 389, 1183, 1184, 1547
MSN Messenger	TCP 6891–6900
PC Anywhere	TCP 5631, 5632
Windows Messenger	TCP 139, 445; UDP 137, 139
Windows Messenger	TCP 6891–6900

in Table 7.3 is by no means comprehensive, but the more important applications are identified and we encourage you to visit ports assignments from IANA (Internet Assigned Numbers Authority) for more detail.

To reach IANA, visit their Web site at: *http://www.iana.org/assignments/port-numbers.* Please note that just because IANA has assigned a port to a specific application, it does not mean that only this application can run from that port. Each vendor is required to show other vendors courtesy (which sometimes they do not) and only use ports that are assigned to them.

For those of you who are interested in more Windows-centric applications, use the chart shown in Table 7.4 of some applications that combine both TCP and UDP ports and are more specific to Windows.

Opening a Port Manually

To manually open a port:

- Click on the **Start** menu, and then click **My Network Places**.
- Under **Network Tasks**, click **View Network Connections**. (Or, you can right-click **My Network Places** on the desktop if it is on your desktop, and then click **Properties**.)
- Right-click the connection that you use for the Internet, and then click **Properties**.
- Click the **Advanced** tab, and then click **Settings**.

NOTE: If the **Settings** button is unavailable, ICF is not enabled on this connection and you do not have to open any ports. (They are all already open.)

- Click **Add** to open a new port.
- In the **Description** box, type a friendly name. For example, type `File Sharing : Port 445`.
- In the **Name or IP address of the computer hosting this service on your network** box, type `127.0.0.1`.

NOTE: You can specify the IP address of an internal computer; however, in most cases, you use 127.0.0.1 for local host.

- In the **External port** and **Internal port** boxes, type the port number. In most cases, this number is the same.
- Click either **TCP** or **UDP**, and then click **OK**.
- Repeat this process for each port to be opened, review Table 7.3 and Table 7.4 (some services require multiple ports), or check the IANA port assignment list.

IPv6 and the Internet Connection Firewall

You have enabled the Internet Connection Firewall and you have both IPv4 and IPv6 interfaces or you simply have IPv6 interfaces. Yet it appears that the Internet Connection Firewall is not doing what you have asked it to do, which is, to block traffic. This is a known issue with Microsoft Windows XP in that additional software is required. This package is in addition to Microsoft Windows XP Service Pack 1 and may be automatically included with Service Pack 2.

Once this additional software is installed, it is possible for you to configure Internet Connection Firewall on your IPv6 interfaces, but you may have to specifically open ports where needed. The software or a specific link to the software is not included with this book because it may change, but at the time of this publication, the software was associated with a knowledge base article. The article number was 817778 and the software was included inside that link as a separate link.

However, the setup switches to effectively install this package are identified here. Additional information should be available in Help from the download.

- /? Show the list of installation switches.
- /u Use Unattended mode.
- /f Force other programs to quit when the computer shuts down.
- /n Do not back up files for removal.
- /o Overwrite OEM files without prompting.
- /z Do not restart when installation is complete.
- /q Use Quiet mode (no user interaction).
- /l List installed hotfixes.
- /x Extract the files without running Setup.

To verify that the advanced networking pack is installed, you need to look for and identify a few system and library files. A list of several of the necessary files follows, but the knowledge base article (the article number is mentioned earlier) has a more comprehensive list.

Date	Time	Version	Size	File name
30-Jun-2003	20:35	5.1.2600.1240	29,952	Ip6fw.sys
30-Jun-2003	20:35	5.1.2600.1240	49,152	Ip6fwapi.dll
30-Jun-2003	20:35	5.1.2600.1240	16,384	Ip6fwcfg.dll
30-Jun-2003	20:35	5.1.2600.1240	40,448	Ip6fwhlp.dll
10-Jul-2003	16:19	5.1.2600.1240	79,872	Iphlpapi.dll
30-Jun-2003	20:30	5.1.2600.1240	48,640	Ipv6.exe
10-Jul-2003	16:19	5.1.2600.1240	54,272	Ipv6mon.dll
30-Jun-2003	20:33	5.1.2600.1240	83,456	Netsh.exe
30-Jun-2003	20:38	5.1.2600.1240	109,056	P2p.dll
30-Jun-2003	20:30	5.1.2600.1240	203,008	Tcpip6.sys
30-Jun-2003	20:38	5.1.2600.1240	26,624	Npcustom.dll

When All Else Fails

When all else fails, you need to spend some time to figure out what failed before you disable anything. The best tools to do this with are ping, tracert, ipconfig, and finally using the Event Viewer.

We assume that you are familiar with how to obtain your IP address using ipconfig. We also assume that you can recognize your local IP address. The method to obtain your default router and DNS servers is documented later, but first let's briefly cover ping.

By using ping you can send pings to your IP address, your default router, and your DNS servers. If you can ping yourself and your gateway (default router), then you have LAN connectivity; if you can ping your DNS servers, then you probably have WAN connectivity (that is, if your DNS servers are not on your local network).

If you fail in pinging anything, you should first traceroute (using tracert) any failed IP address. There are many reasons traceroute could fail, but here are most of the RFC-defined flags you might experience, including their meanings.

- **!H** host unreachable.
- **!N** network unreachable.
- **!P** protocol unreachable.
- **!S** means the source route failed.
- **!F** means that fragmentation is needed, see RFC 1191 for more information.
- **!X** means communication is administratively prohibited.
- **!V** means there has been a host precedence violation.
- **!C** means that a precedence cutoff was in effect.
- **!<number>** means that an ICMP unreachable code was received. Unreachable codes are defined in RFC 1812, which supersedes RFC 1716.

ICMP Error Messages

Here is some information about these errors from RFC 1812, which can be found at the following URL: *http://www.faqs.org/rfcs/rfc1812.html.*

Information about "Destination Unreachable" can be found in Section 4.3.3.1, which talks about a generic error that could mean host, network, or protocol are unreachable. Redirection is spoken about in Section 4.3.3.2, Source Quench is discussed in Section 4.3.3.3, Time Exceeded (this relates to TTL and how traceroute works) can be found in Section 4.3.3.4, and finally Parameter Problem can be found in Section 4.3.3.5.

Specific ICMP query messages and where information can be found about them:

Echo	Section 4.3.3.6
Information	Section 4.3.3.7
Timestamp	Section 4.3.3.8
Address Mask	Section 4.3.3.9
Router Discovery	Section 4.3.3.10

If traceroute received one of the listed errors, it is likely to exit or produce an error response that will probably not be helpful. Therefore, it is important to base your troubleshooting on multiple tools and IP addresses so that you can narrow the problem down when you run into a dead end.

Chapter
8

Internet Connection Sharing in Windows XP

Overview of ICS Functionality

Internet access is an important, sometimes the most important, function of many networks. This chapter focuses on connecting your network to the Internet using Windows XP Internet Connection Sharing (ICS). ICS allows you to provide a single connection or gateway to the Internet used by all computers in the network, as shown in Figure 8.1.

This connection can be a dedicated, "always-on" DSL or broadband connection, or it can be a demand-dial modem based connection. If your network budget does not have room for a multifunction router, or your Internet connection is a single dedicated phone line that you wish to share between five or six computers, ICS is an excellent solution. It eliminates the need for extra hardware (such as a router or multiple modems) and piggybacks on the existing network infrastructure that you already have in place. (This means in a dial-up scenario you do not need a phone jack near each computer that needs Internet access.)

Internet Connection Sharing supplies more than just an Internet connection point for your network, however. It provides many networking components required for connectivity within and outside your local network, and configures them transparently. These components include

- **DHCP Allocator:** Not as feature rich as a full-blown DHCP server, this DHCP service assigns these basic TCP/IP configuration parameters to all DHCP clients on the network:
  - **IP address**
  - **Subnet mask**

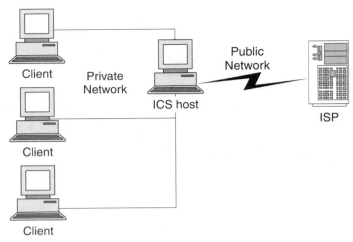

Figure 8.1 A shared Internet connection

- **Default gateway**
- **Domain Name Service (DNS) server**
- **DNS Proxy:** The ICS host provides a modicum of DNS services for your local network. It does not perform as a full DNS server, but rather it resolves Fully Qualified Domain Names (FQDNs) for local network clients. In the event it cannot resolve a name for a client, it forwards locally unresolvable queries to the DNS server it has been configured to use.
- **Network Address Translation (NAT):** NAT provides a mapping service to associate IP addresses and ports on internal and external addresses. NAT ensures that inbound and outbound IP headers are modified appropriately so communication between private and public IP addresses can occur.
- **Autodial:** Automatically dials connections.
- **Application Programming Interfaces (APIs):** For configuration, status, and dial control for programs.

Network Address Translation

In order to connect to the Internet, you must use a unique IP address designated as a public IP address. Typically, a network is assigned public IP addresses by its ISP. Some companies, such as large corporations or ISPs, require large numbers of IP addresses, and these organizations are assigned their addresses directly by

InterNIC. Because IPv4 has a limited number of IP addresses, and each computer that wishes to communicate over the Internet must have a unique and public IP address, the number of available addresses has diminished greatly over the past ten years.

The dearth of IP addresses will be addressed at some point by the implementation of IPv6, but until it is, workarounds must be put in place. One solution is to use private IP addresses on internal networks wherever possible and public IP addresses on external networks. In most networks, a majority of the communications are between hosts on the LAN, with only the occasional external network or Internet session being initiated. As a result, only a few external IP addresses need to be globally unique at any time. NAT is the standard issued by the Internet Engineering Task Force (IETF) that provides the ability to use a private IP address scheme on a local area network and connect to the Internet via an interface with a public IP address. NAT essentially proxies connection requests between internal and external networks. The IP addresses of internal network hosts are converted into public network addresses, and the public IP addresses of inbound connections are converted into a private IP address. This is accomplished by recording source and destination IP addresses in a table and then mapping them to TCP and UDP ports. NAT does have a few drawbacks, which are covered later in this section. For the small office or home network, however, NAT's benefits typically outweigh its negatives.

NAT reuses addresses, so IP address space must be segmented or separated for proper functionality. The reused addresses are those found on the internal network and are also called local addresses. The public network addresses are also called global addresses. Any address can be a global or a local address, but they cannot be both a global *and* a local address at the same time on the same network. If this happens, any routers on a private network are not able to tell the difference between a local or global address. This is one of the reasons that private network IP addresses are not broadcast on the Internet.

NAT Components

NAT is divisible into three separate functions and each function provides an essential component of the total Network Address Translation service. These functions are:

- Translation
- Addressing
- Name Resolution

Translation

The translation component performs the actual mapping of internal and external addresses. The NAT device examines the header of the in- or outbound packet for source and destination IP addresses. It then determines what the appropriate conversion should be and edits the header of the packet before sending it along.

Addressing

NAT provides basic DHCP services for the hosts on the internal network. Some implementations of NAT offer more functionality than others, but Microsoft has opted to forgo many of the options available in other vendors' products in favor of a simple and easy-to-configure implementation. The functionality of NAT in Windows XP Internet Connection Service includes assignment of:

- **An IP address:** An assignment in the private address range of 192.168.0.0 through 192.168.0.255. Other implementations of NAT offer support for private addresses from Class A and B ranges, in addition to the C APIPA range offered by Windows XP ICS.
- **A subnet mask:** 255.255.255.0.
- **A default gateway:** The IP address of the internal network interface on the NAT computer.
- **DNS server:** The IP address of the internal network interface on the NAT computer.

Name Resolution

Network address translation hosts also provide name resolution services to clients on the internal network interface. The IP address of the internal interface is provided to the clients as the name server for that network. In some implementations it provides both WINS and DNS servers, although Windows XP ICS NAT only provides DNS-based services. The NAT host is not actually a name server, however. Instead it forwards inbound name resolution requests to the name server that it is configured to use on the external network interface.

 NOTE: The name server must also be located on the external network. If it is located on the internal network, name server updates will never occur due to the way that NAT proxies name server requests back to its own name server.

How NAT Works

NAT devices straddle the boundaries of the internal network and the Internet and maintain a translation table that matches pairs of internal and external network addresses that have current sessions. Depending on the implementation, multiple NATs can be installed in the same network, but each has to use the same translation table. Cascaded NATs—one NAT that services a network with a NAT that services another network—are not recommended in any implementation. In the event that a single public address supports multiple private addresses, as is the case with Windows XP ICS, dynamically selected TCP and UDP ports are used to make a distinction between hosts on the internal network.

Here is an example of a NAT-ed network. Figure 8.2 shows the communication path.

In this example, the network is using the 192.168.0.0 network for the internal network. An external IP address of a.a.a.a has been assigned to the NAT host. The NAT translates all private addresses to the public address. Computer A in the example uses the address of 192.168.0.10 and initiates a connection to a Web site at Internet host b.b.b.b. IP packets are sent with the destination IP of b.b.b.b and the source IP of 192.168.0.10.

These packets are forwarded to the default gateway and are then processed by the NAT. The NAT examines the packets for source and destination IP addresses. The source address is changed to 192.168.a.a, but the destination is left intact. The new source address is noted in the translation table, along with the port number. The IP packet is then sent on to the destination of b.b.b.b. The

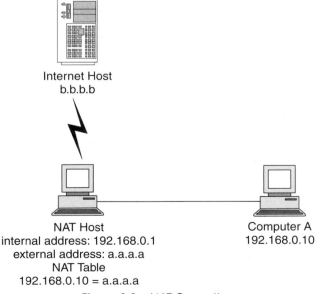

Internet Host
b.b.b.b

NAT Host
internal address: 192.168.0.1
external address: a.a.a.a
NAT Table
192.168.0.10 = a.a.a.a

Computer A
192.168.0.10

Figure 8.2   NAT Operation

Internet host sends a response back to Computer A that is first received by the NAT. The packet contains the destination address of 192.168.a.a and a source address of b.b.b.b.

NAT reviews the mapping of 192.168.a.a to 192.168.0.10 by its port number in the translation table. NAT readdresses the packet to 192.168.0.10, and sends it on, with the source address b.b.b.b intact.

NAT Issues and Considerations

NAT is not intended as a replacement for a routed Internet connection for every network. Instead, it is intended as a tool for administrators of small office and home networks to provide Internet access to the users of the network. It does not require especially advanced networking skills to implement, but there are a few things to consider when implementing NAT on a network:

- **DHCP:** Because NAT provides address assignment, it cannot be used on a private network where a DHCP server or DHCP relay agent is currently in operation. Neither the DHCP clients nor the DHCP relay agent can differentiate between the NAT and the DHCP server when requesting attention from a DHCP server.

- **Name servers:** NAT cannot be run in the same network as another name server. Some implementations of NAT offer the ability to disable the name server component, but Windows XP does not.

- **Inbound connections:** An internal network client can receive traffic from the external hosts it initiates communication with by default. However, special configuration is required to enable connection to internal network hosts initiated by external clients. This is discussed further in Chapter 12, Remote Access.

- **NAT-ed application support:** Many applications run transparently over NAT. Some, however, including many games, do not and therefore require special configuration on the NAT host to run. This is because not all protocol packets can be translated correctly by NAT. This is particularly problematic in applications that embed a source or destination address in the data portion of the packet and with applications that do not use TCP or UDP headers. NAT traversal, an extension to NAT and enabled by Universal Plug and Play, can overcome many of these problems; but it is possible to have a badly behaved application that just does not work well with NAT, particularly one that embeds private IP addresses in the data payload.

- **Demand-dial latency:** Because of the delay that can occur between the time a name resolution request is issued and resolved over a demand-dial connection, some applications may time out and return an unexpected "host not found" error message, even though the remote host is fully operational.

Inbound Connections

Applications and services that expect to be contacted by other computers listen for requests to initiate a connection. An example is a Web server that listens for a request to access HTTP files located on that server. Users on a network are able to make contact with any other service, application, or resource on the network provided the user account being used for access has sufficient permission to access it, and that some network configuration is not blocking access. Users within a NAT-ed network can make transparent connections to both internal and external resources. Users outside the NAT-ed network, however, cannot make a connection. For an external host to contact an internal host, a mapping between the IP addresses of the internal and external hosts must exist in the NAT host's translation table. By default, these mappings are created only by the internal host's attempt to contact an external resource. The external host cannot induce the NAT host to create a mapping in order to initiate contact with an internal network. Effectively this means that a service, a Web site, or a peer-to-peer application, for example, that is set up on an internal network host with an out-of-the-box configured NAT, is not accessible to external hosts.

To enable externally initiated access, the administrator of the network needs to manually configure a port mapping of the external IP address and port of the NAT host to the internal IP address and port used by the service. This permits the NAT to forward inbound packets to the appropriate internal host that is listening for just this type of external traffic.

Problems with Ports Using NAT

Some applications require access to a specific port. Only one application can use a single port/IP address pair at a time. If multiple applications running on different clients on the internal network use the same port and there is only a single external IP address, as in Windows XP ICS, this can be problematic. For example, if two Web servers on an internal network are to be made available to the external network, only one Web server can be accessible at any given moment. Because two internal hosts have the same address and port mappings, the NAT host is unable to determine which packets should go to which server. As a result, inbound requests are sent to the wrong internal client, unless the administrator has configured manual mappings. Even then, there can be problems, as inbound connections expect to use a port that may not be used by the internal application.

Another problem with NAT is that some applications send on one port and receive on another. Unless the administrator configures NAT, only packets for one port are forwarded. For example, Application A on an internal network host sends data to an Internet host from port X. The NAT maps this connection to the internal and external hosts and addresses, and then associates it with that port. When the response for Application A is returned, however, it uses port Z. The NAT receives this inbound packet and checks the forwarding table to see what internal IP address has a connection matched to this source address and port. Because the connection was initially mapped with port X, the NAT drops the traffic, because it believes it to be invalid.

NAT Traversal

As you can see, there are a number of issues with Network Address Translation stemming from its design as an outbound connection proxy and its use of ports and addresses in packets. By means of manual configuration of the NAT translation table, it is possible to overcome some of these problems. However, not all administrators of small office and home networks have the skills or knowledge to make these configuration changes. Additionally, there are a number of application-related issues that can only be resolved by a developer, which no amount of manual configuration of a NAT host can help. In the past, NAT editors were frequently used to make modifications to the IP packets and the actual data payload to ensure that the correct address and port information is included. Some things, however, such as IPSec and H.323, cannot be successfully translated even with a NAT editor, which leads to dropped VPN connections or the inability to conduct an Internet white-boarding session over a NAT-ed connection.

With the proliferation of NAT devices in the market, both hardware and software based, NAT-ing is widely used in networks of many sizes. As part of an attempt to improve user experience, various vendors have joined together to develop the Internet Gateway Device (IGD) specification, which is working to develop a workaround for many of these problems. This workaround is an industry standard called NAT traversal. In a nutshell, it allows the applications on a NAT-ed network to dynamically configure themselves and the NAT host to make the changes needed for a hands-free NAT configuration. The IGD specification falls under the jurisdiction of the Universal Plug and Play Forum.

NAT Traversal API

The magic of the automatic detection of a NAT host and the configuration of a NAT translation table are handled by NAT traversal APIs. These APIs permit network-aware applications to discover that a NAT host is acting as their gateway out of the network and make the appropriate adjustments on that host. Windows XP ICS provides these NAT traversal APIs, and like other industry-standard implementations of NAT traversal, it performs the following tasks:

- Discover if a NAT host is present on the local network.
- Determine the public (external interface) IP address of the NAT.
- Acquire a list of static port mappings for the local network.
- Acquire specific information about static port mapping information for any ports that are needed by applications running on the internal host.
- If the desired external port has not already been assigned, NAT traversal APIs add a static port mapping to the NAT host's translation table.
- If the specified external port is already in use, the NAT traversal APIs can enable or disable a specific port mapping without deleting it.
- If required, NAT traversal APIs can delete static port mappings.

NAT traversal APIs modify the description of a static port mapping that can be viewed by users.

In order to provide this functionality, NAT hosts, also called Internet Gateway Devices, must provide certain information to clients running NAT traversal APIs. The industry standard requirements for a NAT traversal–compatible NAT host are:

- A NAT host may only announce one public interface at a time. Many implementations of NAT permit multiple public interfaces, but NAT traversal APIs only use the first interface.
- A NAT host must provide the ability to create port mappings to permit external hosts to send packets to internal network hosts.
- The NAT host must permit internal host port mappings to use the external interface.
- The NAT host must support different port numbers for internal host and the external interface.
- Any static port mappings must be permanent; that is, they exist until intentionally removed. The NAT must announce itself to NAT traversal clients on the internal network as running Version 1.

NAT Traversal Issues

Although NAT traversal addresses many of the problems associated with Network Address Translation, it is not a panacea. In addition to not fixing all the problems of NAT, new issues have been created by the introduction of NAT traversal. Some of the drawbacks include

- ISPs that use NAT for customer IP address assignment eliminate any benefit of NAT traversal for customers that use a NAT host to share an Internet connection for their internal network. This is known as a cascaded NAT. The problem with cascaded NATs is that the NAT traversal API is only able to detect the presence of a single NAT host on its local network and no additional NAT hosts after that.

  For example, a fictitious company called the Victory Café uses an IP address assigned by its ISP's NAT host. The administrator of the Victory Café network installs a NAT host on the local network to provide a shared Internet connection to the four users of the network. These users cannot benefit from NAT traversal, because although applications that require specific static mappings can pass through the NAT host on the Victory Café network, these mappings cannot be created on the ISP's NAT host. All inbound connection traffic is blocked at the NAT's ISP, and any applications that need specific port mappings are also blocked at the IPS's NAT.

- All applications on the private network may make modifications as necessary to the port mappings of the NAT host. Because applications do not have complete ownership of their port mappings, it is possible for applications to have flaky behavior. If Application A wants to use port X, which is already in use, it can either find an alternate port or it can overwrite the port X mapping. This may unexpectedly disable the application using port X. Furthermore, if an application does not remove its static mappings when it is finished with them, they persist indefinitely. This can cause other applications to have less than optimal performance if they use an alternate port that external clients may not be aware of.

NAT traversal requires the NAT host to support Universal Plug and Play (UPnP). Even if the application is NAT traversal standards compliant, if the NAT host does not support UPnP, NAT traversal cannot work.

Universal Plug and Play

Universal Plug and Play brings the ease of plug-and-play hardware installation to the world of networking. However, UPnP goes far beyond just making the installation of a network a simple process. UPnP is a standard that applies to all types of network devices to make them work "automatically" when connected to a network. This means that when a UPnP device is connected to a network through any UPnP-compatible media, wired or wireless, the device proactively requests Windows to search the network to which it has been attached to discover what services and other devices are available. As these discoveries are made, the UPnP devices self-configure to provide a totally hands-free out-of-the-box experience for users.

UPnP is a standard developed by the Universal Plug and Play Forum. The Forum is an industrial committee composed of companies that design, manufacture, and sell networking gear primarily slated for use within small office and home networks. It was started in 1999 to develop a set of standards for interoperability between UPnP devices and ease of use by users.

By supporting zero-configuration networking and network autodiscovery, UPnP enables data communication between any two UPnP-compliant devices regardless of operating system, development platform, or hardware. UPnP devices can enter and leave a network with no configuration on the part of the user or the network administrator. This makes services like wireless network access in airports and coffee shops and downloading digital photos from a FireWire digital camera possible. Windows XP ICS is UPnP compliant. When enabled, it announces its presence on the internal network and all NAT traversal clients on the network, regardless of vendor, works with it. Non-NAT traversal clients operate with the UPnP-enabled ICS host as well, but they are subject to the same limitations as a plain NAT client.

Installing Universal Plug and Play on Windows XP

Universal Plug and Play is not installed by default on Windows XP. It must be manually installed. To do so:

1. Launch **Control Panel** and double-click **Add/Remove Programs**.
2. Click **Add/Remove Windows Components**. The **Windows Components Wizard** appears, as shown in Figure 8.3.
3. Click **Networking Services**, then click the **Details** button. The **Networking Service** dialog box appears.
4. Put a check in the **Universal Plug and Play** check box, as shown in Figure 8.4.
5. Click **OK** to proceed. When the **Windows Components Wizard** re-appears, click **Next**. UPnP files are installed.
6. When the **Completing Windows Components Wizard** screen appears, click **Finish**.
7. Close the **Add/Remove Programs** window.

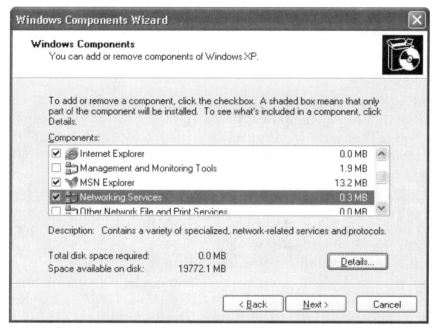

Figure 8.3 Windows Components Wizard

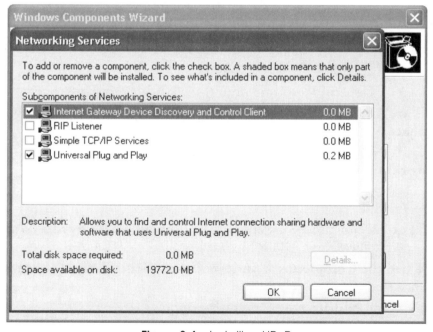

Figure 8.4 Installing UPnP

Configuring Internet Connection Sharing

Windows XP Internet Connection Sharing setup is very straightforward. It is also quite similar to Windows 2000 Internet Connection Sharing. To configure ICS, you need to configure both an ICS host and the clients on the network.

ICS Host Configuration

1. Click **Start**, then **Settings**, then **Control Panel**, and then **Network Connections**.
2. Right-click the connection that you use to connect to the Internet. Click **Properties** on the context menu.
3. Click the **Advanced** tab.
4. Under **Internet Connection Sharing**, put a check in the **Allow other network users to connect through this computer's Internet connection** check box, shown in Figure 8.5.
5. Click **OK**.

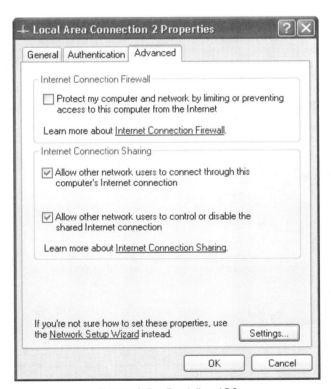

Figure 8.5   Enabling ICS

Client Setup

There are a variety of options for configuring clients to use the ICS host you have just set up.

- **DHCP:** If your clients are configured to use DHCP (the **Obtain an IP address automatically** option is selected in TCP/IP Properties), no additional TCP/IP configuration work is required on your part. If not, simply configure all clients on your network with this setting.
- **Static Addresses:** You can assign a static IP address between 192.168.0.2 and 192.168.0.254 (192.168.0.2 is used by the ICS host), a subnet mask of 255.255.255.0, and a default gateway of 192.168.0.1.
- **Network Setup Wizard:** Run the Network Setup Wizard to configure your clients.

To run the Network Setup Wizard for ICS:

1. Start the **Network Setup Wizard**.
2. The Wizard's Welcome screen, shown in Figure 8.6, appears. Click **Next** to continue.

Figure 8.6 Welcome to the Network Setup Wizard

3. The Wizard prompts you to review the **Preliminary Checklist**. If you have completed all items on the checklist, click **Next**. If after reviewing them you discover you have not completed all the items on the list, click **Cancel** to exit the Wizard. When you have completed the checklist, restart the Wizard.

4. Windows XP detects the ICS host and you are prompted to select that connection, as shown in Figure 8.7. Select **Yes, use the existing shared connection for this computer's Internet access (recommended)**, and click **Next**.

6. If the computer has more than one network connection, the screen shown in Figure 8.8 appears. Select **Let me choose the connections to my network** and click **Next**.

7. Select the connection to the ICS server as shown in Figure 8.9 and click **Next**.

8. Enter a computer description and computer name. The computer name must be unique on the network. For backwards compatibility with other versions of Windows, adhere to the NetBIOS naming convention

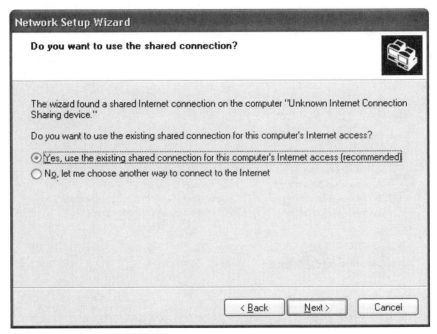

Figure 8.7   Select the connection to the ICS host.

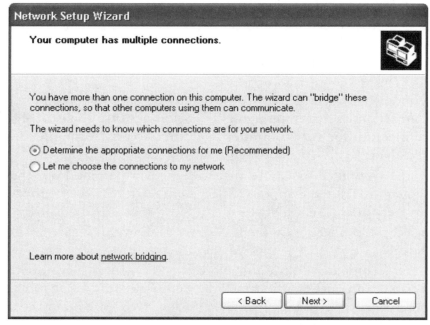

Figure 8.8 Manually select the network connection to be used.

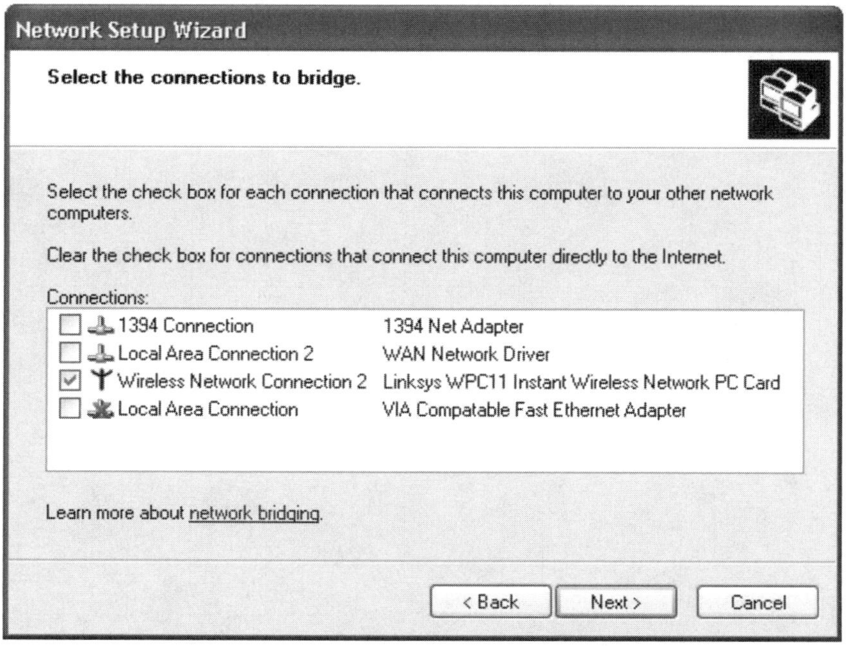

Figure 8.9 Select the interface to the ICS host.

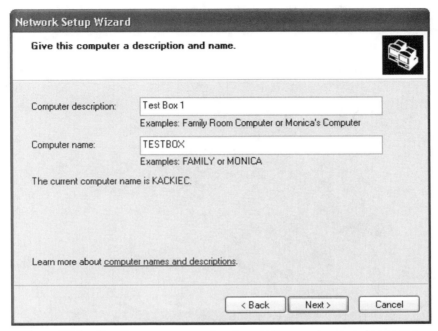

Figure 8.10 Configure a computer description and computer name.

of up to 15 alphanumeric characters, with no blanks, as shown in Figure 8.10. Click **Next**.

9. Enter a workgroup name, which should be the same on all of the networked computers. Once again, use up to 15 alphanumeric characters, with no blanks. The Wizard uses the name MSHOME by default, but you can chose something else, as shown in Figure 8.11. Click **Next**.

10. The Wizard displays the setting selections that you have made, shown in Figure 8.12. Verify that all are correct. If not, click **Back** to change them. When you are ready, click **Next**.

11. The Wizard configures the selected network settings. If the Wizard is running on a Windows XP computer, the screen as shown in Figure 8.13 appears. Select **Just finish the wizard** and click **Next**.

12. When configuration is complete, the Wizard's **Completion** screen appears, shown in Figure 8.14. Click **Finish** to exit.

Creating a Static Port Mapping

To support applications or services, such as a Web site that sits behind an ICS host, you need to create a static port mapping for the ICS host. This

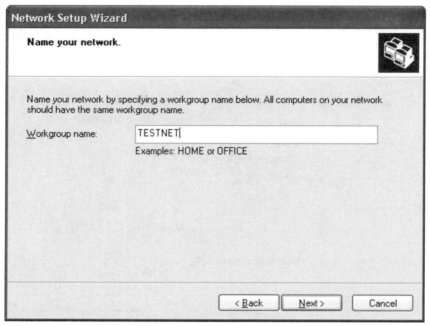

Figure 8.11   Configure a workgroup name.

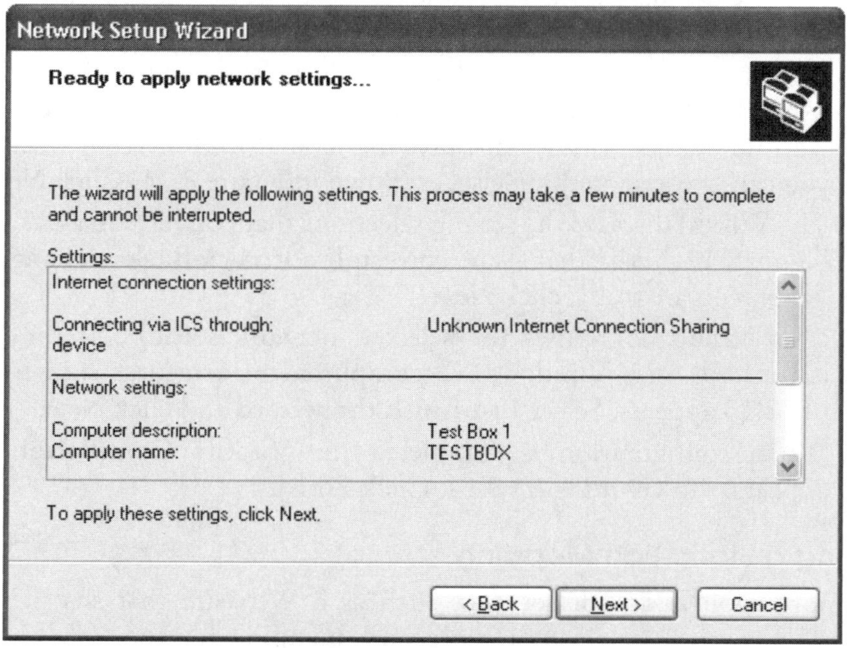

Figure 8.12   Verify settings.

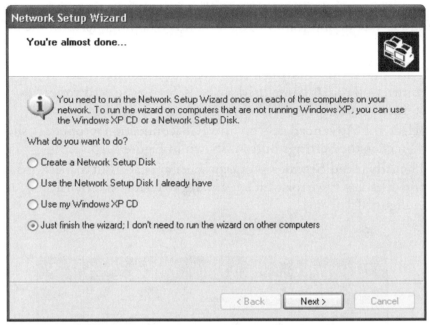

Figure 8.13   Finalizing the Network Setup Wizard.

Figure 8.14   The Wizard completes.

permits users outside the internal network to initiate a session with the host providing the service or application. To create this mapping, perform the following steps.

1. Click **Start**, then **Settings**, then **Network Connections**. Right-click the connection that is configured as the ICS host. Select **Properties** from the context menu.

2. Select the **Advanced** tab on the ICS connection properties sheet, and then click the **Settings** button, shown in Figure 8.15.

3. The **Advanced Settings** property sheet appears. Put a check mark in the box of each service for which you want to enable external access, as shown in Figure 8.16.

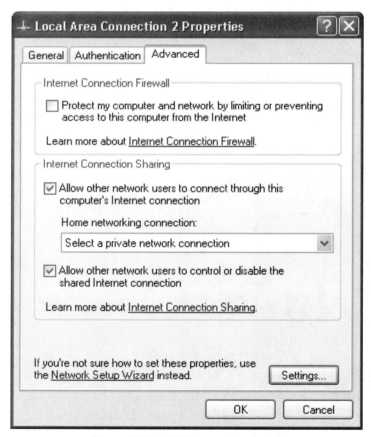

Figure 8.15 ICS Properties sheet

4. Once the check mark has been placed in the box for a service, the **Service Settings** dialog box with the default port mappings for that service is displayed, as shown in Figure 8.17. Enter the name or IP address of the host providing the service. Click **OK** to accept.

5. If the ports for that service do not match what you desire, or if the service you want to configure does not appear in the list, click the **Add** button. A blank **Service Settings** dialog box appears, as shown in Figure 8.18.

6. Provide the following information for the service you are configuring:

   - **Description of the service:** The name of the service you provide. This can be a friendly name.

   - **Name or IP address of the computer hosting this service on your network**.

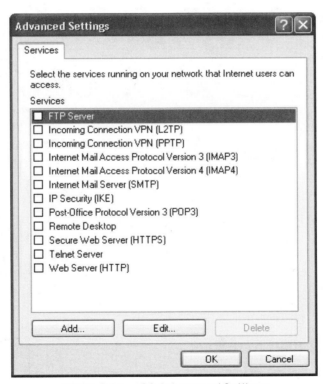

Figure 8.16   ICS Advanced Settings

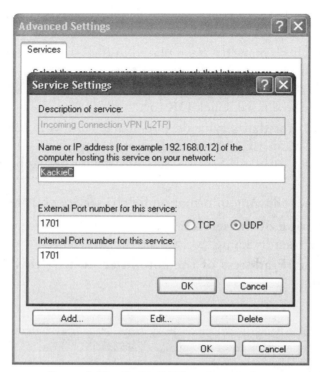

Figure 8.17 Default ICS port mappings

Figure 8.18 ICS Service Settings

- **External port number for the service:** Enter the port that remote hosts use to connect to this application or service. Also specify if the ports are TCP or UDP.
- **Internal port number for the service:** Enter the TCP or UDP ports on the service running on the internal host.

7. Click **OK**, and then close the ICS properties sheet.

ICS Considerations

If you are looking for a simple-to-implement, cost-effective Internet connection sharing service for your small home or office network, Windows XP ICS fits the bill nicely. Configuring ICS beyond these basic options, however, is not possible. Although this makes enabling or disabling its use or setting up applications and services to run through the ICS host a piece of cake, it may make ICS not the best choice for NAT-ing your network. Name resolution and address assignment methods used by ICS may conflict with services currently offered on your network. Keep these things in mind when you are thinking about implementing ICS:

- The default range of IP addresses and subnet mask assigned to the internal network by ICS cannot be changed.
- A static IP address can be assigned, but it is possible for a brief duplicate IP address situation to occur on the network due to the way that ICS assigns IP addresses. The host configured to use the static address is not affected, but the host that receives that IP address dynamically experiences a brief connectivity problem until it is assigned a new address by the ICS server.
- The internal interface of the computer configured for ICS is always set to 192.168.0.1, and it overwrites whatever static IP address was assigned to that interface previously. Any TCP/IP connections between the ICS host and other hosts on the internal network are broken and must be subsequently reestablished. If persistent drive mappings are established on your network clients to connect to the ICS host by its previous IP address, the administrator must change those mappings.
- Only one public address can be assigned to the external ICS interface.
- The ICS computer intercepts all requests for name resolution and forwards them to a DNS server on the Internet.

Conclusion

In this chapter we discussed sharing a single Internet connection among multiple users in a single network. Windows XP provides a tool for this called Internet Connection Sharing. Instead of setting up a separate piece of hardware to act as a router on your network to send traffic between the Internet and your network, you can use ICS to share a single connection to the Internet among all your devices on the local network.

ICS uses Network Address Translation to transfer traffic between the local network and the Internet. Recall from this chapter's discussion that private IP addresses are used in conjunction with ICS on the local network. These private IP addresses are not reachable from the Internet, which means that applications that run over the Internet need some assistance to reach a host running on a network behind ICS. This assistance takes the form of mappings between inbound and outbound applications and the specific ports they use.

From here we move into a discussion of wireless networking. Windows XP provides enhanced support for wireless networking, and this is covered in Chapter 9.

9

Wireless Overview and Enhancements in Windows XP

Wireless networking in its current format first started appearing (standards existed) in 1997. This first version was just referred to as 802.11 and it operated at between 1 and 2 megabits per second (Mb/s). This version of wireless was radio frequency based at 2.4GHz, one of the two commonly used frequencies utilized in 802.11 wireless LAN technologies.

Two commonly used radio frequencies are prevalent in wireless technologies today: 2.4GHz and 5GHz (used in 802.11a). The standard also identified an infrared protocol, but for whatever reason, infrared never took off. This chapter gives information on radio frequencies and talks about the technology behind the two main types of signal dispersal in use in wireless networks today. While it is probably not required for the average user to know about these technologies, it will be important for you to understand their implications when deploying a larger-scale network of wireless technologies.

The 802.11 standard is a member of the IEEE 802 technology family, which many of you recognize as the family in which a lot of your computer Internet technology is based. As shown in Figure 9.1, the IEEE 802 standard has many pieces, including the Logical Link Control (LLC), Media Access Control (MAC) addressing, as well as Ethernet, Token Ring, and many other technologies.

802.11 Basics

There are four components that you need to be aware of that make up the 802.11 substandard. This becomes more important when you begin to deal with larger networks, because it helps determine the layout of your wireless network and whether you support and allow ad hoc or infrastructure or both.

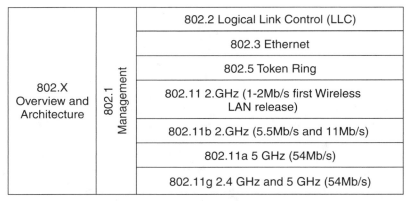

Figure 9.1   802 IEEE overview

Distribution

Distribution is when several wireless access points in an infrastructure mode that you have deployed, such as several access points to cover a larger office, permit wireless client migration around the office. Somehow these access points must communicate with each other by tracking the MAC address and knowing where to deliver frames. This communication channel is covered within the specification between the access points and is typically done using a form of bridging between the access points.

Access Point

As mentioned earlier, when you are in ad-hoc mode, it is a bunch of wireless cards talking to and detecting each other. Whereas in infrastructure mode, you have wireless clients talking to access points, which are like network hubs or bridges that connect these clients back to the backbone network LAN.

Wireless Medium

The wireless medium is the format of the radio frequency (RF) and infrared signal that was defined to allow wireless clients to talk to other wireless clients and to access points. Without this, wireless networks could not function.

Stations

A station is any client that interacts with the wireless network; the clients are separated into their own category because it is important when you understand that it is mobile and therefore can move from one access point to another. (See Figure 9.2.)

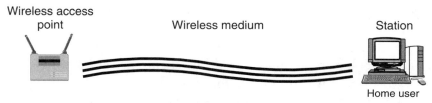

Figure 9.2 Interaction between wireless access point and wireless station

Extensible Authentication Protocol

In this section we talk about the following Extensible Authentication Protocol (EAP) items:

- Overview
- Supported types
- Using Remote Authentication Dial-in User Service (RADIUS)
- Transport Level Security (TLS) and the IEEE 802 Authentication Process

Overview

EAP was created originally as an extension to Point-to-Point Protocol (PPP) and was designed to allow for development of different network access authentication methods.

With point-to-point networking, it is possible to authenticate using Challenge Handshake Authentication Protocol (CHAP), Microsoft Challenge Handshake Authentication Protocol (MS-CHAP), and Microsoft Challenge Handshake Authentication Protocol version 2 (MS-CHAP v2). One of these authentication methods is chosen during the link-establish phase. During the authentication phase, the chosen authentication protocol is used to validate the credentials supplied either by the computer or interactively from the user.

Just as with most protocols and applications during this process, negotiation occurs using a fixed set of messages sent in a specific order. However, with EAP the authentication mechanism is not chosen during the link-establishment phase of PPP. Instead, each peer negotiates during the connection-authentication phase using EAP. When the authentication phase begins, the peers use a specific EAP scheme sometimes referred to as EAP type in RFC 2284.

Once agreed on, EAP allows for the exchange of messages between the client and the server (RADIUS Server). These messages can vary based on chosen parameters of the link state. However, the conversation consists of requests for authentication and expects a specific range of responses. The requests, the responses, and the length of the conversation are wholly dependent upon the EAP type or schema.

EAP was designed a lot like Pluggable Authentication Method (PAM) under UNIX in which plug-in modules at both the client and server can be chosen. To add new types, one must install the libraries associated with that type on both the client and server. Because of this, in some cases, vendors are free to provide better, more secure methods of authentication. (Obviously this leads to vendor diversity for marketing and rights assignment reasons, although that topic is beyond the scope of this book).

It is possible to use such schemes as a Generic Token, a One-Time Password, or an MD5 Challenge for authentication. Using TLS for smart card and certificate support is the accepted practice.

As mentioned earlier, EAP was originally designed as an extension to the Point-to-Point Protocol, but since its inception it has been casually linked to the IEEE 802 link layer, which is available throughout the specification. IEEE 802.1x defines how EAP should be used for authenticating IEEE 802 devices, including the wireless standards (802.11a/b/g). IEEE 802.1x differs from PPP in that only EAP authentication is supported.

Supported Types

There are four commonly supported EAP types within Windows XP. It is, however, possible that other vendors can provide support, and we encourage you to speak to your vendor if none of these work in your environment. These four types are:

- EAP-TLS
- EAP-MD5 CHAP
- RSA SecurID ACE/Agent for Windows
- Protected Extensible Authentication Protocol (PEAP)

EAP-TLS

Transport Level Security is a type that uses certificates. If you are using certificates or smart cards you must use this method. The exchange of messages provides a mutual authentication that is protected against problems with integrity during negotiation. TLS uses a secured private key exchange, which has mechanisms to determine between the client and the server. TLS provides the strongest authentication method available with EAP.

TLS using registry-based computer and user certificates is the default authentication method for Windows XP–based clients for connectivity for the following four reasons:

1. TLS does not require any dependencies on the user's account password.
2. TLS uses certificates, which are reasonably strong (so much better than passwords).
3. With TLS, authentication can occur automatically with no user intervention.
4. TLS uses a form of public key cryptography to protect the exchange and therefore is not susceptible to an offline dictionary attack.

EAP-MD5 CHAP

Challenge Handshake Authentication Protocol is a required type that uses the same handshake as PPP-based CHAP. However, the challenges and responses are sent as EAP messages.

A typical use of this protocol is to authenticate remote access clients using their username and password. You can also use this type to test EAP interoperability, though this EAP type is not suitable for Windows XP wireless clients for the following four reasons:

1. CHAP requires a reversible form of encryption on the password so it can calculate the response. This form of encryption is weaker and is not turned on by default on most account structures, which include local and domain accounts.
2. CHAP cannot authenticate only once; you must authenticate to the wireless access point (or however wireless authentication is achieved) and then again to the domain.
3. CHAP is password-based and therefore users have the ability (and you know they will) to choose weaker passwords, thus resulting in a weaker overall authentication scheme.
4. CHAP is dictionary attack-friendly (that means it is bad). A hacker could capture the CHAP exchange and then spend as long as necessary to attempt to decipher the password.

RSA SecurID ACE/Agent for Windows

The ACE/Agent for Windows is an EAP-based authentication for using tokens (both hardware—those small fobs—and software—using things like your Palm Pilot). This is available both from the vendor and downloadable from Microsoft's Web site.

PEAP

PEAP is a new type of authentication protocol that solves a rather huge problem. With most extensible authentication protocol types, the conversation might be sent in the clear (unencrypted). A hacker with access to the media might be able to inject packets into a conversation or capture some of the EAP messages, such as parts of the authentication, for later analysis and perhaps eventually decipher it. This can be especially problematic with wireless because if you are using radio frequencies, the extent of this network is not necessarily within your office walls; it could extend to the parking lot or maybe even nearby businesses or a residential community. This capture, and eventual dissemination, can occur even when you use Wired Equivalent Privacy (WEP).

PEAP addresses this security issue by first creating a secure channel that is encrypted and has integrity and is also protected using transport-level security. TLS protects the negotiation and authentication for the network access attempt of the client; and because the channel is protected it is not susceptible to an offline dictionary attack.

Extensible Authentication Protocol over RADIUS

Now that you know about the various EAP types that are available, let's spend a little time talking about a secondary authentication protocol that can be combined with EAP to provide pass-through authentication. EAP is able to use RADIUS as a secondary authentication protocol because much like EAP, RADIUS is extensible and has attributes that conform to extensible authentication protocol standards.

You might use EAP over RADIUS in environments where you have already spent the time and resources to build a RADIUS server for other authentication methods. It is important to leverage existing infrastructure components to make transitions easier and to utilize hardware and processes that are already reliable and secure. This use of RADIUS also takes some of the load off the access server, because it is the client and the RADIUS server that perform the authentication, not the access server.

When an attempt is made to authenticate, the client negotiates the use of EAP with the access server. When the client sends its EAP message to the access server, it encapsulates the message as an EAP-Message attribute of the RADIUS Access-Request message and sends it to its configured RADIUS server. The RADIUS server then processes the message and sends back the proper response to the access server, which then forwards it to the client.

EAP, TLS, and the IEEE 802.1x Authentication Process

The following describes the authentication process for a wireless client.

- **Associate and Identify:** The wireless access point or the wireless client attempts to join the network. Either device associating with each other does this. When it is done by the client, it transmits an EAP-Start message. When the IEEE 802.1x process on the access point receives the Start message, the wireless access point will transmit an EAP-Request/Identity management message.

- **Response:** At this point the wireless client determines if a user is logged in so that it can start to build the EAP-Response/Identity. Because in this example a user is not logged on, the computer name is transmitted.
- **Start TLS:** The RADIUS server sends an Access-Challenge message containing the EAP-Request from the wireless client along with the EAP-Type set to EAP-TLS and requests that the communication begin building up the encryption for TLS. At this point the wireless client crafts an EAP-Response that includes the handshake involving TLS.
- **EAP-Request from RADIUS:** The RADIUS server sends an Access-Challenge message containing the original EAP-Request message with the type set to EAP-TLS. This also contains the RADIUS server's certificate.
- **The EAP-Response from the wireless client:** The wireless client sends an EAP-Response with the EAP-Type set to TLS and includes the client's certificate.
- **TLS complete:** The RADIUS server sends an EAP-Request message with the type set to TLS. This message includes the cipher suite and indicates that TLS is complete.
- **Response from the client:** The wireless client sends an EAP-Response message with EAP-Type set to TLS to the access server.
- **EAP-Success from RADIUS:** RADIUS server derives the per-client unicast session key and signing key from the arterial that is a result of the TLS authentication process. Next, the RADIUS server sends an Access-Accept message containing an EAP-Success message, the MPPE-Send key, and the MPPE-Recv key to the access server/access point.

With the MS-MPPE-Send-key attribute, the client unicast session key for transmission to the client can begin. The key may be truncated to the length of the WEP key. The access point/server then uses the key encrypted in the MS-MPPE-Recv key to sign for transmissions to the wireless client that requires signing.

The client derives the per-client session key (the same value that was decrypted from the MS-MPPE-Send-key attribute in the RADIUS message) and the MS-MPPE-Recv-key attribute in the RADIUS message sent to the wireless AP from the key ring that is the result of the TLS authentication process.

Radio Frequencies

While wireless has evolved into something comprehensive and useful in our lives, the standards employed in this technology are straightforward, and while complex, they are easier to comprehend because of these standards. There are two technologies employed for transmission of data, identification, and tracking of stations (STA), and although two exist, only one, radio frequency, is in common use today.

We mentioned earlier that the two frequencies in use today are 2.4GHz and 5GHz. These two frequencies can be either Direct Sequence Spread Spectrum (DSSS) or Frequency Hopping Spread Spectrum (FHSS). While these are big terms they are reasonably simple concepts, and are briefly described here.

Direct Sequence Spread Spectrum

DSSS is a method of spread spectrum that separates by code and not by its frequency. In IEEE 802.11 this spreading is achieved using a chip sequence (+1, -1, +1, +1, -1, +1, +1, +1, -1, -1, -1), which was originally referred to as the "Barker" code. The characteristics of this are that it is robust (against interference), and it is fairly insensitive to multipath propagation problems (also referred to as time-delay spread).

Frequency Hopping Spread Spectrum

FHSS is a technique that is similar to your home cordless phones whereby the coexistence of multiple devices sharing the same frequency area can work at the same time. This is done by each set of devices having a "hopping sequence" where at some random interval, the device will "hop" to a different frequency that presumably is not in use by any other device at that time. If it is, then both devices may experience some interference and therefore need to hop again. The standard defines 79 different hopping channels for North America and Europe and another 23 channels for Japan and Asia.

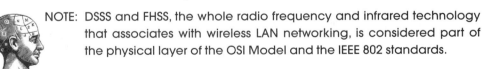 NOTE: DSSS and FHSS, the whole radio frequency and infrared technology that associates with wireless LAN networking, is considered part of the physical layer of the OSI Model and the IEEE 802 standards.

Understanding the 802.11 MAC Sublayer

While discussing radio frequencies, we talked briefly about the technologies that transmit the signal in most wireless products today. However, it is an incomplete description, because you need a better understanding of how the Media Access Control layer works. This section provides you an in-depth explanation because it is important to understand how this works.

It is important because the media access layer is a static definition of resources. In Ethernet, if MAC addresses moved as frequently as they could with wireless technologies (especially when they move from one router bridge to another), then Ethernet would not work the way it is designed to do today.

So, one of the most distinct issues that has to be addressed with wireless is how to keep track of completely mobile and often frequently mobile devices.

At the MAC sublayer, IEEE 802.11 uses the Carrier Sense Multiple Access with Collision Avoidance (CSMA/CA) Media Access Control protocol, which works in the following way.

A wireless station with a frame to transmit first listens on the wireless channel to determine if another station is currently transmitting (carrier sense). If the medium is being used, the wireless station calculates a random back off delay. Only after the random back off delay can the wireless station again listen for a transmitting station. By instituting a random back off delay, multiple stations that are waiting to transmit do not end up trying to transmit at the same time (collision avoidance).

The CSMA standard does not ensure that a collision never takes place, and it is difficult for a transmitting node to detect that a collision is occurring. Additionally, depending on the placement of the access points and the clients, a radio frequency barrier can prevent clients from sensing that another node is transmitting. This is known as the hidden station problem.

IEEE 802.11 provides a better way of detecting collisions and the "hidden station problem" using an acknowledgment (ACK) frame to indicate that a wireless frame was successfully received and the use of Request to Send (RTS) and Clear to Send (CTS) messages. When a station wants to transmit a frame, it sends a RTS message informing the node how much time it needs to send that frame. The wireless AP sends a CTS message to all stations, granting permission to the requesting station and informing all other stations that they are not allowed to transmit for the time reserved by the RTS message. The exchange of RTS and CTS messages eliminates collisions due to hidden stations.

Speed, Function, Form 802.11x

802.11b

With 802.11b changes to the standardization of elements of the physical layer, higher speeds are possible. IEEE 802.11b supports 5.5Mb/s and 11Mb/s using the same frequencies (2.45GHz). DSSS modulation is used to provide the higher rates. A bit rate of 11Mb/s is achievable in ideal conditions, and in less than ideal conditions the system negotiates 5.5, 2, or 1Mb/s.

802.11a

While not commonly used, because of standardization on IEEE 802.11b and the advent of 802.11g, this version also made changes to the frequency and the modulation. OFDM allows data to be transmitted by multiple subfrequencies in parallel. This allows a greater resistance to interference and because more than one data stream is being sent, it is possible for great throughput.

IEEE 802.11a is capable of up to 54Mb/s in ideal situations. In less than ideal situations (or a clear signal), the devices can negotiate 48Mb/s, 36Mb/s, 24Mb/s, 18Mb/s, 12Mb/s, and finally 6Mb/s.

802.11g

While not popularly known, soon after the 802.11b standard was released (sometime in late 1999), the IEEE started work on 802.11g. The final specification included both mandatory and optional features, including some vendor features to allow for competitiveness. Although most usually found at 54Mb/s, it can also be found at lower speeds if there is not a clear signal or if there are less than ideal situations. The additional frequencies in these less than ideal situations include 48Mb/s, 36Mb/s, and 24Mb/s, as well as the lower speeds mentioned in the previous standards.

Additionally, 802.11g uses different modulations than 802.11b. Both Orthogonal Frequency Division Multiplexing (OFDM), found originally in 802.11a, and Complementary Code Keying (CCK), which was originally used in 802.11b, are possible with 802.11g. Typically, OFDM is used in higher data rates and CCK in lower data rates. Including CCK also adds another unique property to 802.11g in that it makes backward compatibility possible, which allows a device to broadcast 802.11g or 802.11b for backward compatibility, as shown in Table 9.1.

Some vendors have used optional support for Packet Binary Convolutional Code (PBCC), which provides for 22Mb/s to 33Mb/s data rates and is included in the standard as an option. Texas Instruments also includes this modulation in something called "802.11b+" that is available from vendors including D-Link and 3Com.

A number of vendors are taking the 802.11g standard further than was envisioned (or approved by IEEE) in that they are using packet-bursting technology that enhances the speed. Other vendors have reported speeds of up to 30 percent greater in mixed networks and 50 percent in 802.11g-only networks.

When a wireless card receives power, it begins to scan across the associated wireless frequencies for access points and other clients. This process is basically an active listening process where the device listens on all channels for beacon

Table 9.1 Backward Compatibility for 802.11b Devices

802.11 comparison	802.11b	802.11a	802.11g
Max. Speed	11Mb/s	54Mb/s	54Mb/s
Modulation	CCK	ODFM	ODFM, CCK (backward compatibility)
Frequencies	2.4 to 2.497GHz	5.15 to 5.35, 5.425 to 5.675, and 5.725 to 5.875GHz	2.4 to 2.497GHz
Acceptable Data Rates	1, 2, 5.5, 11 Mb/s	5.15–5.35 6, 9, 12,18, 24 Mb/s	OFDM (802.11g) 6, 9,12,18, 24, 36, 48Mb/s CCK: 1, 2, 5.5, and 11Mb/s

frames sent by other devices. Assuming the device is set for infrastructure mode, after the scanning finishes the adapter will choose an access point to associate with. This selection can be made automatically by using the Service Set Identifier (SSID) of the network and access point with the best signal strength (highest signal-to-noise ratio). Next the client switches to the assigned channel of the access point and negotiates the use of a logical port.

The process of identifying whether or not the client associates with an access point is determined by the configuration settings. By default the Windows XP client prefers infrastructure mode and to associate with an access point rather than another client. If the signal is too weak, or the error rate too high, Windows XP will, every 60 sections, determine if a different access point on the same network can correct some of these issues.

This process of going through and finding a better access point on the same network is called reassociation. This might be done for a few different reasons beyond weakness, including congestion or other interference. It is important to take this into consideration, because doing so may help you plan your network so that you put the highest concentration of wireless access points in your most heavily populated areas. In planning this, you need to make sure that the subfrequencies do not overlap; but the vendors can provide that information. In more robust products, they can detect other access points and deal with this automatically.

When you link multiple wireless access points, hopefully you create a network that has some overlap. We talked about this overlap and the concern about frequency overlap. This is covered by standards called Extend Service Set (ESS), which also allow a client to roam from one location to another, and therefore from one access point to another, while maintaining network connectivity (and even the same IP address). But there is more—with Windows XP it is not quite that simple.

It is possible for a wireless client to roam beyond your network's ESS, which makes the IP address invalid. With Windows XP, client reassociation is interpreted as a media disconnect, and this event causes a DHCP renewal.

802.11 Authentication

IEEE 802.11 defines the following types of authentication:

- Open System Authentication
- Shared Key Authentication

Open System Authentication

Open system authentication does not provide authentication—only identification using the wireless adapter's MAC address. Open system authentication is used when no authentication is requested or required. Open system authentication is the default authentication algorithm that uses the following process:

- **Identity Requests Initialization:** The client sends an IEEE 802.11 authentication management frame that contains its identity.
- **Identity Acknowledgment:** The receiving node checks the station's identity and sends back an authentication verification frame.

With some wireless access points, you can configure the MAC addresses of allowed clients. This is obviously not secure, however, because the MAC addresses can be spoofed. (It is a trivial exercise of about ten minutes.) By default, a XP wireless client configured to perform open system authentication sends its Media Access Control address as the identity.

Shared Key Authentication

We will discuss IPSec in greater detail in Chapter 18, but for now it is important to note that there are only two main types of IPSec: public key cryptography and private key cryptography. Similarly, there are two types of authentication used in wireless services. The one we discuss here is shared key; and with shared key there is a shared secret (think shared secret from creating a VPN). A shared secret is both the strength and weakness of the system. If the key is handled securely throughout its travels, it is a modestly secure method; if not, it becomes extremely weak.

Shared key authentication uses the following process:

- First, the wireless client sends a data packet consisting of its identity and a request for authentication.
- The authenticating node (probably a wireless access point) responds to the request with a challenge.
- The client responds to the challenge using a WEP encryption key that is derived from the shared key and the authentication secret.
- The wireless access point then reverses this and should be able to find the original challenge text, which results in a successful authentication.
- As we mentioned above, if the key is not handled securely the method becomes very weak. Because the key needs to be manually distributed one can assume that there will be cases where it is handled insecurely. Therefore, and especially in a large network, an organization might consider alternate means.

802.11 Encryption with Wired Equivalent Privacy

Due to the nature of wireless LAN networks (radio frequencies have no boundaries), securing physical access to the network is challenging. Unlike a wired network where a physical connection is required, anyone within frequency range of a wireless access point can send and receive as well as listen for other information being sent, making eavesdropping and remote sniffing of wireless LAN frames (also know as "War Driving") very easy. Wired Equivalent Privacy is defined by the IEEE 802.11 standard and is intended to provide a level of data confidentiality (and security) that is equivalent to a wired network.

WEP provides its services by encrypting the data sent between access point and client (or between any wireless nodes). Setting a WEP flag in the MAC header of the 802.11 frame indicates WEP encryption for an 802.11 frame. WEP provides data integrity for random errors by including Integrity Check Value (ICV) in the encrypted portion of the frame.

WEP defines two shared keys. They are:

- **Multicast/global key**: The multicast/global key is an encryption key that protects multicast and broadcast traffic from a wireless access point to all of its connected devices.
- **Unicast session key:** The unicast session key is an encryption key that protects unicast (UNI = one to one) traffic between a wireless client and a wireless access point, and subsequent multicast and any broadcast traffic that is sent by the wireless client to the wireless access point.

WEP currently uses the RC4 (created by Ronald Rivest of RSA fame in 1987, unfortunately the algorithm was anonymously posted in 1994 on the Web) symmetric stream cipher with both a 40-bit and 104-bit encryption key. 104-bit encryption keys are not exactly in the standards guide though and some providers might not support them.

 NOTE: Some providers, vendors, and implementers have been advising the use of a 128-bit key, but they just end up adding a 104-bit encryption key to the 24-bit initialization vector and call it a 128-bit key.

Understanding WEP Decryption

To produce the encrypted frame, the following process is used:

1. A 32-bit ICV is calculated. The Integrity Check Value provides data integrity for the MAC frame.
2. The ICV is appended to the end of the frame data.
3. A 24-bit initialization vector (IV) is appended to the WEP encryption key.
4. The combination of the IV and WEP encryption key is used as input to a pseudo-random number generator (PRNG). This is then used to generate a sequence that is the same size as the combination of the data plus the ICV.

The sequence that is created by running through the PRNG is also known as the key stream. At this point the IV is added to the front of the encrypted data to create a payload for the wireless MAC frame that is the result of IV + encrypted data + ICV.

To decrypt the wireless MAC payload, the following process is used:

1. The IV is separated from the front of the MAC payload.
2. The WEP encryption key is concatenated to the IV.
3. The concatenated result is used as the input of the same random generated sequence to create a bit sequence of the same size and combination of data and the ICV.
4. The random generated sequence is XORed (mathematically speaking, an exclusive OR statement) with the encrypted data + ICV to decrypt the data + ICV of the payload.
5. The ICV for the data portion of the payload is compared with the value included in the incoming frame. If the values match, the data is considered to be valid (also known as basic authentication and integrity checking).

NOTE: Like most uses of a secret, it can remain constant for a longer duration, while the IV changes periodically and can change as often as
every frame. The periodicity at which IV values are changed depends on the degree of privacy required by the encryption algorithm. Changing the IV after each frame is currently the best practice
to maintain the effectiveness of WEP.

WEP Concerns

As discussed earlier in this chapter, one of the biggest concerns about WEP is
that the determination and distribution of WEP keys are not defined. WEP keys
must be distributed using a secure channel outside the 802.11 protocols (think
about how you receive your credit card; in one envelope is the card, in another is
your PIN). In the virtual world, this is a text string that must be manually configured using a keyboard for both the wireless AP and wireless clients. As mentioned earlier, this is a method that cannot scale well for larger organizations,
and at the same time it presents a significant challenge to the security of the said
model because many people would know the key. Some sort of postinstallation
script or automatic cloning of systems might overcome this.

Additionally, there is no defined mechanism to change the WEP key, either
per authentication or periodically, for an authenticated connection. All wireless
APs and clients use the same manually configured WEP key for multiple sessions. With multiple wireless clients sending a large amount of data, an attacker
can remotely capture large amounts of WEP cipher text and use cryptanalysis
methods to determine the WEP key.

We perceive that the principle limitation of WEP is the lack of a key management system that allows for security in a large infrastructure. Some examples
of this type of network include corporate campuses, with several local buildings,
and public places such as malls, airports, and metro areas. This lack of an automated authentication and key determination service also affects operation in ad
hoc mode where users may wish to engage in peer-to-peer collaborative communication; for example, in areas such as conference rooms (refer to our comments
in Chapters 14 and 15 about using smart cards for added security).

Summary of 802.11 Security Issues

Here are the current seven problems and their solutions for the security issues
that exist with 802.11:

1. There is no per-frame authentication mechanism to identify the source.
   There are several problems with the RC4 cipher; first and foremost it

is a published algorithm, and second, there is no per-frame origin functionality.

2. There needs to be a way to either keep clients from being disassociated through attacks or the information that is passed during authentication and initial setup needs to be less known and more secure. Although there are no easy solutions to the disassociation attack, the best solution for rogue wireless APs is to support a mutual authentication protocol such as EAP-TLS. With EAP-TLS, the client ensures that the wireless AP is a trusted member of the secure infrastructure.

3. There is no per-user identification and authentication. There is a desire to adapt IEEE 802.1x port-based network access control. This allows wireless connections to use the EAP, which allows for user-level authentication before permitting frames to be forwarded.

4. There is no mechanism for central authentication, authorization, and accounting (AAA). By using RADIUS in conjunction with IEEE 802.1x, RADIUS servers provide AAA services for wireless connections.

5. The RC4 stream cipher is vulnerable to known plain-text attacks. As mentioned earlier, the proposed addition or replacement of RC4 with AES solves this problem. If you are unable to wait or implement this solution, however, you can use IPSec to protect your TCP/IP traffic.

6. Some implementations derive insecure or weak WEP keys, which results in poor security. While WEP keys are insecure and probably not very scalable, methods do exist that deal with these problems. We spoke about EAP-TLS as an authentication method, and we also briefly talked about public key cryptography.

7. There is currently no support for extended authentication methods such as tokens, one-time password (OTP) systems, biometrics, or smart cards. This can be solved using the EAP system. It was designed to be extensible for any type of authentication method.

IEEE 802.1x

This addition to the IEEE 802 family defines a port-based network access control system that can be used to provide authenticated network access for Ethernet networks. The port-based access control uses physical characteristics of a switched LAN to authenticate devices attached to a LAN port. Access to the port at the physical layer can be denied if the authentication process fails. As mentioned earlier, it was designed for Ethernet networks, but has been adapted for use with the wireless standard.

Windows XP Wireless Zero Configuration Service

New to Windows XP is the Wireless Zero Configuration Service (ZCS). This service can configure the wireless network adapter with an available wireless network. If there is more than one network in the same area, the user can configure a preferred network order and the computer trys each network in the defined order. It is also possible to eliminate the use of nonpreferred networks and lock out changes.

If an access point is not found, Windows XP can configure the network adapter to use ad hoc mode (remember infrastructure mode is preferred). It is possible for the user to configure the adapter to enable or disable the use of ad hoc mode.

These enhancements are integrated with the security features so that if for whatever reason authentication fails, Windows XP attempts to authenticate with the other attached wireless networks.

Windows XP attempts to perform a shared key authentication if the network has been preconfigured with a WEP shared key. In the event the shared key authentication fails, or the adapter is not configured properly, then the adapter reverts to an open system authentication.

Roaming Support

First introduced in Windows 2000, the media sense feature has been enhanced in Windows XP to allow for the detection of a move to a new wireless access point. This then forces reauthentication to ensure the right access. As mentioned above, this also forces a renewal of the DHCP IP address for the adapter. Within the same Extended Service Set the IP address probably will not change.

Through Windows Sockets extensions, network-aware applications are notified of changes in network connectivity and can update their behavior based on these changes. The autosensing and reconfiguration minimizes the need for mobile IP when a wireless node roams to another subnet.

Windows XP supports IEEE 802.1x authentication for all LAN-based network adapters, including Ethernet and wireless. IEEE 802.1x authentication using the EAP-TLS authentication type is enabled by default.

RADIUS Overview

Remote authentication has always been a concern for larger organizations. In the early days this was done via password, but it was hard to manage and very insecure. There is a lot of history here, but the most commonly deployed protocol is the Remote Authentication Dial-In User Service, which enables centralized authentication, authorization, and accounting for network access.

Originally developed for dial-up remote access, RADIUS is now supported by wireless access points, authenticating Ethernet switches, virtual private network (VPN) servers, Digital Subscriber Line (DSL) access servers, and other network access servers.

Components of a RADIUS Infrastructure

A RADIUS authentication, authorization, and accounting infrastructure consists of the following components:

- Access clients (your workstations)
- Access servers (RADIUS clients, this is the service you are authenticating to)
- RADIUS servers (the actual authentication device)
- User account databases
- RADIUS proxies

Access Clients

An access client is usually a workstation, laptop, or PDA device that requires some level of access to a larger network.

Access Servers (RADIUS Clients)

An access server is any device that provides some access that you want to use. This could be a server, a router, a switch, or anything that can provide some access to a larger network. An access server using a RADIUS infrastructure is also a RADIUS client, sending connection requests and accounting messages to a RADIUS server. Examples of access servers are

- A wireless access point
- A UNIX workstation or server
- A router or switch

It could also be a Windows server that runs Routing and Remote Access and provides some sort of traditional dial-up or virtual private network access to your organization's intranet, mail, or other services.

RADIUS Servers

A RADIUS server is a device that receives incoming authentication requests, and processes per-connection requests or account messages that are sent to it by RADIUS clients or proxies. In the case of connection requests, the RADIUS server processes the list of RADIUS attributes in the connection request. Based on a set of rules and the information in the user account database, the RADIUS server either authenticates and authorizes the connection and sends back an Access-Accept message or sends back an Access-Reject message.

The Access-Accept message can contain connection restrictions that are implemented by the access server for the duration of the connection.

There are hundreds of RADIUS servers out there, from Open Standards–based products to products from companies such as 3COM, Cisco, and of course, Microsoft. The Internet Authentication Service (IAS) component of any Windows server is an industry-standards compliant RADIUS server.

User Account Databases

The user account database is the list of user accounts and their properties that can be checked by a RADIUS server to verify authentication credentials and obtain user account properties containing authorization and connection parameter information.

For Active Directory, IAS provides authentication and authorization for user or computer accounts in the domain in which the IAS server is a member, two-way trusted domains, and trusted forests with domain controllers running a member of the Windows 2000 or Windows 2003 Server family.

If the user accounts for authentication reside in a different type of database, you can use a RADIUS proxy to forward the authentication request to a RADIUS server that does have access to the user account database. Different databases for Active Directory include untrusted forests, untrusted domains, or one-way trusted domains.

RADIUS Proxies

A RADIUS proxy is a device that forwards or routes the RADIUS connection requests and accounting messages from RADIUS clients to RADIUS servers. The RADIUS proxy uses information within the RADIUS message to route the RADIUS message to the appropriate RADIUS server.

A RADIUS proxy can be used as a forwarding point for RADIUS messages when the authentication, authorization, and accounting must occur at multiple RADIUS servers in different organizations.

RADIUS Protocol

RADIUS messages are sent as User Datagram Protocol (UDP) messages. UDP port 1812 is used for RADIUS authentication messages and UDP port 1813 is used for RADIUS accounting messages. Some access servers might use UDP port 1645 for RADIUS authentication messages and UDP port 1646 for

RADIUS accounting messages. Only one RADIUS message is included in the UDP payload of a RADIUS packet.

RFCs 2865 and 2866 define the following RADIUS message types:

- **Access-Request:** This is sent by the RADIUS client to request authentication or authorization for network access.
- **Access-Accept:** This is sent by the RADIUS server in response to the previous Access-Request message. This message tells the client that the connection attempt is authorized, authenticated, and accounted.
- **Access-Reject:** This is the opposite of the Access-Accept message and is also sent in response to the Access-Request message (it is sort of an either-or scenario). A RADIUS server sends this message if either the credentials are not authentic or the connection attempt is not authorized.
- **Access-Challenge:** This is sent by the RADIUS server in response to an Access-Request message. In this situation, the request requires an additional step, and a challenge must be answered.
- **Accounting-Request:** This is sent by a RADIUS client to specify accounting information for a connection that was accepted.
- **Accounting-Response:** This is sent by the RADIUS server in response to the Accounting-Request message. This message acknowledges the successful receipt and processing of the Accounting-Request message.

A RADIUS message consists of a header and any number of attributes. Each attribute specifies a piece of information about the connection attempt. There are attributes that specify the username, a password, and the type of service requested. You can also track and record an IP address or any number of other parameters.

For example, the list of attributes in the Access-Request message includes information about the user credentials and the parameters of the connection attempt. In contrast, the list of attributes in the Access-Accept message includes information about the type of connection that can be made, connection constraints, and any vendor-specific attributes (VSAs).

RADIUS attributes are described in RFCs 2865, 2866, 2867, 2868, 2869, and 3162. RFCs and Internet drafts for VSAs define additional RADIUS attributes.

For PPP-authentication protocols such as Password Authentication Protocol (PAP), CHAP, MS-CHAP, and MS-CHAP v2, the results of the authentication negotiation between the access server and the access client are forwarded to the RADIUS server for verification.

For EAP authentication, the negotiation occurs between the RADIUS server and the access client. The RADIUS server uses Access-Challenge messages to send EAP messages to the access client. The access server forwards EAP messages sent by the access client to the RADIUS server as Access-Request messages. For more information, see "Extensible Authentication Protocol over RADIUS" later in this chapter.

To provide security for RADIUS messages, the RADIUS client and the RADIUS server are configured with a common shared secret. The shared secret is used to authenticate RADIUS messages and to encrypt sensitive RADIUS attributes. The shared secret is commonly configured as a text string on both the RADIUS client and server.

RADIUS Authentication and Accounting

RADIUS messages are used in the accounting, authentication, and authorization of access to devices on your network. How this works is documented in this section.

Access servers, such as dial-up network access servers, VPN servers, and wireless access points, receive connection requests from access clients.

The access server, configured to use RADIUS as the authentication, authorization, and accounting protocol, creates an Access-Request message and sends it to the RADIUS server.

The RADIUS server evaluates the Access-Request message.

If required (for example, when the authentication protocol is EAP), the RADIUS server sends an Access-Challenge message to the access server. The access server or access client processes the challenge and sends a new Access-Request to the RADIUS server.

The user credentials and the authorization of the connection attempt are verified.

If the connection attempt is both authenticated and authorized, the RADIUS server sends an Access-Accept message to the access server.

If the connection attempt is either not authenticated or not authorized, the RADIUS server sends an Access-Reject message to the access server.

On receipt of the Access-Accept message, the access server completes the connection process with the access client and sends an Accounting-Request message to the RADIUS server.

After the Accounting-Request message is processed, the RADIUS server sends an Accounting-Response message.

MS-CHAP v2 Overview

Microsoft Challenge Handshake Access Protocol version 2 is a password-based challenge response mutual authentication protocol. It uses industry-accepted Message Digest 4 (MD4) and Data Encryption Standard (DES) algorithms to encrypt responses.

The authenticating server challenges the access client and the access client challenges the authenticating server. If either challenge is not correctly answered, the connection is rejected.

Although MS-CHAP v2 provides better protection than previous PPP-based challenge-response authentication protocols, it is still susceptible to an offline dictionary attack. A malicious user can capture a successful MS-CHAP v2 exchange and methodically guess passwords until the correct one is determined. Using the combination of PEAP with MS-CHAP v2, the MS-CHAP v2 exchange is protected with the strong security of the TLS channel.

PEAP with MS-CHAP v2 Operation

The Protected Extensible Authentication Protocol authentication process occurs in two parts. The first is the use of extensible authentication protocol and the PEAP type to create the encrypted Transport Layer Security channel.

The second part is the use of EAP and a different EAP type to authenticate network access. This section examines PEAP with MS-CHAP v2 operation, using as an example a wireless client that attempts to authenticate to a wireless AP that uses a RADIUS server for authentication and authorization.

The following steps are used to create the PEAP-TLS channel:

1. After creating the logical link, the wireless AP sends an EAP-Request/ Identity message to the wireless client.
2. The wireless client responds with an EAP-Response/Identity message that contains the identity (user or computer name) of the wireless client.
3. The EAP-Response/Identity message is sent by the wireless AP to the RADIUS server. From this point on, the logical communication occurs between the RADIUS server and the wireless client, using the wireless AP as a pass-through device.
4. The RADIUS server sends an EAP-Request/Start PEAP message to the wireless client.
5. The wireless client and the RADIUS server exchange a series of TLS messages through which the cipher suite for the TLS channel is negotiated and the RADIUS server sends a certificate chain to the wireless client for authentication.

6. At the end of the PEAP negotiation, the RADIUS server has authenticated itself to the wireless client. Both nodes have determined mutual encryption and signing keys (using public key cryptography, not passwords) for the TLS channel.

After the PEAP-TLS channel is created, the following steps are used to authenticate the wireless client credentials with MS-CHAP v2:

1. The RADIUS server sends an EAP-Request/Identity message.
2. The wireless client responds with an EAP-Response/Identity message that contains the identity (user or computer name) of the wireless client.
3. The RADIUS server sends an EAP-Request/EAP-MS-CHAP-V2 Challenge message that contains a challenge string.
4. The wireless client responds with an EAP-Response/EAP-MS-CHAP-V2 Response message that contains both the response to the RADIUS server challenge string and a challenge string for the RADIUS server.
5. The RADIUS server sends an EAP-Request/EAP-MS-CHAP-V2 Success message, which indicates that the wireless client response was correct and contains the response to the wireless client challenge string.
6. The wireless client responds with an EAP-Response/EAP-MS-CHAP-V2-Ack message, indicating that the RADIUS server response was correct.
7. The RADIUS server sends an EAP-Success message.

At the end of this mutual authentication exchange, the wireless client has provided proof of knowledge of the correct password (the response to the RADIUS server challenge string), and the RADIUS server has provided proof of knowledge of the correct password (the response to the wireless client challenge string). The entire exchange is encrypted through the TLS channel created in the first part of the PEAP authentication.

If PEAP-TLS is used, a TLS authentication process occurs in the same way as EAP-TLS, except that the EAP messages are encrypted using the TLS channel created in the first part of the PEAP authentication.

PEAP Fast Reconnect

You can also use PEAP to quickly resume a TLS session. If PEAP Part 2 is successful, the RADIUS server can cache the TLS session created during PEAP Part 1. Because the cache entry was created through a successful PEAP Part 2 authentication process, the session can be resumed without having to perform PEAP Part 1 or PEAP Part 2. In this case, an EAP-Success message is sent immediately for a reauthentication attempt. This is known as fast reconnect. Fast reconnect minimizes the connection delay in wireless environments when a wireless client roams from one wireless AP to another.

PEAP Support in Windows

PEAP-MS-CHAP v2 and PEAP-TLS are provided with Windows XP SP1, as part of enhanced EAP and IEEE 802.1x support. This allows Windows XP wireless clients to use PEAP with MS-CHAP v2 for secure wireless access—with passwords rather than certificates. The IAS networking component provided with Microsoft 802.1x Authentication Client for Windows 2000 also supports PEAP with MS-CHAP v2, allowing an IAS server to authenticate wireless clients running Windows XP SP1 or Microsoft 802.1x Authentication Client.

PEAP with MS-CHAP v2 requires certificates on the IAS servers but not on the wireless clients. IAS servers must have a certificate installed in their Local Computer certificate store. Instead of deploying a PKI (Public Key Infrastructure), you can purchase individual certificates from a third-party CA (Certificate Authority) to install on your IAS servers. To ensure that wireless clients can validate the IAS server certificate chain, the root CA certificate of the CA that issued the IAS server certificates must be installed on each wireless client.

Windows XP includes the root CA certificates of many third-party CAs. If you purchase your IAS server certificates from a third-party CA that corresponds to an included root CA certificate, no additional wireless client configuration is required. If you purchase your IAS server certificates from a third-party CA for which Windows XP does not include a corresponding root CA certificate, you must install the root CA certificate on each wireless client.

IAS and Remote Access Policies

This section describes the following topics:

- IAS overview
- IAS as a RADIUS server
- Remote access policies
- Remote access policy conditions and restrictions
- Dial-in properties of a user or computer account
- Authorizing access

IAS Overview

Internet Authentication Service in Windows 2000 and 2003 Server is the Microsoft implementation of a RADIUS server. IAS performs centralized connection authentication, authorization, and accounting for many types of network access, including wireless, authenticating switch, dial-up, and virtual private network remote access, and router-to-router connections. IAS supports RFCs 2865 and 2866, as well as additional RADIUS extension RFCs and Internet drafts.

IAS enables the use of a heterogeneous set of wireless, switch, remote access, or VPN equipment, and can be used with the Windows 2000 Routing and Remote Access service.

When an IAS server is a member of an Active Directory–based domain, IAS uses Active Directory as its user account database and is part of a single sign-on solution. The same set of credentials is used for network access control (authenticating and authorizing access to a network) and to log on to an Active Directory–based domain.

Different IAS configurations can be created for the following solutions:

- Wireless access
- Organization dial-up or VPN remote access
- Outsourced dial-up or wireless access
- Internet access
- Authenticated access to extranet resources for business partners
- IAS as a RADIUS server

IAS can be used as a RADIUS server to perform authentication, authorization, and accounting for RADIUS clients. A RADIUS client can be either an access server or a RADIUS proxy.

When IAS is used as a RADIUS server, it provides the following:

- A central authentication and authorization service for all access requests that are sent by RADIUS clients. IAS uses a Windows NT Server 4.0 domain, an Active Directory–based domain, or the local Security Accounts Manager (SAM) to authenticate user credentials for a connection attempt. IAS uses the dial-in properties of the user account and remote access policies to authorize a connection.
- A central accounting recording service for all accounting requests that are sent by RADIUS clients. Accounting requests are stored in a local log file for analysis.

Remote Access Policies

In Windows NT versions 3.5, 3.51, and 4.0, authorization was based on the "Grant dial-in permission to user" option in either User Manager or the Remote Access administration utility. For IAS in Windows 2000 or Windows 2003

Server, network access authorization is granted on the basis of user account dial-in properties and remote access policies.

Remote access policies are an ordered set of rules that define how connections are either authorized or rejected. For each rule, there are one or more conditions, a set of profile settings, and a remote access permission setting.

If a connection is authorized, the remote access policy profile specifies a set of connection restrictions. The dial-in properties of the user account also provide a set of restrictions. Where applicable, user account connection restrictions override the remote access policy profile connection restrictions.

Remote Access Policy Conditions and Restrictions

Remote access policies validate a number of connection settings before authorizing the connection, including the following:

- Group membership
- Type of connection
- Time of day

Advanced conditions include the following:

- Access server identity
- Access client phone number or MAC address
- Whether unauthenticated access is allowed

After the connection is authorized, remote access policies can also be used to specify connection restrictions, including the following:

- Idle time-out time
- Maximum session time
- Encryption strength
- Authentication method
- IP packet filters

Advanced restrictions include the following:

- IP address for PPP connections
- Static routes

Additionally, you can vary connection restrictions based on the following settings:

- Group membership
- Type of connection

- Time of day
- Authentication methods
- Identity of the access server
- Access client phone number
- MAC address
- Whether unauthenticated access is allowed

For example, you can have policies that specify different maximum session times for different types of connections or groups. Additionally, you can specify restricted access for business partners or unauthenticated connections.

Computer Authentication and User Authentication

To successfully authenticate a Windows XP computer with a wireless access point, you must have a computer certificate, a user certificate, or both installed. Wireless clients running Windows XP can use EAP-TLS to authenticate the computer or the user logged on to the computer.

To authenticate the computer, the computer running Windows XP submits a computer certificate (along with its chain) stored in the Local Computer certificate store during EAP-TLS authentication. The Local Computer certificate store is always available, regardless of who or when someone is logged on to the computer. More importantly, the Local Computer certificate store is available during the computer's startup process.

To authenticate the user logged on to the computer, the computer running Windows XP submits a user certificate stored in the Current User certificate store during EAP-TLS authentication. The user's certificate store is only available after the user has successfully logged on to the computer using the proper credentials. Each individual user that logs on to the computer has a separate user certificate store. The user certificate is not available during the startup process.

Without an installed computer certificate, a Windows XP wireless client computer that starts up within range of a wireless AP associates with it, but authentication fails. A user can log on to a computer that does not have wireless LAN network connectivity using cached credentials. Once successfully logged on, the user's certificate store becomes available, and the subsequent authentication with the wireless AP succeeds using the installed user certificate.

The following registry setting controls the computer and user authentication behavior of Windows XP:

Key: HKEY_LOCAL_MACHINE\Software\Microsoft\EAPOL\
Parameters\General\Global
Value type: REG_DWORD

Valid range: 0–2
Default value: 0
Present by default: No
Values:

0 - **Computer authentication mode:** If computer authentication is successful, no user authentication is attempted. If the user logon is successful before computer authentication, then user authentication is performed.

1 - **Computer authentication with reauthentication:** If computer authentication completes successfully, a subsequent user logon results in a re-authentication with the user certificate. The user logon has to complete in 60 seconds or the existing network connectivity is terminated. The user certificate is used for subsequent authentication or reauthentication. Computer authentication is not attempted again until the user logs off the computer.

2 - **Computer authentication only:** When a user logs on, it has no effect on the connection. 802.1x authentication is performed using the computer certificate only.

The exception to this behavior is that if you have a successful user logon and roam between wireless APs, then user authentication is performed.

For computers running Windows XP (prior to SP1), the default value of the AuthMode setting is 0. For computers running Windows XP SP1, the default value of the AuthMode setting is 1.

For changes to this setting to take effect, restart the Wireless Zero Configuration Service.

Obtaining a Certificate for IEEE 802.1x Authentication

The following methods can be used to obtain certificates for Windows XP wireless clients and IAS server computers:

- Autoenrollment
- Request a certificate via the Web
- Request a certificate using the Certificates snap-in
- Import a certificate using the Certificates snap-in

Autoenrollment

Certificates have grown in popularity and one of the additions that has seen a lot of action is the Simple Certificate Enrollment Process (SCEP). Microsoft has introduced something similar to this within IAS and we describe it in this section.

Autoenrollment is the automatic requesting and issuing of certificates based on Computer Configuration Group Policy. By configuring the Automatic Certificate Request Settings Group Policy setting (found under Computer Configuration\Windows Settings\Security Settings\Public Key Policies), you can have the computers that are members of the domain system container for which the settings are configured automatically request a certificate of specified types when Computer Group Policy settings are refreshed.

For wireless client access and for the IAS server, configure the Automatic Certificate Request Settings Group Policy setting to automatically request the "Computer" certificate. The "Computer" certificate (as named in the Certificate Template dialog box of the Automatic Certificate Request Setup Wizard), is stored in the Local Computer certificate store of the member computer and contains both the User Authentication and Server Authentication certificate purpose.

EAP-TLS in Windows requires that the certificate offered for validation by the authenticating client contain the Client Authentication certificate purpose and that the certificate offered for validation by the authenticating server contain the Server Authentication certificate purpose. If both of these conditions are not met, the authentication fails.

Because the autoenrolled "Computer" certificate contains both the Client Authentication and Server Authentication certificate purposes, it can be used by both a Windows XP wireless client to perform computer authentication and by the IAS server as the authenticating server.

Request a Certificate Via the Web

Requesting a certificate via the Web, also known as Web enrollment, is done with Internet Explorer. For the address, type `http://CA-Server/certsrv`, where CA-Server is the computer name of Windows Certificate Authority (either Windows 2000 or Windows 2003 Server). A Web-based wizard takes you through the steps of requesting a certificate.

Note that the location where the certificate is stored (whether it is the Current User store or the Local Computer store) is determined by the Use local machine store check box when performing an advanced certificate request. By default, this option is disabled, and certificates are stored in the Current User store. You must have local administrator privileges to store a certificate in the Local Computer store.

Request a Certificate Using the Certificates Snap-In

Another way to request a certificate is by using the Certificates snap-in. To request a certificate to store in the Current User store, open the **Certificates-Current User\Personal\Certificates** folder, right-click the **Certificates** folder, point to **All tasks**, then click **Request New Certificate**. A Certificate Request Wizard guides you through the steps of requesting a certificate. For wireless access, the certificate requested for the Current User store must have the Client Authentication certificate purpose.

To request a certificate to store in the Local Computer store, open the **Certificates (Local Computer)\Personal\Certificates** folder, right-click the **Certificates** folder, point to **All tasks**, then click **Request New Certificate**. A Certificate Request Wizard guides you through the steps of requesting a certificate.

For wireless access, the certificate requested for the Local Computer store must have the Client Authentication certificate purpose. For the certificate for the IAS server, the certificate requested for the Local Computer store must have the Server Authentication certificate purpose.

Import a Certificate Using the Certificates Snap-In

All of the preceding ways of requesting a certificate assume that network connectivity already exists, such as using the Ethernet port on a laptop. For those configurations where the only network connectivity is wireless, which cannot be obtained without certificates, you can also import a certificate file from a floppy disk, CD-ROM, or other recordable media using the Certificates snap-in.

To import a certificate to store in the Current User store, open the **Certificates-Current User\Personal\Certificates** folder, right-click the **Certificates** folder, point to **All tasks**, then click **Import**. A Certificate Import Wizard guides you through the steps of importing a certificate from a certificate file. For wireless access, the certificate imported into the Current User store must have the Client Authentication certificate purpose.

To import a certificate to store in the Local Computer store, open the **Certificates (Local Computer)\Personal\Certificates** folder, right-click the **Certificates** folder, point to **All tasks**, then click **Import**. A Certificate Import Wizard guides you through the steps of importing a certificate from a certificate file.

For wireless access, the certificate imported into the Local Computer store must have the Client Authentication certificate purpose. For the certificate for the IAS server, the certificate imported into the Local Computer store must have the Server Authentication certificate purpose.

Group Policy and IEEE 802.1x Authentication

Group Policy settings define the various components of the user's desktop environment that a system administrator needs to manage; for example, the programs that are available to users, the programs that appear on the user's desktop, and Start menu options. Group Policy settings you specify are contained in a Group Policy object, which is in turn associated with selected Active Directory container objects—sites, domains, or organizational units. Group Policy includes settings for User Configuration, which affect users, and Computer Configuration, which affect computers.

IEEE 802.1x and Computer Configuration Group Policy

Updates to Computer Configuration Group Policy occur when the computer starts, achieves network connectivity, and locates a domain controller. The computer attempts to download the latest Computer Configuration Group Policy based on the computer's membership in a domain system container.

If a Windows XP wireless client does not have a computer certificate installed, it cannot authenticate to a wireless AP to obtain wireless LAN network connectivity. Therefore, the attempt to locate a domain controller and download the latest Computer Configuration Group Policy fails. This event is recorded in the event log.

The solution to this problem is to install a computer certificate on the Windows XP wireless client so that wireless LAN network connectivity is present during the location of the domain controller and the download of the Computer Configuration Group Policy.

IEEE 802.1x and User Configuration Group Policy

Updates to User Configuration Group Policy occur when a user supplies correct credentials and logs on to the domain. If a computer certificate is not installed (and the computer has not authenticated itself against the wireless AP), the logon uses cached credentials. After the user certificate in the user's certificate store becomes available, the Windows XP wireless client attempts to authenticate against the wireless AP. Depending on how long the wireless authentication takes, the download of the User Configuration Group Policy might also fail. This event is recorded in the event log.

The solution to this problem is to install a computer certificate on the Windows XP wireless client. With an installed computer certificate, the Windows XP wireless client has wireless LAN network connectivity during the entire log-on process, and therefore should always be able to download the latest User Configuration Group Policy.

Chapter

10

Wireless Configuration

As we discussed in Chapter 9, IEEE 802.11 is roughly the wireless equivalent of Ethernet; it functions much the same and includes the same standards and technology. IEEE 802.11 also uses the media access control (MAC) and Logical Link Control (LLC) functionality in similar ways. While the similarities at 35,000 feet are easy to spot, when you get down to ground level neither is anything like the other.

In this chapter we briefly talk about a couple of issues and assume that you have read Chapter 9 in its entirety. We also hope that you have picked up books such as *Microsoft Windows XP Professional Resource Kit, Second Edition* and *Windows XP Professional Security* and perhaps a couple of books on wireless networking, and reviewed them.

Also in this chapter we discuss configuring your wireless network (from the perspective of your Windows XP Professional Workstation).

 NOTE: Because we are working with three distinct standards (802.11a, 802.11b and 802.11g) and because there are at least 30 different vendors who offer wireless accessories for Windows XP, we do not discuss any of those vendors' tools, how to perform specific hardware configurations for those vendors, or go into the drivers and support issues of making the hardware work.

Configuring Your Wireless Network

The first step is the installation and configuration of the hardware that you are going to use for your wireless network connection. It probably involves inserting your hardware. Now this insertion takes one of two major forms. With a desktop or workstation you remove some sort of cover and get into your workstation and insert a PCI card. If you are working with a laptop, then it is a simple matter of inserting a PCMCIA card. As new technologies evolve, wireless will propagate; new laptops featuring Intel mobile processors already come with wireless built in.

NOTE: For obvious reasons, inserting hardware into a desktop or workstation can be risky. You should, at a minimum, be sure you are not carrying any sort of static charge (use an antistatic wrist strap found at any computer store or consumer electronics outlet). You should also be aware that working on your computer while an active current is plugged into it is very unsafe; you should power down your workstation and unplug it from any live current before working on it. Finally, hardware is sensitive to damage. That means that if it does not fit where you are trying to put it, you are probably doing something wrong, so read the instructions.

There are essentially two main ways to go about this configuration, depending on whether or not you are using the "Windows XP" way or the classic way available in Windows 2000. We document both, but start with the new way available at this time only in Windows XP and Windows 2003 Server.

You begin by clicking on your **Start** menu, found in the lower left hand corner, which shows you the screen shown in Figure 10.1.

You then need to choose **Control Panel** as shown in Figure 10.1, which presents the image shown in Figure 10.2.

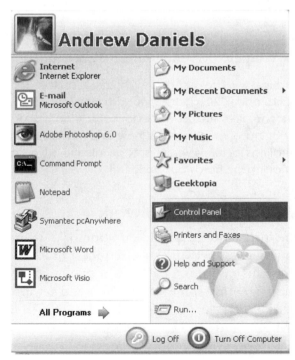

Figure 10.1 Click the Start menu and select Control Panel.

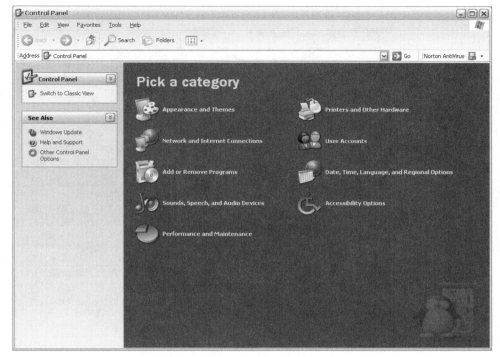

Figure 10.2   The Control Panel

In Figure 10.2, you see nine possible choices. We choose **Network and Internet Connections**, which presents the screen shown in Figure 10.3.

In Figure 10.3, we see five options in the area to the right. Under **Pick a task** we have three, none of them really help us do what we want to do today. We need to navigate to **or pick a Control Panel icon** and choose **Network Connections**, which opens up the dialog shown in Figure 10.4.

In Figure 10.4, we are again presented with a few options; most notably we see that **Wireless Network Connection** is listed instead of **Local Area Connection**. This is where we make all the local changes to our wireless connection that are covered in this chapter.

Now for us to really be able to see what is going on, we have zoomed in on Figure 10.4 and brought into focus the important area shown in Figure 10.5.

Now to continue with the configuration, we begin by double-clicking on **Wireless Network Connection**, which brings us to the dialog shown in Figure 10.6.

In Figure 10.6, we see that there are two listed under **Available wireless networks**. If you do not currently have any wireless networks in proximity to your workstation, then you will not see this information. In this case, both our

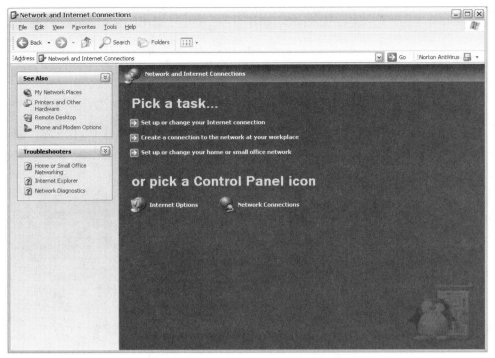

Figure 10.3 Network and Internet Connections

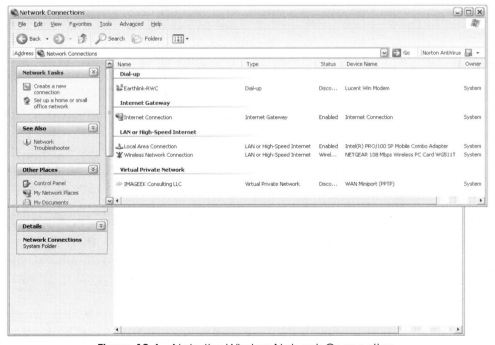

Figure 10.4 Note the Wireless Network Connection.

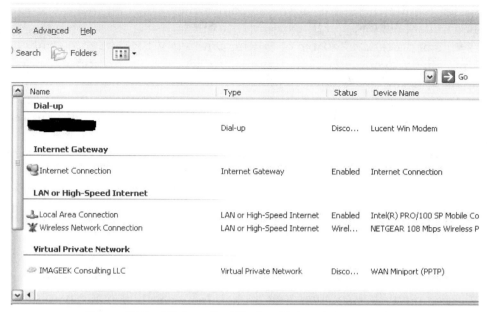

Figure 10.5   Click on the Wireless Network Connection.

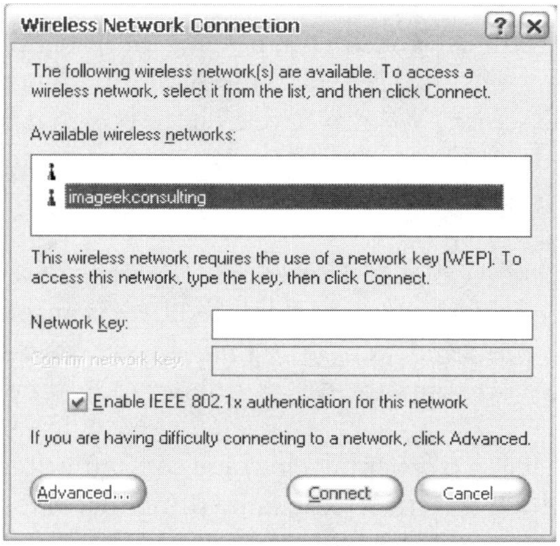

Figure 10.6   Available wireless connections

networks require the use of a Wired Equivalency Privacy (WEP) key as described in detail in Chapter 9.

While networks are capable of existing without WEP, doing so is only marginally easier to your users and significantly less secure. As also discussed in Chapter 9, doing so encourages intruders on your network. Because wireless can, and typically does, extend the boundaries of your physical office, intruders could be in the parking lot or they could be across the street and you would never know it.

Also found on this screen (Figure 10.6) is the use of IEEE 802.1x authentication that we discussed in Chapter 9. At this point, you do not need to do much else in terms of configuration unless you have more complicated options. We assume you do. Let's take a look at the **Advanced** area and examine more closely the properties of this connection.

Before we do, though, there is something interesting about Figure 10.6. Notice in the **Available Wireless Networks** that there are two entries listed; but only one has a name, the other just has the little access point in front of it. This is an access point that does *not* have an SSID. The SSID is one way to disguise networks. If you do not broadcast your SSID, and the person that tries to get on your network cannot determine it by sniffing or by social engineering, then they move on to an easier target. Just like WEP, this is a way to secure your network from intrusion.

As we move on to the advanced area, notice that in Figure 10.7 we see a little bit more information. First, we see the same **Available Networks** section in the upper portion of the screen. We also have a check box that indicates whether or not Microsoft Windows should be in charge of configuring your connection. For most users this is going to be fine. However, we are going to examine all the options.

You not only have **Available Networks**, but also now you have a section called **Preferred Networks**. Any network listed here is automatically configured to use. If you have preferred networks that do *not* have WEP, then you are asked to verify that you want to use an unencrypted network as a preferred network.

At the top you have two other tabs in these configuration properties that you can use: **General**, which is virtually the same thing that is found on any network connection, including hardwired connections, and **Advanced**. Issues such as the Internet Connection Firewall, discussed in Chapter 7, and Internet Connection Sharing, discussed in Chapter 8, are covered under the **Advanced** tab.

For your reference we show this screen in Figure 10.8.

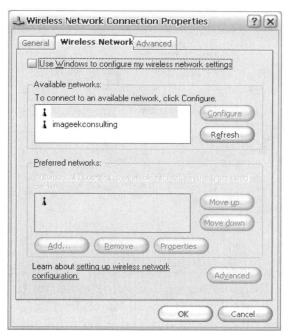

Figure 10.7   Wireless Network Connection Properties sheet

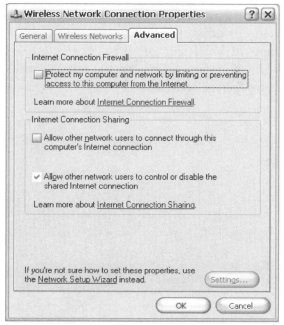

Figure 10.8   Sharing control of an Internet connection.

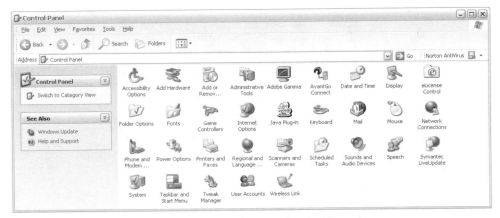

Figure 10.9 The classic Control Panel

There are two ways to display the Control Panel. Figure 10.9 shows the Classic View. Basically all the screens are going to be similar except that during this process we use the traditional Control Panel view.

Figure 10.9 shows the view of the "classic" control panel, which might not look this way if you have applied any of the settings discussed in Chapter 15, System Hardening. If you click on **Network Connections** on the far right of the second row, it takes you to the same place as shown in Figure 10.4.

Now that we have covered traditional networking technologies supported by Windows XP, we begin to examine other network services. The following chapters include coverage of a variety of alternative connectivity options such as modems, telephony, and remote access. Quality of Service as supported by Microsoft in Windows XP is also included.

Chapter

11

Windows XP Telephony

Windows XP joins a large number of products on the market offering IP telephony solutions. IP telephony provides the ability to combine voice, video, and data communications into a single network rather than maintaining separate networks for each of these communications types. These services utilize IP networks of all sizes: from small LANs to Campus Area Networks and Metropolitan Area Networks to Wide Area Networks and the Internet. Not only are the communications paths combined into a single network, but also the applications themselves have been converged. Voice and video services have been combined to provide IP conferencing, data and voice services join to create computer-based telephony solutions, and in one of the most familiar convergence applications, Voice over IP services (VoIP), where users of computers connected via IP-based networks can communicate via voice without the need for standard telephone equipment.

Windows XP does not offer the vast array of features found in IP telephony equipment manufactured by companies specializing in IP telephony. It does, however, offer many features that work well in small networks as well as use standards-compliant technology to make Windows XP telephony interoperable with other standards-compliant devices and equipment. In addition to these IP telephony services, Windows XP also makes it easy to use both standard dial-up Public Switched Telephone Networks (PSTN, also known as POTS—Plain Old Telephone System) and Integrated Services Digital Networks (ISDN). It is also possible to integrate Windows XP with computer-based client/server telephony solutions and Private Branch Exchange (PBX) systems. This chapter covers these topics, and includes operational details and step-by-step configuration information. We start with a look at the Telephone Application Programming Interface (TAPI), which enables much of the telephony functionality in Windows XP.

Telephony Application Programming Interface

TAPI is a set of application programming interfaces. APIs allow multiple Windows applications to share telephony devices with each other. Telephony Application Programming Interface was developed by Microsoft and Intel in the mid-1990s and is available in all versions of Windows. Windows XP uses TAPI version 3.1 and TAPI 2.1 to provide backward compatibility with older versions of Windows. TAPI 3.1 provides a wide range of telecommunications functionality to software applications including speech recognition, text-to-speech, tone detection, tone generation, file recording, and file playback.

TAPI provides the telephony infrastructure for all communications- and connection-related functions between a computer and a telephony network. This includes PSTN functions such as managing the interface between the computer and the phone line to ensure that calls are dialed or answered, conducted, and ended in the appropriate manner. TAPI also provides these same types of communications management services for ISDN, PBX, and IP telephony.

Service Providers

TAPI uses service providers to enable communication between TAPI-compliant applications and TAPI hardware. A TAPI service provider can be thought of as essentially a driver. There are two TAPI service providers in TAPI 3.1: Telephony and Media.

Telephony Service Providers

Telephony service providers (TSPs) handle the interaction between the telephone network and the modem or other hardware device that connects a computer to the telephone network. The TSP is responsible for the basic functions such as dialing or answering calls, caller ID, or callback. The specific functionality available in a TSP varies according to the vendor of the TSP. Features available in one particular vendor's TSP may not work with the feature set available in the TSP of the computer to which the TSP is connected.

Media Stream Providers

Media stream providers (MSPs) provide the link to the actual content a connection is sending. The MSP is the TAPI component that allows the telephony device to be accessed by various TAPI applications and allows direct control over the stream of data flowing over the connection.

IP Telephony

IP telephony is the integration of voice, video, and data into a single network and application or suite of applications. These applications replace conventional mechanisms for communication, such as telephones or television broadcasts, with computers and the appropriate communication device for that application. Data from the applications is decomposed into packets. The resulting data stream is sent over an IP connection to another computer, which reconstructs data packets, and the user is able to hear, see, speak, or otherwise collaborate in real time with the other user.

Windows XP supports three IP telephony methods:

- Session Initiation Protocol (SIP)
- H.323 protocol
- IP multicast conferencing

Session Initiation Protocol

SIP is an ASCII-based signaling protocol for setting up connections for various types of telephony applications, such as conferencing, that require real-time connections. Originally developed as a component of the Multicast Backbone (MBone) experiment, it deals strictly with locating and connecting two or more ends of a telephony call. It is used primarily for voice-related applications and handles only the signaling functions of these applications. Another application handles the actual streaming of data.

Because it is designed to be used within an existing TCP/IP network (MBone), SIP uses many existing IP protocols and is intended to be scalable and widely interoperable with many diverse users and environments. Session Initiation Protocol is described in detail in the Internet Engineering Task Force (IETF) Request For Comments (RFC) 2543.

SIP Architecture

SIP is made up of a number of components that can be divided into these two main groups:

- User Agents
- Network Servers

Each group is responsible for performing specific types of tasks.

User Agents

SIP User Agents are the endpoints of the connection. Think of these agents as the parties involved in a phone call. One party initiates the call to the other party. There are two types of User Agents: the User Agent Client (UAC) and the User Agent Server (UAS).

The UAC is also known as the Caller and is the endpoint that initiates a session request. The UAS is the endpoint, the party that is being called, and is also known as the Callee.

Users in a SIP network are identified by unique SIP addresses. A SIP address is similar to an e-mail address. It uses the format of `sip:username@sipdomain.com`.

Network Servers

There are three types of intermediary servers in the SIP network. They are the:

- Proxy Server
- Redirect Server
- Registration and Location Server

Each of these servers performs a different function, but they can be located on the same physical machine. These servers are responsible for locating the correct endpoint and passing a request to that endpoint. This is analogous to calling directory assistance on the telephone and having the operator connect the call for you. In addition to the connection-related services, the SIP network servers also perform the directory-building services.

The SIP proxy server receives a connection request and forwards it to the next-hop SIP server or UAS in the SIP network. It can also perform authentication, authorization, and accounting (AAA) related functions for billing purposes, as well as other networking functions like routing and security. If a UAS has moved, SIP redirect servers provide the address of the requested UAS back to the UAC, rather than forwarding the request directly. Finally, the registration and location server is used to catalog the directory of servers and location addresses.

How SIP Works

The first step is for users to register their SIP addresses with their configured registration server, as shown in Figure 11.1. The location information registered can be updated as a user moves to a different location.

When a UAC makes a call, the request is sent to a SIP server to be connected to the caller. The request includes the source and destination SIP addresses. The

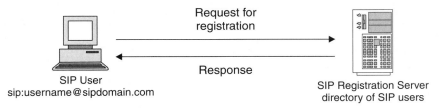

Figure 11.1   SIP user registration

SIP proxy will forward the request to the next proxy in the route to the final UAS, or directly to the UAS. If the SIP proxy forwards the packet to the next hop, but the UAS has moved, the SIP redirect server will provide any new Callee address information it may have. The SIP redirect server will refer this information directly back to either the Caller or the SIP proxy (whichever component had contacted the SIP redirector), so that the request can be modified to show the new address. This process is shown in Figure 11.2.

A growing number of commercial SIP service providers provide Voice over IP services for businesses and individual users that do not wish to set up their own SIP infrastructure. A list of service providers and additional information can be found at *www.sipcentre.com*.

H.323 Protocol

H.323 is a signaling and call control standard published by the International Telecommunications Union (ITU). It is an application layer protocol that provides voice, video, and data communications over IP networks. It offers the ability to manage multimedia communications over local area networks and the

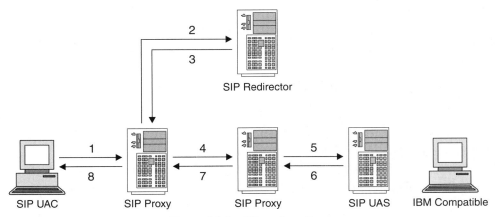

Figure 11.2   SIP call routing

interface between IP networks and other types of networks as well, including Signaling System 7 (SS7). H.323 does not, however, provide Quality of Service (QoS) features. At its most basic level, it can be thought of as a way to send and receive multimedia communications between an IP network and a telephone network, rather than simply converging the two separate networks into a single network.

Because H.323 is an industry standard, products from all H.323 standard-compliant vendors interoperate. It is part of the H.32x series of communications standards. The H.32x series also includes standards for ISDN and PSTN communications, as well as IP networks. H.323 can be used in computers and related hardware, teleconferencing equipment, and telephone handsets to provide a broad range of product and implementation choices.

One of the features that H.323 offers is the ability to throttle the amount of network bandwidth that is available for conferencing. Although it does not provide guaranteed service for real-time communications, its network management tools can handily prohibit conferencing from hogging a network. It also supports multicasting, which can further reduce the amount of bandwidth used for conferencing in a network.

There are four main components of an H.323 system:

- **Terminals:** The endpoints of an H.323 system. A computer running Windows XP can act as an H.323 terminal and can be configured to connect to specific gateways and gatekeepers. Voice handsets can also be terminals.

- **Gateways:** The gateway provides many functions, the most important of which in Windows XP is the setting up of connections between analog PSTN terminals.

- **Gatekeepers:** Provide address; both translation from LAN terminals and gateways to IP or IPX addresses, and bandwidth management.

- **Multipoint Control Units:** Supports conferences among three or more terminals by handling the negotiations among all terminals to determine common capabilities for audio and video processing.

The architecture of an H.323 network is shown in Figure 11.3. All of the various components working together in a single system and managed by a single gatekeeper are called an H.323 zone.

In addition to the listed components, an H.323 network may include a directory service. The directory service provides name resolution for an H.323

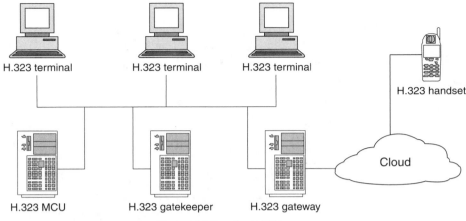

Figure 11.3   An H.323 zone

network by translating user or computer names into IP addresses. Microsoft has incorporated H.323 directory services support in the Active Directory and Microsoft Site server.

IP Multicast Conferencing

Windows XP includes a Multicast Conference Service provider. This TAPI 3.1 service provider provides support for IP multicasting of audio and video streams. Multicasting is one of the methods of performing point-to-multipoint delivery or delivering the same data to multiple destinations on a network.

Multicasting sends messages to a multicast address. A copy of the data is sent to that address, and only the computers that have been configured to listen for it are disturbed. This is different from unicasting, whereby a copy of the data is sent to each computer on the delivery list, which can utilize a great deal of bandwidth. It also differs from broadcasting, in which only one packet is sent, but all hosts on the network receive it.

Multicast messages are limited by boundaries, based on the TTL value of the IP header or the range of IP class-D addresses used, called the Multicast Scope. If the TTL has been exceeded, the packets are silently discarded. Multicasting uses datagrams, which means that neither delivery of packets nor the order in which they are received is guaranteed. It is strictly a best-effort delivery method. All routers between multicast server and clients support IP multicasting, as shown in Figure 11.4.

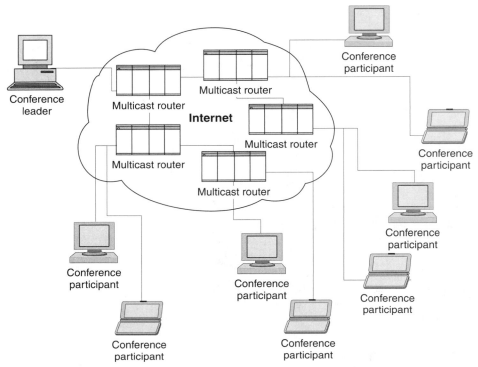

Figure 11.4 Participants in an IP Multicast conference

Telecommunications Services

Windows XP supports a number of widely available telecommunications connectivity services. These are discussed in this section. Broadband solutions such as DSL and cable access are not covered in this chapter because they are run into the home or office as Ethernet IP connections, rather than telephony-based connections.

Public Switched Telephone Network

PSTN or POTS, as it is also known, is exactly what it sounds like: analog dial-up service that supports both voice and data. Typically used for dial-up access to an ISP, it can also be used for directly dialing another computer. The equipment required for this type of connection is just a computer, a modem, and the phone line. PSTN sends data at speeds between 52K and 56K on copper cable. In the United States, however, this is limited to 53Kb/s by the Federal Communications Commission.

Bandwidth is not guaranteed on a PSTN connection. It varies constantly by place, by connection, and by provider. You have no doubt experienced this when dialing up an ISP and getting a connection with a different speed each time you connect. If your bandwidth needs are high, consider a digital line. Guaranteed bandwidth comes at a price, however—high-speed digital connections can be expensive. Low-priced digital solutions such as DSL are not available in all locations.

Multilink can be used to aggregate multiple dial-up lines to provide an alternative to higher-speed leased lines where cost or availability of these high-speed lines is an issue. Multilink is discussed later in this chapter. For smaller networks in areas where high-speed broadband access is not available, using multilink to combine multiple modems with multiple phone lines may provide enough bandwidth for the network's needs.

Integrated Services Digital Network

In addition to supporting dial-up service, Windows XP supports Integrated Services Digital Network service. ISDN is a higher-speed alternative to analog phone service via PSTN. ISDN is a digital dial-up service that was introduced in 1984 as a way to bring digital service to the last mile joining customer and telephone company infrastructure. It can send voice, video, and data at speeds from 64Kb/s to 128Kb/s over the existing copper telephone wiring.

ISDN is widely available, but it is not available everywhere. ISDN is not always called ISDN, either. Just like athletic shoe companies and CPU manufacturers, telephone companies like to use product brand names for marketing purposes. As a result, when you contact your local phone company to ask about ISDN, you may be told about a product that is ISDN with an alias, like Freedom Connect or FlexPlus.

ISDN uses channels to send data. These channels each offer a different group of functions. The two ISDN channels are:

- B-channels
- D-channels

B-Channels

The B-channel sends the payload of voice, video, or data. The throughput on a B-channel ranges from 56Kb/s to 65Kb/s, depending on the carrier. The average speed, however, is 64Kb/s. It is sometimes called the bearer channel.

D-Channels

The D-channel is used for the basic functions of establishing and ending calls, as well as other maintenance tasks. The size of the D-channel is dependent on the number of B-channels it supports.

Service Options

There are two main ISDN offerings that are based on B-channel groupings. They are Basic Rate Interface (BRI) and Primary Rate Interface (PRI). BRI, also called 2B+D, uses two B-channels with one 16Kb/s D-channel. The B-channel, as you now know, is responsible for the actual data transmission, while the tasks of maintaining the call are left up to the D-channel. This means that if both B-channels are the industry-average 64Kb/s type, this connection will be able to provide 128Kb/s of data throughput. It is possible to purchase a single B-channel plus a D-channel for support from some telephone companies; if this is the case you will be limited to only the throughput of the B-channel. BRI is better suited for smaller networks, such as small business offices or home offices.

PRI is a much larger service. It utilizes 23 B-channels and a single 64Kb/s D-channel. The total bandwidth made available by a PRI service is nearly equivalent to a DS-1 circuit. This level of service is suitable for larger networks with greater bandwidth needs, or smaller networks that send or receive large amounts of data.

Private Branch Exchange

A Private Branch Exchange (PBX) is a private telephone system that enables calls into a single phone number to be switched to another line internally, or permits the direct dial access of an internal line, dependent on the PBX system in use. The phone switching service is performed automatically with the assistance of the PBX equipment. PBX functions are typically handled in-house, and provide the ability to share a few phone lines among many users, as well as provide features like voice mail, call transferring, and call parking. Before automated PBX systems were available, switchboard operators handled the switching services of answering and forwarding calls. Operators would literally plug in a cable to answer an inbound call, and then connect or switch that call to another line by means of plugging the other end of the cable into the corresponding spot on the switchboard for the appropriate line.

A variety of vendors offer hardware and software PBX products, and Microsoft is no exception. With TAPI 3.1 in Windows XP, typical features that a PBX offers, such as caller ID and voice mail, can be controlled directly from the

Windows XP workstation. As an example, one PBX integration product for Windows XP brings up a dialog box on the monitor screen that displays the source number of the call that is ringing on the telephone handset. It also forwards voice mails directly into the user's e-mail inbox, permitting the user to collect messages either via their workstation or the telephone.

Configuring Telephony Parameters

From here we move into how to configure telephony and conferencing options within Windows XP. Windows XP installs and configures many plug-and-play devices automatically. However, some devices may not be detected properly, or additional configuration options beyond the default selections may be required to use certain features.

 NOTE: Remote access features are covered separately in Chapter 12.

Modem Installation

The first step is to physically install the modem. Power down the computer, pop in the hardware, and restart the computer. Windows XP should detect and install it automatically. If your modem has installed automatically, skip ahead to the next section, Modem Configuration, for assistance with advanced settings. However, if it is not detected or an incorrect modem type is detected, use these steps to complete the installation.

To install a modem:

1. Click **Start**, then **Settings**, then **Control Panel**.
2. From within **Control Panel** click **Phone and Modem Options**. The dialog box shown in Figure 11.5 appears.
3. Click the **Modems** tab of the **Phone and Modem Options** dialog box, then click the **Add** button. The **Add Hardware Wizard** appears as shown in Figure 11.6.
4. You can click **Next** to let Windows XP try to detect your modem, but if it did not detect your modem the first time around, it will not now, either. You can save a couple of minutes by putting a check mark in the check box for **Don't detect my modem; I will select it from a list** and then clicking **Next**.

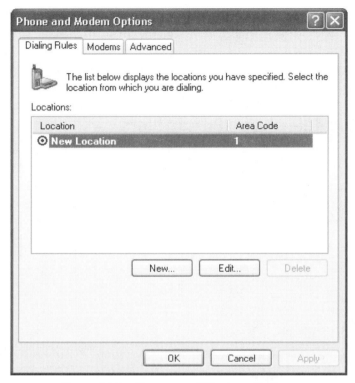

Figure 11.5 Phone and Modem Options

5. If your modem is listed in the next window shown in Figure 11.7, select it and skip to step 7. If it does not appear, or you want to use an alternate driver, click **Have Disk**.

6. If you click **Have Disk**, the dialog box shown in Figure 11.8 appears. **Browse** to the location of the files for your modem and click **OK**.

7. The correct modem should appear in the dialog box, as shown in Figure 11.9. Click **Next**.

8. Select the **COM port** your modem is attached to and click **Next**. Windows XP installs the modem on the port you indicate.

9. When the port assignment process is complete, click **Finish** to complete the modem installation.

 TIP: Always look for hardware that is on the Windows Hardware Compatibility List, found at *http://www.microsoft.com/whdc/hcl/default .mspx*. Regardless of the version of Windows you use, shopping from the HCL saves you the trouble of spending hours trying to get a non-Windows Logo device to work right and play well with the rest of the computer.

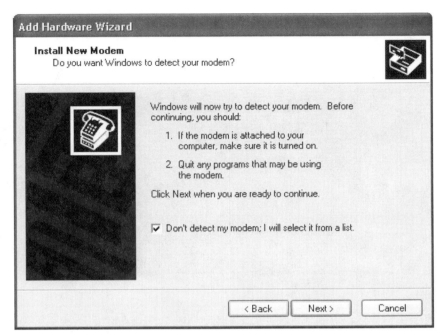

Figure 11.6 Add Hardware Wizard

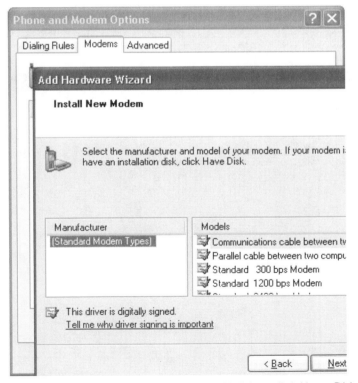

Figure 11.7 Select your modem from this list or click Have Disk.

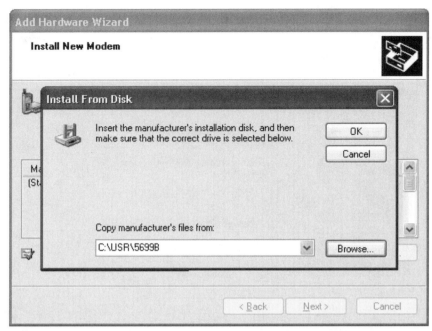

Figure 11.8 Browse to the location of the modem files.

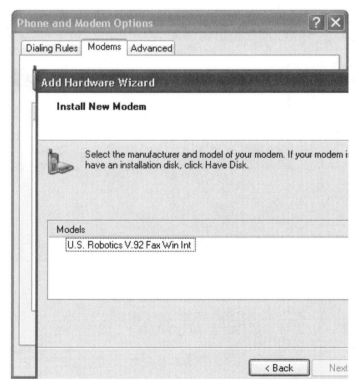

Figure 11.9 Ensure the correct modem appears.

Integrated Services Digital Network Configuration

The installation of an ISDN adapter is very similar to the installation process for modems or any other plug-and-play device: Shut down the computer and install the adapter. Boot up and install the driver as prompted by Windows XP. If it does not detect the adapter, or detects the incorrect adapter, run through the Add Hardware Wizard in the Control Panel. When the installation is finished you are prompted to configure the ISDN adapter for use with your phone service.

The information you need to provide is:

- **Switch type:** The vendor of the telephone company's switch to which your line will be connected.
- **SPID (Service Profile Identifier):** The ID or phone number for the ISDN line.
- **Telephone number:** The number or numbers of the ISDN line.

Your telephone company can provide you with all this information.

Modem Configuration

Once a modem is installed, a number of additional options must be configured before it can be used. Specifically, you need to set up dialing instructions to be used by the modem for how it needs to use prefixes, calling card numbers, and line access codes to make an outbound call. These options and their associated parameters are covered in this section.

Location

Location refers to the location from which a modem will be dialing and the dialing rules for that location. The dialing rules are the way a connection is to be dialed when the computer is in a given location. Multiple locations can be configured on a computer to correspond to different workplaces or different connections within a single workplace. For instance, you may use your laptop to dial up your ISP while in a hotel and again from a remote office.

Dialing rules are available to all modems installed and can be selected at the time you start a dial-up connection. You can configure as many locations as you need on a given computer.

To configure a location's general properties:

1. Open **Phone and Modem Options**.
2. From the **Dialing rules** tab click the **Add** button. If you are editing an existing location click the **Edit** button. For the sake of this discussion we

focus on adding a new location, but the instructions for editing an existing location are identical.

3. The **New Location** dialog box appears, as shown in Figure 11.10. Type the dialing information when prompted.

On the **General** tab you will be prompted for the following information:

- **Location name:** A user-friendly name describing the location, such as Indianapolis office or San Francisco client.
- **Country/region:** The country from which you are dialing.
- **Area code:** Enter an area code if applicable.
- **Dialing rules:** Enter specific details impacting the way a call must be dialed, including access numbers for outside lines and long distance or international calls if required.

Figure 11.10   Adding a new location

- **Disable call waiting:** Call waiting can unexpectedly disconnect or otherwise disrupt a dial-up session. If call waiting is available on the line you are dialing from, you should disable it.
- **Dial using tone or pulse:** Select as appropriate for the line you use to dial out on.

Area Code Rules

On the **Area Code Rules** tab you are prompted to input data related to how phone calls should be dialed in the geographic area you are calling from, rather than the specific line you are calling from. These rules are helpful when you regularly dial certain phone numbers in your area code that require the area code to be used, while other numbers in that area code do not require the area code. They can be particularly handy for users that make international calls with tricky prefix combinations.

An example is a large geographic area that is covered by a single area code. When you dial prefixes in your local area, no area code is required. However, calls to locations outside the local area require 1 + area code + the number.

Area code rules work on an exclusion basis. This means that any rule that you create applies to either all prefixes in that area code or only to those that you specify. For example, you may create a rule that includes only the 555 prefix in the 650 area code.

To make these modifications:

1. Click the **Area Code Rules** tab on the **New Location** dialog box, shown in Figure 11.11.
2. Click the **New** button and provide the required information, shown in Figure 11.12. This information is used only for this location. If you use the same area code rules for multiple locations, you have to recreate them for each location.

Calling Cards

Calling Card information may be entered and stored in encrypted form for each location, as shown in Figure 11.13. Click the **Calling Card** tab and either use an existing card type or enter a new one. Provide the account number and PIN for your card and then click **OK**.

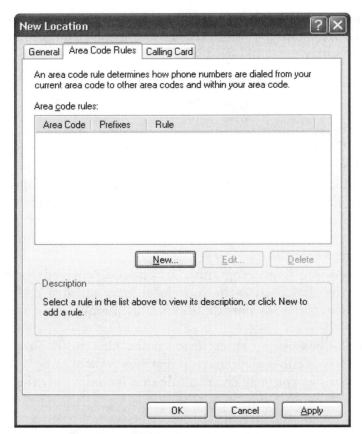

Figure 11.11 Area Code Rules

NOTE: Once the card number and PIN have been entered, they are not displayed again.

Modem Properties

It may become necessary to modify the default settings for your modem. If this is the case, refer to the following section for instructions.

To view the properties sheet for a modem:

1. In **Control Panel**, click **Phone and Modem Options**.
2. Select the **Modem** tab.

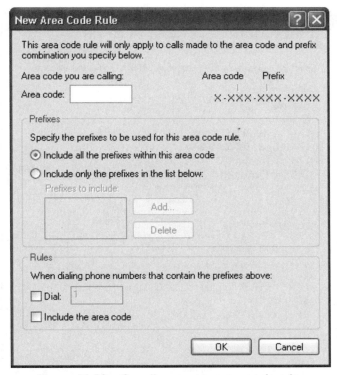

Figure 11.12 Creating a new area code rule.

3. Select the modem or device you want, and then click **Properties**. The properties sheet will appear as shown in Figure 11.14.
4. Adjust modem settings as desired on the available tabs. The most commonly used are on the Modem and Diagnostics tabs.

General Settings

General Settings cover the most frequently used settings for a modem. The following list describes the options available on the Modem tab:

- **Port:** The COM or LPT port to which a modem is attached.
- **Speaker volume:** Sets the volume for the telephone speaker. All line noise including dial tone, connection negotiation, and voices are transmitted through this speaker.
- **Maximum speed:** Sets the highest speed at which Windows XP Professional communicates with the modem. Slower computers should select a

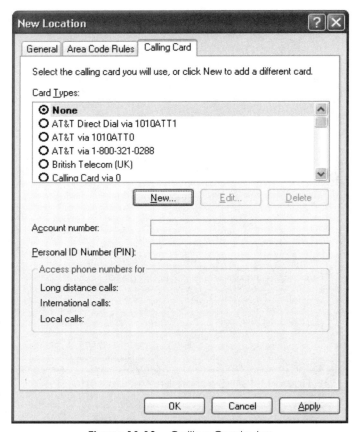

Figure 11.13   Calling Card rules

lower setting to prevent data loss, while a faster computer can safely select a higher speed.

- **Dial control:** Choose whether or not you wish to wait for a dial tone before dialing.

Diagnostic Settings

If you are experiencing difficulty with a modem dropping or failing to negotiate a connection, diagnostics can help you by providing a log file to review in conjunction with the modem documentation or other support materials from your modem hardware provider. The following options shown in Figure 11.15 are available for diagnostic purposes.

Figure 11.14   Modem Properties sheet

- **Modem information:** Provides vendor-specific hardware information.
- **Query modem:** Sends AT commands to the modem and displays the responses in the window provided.
- **Append to log:** Choose this option if you want to record all calls in modemlog.txt. If this option is not selected, the most recent call overwrites the last call.
- **View log:** Opens modemlog.txt in Notepad, as shown in Figure 11.16.

Creating a Dial-up Connection

Now that you have installed your hardware and configured the dialing rules to be used by the modem, it is time to create a dial-up connection. In this section we look at the options for configuring a Windows XP computer as a dial-up client. Dial-up connections are made in the Network Connections folder. A

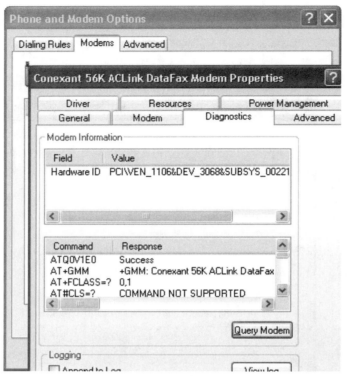

Figure 11.15 Diagnostic settings

```
ModemLog_Conexant 56K ACLink DataFax Modem - Notepad
File  Edit  Format  View  Help
05-22-2003 21:00:43.783 - File: C:\WINDOWS\System32\tapisrv.dll, Version 5.1.2600
05-22-2003 21:00:43.783 - File: C:\WINDOWS\System32\unimdm.tsp, Version 5.1.2600
05-22-2003 21:00:43.783 - File: C:\WINDOWS\System32\unimdmat.dll, Version 5.1.2600
05-22-2003 21:00:43.783 - File: C:\WINDOWS\System32\uniplat.dll, Version 5.1.2600
05-22-2003 21:00:43.783 - File: C:\WINDOWS\System32\drivers\modem.sys, Version 5.1.2600
05-22-2003 21:00:43.793 - File: C:\WINDOWS\System32\modemui.dll, Version 5.1.2600
05-22-2003 21:00:43.793 - File: C:\WINDOWS\System32\mdminst.dll, Version 5.1.2600
05-22-2003 21:00:43.793 - Modem type: Conexant 56K ACLink DataFax Modem
05-22-2003 21:00:43.793 - Modem inf path: oem9.inf
05-22-2003 21:00:43.793 - Modem inf section: ModemXP
05-22-2003 21:00:43.793 - Matching hardware ID: pci\ven_1106&dev_3068&subsys_0022103c
05-22-2003 21:00:44.063 - 115200,8,N,1, ctsfl=1, rtsctl=2
05-22-2003 21:00:44.063 - Initializing modem.
05-22-2003 21:00:44.073 - Send: AT<cr>
05-22-2003 21:00:44.083 - Recv: <cr><lf>OK<cr><lf>
05-22-2003 21:00:44.083 - Interpreted response: OK
05-22-2003 21:00:44.093 - Send: AT&FE0V1S0=0&C1&D2+MR=2;+DR=1;+ER=1;W2<cr>
05-22-2003 21:00:44.093 - Recv: <cr><lf>OK<cr><lf>
05-22-2003 21:00:44.093 - Interpreted response: OK
05-22-2003 21:00:44.103 - Send: ATS7=60M1+ES=3,0,2;+DS=3;+IFC=2,2;X4<cr>
05-22-2003 21:00:44.103 - Recv: <cr><lf>OK<cr><lf>
05-22-2003 21:00:44.103 - Interpreted response: OK
05-22-2003 21:00:44.103 - Waiting for a call.
05-22-2003 21:00:44.113 - Send: ATS0=0<cr>
05-22-2003 21:00:44.113 - Recv: <cr><lf>OK<cr><lf>
05-22-2003 21:00:44.113 - Interpreted response: OK
05-22-2003 21:00:44.113 - 115200,8,N,1, ctsfl=1, rtsctl=2
05-22-2003 21:00:44.113 - Initializing modem.
05-22-2003 21:00:44.123 - Send: AT<cr>
05-22-2003 21:00:44.123 - Recv: <cr><lf>OK<cr><lf>
05-22-2003 21:00:44.123 - Interpreted response: OK
05-22-2003 21:00:44.133 - Send: AT&FE0V1S0=0&C1&D2+MR=2;+DR=1;+ER=1;W2<cr>
05-22-2003 21:00:44.133 - Recv: <cr><lf>OK<cr><lf>
05-22-2003 21:00:44.133 - Interpreted response: OK
05-22-2003 21:00:44.143 - Send: ATS7=60M1+ES=3,0,2;+DS=3;+IFC=2,2;X4<cr>
05-22-2003 21:00:44.143 - Recv: <cr><lf>OK<cr><lf>
```

Figure 11.16 Modemlog.txt

Wizard is used to create the initial dial-up connection. However, you can modify it at any time.

To create the dial-up initial connection:

1. Click **Start**, **Settings**, **Control Panel**, and **Network Connections**.

2. Click **Create a new connection** in the upper left-hand corner of the **Network Connections** window as shown in Figure 11.17.

3. The **New Connection Wizard** starts. Click **Next** to continue.

4. Select **Connect to the network at my workplace** as shown in Figure 11.18, then click **Next**.

5. Select **Dial-up connection** from the next screen and click **Next**.

6. Provide a name for the connection as requested and click **Next**. This is a friendly name and can be descriptive of the connection or the party you are calling, as shown in Figure 11.19.

7. Enter the phone number you are calling. Be sure to take into account any dialing rules you have specified for the location you are using with this

Figure 11.17   Create a new connection

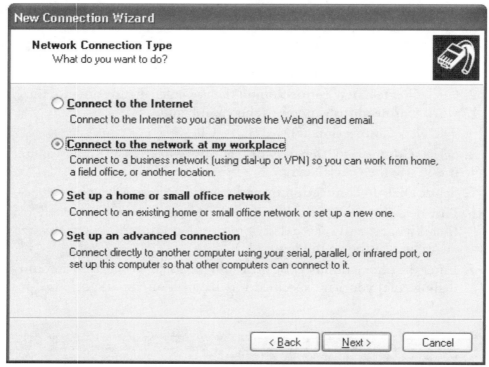

Figure 11.18 Select Connect to the network at my workplace to create a dial-up connection.

dial-up connection to ensure that the two settings do not conflict with each other. Click **Next** to continue.

8. If you wish to **add a shortcut to this connection to the desktop**, put a check in the box provided, as shown in Figure 11.20. If you do not want to create a shortcut, you will access this item from within Network Connections in Control Panel.

9. Click **Finish** to complete the Wizard. The **Connect to Dial-up Connection** dialog box will appear, as shown in Figure 11.21. You are now ready to use this connection or to continue performing advanced configuration.

Connection Properties

In this section we examine the properties of a dial-up connection. All options are not covered in this chapter, however; some of them are discussed in other chapters dealing with Remote Access, Internet Connection Sharing, and the Internet

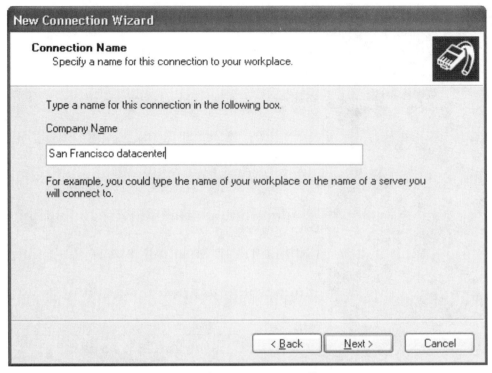

Figure 11.19 Specify a connection name.

Connection Firewall. Because there are so many configuration options available, you may find that you prefer to create a different connection for each way you connect to the same ISP or remote office. Just follow the Dial-up Connection directions above to create as many connections as you need to the same number. Then follow the next directions to customize each connection accordingly.

To access the properties sheet of a dial-up connection:

1. Open the **Network Connections** folder and right-click the desired dial-up connection.
2. Select **Properties** from the context menu.
3. The **Dial-up Connection Properties** sheet appears, as shown in Figure 11.22.

General Tab

The General tab is the place to modify basic things about the connection. Windows XP supports the use of multiple devices to make a single connection to one or more phone numbers. (You must have a separate phone line for each modem

Figure 11.20 Check the box to create a shortcut on the desktop.

to be used in this type of connection.) On the General tab you can specify the modem(s) or another device to be used to create the connection, and what phone number or numbers should be dialed by each modem, including alternate numbers for each modem.

You can also specify if dialing rules should or should not be used by this connection. Dialing rules are the location-specific rules for area code, calling cards, local line access, and so forth that you specified as part of the Phone and Modem properties in Control Panel. You can also access those locations from a connection's properties sheet for modification. If you enjoy the convenience of monitoring a connection's status from the taskbar, put a check in the box for **Show icon in taskbar when connected**.

Connection-specific configuration changes can be made for each modem you select by clicking the **Configure** button. The **Modem Configuration** dialog box appears, and is shown in Figure 11.23.

Figure 11.21   The completed dial-up connection

The Modem Configuration dialog box is where you set various options for configuration speeds and modem protocols. If you want to view the connection as it is created, you can opt for a terminal window to be opened before dialing. You can also include the path to a specific script that may be required by the remote server you are accessing.

Options Tab

The Options tab, shown in Figure 11.24, is where you can configure whether you want to view connection attempts while in progress, to be prompted to supply various user credentials, and to view domain log-on information. You can also specify if you want to be prompted for the phone number to be dialed, which allows the number to be verified and modified if needed before use. This can be helpful in situations where you always dial the same number for your office remote access server and only want to configure connection-specific settings once, regardless of from where you dial. Doing so can let you determine if

Figure 11.22 Dial-up connection Properties

you need to dial 9, 1 + area code, or any other special information that may vary from location to location. Your users may prefer this method as well—instead of trying to remember which connection or location they need to use from which location, or which connection has which characteristics.

Redial attempts are configured here as well. You may specify a specific number of attempts, the length of a pause to be placed between attempts, and how quickly the call should be dropped if the line is idle. This is a great feature if you are subject to per-minute long distance or usage charges. If you are distracted and leave the computer for an extended period, you do not incur huge charges for the time you are not actually using the service.

Selecting the option for redialing if a connection is dropped is ideal for situations where the telephone service is unreliable or some other problem causes your call to be unexpectedly interrupted. This is also helpful for virtual private networks, which are notorious for dropping connections.

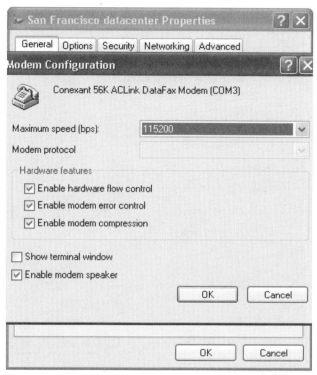

Figure 11.23 Configure connection-specific modem options

If you are using an X.25 connection, this is where you configure it. X.25 uses packet-switched networks to send data from point to point. It is more popular outside the United States. X.25 speeds are 56Kb/s in the United States and up to 64Kb/s in European countries. The parameters to configure X.25 are network name, X.121 address, and other information such as user data and facilities. Your X.25 provider can give you this information.

Security Tab

On this tab, shown in Figure 11.25, you configure authentication and data security appropriate for the connection you are editing. Secured, unsecured, or smart card authentication is configured here.

To configure more complex security options, click the **Advanced** button. These security protocols are discussed in Chapter 12. Only configure these settings if you know that your remote server supports them. Otherwise, your connection may fail.

Figure 11.24 Configuring dialing options.

The final option on the Security tab is to specify if you would like to run a terminal window during logon and if a specific log-on script should be run. This script option is different from the options available in the modem properties windows. In this instance, the script you are running deals with the actual authentication and authorization process of the connections, and the administrator of the remote computer to which you are connecting specifies its use. The modem scripts govern how the connection is to be set up on the local computer.

Networking Tab

The Networking tab is where specific settings for this connection are configured. The choice of dial-up server used to provide the protocols and services are all configured here, in the same way they are for a network interface. For additional information on protocol-specific configuration, refer to Chapter 5, TCP/IP Configuration and Chapter 6, Other LAN Protocols and Heterogeneous Networking.

Figure 11.25   Security settings for dial-up connections

Additional Parameters

Within the Network Connections folder you find additional advanced configuration parameters. These are located on the **Advanced** menu, as shown in Figure 11.26.

Operator Assisted Dialing

Occasionally you may require an operator's assistance when dialing a connection. Selecting this option permits that to happen. To do so:

1. Pick up the phone handset.
2. Click the menu option for **Operator Assisted Dialing**.
3. Open the dial-up connection to be used.
4. Dial the operator.
5. After the operator has connected the call, click **Dial** on the dial-up connection dialog box.

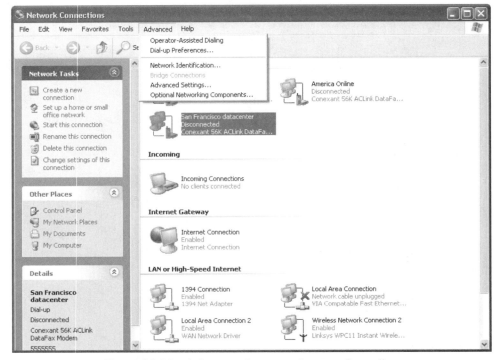

Figure 11.26   Advanced connection configuration

6. Once you hear the squeal of the modem making a connection attempt, you may hang up the handset.

Dial-up Preferences

The Dial-up Preferences menu option shown in Figure 11.27 provides a dialog box where configuration options for autodial and callback are made.

- **Autodial:** Permits you to have your computer automatically dial a connection for you when you try to reach resources not available locally. It is configured by location, so that this feature can be enabled or disabled easily depending on where you are.
- **Callback:** If the server you are dialing into is configured to call back any remote access attempts, you can set up how that is to be handled in this dialog box.

TIP: To save time and effort, you can create a copy of a dial-up connection simply by right-clicking the desired connection and selecting **Create copy** from the context menu. An exact copy of the selected connection is created.

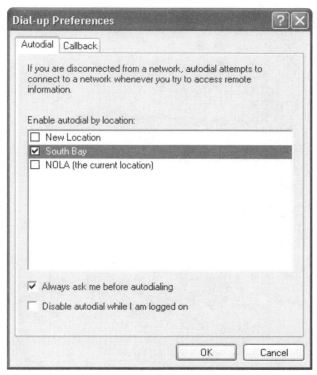

.**Figure 11.27**   Configuring autodial and callback.

IP Telephony Configuration

Earlier in this chapter, H.323 was discussed as an IP telephony protocol. Windows XP can be configured as an H.323 client, either when connected to the Internet or in a network where an H.323 gateway is used. In this section the configuration of a Windows XP client to participate in an H.323 network is reviewed.

To participate in an H.323 network, you need to specify a gateway, a proxy, or a gatekeeper, as shown in Figure 11.28. The item or items you choose to configure are dependent on the architecture of the H.323 network you wish to use.

To configure these settings, open the **Configure H.323 Service Provider** dialog box by performing the following steps:

1. In **Control Panel**, click **Phone and Modem Options**.
2. Click the **Advanced** tab, and then select **Microsoft H.323 Telephony Service Provider**.
3. Click the **Configure** button.

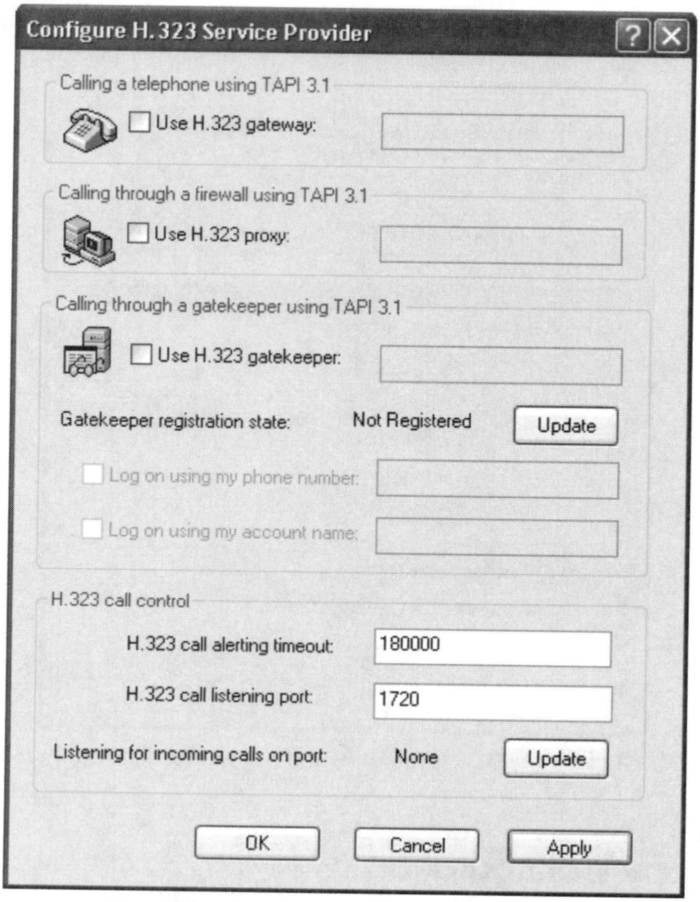

Figure 11.28   Configuring H.323 services.

4. If you plan to make a call to a telephone using TAPI, check the **Use H.323 gateway** and supply the name or IP address of the gateway in the text box.

5. To reach H.323 resources outside a firewall that supports H.323, such as Microsoft Internet Security and Acceleration Server, or to reach a proxy directly, put a check in the **Use H.323 proxy** check box. Provide the computer name or IP address of the interface proxy or firewall that faces this workstation.

6. If you plan to use a gatekeeper's services, put a check in the **Use H.323 gatekeeper** check box, and provide the information requested regarding the gatekeeper's configuration.

Conclusion

In this chapter you learned that Windows XP provides users the ability to combine voice, video, and data communications into a single network, rather than maintaining separate networks for each of these communications types. Windows XP alone does not provide all of the infrastructure needed to implement this type of communications convergence, but it does integrate seamlessly with Windows 2000 and other third-party provider IP telephony solutions.

Windows XP also continues Microsoft's long-standing support for both standard dial-up Public Switched Telephone Networks and Integrated Services Digital Networks, as well as integration with PBX systems. This chapter covered these dial-up functions from the perspective of the outbound connection. In the next chapter, we discuss how to configure and manage inbound connections on a Windows XP computer. We also present tools to automate the dial-up configuration of multiple remote users.

Chapter
12

Remote Access

A greater number of workers are telecommuting to work now than ever before. As a result it is important to be able to easily connect to remote networks and computers. Virtual Private Networks (VPNs), accessed via the Internet, and dial-up connections to a server are the most common ways for remote users to connect to another network. Large networks have the luxury of installing expensive and feature-rich network access solutions to provide for the needs of their remote users. Smaller networks, however, do not always have the budget for this and solve their remote access problems differently. Regardless of the size of the network, the end user's computer must be configured to correctly make the connection to the network.

Windows XP provides basic inbound and outbound connection services to your users. In Chapter 11, we discussed how to set up dial-up connections on Windows XP. In this chapter, we talk about how to set up Windows XP to accept inbound connections, the security options for outbound connections, and the benefits and basics of Connection Manager and the Connection Manager Administration Kit.

Before we move on to those topics, let's discuss the different types of remote access. The first is *host only access*, also called *point-to-point remote access connectivity*. This type allows the remote user to access resources only on the host that answers the remote access call. The second type is called *point-to-LAN remote access connectivity*. This type allows the remote user to access resources on the host that answers the call, as well as any other resources on the remote network just as if they are physically part of that LAN.

Another distinction to make is the difference between remote access and remote control. Remote access provides access to remote network resources. With the appropriate configurations and permissions in place, a remote access connection can be used to gain access to and subsequently manipulate a remote computer. However, remote access alone does not offer this ability. It is simply a method of access, and you need to have a remote access connection to be able to remotely control a computer. Remote control is software, such as pcAnywhere, or Windows XP Professional's Remote Desktop, that allows remote users to run applications or perform other actions on a remote computer just as if the user were physically present at that computer.

Inbound Connections

Windows XP supports up to three simultaneous inbound connections from dial-up, VPN, and direct-connect clients (but no more than one of each type at a time). In this section we review how to set up and configure dial-up and direct-connect inbound connections.

A bare-bones Point-to-Point Protocol (PPP) server is part of Windows XP TCP/IP, for the purpose of terminating inbound calls. Before getting into the creation of the actual connection, we look first at PPP.

PPP is responsible for the logical link between a client and server. Once the physical connection is set up between two computers, PPP steps in to negotiate how they will communicate and to encapsulate the LAN protocols to be sent over this link. It is an industry standard remote access protocol, which means any PPP-compliant client can talk to any PPP-compliant server, regardless of the operating system.

The connection negotiation process for PPP has four phases:

1. Link configuration
2. Authentication
3. Callback
4. Protocol configuration

This is a logical progression of steps. During link configuration, connection "business decisions" are made. These include how the client is to be authenticated, if compression is to be used, and so on. Once those decisions are made, the PPP server proceeds to use the authentication method previously agreed upon to verify the identity of the client. When authentication is successfully completed, and if the server has been configured to use callback, the call is terminated and the server calls the client back at the specified number. Finally, the network protocol to be used on the remote LAN is negotiated.

Callback is a useful option for a couple of reasons. First, it allows the user to limit long-distance charges related to dialing in to a remote server, by having the remote server terminate the call and recalling the client. Second, it provides an extra layer of security if you have configured the server to only call back specified numbers, preventing intruders using war-dialers from accessing your dial-up server.

Creating Dial-up Connections

Windows XP supports inbound dial-up connections to Public Switched Telephone Network (PSTN) modems, Integrated Services Digital Network (ISDN) adapters, and X.25. Assuming that you have installed and configured your hardware and arranged with a service provider for some type of dial-up service, you are ready to set up your Windows XP Professional computer for this type of remote access. Inbound connections are set up in the Network Connections folder. A wizard is used to create the initial connection. You can, however, modify it at any time.

To create the initial connection:

- Click **Start**, **Settings**, **Control Panel**, and **Network Connections**.
- Click **Create a new connection** in the upper left-hand corner of the **Network Connections** window as shown in Figure 12.1.
- The **New Connection Wizard** starts. Click **Next** to continue.
- Select **Set up an Advanced Connection**, then click **Next**.

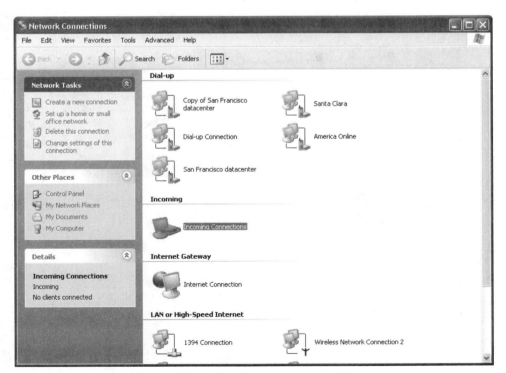

Figure 12.1   Create a new connection.

- Select **Accept Incoming Connections** from the next screen and click **Next**.
- Select the devices you wish to use for this connection, as shown in Figure 12.2, and click **Next**.
- Specify whether you do or do not wish to accept VPN connections over this link and then click **Next**.
- Put a check mark in the box for each of the users that you want to have access to this computer, as shown in Figure 12.3. Specific user configuration options are covered in the next section. Click **Next**.
- Select all the protocols, clients, and services that you wish to be available over this connection, as shown in Figure 12.4. Click **Next**.
- Click **Finish** to complete the Wizard. The newly created connection appears in Network Connections when it is completed.

Configuring Inbound Connection Properties

There are many other configuration options beyond what are presented in the Connection Wizard, and these are discussed in this section.

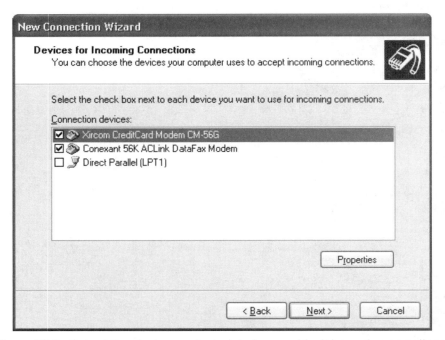

Figure 12.2   Select the device or devices to be used for inbound connections.

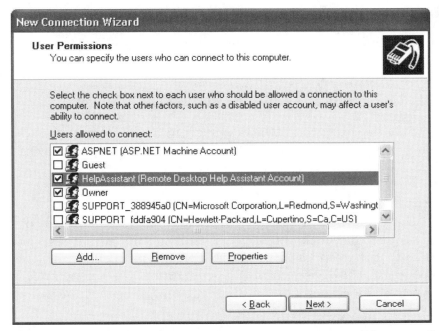

Figure 12.3   Specify users who are granted remote access over this connection.

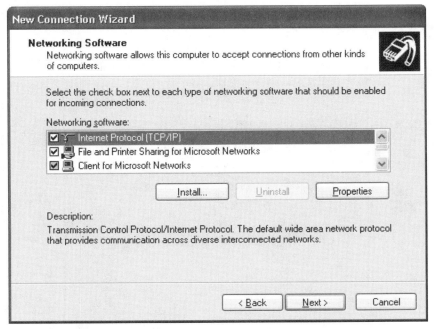

Figure 12.4   Enable protocols, clients, and services over this interface.

To access the properties sheet of a dial-up connection:

- Open the **Network Connections** folder and right-click the desired dial-up connection.
- Select **Properties** from the context menu.
- The **Connection Properties** sheet will appear

There are three tabs on the incoming connections property sheet: General, Users, and Networking. Each has a variety of parameters that may be configured.

General

The General tab, shown in Figure 12.5, is where you can modify the devices for a specific connection, including if you will allow VPN connections and if you would like an icon to appear in the task bar when connected.

If you replace the device used for this connection with a new device, the connection will no longer respond to inbound connections. The new device must

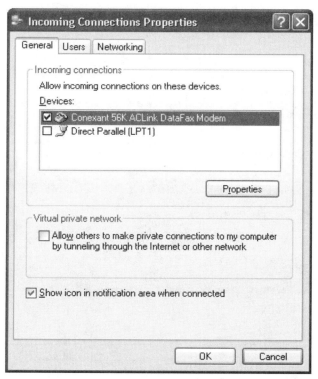

Figure 12.5 You can change the devices used for this connection at any time.

be associated with this connection, which can be done easily by putting a check mark in the box for the appropriate device. Alternatively, if you have installed a new device that you would like to add to a connection, or want to move the connection to a different device, you can do that here by checking the correct box. It is also possible to configure basic functions of the devices by clicking the **Properties** button. One particularly useful option is disconnecting an idle call, or a call that is not connecting properly. Since Windows XP only allows one inbound connection of a given type, tying up a line with a call that is not "productive" is an inefficient use of resources if you have multiple users who can be trying to reach the same connection.

Users

Each user that needs remote access must be explicitly granted that access, as shown in Figure 12.6.

If you want to add a user, click the **New** button. If you want to modify an existing user account, select that account and then click the **Properties** button. The user's property sheet will appear. Configure the username and password as

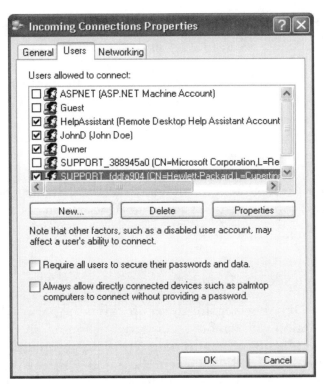

Figure 12.6   Grant remote access on a user-by-user basis.

desired for this remote user, and then click the **Callback** tab to set any callback options you may wish.

Callback is useful for a couple of reasons. It can provide a level of security beyond just verification of the username and password. If a fraudulent user calls in and guesses a username and password combination, there is still a chance to head him or her off if the computer is configured to call back to a preconfigured number. If your users travel frequently and you want to lower the number of long-distance calls the remote users can make, setting Callback to **Set by Caller** allows a sort of "follow me" remote connection.

There is a caveat with Callback. Because you can only associate one callback number with a client, clients with multilink capabilities who are required to use callback will be unable to take advantage of line aggregation, unless all the devices on the client use the same number as configured on the dial-in host.

Networking

The Networking tab is the home of the usual group of services, clients, and protocols. You can offer any combination of these items to your remote users by clicking the check box for each protocol, service, or client to be used by your remote access connections.

The most important options to configure in this area are how clients are assigned a network address and if they are to be granted point-to-point remote access or point-to-LAN access. To configure these options, select **Internet Protocol (TCP/IP)** on the **Networking** tab and click **Properties**. The **Incoming TCP/IP Properties** dialog box appears, as shown in Figure 12.7.

To limit users to resources on the computer providing remote access services, remove the check mark in the box for **Allow callers to access my local area network**. If incoming connections need to reach network resources, however, leave this checked.

Addressing is the next item to configure. When a remote client connects to this remote access computer, it is assigned an IP address in one of three ways:

- By a DHCP server
- From a pool of IP addresses
- The user provides the IP address

If you have a DHCP server already set up, this is the preferred option. When you select this option, the remote access service running on the Windows XP computer accepting inbound connections retrieves a group of IP addresses from the DHCP server. The first IP address in the group is assigned to the first client that connects, and the remaining IP addresses are assigned to clients in the order

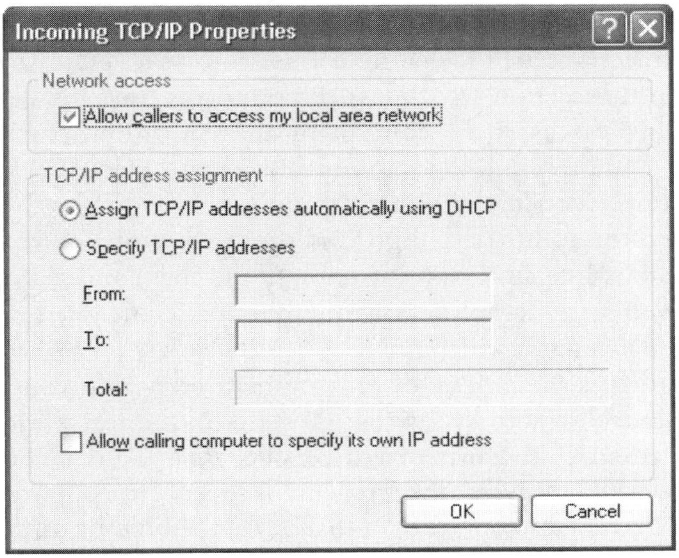

Figure 12.7 Configuring remote access client access and addressing.

that they connect. When clients disconnect, the IP addresses return to the pool of available addresses and are ready for the next inbound connection request.

In the event that a DHCP server is unavailable or is unreachable, Windows XP resorts to assigning APIPA (Automatic Private IP Addressing) addresses. If the remote network is also using APIPA-assigned addresses, this is not a problem. However, if the remote network uses a different range of IP addresses than the dial-up user is using, only the resources on the computer with the inbound connection are available. Additionally, as you may recall from Chapter 5, APIPA only assigns IP addresses and subnet masks. This means that communication off the local network subnet is not possible, even if the local network is also using APIPA.

If you choose to use a pool of IP addresses, ensure that a DHCP server on the remote network is not also handing out those IP addresses. Also, be sure that the range does not include IP addresses already in use on the remote network. This eliminates the hassle of troubleshooting intermittent duplicate IP address problems. The same thing holds true of IP addresses that are assigned by the user.

IPX/SPX protocol configuration is configured the same way. Just select the protocol, click **Properties**, and then provide the requested information regarding network access and address assignment.

Outbound Connections

Outbound connections are the dial-up connections that you learned to create in Chapter 11. In this section we discuss the protocols used for PPP authentication. Chapter 16 discusses the concept of authentication, particularly in the context of the Windows XP logon, in greater detail. However, for the sake of discussion, a brief overview of authentication is provided here. It is useful to understand how the authorization processes for each protocol work. This information can help with troubleshooting on both the client and server sides, as well as providing you with some ideas about how to secure your network when remote access services are available.

Authentication is the process of proving that the person you are communicating with is indeed who they say that they are. In the real world this involves providing credentials in the form of a driver's license or other identification card. In the virtual world, however, other credentials must be used. For security's sake, the credentials should also be strong—that is, they should be difficult to obtain, difficult to forge, and difficult to use by unauthorized parties.

Windows XP provides over a half-dozen PPP authentication protocols for dial-up clients. This enables the use of a wide range of PPP servers running just about any operating system, including down-level Windows versions, Linux, Solaris, and so on. When you are configuring a dial-up connection for a PPP server, select the most secure protocols and level of encryption allowed by the server to be called. Most remote access servers will negotiate for the highest level of mutually compatible authentication protocol, if multiple protocols have been selected on the client.

 NOTE: If there is a protocol or encryption mismatch between the client and PPP server (that is, there is no common authentication protocol or encryption setting between client and server), the connection will fail. Be sure to verify all settings with the administrator of the PPP server to which you are connecting.

To select these protocols:

- Open **Network Connections** from within **Control Panel**.
- Right-click the desired dial-up connection and select **Properties** from the context menu.
- When the **Properties** sheet appears, click on the **Security** tab.
- Click the **Advanced** radio button, and then click **Settings**.
- Select the desired level of **Data encryption**.
- Check the boxes for the appropriate protocols, as shown in Figure 12.8.

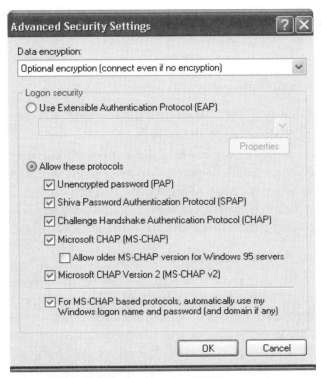

Figure 12.8   Configuring PPP protocols.

The protocols are arranged into two options—Extensible Application Protocol (EAP) and all other protocols. We now look at the function of each of the protocols in order, from weakest to strongest.

Password Authentication Protocol

Password Authentication Protocol (PAP) uses clear text passwords for authentication, and as a result, is the least secure PPP authentication protocol. The passwords are stored in clear text form on both client and server, and are transmitted from client to server in clear text. Anyone monitoring the connection between a client and server during the PAP authentication process can pull the passwords right off the line and use them for unauthorized access.

It is the last protocol negotiated for during the link connection phase and for this reason is often called the protocol of last resort. PAP does not permit users to change passwords during the authentication process. If a user's password has expired, the administrator must reset the password for the user. Additionally, PAP does not offer any protection from replay attacks. Neither the client nor the server offers any sort of session-specific information that will prevent an unauthorized user from impersonating the client or the server.

How It Works

The PAP authentication process is as follows:

- The client sends a PAP Authenticate-Request message containing the username and password to the server.
- The remote access server reviews the request. If the username and password match the credentials stored on the server, the server returns a PAP Authenticate-Ack message to the client and the connection continues. If there is not a match, the server returns a PAP Authenticate-Nack message to the client and the connection is terminated.

Shiva Password Authentication Protocol

Shiva Password Authentication Protocol (SPAP) offers two-way reversible encryption during the PPP authentication process. It is more secure than sending clear text passwords over an open communication line, but only just slightly. SPAP passwords are encrypted, but the same encrypted password is used every time a connection is attempted, leaving the server vulnerable to a replay attack. It does not provide mutual authentication either, so the client is left vulnerable to a server impersonating the authentic server. It is recommended that SPAP be used only where absolutely necessary, such as when connecting to a Shiva remote access server that does not support any authentication protocol with a stronger level of security.

How It Works

The SPAP authentication process is as follows:

- The client sends a SPAP Authenticate-Request message containing the username and encrypted password to the server.
- The remote access server decrypts the password and reviews the request. If the username and password match the credentials stored on the server, the server returns a SPAP Authenticate-Ack message to the client and the connection continues. If there is not a match, the server returns a SPAP Authenticate-Nack message to the client and the connection is terminated.

Challenge Handshake Authentication Protocol

Challenge Handshake Authentication Protocol (CHAP), is the first of the three challenge-response protocols available in Windows. It is an industry standard

PPP authentication protocol that is based on RFC 1994 and is widely used by many remote access vendors. CHAP uses an MD5 hash to encrypt passwords. This eliminates the sending of clear text passwords over the wire as happens with other lower-security authentication protocols like PAP. It uses a shared secret, a password known by both the client and server, to authenticate users. Although the password is encrypted for transit, the password must be available in a clear text format on the client and server.

CHAP does have a few disadvantages. The user cannot change CHAP passwords during the authentication process. If a user has an expired password, administrative intervention is required to change the password so that the user can log on. CHAP is also vulnerable to dictionary attacks. For this reason it is sensible to implement a password policy requiring strong passwords (more than eight characters, mixed-case, contains both letters and numbers, and so on). Finally, CHAP only provides client authentication, meaning that while the server requires the client to be authenticated, nothing is protecting the client from a fraudulent remote access server masquerading as a legitimate network resource. Microsoft recommends using MS-CHAP or MS-CHAP v2 instead.

How It Works

CHAP authentication takes place as follows:

- The remote access server sends the client a CHAP-Challenge message. This message contains a unique session ID and challenge string.
- The client sends a CHAP-Response message containing the encrypted session ID, the encrypted challenge string, and encrypted password, as well as the client's username in clear text.
- The server hashes the challenge string, session ID, and client password and compares them to the encrypted data sent from the client. If they match, a CHAP-Success message is sent; if they fail, a CHAP-Failure message is sent.

MS-CHAP

MS-CHAP, also known as MS-CHAP v1, began as an initiative within Microsoft to fix some of the vulnerabilities with CHAP. The result was so successful, relative to the security of CHAP, that many remote access server vendors began incorporating support for MS-CHAP in their products as well.

The primary advantage of MS-CHAP over CHAP is that plain text client passwords are not required on the server that performs remote access authentication. Instead, MS-CHAP stores a reversibly encrypted MD4 hash of the password on both the client and server.

How It Works

MS-CHAP functionality is as follows:

- The server sends a CHAP-Challenge message to the client. It contains the session ID and a randomly generated, connection attempt–specific challenge string.
- The client sends a CHAP-Response message containing the username in clear text, and the challenge string, session ID, and client password as an MD4 hash.
- The server reviews the response. If the client's hash matches the server's hash, a CHAP-Success message is sent and the connection is continued. If there is no match, however, the server sends a CHAP-Failure message and terminates the connection.

MS-CHAP v2

MS-CHAP v2 is the last of three challenge-response protocols supported by Windows XP. It is also the strongest. It was developed as a response to the number of vulnerabilities and drawbacks to CHAP and MS-CHAP v1. A unique challenge string is generated for each connection. This string, plus the client's password, are used as the basis for the crypto key used for the challenge response. The result is a session-specific key. Furthermore, in addition to the initial data encryption key, different keys are used for sent data and received data. Mutual authentication of client and server is provided by MS-CHAP v2, so clients are protected from fraudulent servers impersonating the real remote access server. Changing a password during the log-on phase is supported as well, eliminating some level of administrative burden in that regard.

How It Works

MS-CHAP v2 authentication runs like this:

- The server sends a CHAP-Challenge containing a session ID and randomly generated challenge string to the client.
- The client sends a one-way MD4 hash of the server's challenge string as CHAP-Response to the server. The client also sends its own CHAP-Challenge message that contains the username and its own randomly generated challenge string.
- The server reviews the client's response. If the server's local hash matches the server's hash received in the response, a CHAP-Success message is sent to the client. If no match is found, a CHAP-Failure message is sent.

- If the match is a success, the server will also send a CHAP-Response message to the client in response to the client's CHAP-Challenge message. This message is a hash based on both the client's and server's challenge strings, as well as the encrypted client response and password.
- The client examines the response from the server. If there is a match, the connection will be completed. If not, the client will terminate the connection.

Extensible Authentication Protocol

EAP is a flexible authentication protocol, just as the name implies. It allows a variety of different authentication mechanisms to be used for a custom fit. MD5-CHAP and smart cards are the two mechanisms provided in Windows XP by default. Because EAP is an extensible platform, new plug-in authentication modules can be created to solve future security problems.

Recall that during PPP connection establishment, the authentication protocol is one of the items negotiated and settled upon. When EAP is used, only EAP is specified at that time. The exact authentication mechanism to be used is negotiated as part of the EAP negotiation process. This process is a series of messages requesting authentication and the corresponding information sent in response. The content of these messages is not subject to harsh restrictions, thus supporting the ability to provide new authentication mechanisms. Developers can easily create new mechanisms, and these mechanisms can be layered.

Layering allows the use of multiple credentials to be provided in an authentication session, and authentication is granted based on properly supplying each of the requested credentials. An example of such an application is token cards, which require a username, a password, and a token to be provided.

MD5-CHAP

MD5-CHAP or MD5-Challenge is EAP that uses Challenge Handshake Protocol for authentication during the connection negotiation phase, rather than later at the link negotiation phase.

How It Works
The steps of MD5-CHAP authentication are as follows:

- The server sends an EAP-Request message to the remote client. This request asks for the identity of the client.
- The client sends an EAP-Response message back to the server. This message contains the client's identity.

- The server sends another EAP-Request message containing the MD5 challenge string to the client.
- The client then replies with an EAP-Response message. This message contains the MD5 hash of its username and password.
- The server sends a success message to the client if the previous response was correct.

EAP-TLS

Transport Layer Security (TLS) is a supported EAP plug-in with Windows XP. If you intend to use smart cards for authentication, you are required to use EAP-TLS. TLS is modeled on Secure Sockets Layer (SSL) and provides these features:

- Client-only and mutual authentication
- Private keys for message encryption
- Secure key exchange
- Negotiation of encryption algorithm
- Message integrity and authentication

Connection Services

There are three relatively undocumented tools available to assist administrators supporting multiple users using dial-up and VPNs. Rather than having users configure their own connection settings manually, or you performing this task for them, you can use Connection Manager to distribute this information to your users in the same way that MSN does. Many other commercial ISPs also use Connection Manager to distribute connection settings to their customers in a self-contained installation package. You can do the same thing, without any advanced software engineering skills.

The client-side tool is Connection Manager, which is a preconfigurable client dialer included in Windows XP Professional that contains all parameters and settings required to connect a computer to a particular remote service. Connection Manager provides these preconfigured connections for remote users to access an ISP, a VPN, a private remote access server, or some other remote resource. Its features and benefits are much more advanced than the basic dial-up networking options discussed up to this point.

The second tool is the Connection Manager Administration Kit, which allows the administrator to preconfigure and distribute remote connection information for these remote services to users easily. You can use Connection Manager, a component of the Microsoft Windows 2000 Server operating system, to provide customized remote access to your network through dial-up or virtual private network connections.

The third tool is Connection Point Services (CPS), components of which are found in both Windows XP and Windows 2000. CPS allows you to configure and distribute a phone book with the Connection Manager packages, so that users can find the most convenient dial-up access number and subsequently automatically download updated connection numbers. Phone books store the access numbers for remote servers. If these numbers change frequently, perhaps because you are adding more remote access points to your network, users can automatically download updated phone books. CPS requires Internet Information Server running both WWW and FTP services for phone book distribution. CPS is made up of two components:

- **Phone Book Service (PBS):** The distribution point for new phone books; requires IIS 5.0. Connection Manager queries for and downloads new phone books from the PBS server without user intervention. This eliminates phone calls and e-mails from users requesting new numbers or access numbers for new locations. The connection to the PBS server is via the WWW service.
- **Phone Book Administrator (PBA):** PBA is used to create phone books. Phone books are collections of the remote access points available for use by your users. The phone books (available on both the Windows XP Professional and Windows 2000 CDs), can be created on either a workstation or a server and are uploaded via FTP to the PBS server.

How these components are related to each other is diagrammed in Figure 12.9.

Connection Manager 1.2 is used on Windows 2000, while Connection Manager 1.3 ships with Windows XP Professional components. You cannot create a Connection Manager service profile on a Windows XP computer. It can only be performed on a Windows 2000 server. However, the service profile package interfaces with the components on the Windows XP computer to update the feature set to version 1.3 functionality.

A number of improvements and enhancements have been made in version 1.3, including

- Multiple simultaneous instances of Connection Manager service profiles
- Connection logging
- Selection of VPN servers
- Support for terminal windows
- Better support for ISDN

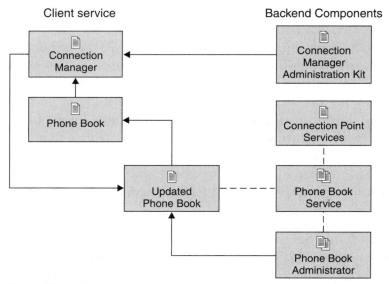

Figure 12.9 Relationship of the connection services components

- Automatic route addition
- Split tunneling
- Connection settings favorites list
- Callback

We now discuss the configuration of the components needed for a fully functional connection service. Even if your service is not large enough to justify the implementation of a PBS server, this is good information to have; preconfiguring, and subsequently securing from fiddling fingers even remote access clients, can save you a great deal of administrative work in the long run.

Configuration of Connection Point Services

We discuss Connection Point Services first. The rationale behind this is that the selection of a phone book and a phone book server is part of the service profile creation phase of the Connection Manager Wizard, which means it needs to be configured first (or the service profile has to match the CPS component configurations exactly).

Connection Point Services are extremely helpful in networks that experience frequent changes in remote access numbers. For example, you have outsourced your remote access to an ISP, but provide a VPN connection into your own network over this ISP link. The ISP regularly adds new access numbers. Historically, distribution of this information has been difficult—e-mails and phone calls to the help desk, or visits to Web sites to get this information were all common. With CPS, however, rather than requiring the users to create and update their own phone books or dialing instructions, you can create and publish a new phone book any time the ISP gives you their new info, and all users will download this phone book the next time they connect.

System Requirements

CPS is a Windows 2000 Server component, and as such it requires a Windows 2000 server running IIS 5.0. Both the WWW and the FTP services must also be running. The FTP service only needs to be running when you upload a new phone book; so if you prefer to disable FTP for security reasons on a general basis, CPS will not interfere with this. It only needs to be enabled for the amount of time it takes for the phone book to upload—a few minutes at the most. You cannot, however, uninstall FTP. Doing so uninstalls CPS.

Installation

Connection Point Services are installed via the Add/Remove Windows Components Wizard. The following instructions guide you through the process.

- On a Windows 2000 server or Windows 2000 Advanced server, click **Start**, **Settings**, and then **Control Panel**. The **Control Panel** appears.
- Double-click the **Add/Remove Programs** icon and then click **Add/Remove Windows Components**. The **Windows Components** screen appears.
- Select **Management and Monitoring Tools** and then click the **Details** button. The **subcomponents** Dialog Box appears as shown in Figure 12.10.
- Click to put a check in the **Connection Manager Components** check box. Click **Next**.
- Click **Finish**. The Wizard completes.

Now that the server component has been installed, you install the Phone Book Administrator. This is found on both the Windows XP and Windows 2000 Server CDs.

- Pop in the appropriate CD and navigate to the **\VALUADD\MSFT\MGMT\PBA** directory, as shown in Figure 12.11.
- Double-click **PBAINST.exe**. The **Phone Book Administrator Installer** is launched.
- Click **Yes** when prompted to install the Phone Book Administrator.
- Click **OK** when the process is completed.

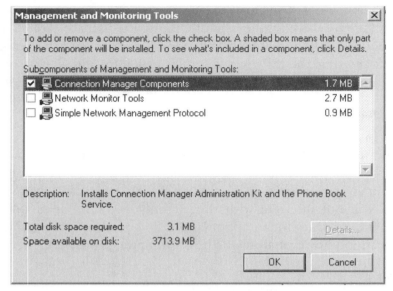

Figure 12.10 The Windows 2000 Server Add/Remove Windows components

Security

With the CPS installed, it is a good idea to do some work to secure the server. This section covers suggested permissions and accounts for the phone book administrators.

First, we talk about folder security. You should change the permissions on the following folders to allow administrator-only access:

- C:\Program Files\Phone Book Service
- C:\Program Files\PBA

To do so:

- Right-click the **folder** icon on the Windows 2000 server; then select **Properties** from the context menu. Click on the **Security** tab and add the appropriate users or groups.
- Remove the check mark for **allow inheritable permissions from parent to propagate to this object**.
- Repeat for the other folder.

Next you need to allow **temporarily is best** write access to the FTP virtual directory used for Phone Book Services. It is advisable to perform this just before uploading a phone book and remove this access immediately after the

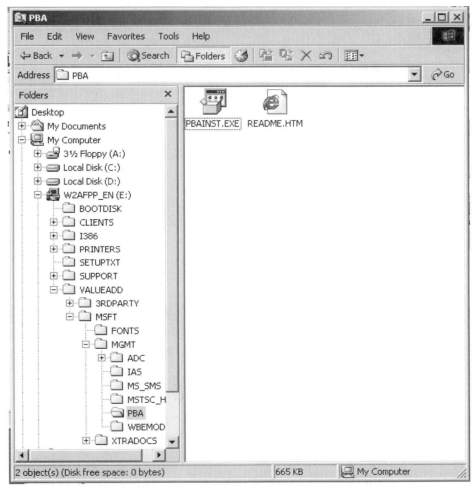

Figure 12.11 Phone Book Administrator is found on the Windows 2000 Server and Windows XP CDs.

upload is complete. This is accomplished via the Internet Services Manager, as follows:

- On the Windows 2000 server, click **Start**, **Programs**, **Administrative Tools**, and then **Internet Services Manager**. The **Internet Services Manager** console appears, as shown in Figure 12.12.
- In the left pane, double-click **Internet Information Services**, and then double-click the appropriate server name.
- Double-click **Default FTP Site**, then right-click **PBSData**. Select **Properties** from the context menu.

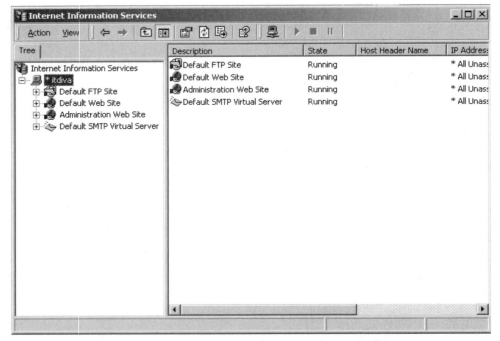

Figure 12.12   The Internet Services Manager console

- Click the **Virtual Directory** tab and place a check mark in the **Write** check box, as shown in Figure 12.13.
- Click **OK**.

Finally, we limit access to the FTP service. Determine which users who have accounts on the Windows 2000 server will have a need to publish phone books. Once you have this information, follow these instructions:

- In the **Internet Services Manager** console, right-click the **Default FTP Site** and select **Properties** from the context menu.
- Select the **Security Accounts** tab as shown in Figure 12.14. Click to remove the check mark in the **Anonymous access** check box. When prompted, click **Yes** to verify this action.
- Click the **Add** button and add the appropriate user accounts that will be permitted to publish phone books. Click **OK** when done. You have now completed the setup of Connection Point Services on a Windows 2000 server.

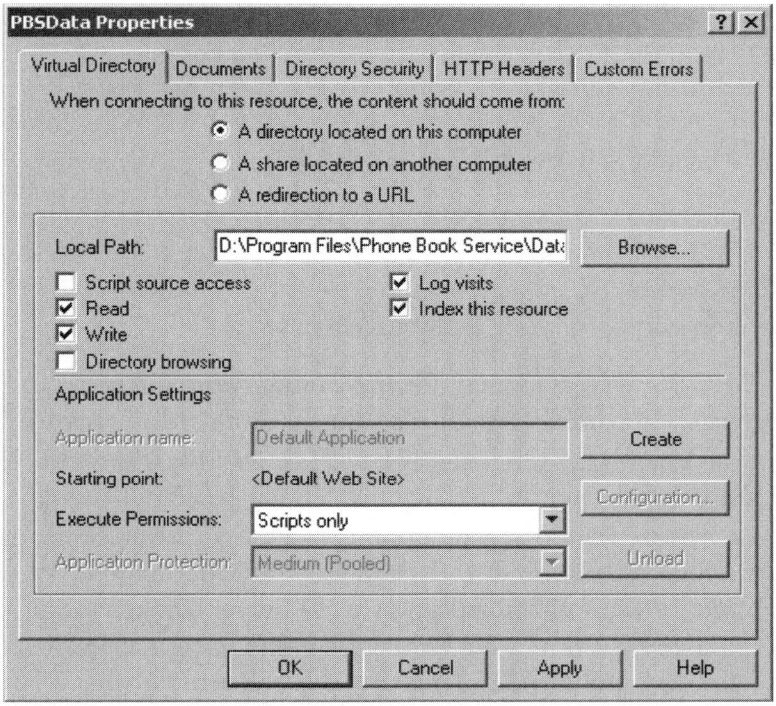

Figure 12.13   Setting write access for the PBS Virtual Directory.

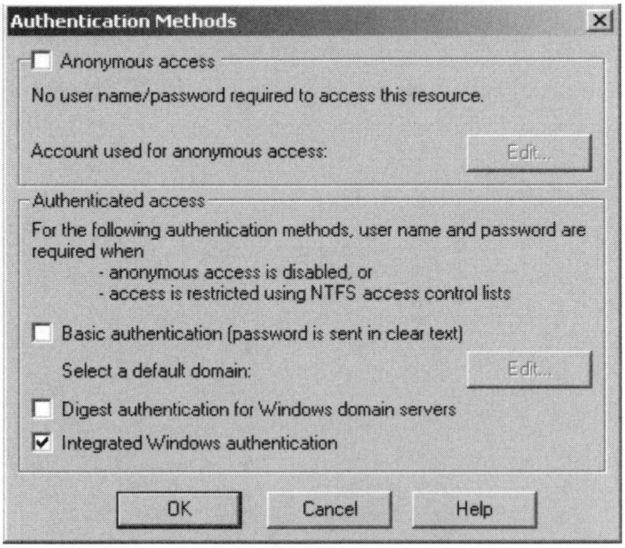

Figure 12.14   Prohibiting anonymous FTP connections to the PBS server.

Connection Point Services Administration

Administration of Connection Point Services has two parts:

- Creating a phone book
- Publishing a phone book

We cover both tasks in this section.

Create a Phone Book

To build a phone book for your remote access users:

- On the PBS server, launch **Phone Book Administrator**. Click **Start**, **Programs**, **Administrative Tools**, **Phone Book Administrator**.
- Click the **File** menu, then select **New Phone Book**. The **Add New Phone Book** dialog box appears, as shown in Figure 12.15.
- Supply a name for the phone book in the **New phone book name** field. The naming restrictions are the typical DOS file naming conventions: a maximum of eight characters and the following characters are prohibited: * = \ / : ? ' " < > |. This is the name reference in the Connection Manager, but not a name the user has to remember, which is good, because you do not have a lot of flexibility to create a user-friendly name here.
- In **Phone Books**, select the new phone book and click the **Tools** menu. Click **Options** to open the **Options** dialog box. Provide the CPS server address and username/password for the appropriate account that will FTP the phone book to the PBS server.
- Add a network access or point-of-presence (POP) server to the new phone book by selecting the phone book in the phone books list. Click the **Edit**

Figure 12.15　Adding a New Phone Book.

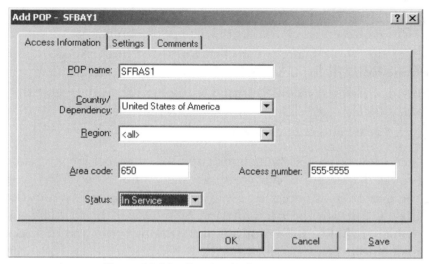

Figure 12.16   The Add POP dialog box

menu and select **Add POP**. The **Add POP** dialog box appears, as shown in Figure 12.16.

Provide the following information on the **Access Information** tab:

- **POP name:** The identity of the POP server.
- **Country/Dependency:** The country where the POP server is located.
- **Region:** Can be used to provide optional geographic location information.
- **Area code:** The POP's area code.
- **Status:** You can specify if this POP is in or out of service. This is helpful if a server is taken offline for temporary administrative work.

Repeat for each remote access server in your network, and click **OK** when you are done.

Publishing a Phone Book

Now that you have successfully created a phone book, you need to make it available to your users by publishing it to the PBS server.

NOTE: You must have FTP write access enabled for the PBSData Virtual Directory for this to work. If you have not done this yet, go ahead and do it now. When you reach the end of the instructions, remove write access from this directory.

- Open **Phone Book Administrator**.
- In **Phone Books**, click the appropriate phone book.
- Select the **Tools** menu; then click **Publish Phone Book**. The **Publish Phone Book** dialog box appears, as shown in Figure 12.17.
- Provide or browse to the **Release Directory**. This is the where the files are to be stored.
- Click **Create** and then click **Post**.

You have now created a phone book and made it available for distribution to your designated users. You can create as many phone books as needed and update them as often as necessary. From here we look at the Connection Manager and walk through the configuration of the Connection Manager service profiles, which include information about the phone books and PBS servers that remote clients will use.

Connection Manager

In this section, we review the requirements for running Connection Manager and how to configure a Connection Manager service profile. A service profile contains all the information needed by a client to connect to a service and can automate some tasks that users normally perform while connecting. There is a Wizard to walk you through each of the options, which requests fairly detailed information from you.

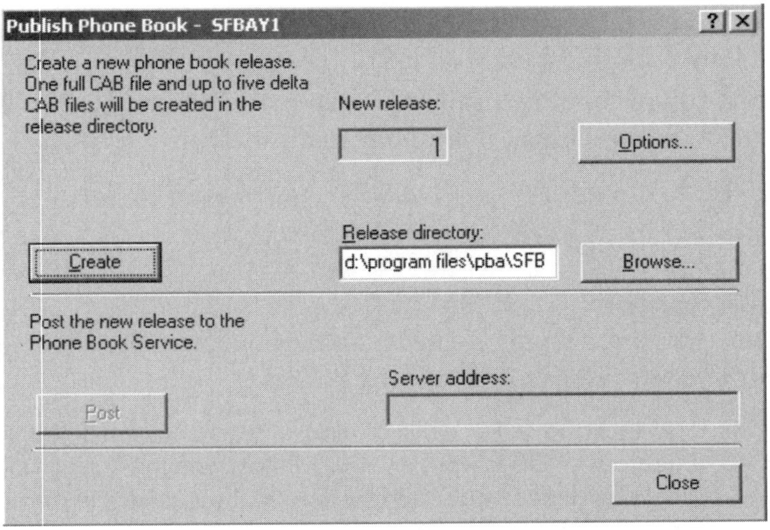

Figure 12.17 Publishing a New Phone Book.

Requirements

Connection Manager clients are supported in Windows XP, Windows 2000, Windows NT 4.0, Windows Me, Windows 98, and Windows 95. These clients need 1MB of free disk space, a service profile, and the Connection Manager software (previously installed by the supported OSs, or can be distributed as part of the Connection Manager install package). The service profile is built with the Connection Manager Administration Kit on a Windows 2000 server or Windows 2000 Advanced server. Phone books are included as part of the service profile. If phone books have not been created at the time the service profile is created and distributed, the service profile must be updated and redistributed to your clients when the phone book is available.

Configuring a Service Profile

To configure a service profile, you need to supply a good deal of information about the connection you are creating. It is a good idea to compile this information in advance, to speed up the profile creation process, because this is a long and detailed process. First though, you need to install Connection Manager Administration Kit (CMAK) on a Windows 2000 server or Windows 2000 Advanced server.

If you did not install the Connection Manager components in the last section:

1. On a Windows 2000 server or Windows 2000 Advanced server, click **Start**, **Settings**, and then **Control Panel**. The Control Panel will appear.
2. Double-click the **Add/Remove Programs** icon, and then click **Add/ Remove Windows Components**. Select **Management and Monitoring Tools**, and then click the **Details** button. The **Subcomponents** dialog box appears.
3. Click to put a check in the **Connection Manager Components** check box. Click **Next**.
4. Click **Finish**. The Wizard completes.
5. To start the CMAK Wizard, click **Start**, **Programs**, **Administrative Tools**, **Connection Manager Administration Kit**. The Connection Manager Wizard will start. You will need to supply the requested information listed below.
   - **Service profile source:** Specify if you want to create a new profile or edit an existing profile. You can create as many profiles as needed to support the various types of connections your users require. Alternatively, changes can be made to existing connections to support service changes.

- **Service and file names:** The service name is the user-friendly name to give the profile. It can have a maximum of 40 characters and is displayed in the Connection Manager's title bar, dialog boxes, and the task bar when it is running. The file name is applied to all files associated with the profile and must adhere to standard 8.3 file names. Both names must be unique on the computer on which they are running.

- **Merged service profiles:** The CMAK allows you to combine existing profiles into a single new profile. This provides the ability to allow all types of services—VPN, dial-up, and ISP—to be contained in a single service profile rather than separate profiles. It is also a good way to clean up the assorted profiles that users may have and distribute a single profile to everyone when any of the incorporated profiles changes. Doing so can eliminate some of the confusion users have about which profile to use and which one is the most up-to-date version.

- **Support information:** This is where you can provide a help desk phone number or a pager number for technical support. Again, this is a nice feature for users who may be unable to get online to locate a corporate directory for this information.

- **Realm name:** If your service utilizes an authentication provider such as an ISP's RADIUS server, you provide this information here. Consult your service provider for specific configuration details.

- **Dial-up networking entries:** If you would like to customize the network and dial-up connection that you specified in the Phone Book Administrator or Connection Point Services, you can do so here, specifying name servers to be used and scripts to be run when a particular connection is used.

- **VPN support:** If you have a VPN connection as part of your service offering, you specify that you wish to do so here.

- **VPN connection:** If you included a VPN connection, you provide the complete configuration details of the VPN connection to be used here on this screen.

- **Connect action:** Specify any preconnection/pretunnel and/or postconnection/posttunnel actions to be performed, such as downloading new phone book entries.

- **Auto applications:** These are applications to be run after the connection (dial-up, network, or VPN) has been established. If the primary reason for users to connect to a network is e-mail, for example, then you can specify an e-mail application to run automatically.

NOTE: If the user closes the auto application, Connection Manager auto-matically begins the disconnection process. This could be useful when there are more users than available connections or licenses on the remote access point, but annoying to users who accidentally closed the application and must reconnect to the service.

- **Custom graphics:** Here is a way to customize the appearance of the dialer. A bitmap has been provided for use by default, but if you want to change this to a corporate logo or other image, you may. These graphics appear in both the Log on and Phone Book dialog boxes. The log-on bitmap is displayed at 330 × 141 and the Phone Book bitmap is displayed at 114 × 304. The graphic is limited to a 256-color image.

- **Phone book:** Select one of the three options for phone book distribution:
  - Include a phone book and allow users to automatically download the latest phone book.
  - Include a phone book, but do not allow users to automatically download the latest phone book.
  - Do not include a phone book, but allow users to download the phone book and updates at a later time.

- **Icons:** This is another way to customize the appearance of the dialer. These icons appear in the title bar, as the program icon, and in the status area. You can specify that you want to have one or more of these icons replaced by graphics of your choosing. The program icon is displayed at 32 × 32, while the title and status bar icons are displayed at 16 × 16. All are limited to 16 colors.

- **Status-area-icon menu:** Right-clicking the status icon in the tray area of the task bar brings up a customizable context menu. As a convenience to your users, you can add shortcuts to applications that are used with this connection.

- **Help files:** If you have created a customized help file for your users, you can substitute it for the default help files. This is a great place to put all the FAQs that your help desk or administrative staff has compiled for remote users.

- **Connection Manager software:** Windows XP uses version 1.3 by default. By selecting this option, you force the client to use version 1.2 instead. This might be useful in some scenarios, but if you are trying to take advantage of the newest version of Connection Manager software available in Windows XP, do not opt to include version 1.2 files.

- **License agreement:** If you want to distribute an agreement that users must consent to before installing your connection profile, include that information here. If you are providing this for corporate users, you may wish to include your acceptable use policies in this area.

- **Additional files:** If you want to include extra software, such as documentation, license files, frequently used utilities, or client access software for corporate databases, you can do so here. It saves the user the trouble of having to locate and download these files themselves. The more files you include, the larger the distribution file, so keep this in mind when determining the method of distribution (such as CD, floppy, or download).

When all information is entered, the wizard builds your profile. The wizard creates a number of files and folder in \Program Files\CMAK\Profiles\ <service_profile_name>. Only the .exe file is required for distribution. Many other configuration options can be selected if you manually edit the files used to build the profile. Consult the Connection Manager Administration Kit Guide to find the complete list of options and instructions.

Conclusion

In this chapter you learned how to configure Windows XP inbound connections, the security options for outbound connections, and the benefits and basics of Connection Manager and the Connection Manager Administration Kit. Windows XP supports up to three simultaneous inbound connections from dial-up, VPN, and direct-connect clients (but no more than one of each type at a time). A bare-bones PPP server is included in Windows XP TCP/IP for the purpose of terminating inbound calls, and it supports over a half-dozen PPP-authentication protocols for dial-up clients. This enables the use of a wide range of PPP servers running just about any operating system, including down-level Windows versions, Linux, Solaris, and so on.

Connection Manager is a preconfigurable client dialer included in Windows XP Professional that contains all parameters and settings required to connect a computer to a particular remote service. Connection Manager provides these preconfigured connections, or service profiles, for remote users to access an ISP, a VPN, a private remote access server, or some other remote resource. A Connection Manager service profile contains all the information needed by a client to connect to a service and can automate some tasks that users would normally perform while connecting. The service profile is built with the Connection Manager Administration Kit on a Windows 2000 server or Windows 2000 Advanced server. Connection Manager clients are supported in Windows XP, Windows 2000, Windows NT 4.0, Windows Me, Windows 98, and Windows 95.

The next chapter moves us out of the world of telephony and back into "traditional" Ethernet-based networking, beginning with Quality of Service features.

13

Quality of Service

This chapter covers Quality of Service (QoS) as it is implemented in Windows XP. It provides a general overview of QoS and a look at how it functions within Internet Connection Sharing (ICS) and in conjunction with modems and remote access services. The chapter concludes with a discussion of how to configure various parameters associated with QoS. Windows XP does not offer the entire range of features offered by Windows 2000, Windows 2003 Server, or other operating systems, applications, or network devices, but it is a functional QoS implementation and can be used reliably for service improvements in certain instances where lack of bandwidth, increased latency, and jitter can degrade performance of an application.

Overview of QoS

Quality of Service is the term assigned to a specific group of techniques for improving network throughput for a given application or service. It allows you to fine-tune network response for applications such as real-time video that do not tolerate delays in transmission well. This is particularly useful when the application is running over a slow network link, such as a dial-up connection.

QoS is defined in IETF RFC 2212. The RFC does not specify the implementation level details of QoS, but rather it defines the specific functionality required in any given QoS implementation. QoS works by reserving or allocating a portion of bandwidth to a designated application. When that application is functioning, Windows XP will make up to the specified amount of bandwidth available to the application.

For example, a streaming media application has a reservation level of 13 percent. This means that 13 percent of the bandwidth available on the QoS-enabled interface that application is using is dedicated to it. It does not mean that that bandwidth is unusable for any other application at that time, however. Windows XP simply prioritizes demand based on QoS settings. An application with reserved bandwidth gets to cut to the head of the line, for as much bandwidth utilization as it has been allocated. If it only needs 9 percent, the remaining 4 percent is used by any other application that needs bandwidth, until such time that the QoS application needs some or all of the remaining bandwidth.

Note that this is contrary to a pesky rumor floating around out there that says the allocated bandwidth is only usable by the QoS application and it cannot be used by any other application. A number of technical articles and newsgroups have incorrectly claimed that Windows XP always reserves 20 percent (the default allocation) of the available bandwidth for QoS. All bandwidth is available to be shared by all applications unless an application has specifically requested priority handling. This allocated bandwidth is still available to other programs unless the requesting program is sending data.

There are several benefits to using QoS-enabled applications and network devices. QoS gives administrators more control over the traffic in their networks. By guaranteeing mission-critical applications a specific slice of the network pie, the administrator can potentially improve the performance of the applications as well as the user experience. As every administrator knows, user perception of network speed and availability of critical resources is often more important than the actual level of availability. By this we mean an application that runs with no delays at 3:30 A.M. when there is no other traffic on the network, but runs with a slight delay during normal business hours, is perceived as slow and unavailable. Upgrading a network may not be practical for financial or logistical reasons, but by using QoS the perception of increased speed and availability of a key corporate application is increased without the major costs and effort associated with a network upgrade. It may not be a permanent fix to the congestion and latency problems a given network has, but it can certainly be an effective stopgap measure.

Both Windows XP Professional and Home provide QoS services, but to varying degrees. Both provide a QoS packet scheduler for traffic handling. Only Windows XP Professional, however, allows advanced configuration of the packet scheduler, which is performed through Group Policy. Configuration is covered later in this chapter.

How QoS Works

The rules of supply and demand apply to available network bandwidth and network traffic in much the same way as they do to housing, jobs, or electronics. When supply is high, but demand is low, everyone can get what they want easily. When demand is high, but supply is low, there is a cost associated with acquiring the desired item. An application that runs over a network produces traffic. This traffic needs to be able to be transmitted over the network to client computers. If there is not much other traffic on the network, this may be accomplished without a hitch. However, if there is a lot of traffic or slow links that create bottlenecks in the flow of data, the application data may suffer as a result. Some applications can handle some packet loss or delays, while others are sensitive to both delay and packet loss. When the intermediary network cannot handle all the traffic that is flowing over it for whatever reason, it is possible that an application may fail or perform poorly. In those cases, it is important to provide some sort of helping hand to the network by either expanding capacity (increasing supply), reducing the amount of traffic on the network (reducing demand), or providing some mechanism to provide better service to certain types of traffic (prioritizing the load). Think of this prioritization as VIP treatment for a specific application's traffic.

On the supply side of the equation, consider that networks are made up of a number of devices, and the whole end-to-end connection between any two computers is not going to be able to function any faster than the slowest point in between. Traffic may flow quickly and easily over a network, but the device, or interface on a device, that forwards the traffic may be overwhelmed by the load it is under, or it may be working improperly for some reason—faulty hardware or incorrect configuration, for example. Traffic signals on city streets are a real-world analogy for this situation. We have all traveled down a street with no real traffic to speak of, but nevertheless had to stop at every single light for six or eight blocks, with no cars crossing the intersection. Alternatively, we have all also been at super-congested intersections where the lights only allow two cars to pass before changing from green to red. In these situations, it does not matter what the speed limit is on the interstate. The plain and simple fact that you have to stop wherever the traffic signals are red means that your trip may be longer than you had anticipated.

Now let us take this traffic analogy a little farther. You know that certain types of traffic get the right of way on roads and in intersections. Emergency vehicles like police cars, fire trucks, and ambulances are examples of this type of traffic that can pass all other cars and carry on its way. Flashing lights, sirens, and other markings identify these vehicles, and it is well-known to all drivers that these vehicles have the right of way. In a network, specific application traffic can be marked for priority handling. All the network devices that it passes through are then able to allow that traffic to move to the head of the line and be forwarded on to the next point along the way, before any lesser priority traffic is forwarded.

QoS provides this special handling of traffic. First, traffic is separated into separate groups called *flows*. The division of traffic into flows is based on classification of the packets that are being transmitted. Next, each flow is directed into a different forwarding queue on the appropriate interface on the network device. And finally, each queue is allocated a specific amount of bandwidth according to an algorithm that takes into consideration the priority of the queue. Packets from each queue are forwarded according to this algorithm.

There are many different mechanisms for implementing traffic handling and control. Different vendors, and even different versions of Windows, offer different types of traffic control mechanisms. The one thing that is common to all QoS implementations, however, is that QoS must be provisioned on every interface of every network device from end to end of the network for this service to be of any benefit. This includes every network card, every switch, and every router, as well as every WAN link hardware device that will be traversed. Simply enabling a single computer here or there does not typically provide any benefit, as the intermediary devices do not know to provide the level of guaranteed service that an application expects to get. In addition, the application receiving QoS service must be QoS aware, and have a QoS management, administration, and provisioning server, such as Admission Control Service (ACS) server running on a Windows 2000 server.

Traffic Handling

There are a number of traffic handling mechanisms in use today. Different vendors have chosen to implement different mechanisms. All traffic handling mechanisms can be categorized as either per-conversation or aggregate mechanisms. The former is a much more granular level of flow control—each flow is kept separate from other flows. Aggregate mechanisms, on the other hand, combine multiple flows into a single aggregate class. Like-priority flows are bundled with other like-priority flows. Let's now take a look at several traffic handling mechanisms used within Microsoft implementations of QoS.

Differentiated Services

Large routed IP networks that carry a great deal of traffic use Differentiated Services (Diffserv) for traffic handling. Diffserv is an aggregate mechanism, which means traffic with similar priorities is grouped together in service queues. The way this traffic is grouped is based on the value of a specific field in the IP packet header. This field, the Diffserv codepoint (DSCP), contains a value assigned by a Diffserv-network entry point QoS host or router. That field is read by other routers on the Diffserv network (all of which must support Diffserv), and the packets are assigned to the appropriate queue based on the value of the field. DSCP is configurable in Windows XP Professional.

802.1p

Smaller networks, including LANs, use 802.1p for traffic handling. 802.1p assigns a value to a field in the Ethernet header that is then used for flow aggregation. The entry point host or router in a LAN (which could also be a Diffserv router on a WAN interface), provides this value and each LAN forwarding device reads this field and forwards the packet according to its priority.

As you can see from this coverage of 802.1p, a significant amount of infrastructure must be QoS compatible for effective use. All switches, bridges, hubs, and network adapter cards on servers and workstations must support 802.1p or the benefits of QoS are lost.

 NOTE: RSVP signaling, a QoS provisioning signaling protocol supported in Windows 2000, has been turned off in Windows XP. RSVP messages received by Windows XP are silently discarded and no error message returned.

QoS in Windows XP

Internet Connection Sharing

When the QoS Packet Scheduler is installed, Windows XP automatically and dynamically provides QoS service over an Internet Connection Sharing Interface. No user intervention is required.

Recall that TCP utilizes sliding windows to transmit and receive data. The size of the windows is negotiated between the two computers involved in the data transaction, with the receiver setting the size for the connection. The size of a computer's sliding window is typically based on the speed of its network. In the event that a computer is running on a fast network, but makes a TCP connection to a computer on another network, there could be delays in transmission. The reason for this is that the receiver's computer is unable to take into consideration the speed of the intermediary network, which can yield a mismatch of window sizes for the actual network connection.

If the receiver is behind an ICS host, however, this problem is alleviated by the QoS Packet Scheduler. The QoS Packet Scheduler automatically adjusts the receive window size to something that is appropriate for the slow link the ICS host is connected to on its external interface. This window size takes precedence over any window size stated by the ICS client/receiving computer.

Dial-up Networking

Another area where Windows XP QoS Packet Scheduler automatically provides QoS services without user intervention is on dial-up connections. As much as we would all like to have high-speed Internet access anywhere, anytime, this is just not possible. Either there is no last-mile infrastructure in place at that location, or the service is not enabled, or the service is not accessible by a given user. Whatever the reason, dial-up links are frequently utilized to provide connectivity.

Slow dial-up speeds can induce more latency than the speed of the actual link itself would indicate. Recall that TCP connections are guaranteed deliver connections. This means that when a packet is sent, an acknowledgment of receipt is required. Applications are given access to the link in the order in which they request it—the first to come is the first served, and it gets full access to the link! If too much data remains unacknowledged, however, the remaining applications that attempt to use this link are delayed as well, even though the link is sitting idle, because they cannot send data until a set amount of sent data has been acknowledged. Microsoft has implemented an algorithm invented at Ford Aerospace in the early 1980s by John Nagle in its TCP/IP stack. The Nagle algorithm, called *tinygrams,* was created as a way to avoid problems with small packets on Ford's private TCP/IP network. As the use of TCP/IP spread, the use of Nagle's algorithm spread as well, and it is now defined as a standard in RFC 896. Nagle's algorithm states that a TCP connection can have only one outstanding unacknowledged small segment at a time.

There are a number of ways to overcome the problems associated with this latency in packet delivery over a slow link, sometimes called *nagling.* These typically involve manual reconfiguration of the registry, and that is not something you want your users to be doing for themselves. In Windows XP, a deficit round robin (DRR) scheme is used to ensure that all applications get a fair shot at sending data. The QoS Packet Scheduler automatically sets up DRR when a slow link is used for transmission. Data flows are created and data is sent to each flow. Each flow is in turn offered service, or access to the network, to ensure that all applications are given access to the link.

Diffserv

Windows XP Professional supports Diffserv. These options are configured through Group Policy and must match your total QoS infrastructure configuration requirements. If you don't have a QoS infrastructure in place, enabling and configuring Diffserv does not do anything for you. The QoS options available for configuration are

- Limit reservable bandwidth
- Limit outstanding packets
- Set timer resolution

- DSCP value of conforming packets
  - Best effort service type
  - Controlled load service type
  - Guaranteed service type
  - Network control service type
  - Qualitative service type
- DSCP value of nonconforming packets
  - Best effort service type
  - Controlled load service type
  - Guaranteed service type
  - Network control service type
  - Qualitative service type
- Layer-2 priority value
  - Nonconforming packets
  - Best effort service type
  - Controlled load service type
  - Network control service type
  - Qualitative service type

When these features are enabled, a key is created in the registry. At the time they are configured, the appropriate configuration value is stored in the registry.

Configuring QoS

There are two phases in the configuration of QoS. First, the QoS Packet Scheduler must be installed. Second, specific QoS parameters may be set, if appropriate for your network. Both of these phases are covered in this section.

Installing QoS Packet Scheduler

To install QoS Packet Scheduler for Windows XP, follow these instructions:

1. Click **Start**, then **Network Connections**, then right-click the local area connection on which to install the QoS Packet Scheduler. Select **Properties** from the context menu.
2. Click **Install**, click **Service**, and then click **Add**.
3. Click **QoS Packet Scheduler**, and then click **OK**.
4. The QoS Packet Scheduler appears in the properties sheet for that interface, as shown in Figure 13.1.

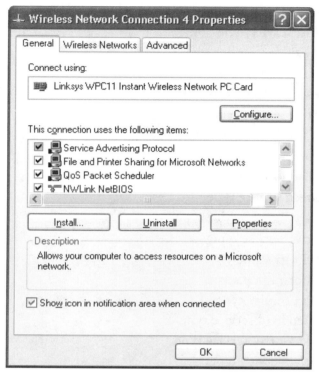

Figure 13.1 QoS Packet Scheduler successfully installed

Configuring QoS Options

QoS options are configured within Group Policy on Windows XP Professional. To edit settings, follows these instructions:

1. Click **Start**, then **Run**.
2. Type **gpedit.msc**, then click **OK**.
3. Navigate to **Computer Configuration**, then **Administrative Templates**, then **Network**. Click on **QoS Packet Scheduler**, as shown in Figure 13.2.
4. Double-click on the item desired and configure appropriately.

Conclusion

In this chapter, we covered Quality of Service within the context of Windows XP. QoS is a set of mechanisms that are intended to provide improved network throughput for applications that are QoS aware. Windows XP does not offer the full complement of QoS features that Windows 2000 and Windows 2003 Server provide, but it does offer a number of configurable and automatic QoS

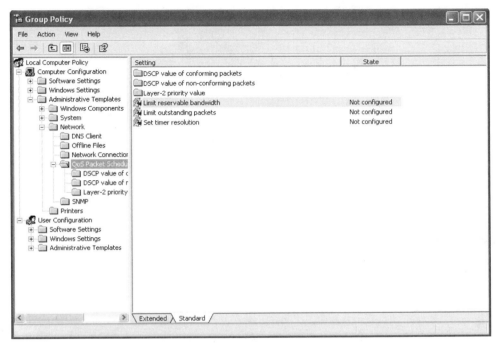

Figure 13.2   Locating QoS in Group Policy.

services. When the QoS Packet Scheduler is installed, Windows XP automatically and dynamically provides QoS service over an Internet Connection Sharing Interface with no user intervention required. Windows XP QoS Packet Scheduler automatically provides QoS service on dial-up connections using a DRR scheme. The QoS Packet Scheduler automatically sets up DRR when a slow link is used for transmission. And finally, Diffserv is supported in Windows XP for use within networks with an existing QoS infrastructure.

From here we move from general networking topics and transition into securing your network assets with Windows XP, building upon the information in this and the previous chapters. The next chapter introduces network security with a discussion of general security practices and makes recommendations for a baseline security policy.

Chapter

14

General Security Practices

A good security practice begins with the fundamentals, and in most cases this involves an examination of a common set of widely accepted basic practices and principles. This chapter provides some structured guidelines, but these guidelines only provide one perspective to a potentially complex area. In your quest for knowledge about security principles and practices, however, do examine several opinions and form an educated response to the greater problems that security can help resolve.

The goals of this chapter are based entirely on the premise that security can be planned and controlled if its basis is simple, straightforward, and easy-to-understand principles and practices. As this chapter progresses, you learn many of the essential security principles common to most security infrastructures. Based on these principles, it should be possible to apply some of this knowledge through the examples provided. It is strongly recommended that as you develop your practice, you formulate a plan to accomplish this by taking several principles that we discuss, and concepts that we outline, to create an effective and sensible practice for your organization.

Other chapters in this book expound on some of these principles and how they relate to Microsoft Windows XP. This chapter attempts to focus on something above an operating system, network, or an organization. The hope is that if and when a majority of individuals on the Internet begin to follow generally accepted practices, it will be a safer and more fun place to be.

Defining Good Security Practices

Fundamentally speaking, good security is common sense and straightforward changes to your habits, applications, systems, and networks that prevent the release of private, confidential, and proprietary information and resources that your organization pays for. Hackers, crackers, or unauthorized invaders of any kind want the information you have or they want to use your systems to gain access to resources that you have control of or your company pays for.

The unauthorized use of your systems is sometimes for personal gain, but often it is used to launch attacks against others. This puts you in the middle of a huge problem in which your hardware and software is used to attack others. This is an important distinction, because if your property is involved in attacks against others, it is possible for a governing or legal body to request and in most cases, seize your assets in their investigations.

Therefore, your goals are to protect your information (including confidential, proprietary, and private assets), systems, and networks from both internal and external threats. This is primarily so that your business does not suffer and you do not inadvertently assist in illegal activities of harming innocent people.

Unfortunately, you cannot know how or when hackers will attack you because their methods change from week to week. But by setting principles and practices that guide your activities, you can keep your systems secure and more or less trouble free.

You can patch an IIS exploit with a Microsoft-released hotfix, and the next week another exists, and you are no less exposed and vulnerable, and in some cases you can be more at risk. To combat this, set a daily practice by which your staff checks for new patches on *www.microsoft.com/security,* and applies them to your staging environment where they are then tested for 24 hours, at which point a change is commenced to apply the patches. This way you are on alert and can at least head off these vulnerabilities at the pass. You still might need to do patching on a weekly, if not a daily, basis but at least you have a solid method for dealing with vulnerabilities as they arise.

Additionally, there are now new tools available that are capable of helping you with the onslaught. Sometimes called *Patch Management Systems,* they are designed around a client-server approach and automatically check for the presence of the most current patches. If patches are missing, the system applies patches of certain types. These systems have features such as rollbacks and approval processing that can help you streamline and automate your needs.

Without an effective, timely patching policy to deal with evolving threats, your systems can and will be compromised. With security it is always just a matter of time. With the advent of some of these tools, you have ways to improve reliability and improve your security as well as continue to keep the latest upgrades available to your users.

Remember, to be successful, you have to have a strategy to follow your practices. Figure 14.1 shows the relationship between all the components of a good security strategy.

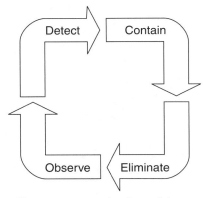

Figure 14.1   The components of a solid security strategy

For some reason, there are two classes of individuals: those who fear insecurity and those who do not. While security can be a point of mystery, complexity, and difficulty in an environment, it is usually because an individual or company has chosen to ignore, deprive, or suffocate their security practice. Just as you have been taught to afford proper respect for the law, wild animals, fire, and weapons, you must also afford a proper respect for security by paying it some attention on a regular basis; most importantly, pay attention to what it is telling you, by reviewing the logs and alerts that your devices produce.

Many times companies are in a position where they have no security and are in a critical situation. Sometimes a company either had or has a security system that is not being properly maintained. In some cases, they can experience outages that cost them thousands (or millions) of dollars an hour.

When you think of the pure justification and cost versus benefit of security, some companies have a harder time justifying a sustained, funded, supported security practice. But just as with your insurance policies for your home, car, and most other valuables, the biggest justification is one that you hope is never needed. A security budget has benefits beyond the loss scenario: it can help you realize how your costs are being used, from why an Internet connection spikes in utilization at 10 A.M., to why a particular project is not getting done fast enough, and even to why a server keeps crashing.

In daily life, there are people driving the streets without an auto insurance policy, which puts you at risk. Thankfully, there are laws in place that require it in most states. You could and should think of Internet security in the same way. If those traveling the Internet highway are not paying attention, then they are putting you at risk because someone will come along and use their resources against others.

Over the years, security has been a high-priority issue for some and not for others. Its importance in the enterprise cannot be explained away as not having a return on investment or being prohibitively expensive. Neither is the case, and neither statement is in the right context.

It is possible to deploy an effective security solution without having to hire additional personnel or spending hundreds of thousands of dollars on security devices. Security can be had for a fraction of that cost, but a trade-off does exist: the more integrated and flexible solutions cost more, and rightfully so.

This chapter, and this book for that matter, is not a definitive guide. It is recommended that you read others on the subject and look into incorporating several approaches into your security proposals. Universities typically do not hire their own graduates to teach because they are looking for the broader perspective. For similar reasons, you should review several approaches when developing your security practice.

While this is not a definitive guide, it is useful as either a fundamental guide or a great supporting work to help you develop an effective plan. Basically, there are many accepted practices that can be implemented, and they can be implemented in many ways and still be effective.

This chapter attempts to explain the concept surrounding the known versus the unknown and how being logical, calm, and prepared can benefit you in a crisis. This chapter may seem a bit preachy, because there is more on theory than actual practical steps you can take; however, it will put you on the right course. The following chapters provide more practical and in-depth coverage where possible.

Tenets of Security

Without a doubt, there are three statements or lists that we describe, for lack of a better word, as "tenets" of security. These statements and lists cover the essence of a good practice, and if expanded, provide a logical, straightforward approach to security in your enterprise.

Our first topic is what we consider to be eight focuses or areas of computer security; each area or focus can and should have a set of regularly followed steps and an emergency action plan for dealing with immediate, pending threats to that security practice.

Each type of security represents an area that you may want or need to address. Not every type is one that this book is able to adequately provide you an answer for, since some areas of security are not resolved by a solution provided by the operating system; and this book is mostly focused at how to work with Microsoft Windows XP. Others may involve user awareness training, management consensus or tools that exist above and outside the operating system.

At this stage we identify the security category and explain what it might mean to your enterprise.

Accountability

Accountability is by far one of the cornerstones of security, and part of the acronym AAA for Authentication, Authorization, and Accounting—accounting for the actions of your users (be they customers, vendors, partners, or employees) and how (also when, where, and why) those users access a specific resource within your environment. Accountability can also be tracking what your systems do and how the utilization of your resources is allocated.

Typically, in most environments administrators know that a server has been accessed, but often how and who accessed that server in the past is difficult to reconstruct. Accountability can and should include not only who is accessing, but also what they are accessing. Many environments use multiple-user login accounts, which makes it even more difficult.

Accountability on Windows XP should be the creation and management of individual user accounts, including controlling who has administrative rights and what account they run. This is viewed in further detail in this chapter and also in Chapter 15 on System Hardening.

Accountability also has to involve, at some level, a user's understanding of your policies: what is accepted and what is not accepted. Your specific mileage may vary, but you should have some assistance from the human resources department in how employees are approached regarding policies and procedures.

Analysis

There are a lot of organizations that spend enormous amounts of money to identify and track security events, but the amount of time and resources dedicated to analyzing intrusions, compromises, and other security information is significantly lacking. Security is much like evolution—new exploits, risks, and threats sometimes appear out of thin air. You need to analyze these events and apply lessons learned from these logs and events.

As much as analysis is neglected, it is also very common that proper correlation is not done, which makes the analysis much more difficult. Most security attacks begin with probes and other tactics that help attackers define your infrastructure. The only way you can prepare is to identify these initial probes and continue to update your infrastructure as new attacks are identified.

There are several ways to approach this. The first is through diligent log viewing and alert configuration. This, however, puts a great burden on systems staff. The second is using some correlation and prioritization software to raise the threshold for alarms. These software platforms are a medium-cost solution that more intelligently deal with these log entries and in most cases also provide very comprehensive and useful reporting. Finally, there are several companies that offer log analysis and reporting, and as part of those services they perform a level-one analysis and reach out to you when it is appropriate.

The most important thing in any infrastructure is to identify and justify the needs your organization has. While an effective security plan is essential, how complex and involved it is really depends on your risks, assets, and the tools you have deployed. A lot of companies have typically deployed just a firewall. Most do not even monitor it for unusual things and that is a big mistake! The mistake is to not continue to monitor, update, and analyze these devices on a regular ongoing basis.

It is extremely dangerous for an organization to ignore the importance of updated, comprehensive security architecture. Many companies are completely unaware of their risks and notice them only when they find they have lost valuable information, such as employee records, customer credit card information, or important intellectual property. The pity is that in most cases nothing can be done about it.

In many organizations employees specifically assigned to deal with the corporate security issues find the infrastructure deployed confusing. Some ignore most of the alarms and alerts that are generated by those devices. For such companies, where you cannot justify a full-time security staff, outsource! Find a reputable security management vendor and help them define your needs and requirements.

Unfortunately, this is not the practice. The overwhelming prevalence of alarms, the confusion caused by their meanings, and a lack of understanding of the importance of these alarms are more to blame than sheer corporate callousness about safety.

While it is good to see more security infrastructure deployed, the most important thing in any security infrastructure is that someone pays attention to those alarms and works to reduce them by finding the causes and resolving those issues. Just as most security issues boil down to either a misconfiguration or an exploit that is patchable, most alarms are also eliminated with just a bit of care and due diligence.

Any security practice can only be effective with trained staff, whether they are employees in your company or an outsourced security firm. It is essential to properly review whatever security infrastructure you employ on a regular basis. It is equally essential that logs and alerts generated by the devices you have deployed are also reviewed and, where possible, the problems detected are corrected.

Access Control

This is typically thought of as part of the AAA system, but in fact it is a bit more than all of those. Access control is the process of taking an authenticated, authorized user who has been accounted for and determining specifically what level of access they should have to a specific system, resource, or asset. For example, Jane Doe is a contractor who can log in to the domain, but cannot access the Exchange server for local login, or access the finance network share. Access control is a combination of the three principles, and covers how, when, where, and why people access systems.

When contemplating access control, you need to remember that it should be acceptable in your organization to follow the least-access principle. If you do not need access, then you should not have it. This protects both the employee and the employer. With the least-access principle you also limit the number of users (and their accounts) that can be compromised. Most sites provide a lot more access to their users than they should and when something goes wrong, it is rarely possible to locate who might have been involved.

Authentication

Authentication (also part of AAA) is the process by which user John Doe is different from Jane Doe or John Jones. It is the practice of not only knowing who your users are, but giving them appropriate authority on your systems.

Authentication can be simply a username and password that provides a rudimentary approach to the concept "something you know," or it can be two or more factor authentication using products such as RSA's SecurID tokens or CryptoCards from Evidian (which adds the element of something you have, a token). Truly secure systems add a third factor, sometimes referred to as something you are (your fingerprint, retina scan, or other biometric identification).

Using newer technologies, authentication has been taken to the next level with security implementations using PKI, where not only is a user authenticated to use a specific network or system, but is also authenticated to access a subset of the information found on that system (such as personnel records or financial records).

While this does increase some of the complexity of authentication, it decreases administrative overhead by allowing users to be created and deleted in a more controlled and simpler manner. With a single authentication mechanism, it is a one-time add or delete, whereas others have to run around to all the important machines and make changes.

A sound authentication system also allows a more granular control structure. It means you need to dedicate fewer resources to specific tasks. (For example, in most organizations they allocate specific resources to finance, others to billing, and still others to general purpose; if they could share this system, they would find that they could buy or build one server that can be shared instead of having 16 servers that cannot.)

Authorization

This is the process by which a user is matched to their login credentials. This can also be the process whereby access to a specific object is checked (Is John Doe an administrator? Is Jane Doe a server operator?).

Simply put, it is how users are checked against some system credential process to determine if they are authorized to use that resource. It can and does go beyond that, though, as it is also the process where a local, normal user is different from a remote, normal user, and administrative privileges are sorted out.

Authorization can and should also cover legal warnings. It is important for you to inform your users where they can find the policies that bind them, more so for nonemployees, but nevertheless as reminders for employees as well.

A legal warning is not foolproof, but it is even less so if you do not identify that the illegal behavior is targeted at your company. Assuming you take the individual who was hacking your systems to court to recover damages, they can argue that they did not know they were affecting you because you did not identify your assets. If your legal warnings are too generic, they can also argue that they mistakenly thought they were logging into their own system.

You can find all you need to know about the United States Code online, but you need the following information: Title 18 USC 2701 (a) covers unauthorized access to electronic devices, and Title 18 USC 2511 (a), (b), and (c) cover monitoring activities.

Availability

Just as with analysis, system availability is rarely listed among the values most security organizations hold true. An effective security posture, however, is quite simply one that encourages, augments, and protects your business, and it is impossible to do that without having your systems available for use by your employees.

Every part of your security infrastructure can help to enable the user, and can even be justified in how a central authentication provides redundancy, high availability, and centralized management. It can also help you when the time comes to grow or shrink, add or remove users.

You can easily implement a secure system that can be user-friendly and highly available in the event of a catastrophe. When considering your next control mechanism, do not hesitate to apply rules around making the system available and not limiting your business operations.

Remember, if the device is secure and no one can use it, it is hard to continue to justify the cost of that asset. Also, your users are more likely to help with the security mission if they feel that security has helped them by making it easier to access their work. For example, single sign-on has always been very popular with users because it simplifies their need for passwords and remembering different connectivity details.

Confidentiality

This is a tough concept for the security personnel, but more so for anyone who has any level of access. Sometimes it is necessary for one person in a company to be assured that they have a completely private, secure communication with another. Therefore, every effort must be made to ensure that no one is eavesdropping on a conversation or duplicating information meant for a more restrictive audience.

There are many tools available to help you ensure confidentiality, but more than anything it requires diligence and user participation in your security plans. Tools alone cannot absolutely solve your confidential access problem; a determined user can still find a way in.

One of the common concerns raised with the most used confidentiality pattern encryption is that there needs to be a way for the legal and human resource departments to gain access to all information an employee has been working on or with. This is why you have to be very careful when you set up your encryption by forcing site keys, and even collecting and keeping safe a copy of private keys and passwords for your employees for an emergency.

Integrity

Integrity is one item that is often overlooked. It means knowing that the data you have received from a source is really from that source and not someone trying to pretend to be that source. There are a lot of ways you can accomplish this throughout the security infrastructure. The most common way is through the use of IPSec protocol suite, specifically, authentication headers, which is available within the Windows XP operating system for setting up VPNs. We address this concept in more detail in Chapter 18, Virtual Private Networks.

Nonrepudiation

Nonrepudiation is using some means that is trusted (like a certificate authority) to validate and verify that an electronic document, transaction, or connection is coming from the person identified in the request. Also, nonrepudiation attempts to make statements like "this e-mail came from Jane Doe and has not been altered." So it is an effective tool to certify the validity of e-mails and other communications. This topic is discussed mainly in VPN technology circles, but it should concern all users of network security measures. Understanding nonrepudiation is essentially understanding how you are legally referenced and how easy it is to forge an e-mail address without it. It is an important concept because it helps you know who is who and what is what in your environment. Because the technology moves so fast and there is a need to validate as much in your environment as possible for legal, civil, and criminal reasons, it is important to spend a little time understanding and applying this concept in your office.

Especially in the present business climate, assurance is based on nonrepudiation, and it is essential that you identify the individual or individuals who are involved in a transaction. This way you know who to talk to when an issue needs to be resolved.

Prevention

Prevention is obviously a trickier subject. It takes detection to a logical next step and is difficult to implement. Newer tools take advantage of rudimentary Artificial Intelligence (AI) in programs. This is sometimes referred to as neural networking. While not truly AI, these tools are smarter than earlier programs because they compare the expected to the received and determine if that which is received is far enough off-track to warrant an alert or log entry.

This is a very good advancement in security technology. The technology is in its infancy, but as it develops it will be easier to build programs and rules, analyze data, and weed out false alarms and false positives.

Another category is a set of principles that every administrator should hold dear and true to their jobs. They are statements that should probably be propagated throughout your company and supported by every employee, contractor, vendor, and partner. These general statements, while brief, describe security at its core.

- **Security is everyone's job.** As soon as someone forgets to lock his or her session, bolt the door, turn on the alarm system, or shred a sensitive document, your job of protecting the enterprise becomes next to impossible. You must convince each and every one of your users that their participation in your company's security posture is absolutely critical to its success.

- **Security is only as good as its weakest link.** This statement is the same as the previous one, but more specifically stated: If you lock the back door securely, but leave the front door open, then locking the back door had no significance in your grand scheme. Therefore, you must make sure that whatever you do, it is proportionate, measured, and even throughout your entire enterprise.

- **Security is best in layers.** To compensate for possible failures of the first two principles, if possible, it is best to have redundant, overlapping systems in place. Having a lock on the door is great, but having a lock on a door with an alarm system in case that lock is circumvented is even better. Having a camera or a physical security presence increases your ability to protect your assets.

- **Security measures like locks are sometimes not very effective against dishonest people.**

- **Some security measures can and will be broken. Expect it.**

Knowing the Threats

To truly understand your threats you need to fully quantify three things. The first thing that you should do is to calculate and appreciate your assets: What exactly are you trying to protect? A lot of business managers have a hard time justifying the cost of security, but the justification comes from having a clear, concise strategy for dealing with their greatest risks and most likely threats. Security does not always prevent security problems. Sometimes it contains them or alerts you so that you can take a proactive stance against those threats.

Second, you should have some understanding of how intrinsically valuable those assets are. Sometimes assets have a negative value; this means that losing the asset is not as bad as the press that you receive for losing it (such as customer confidence information). Other times, the asset has a significant positive value, like customer contact data such as e-mail addresses, or billing information such as credit cards. It may be as simple as payroll information being discussed between human resources and finance.

Finally, you have to remember that while security is in part an insurance policy against catastrophic events, that is by no means its only advantage, justification, or purpose in your company. There is a great deal that an effective security practice can do for you. It can, without a doubt, help you contain costs, improve efficiency, help you automate, and reduce the time some of your computer and IT tasks take, thus improving the overall environment. It also helps you become a better consumer. And in the end, it helps all of us against the few who wish to bring chaos and destruction to our collaborative efforts.

You can and will be more successful if you spend a portion of your budget and some of your resources to bring your security practice up to a level that is reasonable and meets or exceeds the standards of due care and due diligence.

Classification and Containment

A final principle that is important in security is accurate classification and effective containment. While it is clear why this principle is important, the problem is that most professionals entrusted with this task are not properly trained or lack a good basis for making the requisite decisions.

Classification

Essentially it is the practice of taking an alarm, event, alert, or issue and making some initial statements and applying labels to it.

Dissecting an event or issue (classification) can be done in a lot of ways, but a good set of requirements are:

1. Priority
2. Severity
3. Type
4. Timestamp
5. Owner

Typical priority levels are identified by some sort of system that tracks issues. This could be any of the ticketing systems or simply internal levels you use to classify those attacks and issues. We normally use numbers and usually have three levels: Priority One (most serious/time sensitive), Priority Two, and Priority Three.

Usually Priority Three are events that are not a risk to you, but you would like more information about them and could spend a week or two seeking additional sources. Priority Two typically means that it should be resolved within four hours, and should be immediately escalated one level in management. Finally, Priority One should require that a director or vice-president be aware of the event and it should be actively worked at until the issue has been resolved.

A good set of severity levels is low, medium, high, and critical and should be color coded, with red being critical, orange being high, yellow being medium, and green being low.

Type refers to the specific kind of event that has occurred: Alarm, missing data, unusual access patterns, and the like are all specific types of events that can be listed in a classification record.

Timestamps are usually just a classification that you can use to sort your issues. The important thing with a timestamp is that it should be as accurate as possible; if you are not using NTP (Network Time Protocol) to sync your time-servers, you should.

Owner can be either an individual or a group. Usually a specific person is the best way to track this, though you work within your own system.

Containment

As the name implies, the first and most serious task you have in any event that could cause damage to you or someone else is to contain that event from causing further damage. In some situations it is not unusual for someone to contain a situation by powering off the offending server or trying to clean up the situation. However, it is really important to contain and not do harm or modify the systems in question so that a proper forensics investigation can be completed.

Chapter

15

System Hardening

This chapter covers six key areas that are critical in determining your success as an administrator of systems:

1. Introduction to System Security
2. Basic Service and Application Tuning
3. Service and Application Auditing
4. Registry Tweaking
5. Performance Enhancements
6. Automatic System Recovery

Introduction to System Security

System hardening is something that often does not happen or goes incomplete on systems, and creates a great expanse for hackers, crackers, and the like to gain access to your environment.

From a scenario standpoint, the who, why, and where are various in type or form as discussed in Chapter 14. It could be someone from your team who is disgruntled; it could be your boss who feels left out of some decisions in the chain of command. It could be someone from accounting, finance, or some other department; and as always it could be someone from outside your organization.

There are many horror stories of servers and workstations hacked, compromised, or invaded, which leave the owner of the system to start from scratch and rebuild. In the past, Microsoft Corporation paid less attention to the security of their operating systems. Of course, when a patch was necessary they created it; when someone alerted them to a vulnerability, they tried to deal with it. However, no holistic approach to security existed until after Windows 2000 was released. Most of the tools and strategies developed with Windows 2000 are carried forward to XP.

This chapter identifies some resources available to you to help protect your company's investment. As stated previously, this book is not necessarily designed for a home computer, because it goes into details of how to apply these thoughts, ideas, and tools in mass quantities. However, none of these tools are specifically prohibited for use on one or two computers. You may have to read up on the tool itself to see how it might apply to you.

We focus on Windows XP Professional. Home Edition cannot participate in domains and is not a wise choice for a corporate environment, and because it is crippled in several key areas it is not covered here.

As a bonus we cover tools that Microsoft Corporation has released that will help you make these changes more automatically including the Microsoft Baseline Security Analyzer (MBSA) and the components related to this tool. We also cover the Microsoft Security Toolkit that you have to order (U.S. customers can receive it free at the time of this publishing).

Basic Service and Application Tuning

Standard caveats apply here (caveat emptor—buyer beware, use at your own risk). Before you do anything recommended in this chapter, or in this book for that matter, know: 1) what you are doing and 2) test it in a nonproduction, controlled environment. We cannot be responsible for every possible scenario that you may encounter. We cover the basics, but it is possible that there is a unique requirement in your environment.

Our first topic is probably one of the most important ones. As you may know, security of a system becomes infinitely easier with fewer services installed and running that you have to keep patched, secured, and supported. So the easiest, most secure approach is to disable anything you do not use.

If, for whatever reason, you disagree with that approach, or believe that doing so might limit your functionality, we outline some of the riskier services and applications that you should consider disabling or removing. Remember that the goal is secure functionality or it will be impossible to limit your exposure.

We attach no prioritized importance to these specific services and they are listed alphabetically so you can approach them from a top-to-bottom checklist. Each of these services are specifically identified for what they do; that way you can make an intelligent decision on whether or not these services should remain.

Service-by-Service Checklist

There is no real guide on what to do service by service, but essentially the way you secure your system is to understand it: You need to know what services are needed, where those services extend, what risks those services present, and whether the benefit of a service outweighs the said risk.

There are two types of services that can be found in Windows XP: those that are installed by default and those that are commonplace in most installations. The service-by-service listing that follows includes whether the service is installed by default or not, as well as our recommendations.

This breakdown also goes a bit further in helping you to understand why we believe a specific service should or should not be disabled. We list our concern with regard to the severity of the vulnerability or exposure the service presents to your server, and in some cases your overall organization.

ClipBook Service

Installed by default (Professional)
Recommendation: Disable
Severity: High (network abuse)

The clipboard service has been around essentially since Windows became popular. In later versions of the operating system, Microsoft introduced the ability through the ClipBook service of sharing this "clipboard" across your intranet or LAN.

Most uses for the clipboard are basic and necessary, but rarely does anyone have a need to share those clips across multiple computers, so we recommend that you disable the service. If it is needed, firing up the service takes a few seconds, so the overhead is worth the lowering of the risk.

COM+ Event Subsystem

Installed by default (Professional)
Recommendation: Manual
Severity: Low

The history of the COM object began with object linking in the late 1980s and developed to be a core component of the ActiveX infrastructure that Microsoft incorporated in most of their technologies.

However, the COM+ Event Subsystem deals more specifically with the distribution of events that subscribe to COM+ components. One area that is specifically affected is Windows' ability to provide log-on and log-off notifications, therefore leaving it in a manual state may prove to be less bothersome than completely disabling it.

COM+ System Application

Installed by default (Professional)

Recommendation: Manual

Severity: Low

The COM+ System Application controls the Event Subsystem and therefore whichever decision you go with for the Event Subsystem, you should also follow for the System Application service.

The likelihood that the service will be abused is low, but definitely not irrelevant. Leaving it manual with a comprehensive network security process in place (including firewalls and intrusion detection) should be sufficient.

Error Reporting Service

Installed by default (Professional)

Recommendation: Disable

Severity: Medium (information dispersal)

In a home environment it is likely that you will want to report errors back to Microsoft, which might have an impact in future patches and fixes. But in a corporate environment it is less likely that you want your users reporting issues outside your IT organization. The user might be frustrated by the experience, and you may remain unaware that a problem occurred.

Fax Service

Not installed by default (Professional)

Recommendation: Disable (if installed)

Severity: Medium (information dispersal)

The fax service is not installed by default. If you have it installed and are not using it, then disable it. By disabling it, you make it impossible to send or receive faxes directly by the operating system. If you use a third-party faxing software it may still be possible with this disabled for you to receive faxes. This depends on how the fax software interacts with the operating system and your fax device.

FTP Publishing Service

Not installed by default (Professional)

Recommendation: Disable (if installed)

Severity: High (network abuse)

For obvious reasons, primarily because passwords and usernames are sent in clear text and, in most cases, anonymous access must be granted, the FTP publishing service is a security risk. Disabling this does not limit your ability to FTP to other sites, it just prevents users from setting up their own FTP service on the workstation or server where you disable the service.

Help and Support Service

Installed by default (Professional)

Recommendation: Disable

Severity: Low (configuration changes)

This limits access to Microsoft's online help; however, access to local help services remains unaltered. It is preferable that user education and support is centrally controlled. You may not want your users to make modification to their systems that you may or may not be aware of, because it increases your support burdens.

Human Interface Device Access

Installed by default (Professional)

Recommendation: Disable (default)

Severity: Low

This is an accessibility feature meant for devices that assist workers who have special accessibility needs, for use with devices such as eye motion tracking, voiceprint, and other such devices. At the time of the writing of this book, no such devices have been qualified for use with this service. In any case, unless you have a need for it, keep it disabled.

Internet Information Server (IIS) Administrative Service

Not installed by default (Professional)

Recommendation: Disable (if installed)

Severity: Medium (network abuse)

The IIS administrative service gives your local users the ability to control locally and (if they have the necessary permissions) remotely installed FTP, WWW, and Mail (SMTP) services. We assume you have a central server for those services and they should not be installed on workstations.

Some applications, typically multiuser services, although designed to interoperate with Web applications, may require this service.

IMAPI CD-Burning Service

Installed by default (Professional)

Recommendation: Disable (unless CD burner installed)

Severity: Low

This service is designed specifically to give you a native ability to "drag and drop" to a CD-R or CD-RW burner. If neither is installed by default, then disable it. There is no significant network risk with this service so if you want to leave it in the manual state (the default), no harm is done.

Indexing Service

Installed by default (Professional)

Recommendation: Disable

Severity: Medium (network abuse)

The indexing service creates tables and indexes that make rapid file access quicker if you have access to querying languages. We list this as a disable-by-default because of security risks generated by this service. All the listed risks require local privileges, so if you are doing a good job of securing guest and remote access, leaving it manual should cause you no harm.

Internet Connection Sharing

Installed by default (Professional)

Recommendation: Disable (unless using ICF)

Severity: High (network abuse, information dispersal)

Internet Connection Sharing is a very dangerous function, because it can dramatically impact the confidentiality and integrity of your systems. If you need this functionality, then be sure to properly configure the included Internet Connection Firewall (ICF) service. Chapter 12, Remote Access, covers this in greater detail.

Basically, the ICF should be used only in conjunction with a network-based firewall sitting on the perimeter of your network; Microsoft still has much to do to bring the ICF to an acceptable standard for firewalls.

Logical Disk Manager

Installed by default

Recommendation: Disable (unless installing new disks)

Severity: Low

The Logical Disk Manager is the service under Control Panel (Classic View), Administrative Tools, Computer Management, under the Storage tab called Disk Management. If you envision doing repartitioning, reformatting, or adding disks then enable this; but if you do not, turn it off until you need it.

While there is no inherent risk to leaving this service on from a network perspective, it is a service that can potentially be exploited on the local network. It may also be possible for Trojans to cause damage to your disk subsystem if it is turned on or enabled.

Logical Disk Manager Administrator Service

Installed by default

Recommendation: Disable (unless installing new disks)

Severity: Low

This is the same as Logical Disk Manager, typically used for mass-storage device changes. Whichever direction you took for the preceding service, follow the same here because they really are not effective unless both are active.

Message Queuing Triggers

Not installed by default

Disable (if installed, related to message queuing service)

Severity: Low

The message queuing triggers work with the message queuing service and is responsible for distributed transactions across multiple systems. If you do not know what it is, what it is for, or why you want it, then turn it off.

Messenger Service (*not* MSN Instant Messenger)

Installed by default

Recommendation: Automatic (automatic by default)

Severity: Medium (must enable security policy and restrictive administrative rights)

As a general rule disabling this service makes a lot of sense, but in a corporate environment there are reasons (most of which are not used frequently enough) for you to notify your users that something is happening. Depending on corporate policy, this service is an excellent tool to notify users of pending mail outages, network printer problems, or just any sort of outage that might affect more than one user. It is possible to use this service in advanced mail filtering, but few have actually implemented it in that manner. The messenger service is a mostly obsolete service from fragmented, disjointed workgroups.

 TIP: Remember, messages can queue for a user even if they are not logged on, therefore if you use this service remember to time and date your messages and include information about where a user can seek updates concerning a problem to which you have alerted them.

Software Shadow Copy Provider

Installed by default (Professional)
Recommendation: Disable (manual by default)
Severity: Low

A legacy application that Microsoft has continued to include and has recently updated is the Microsoft Backup Service. The shadow copy service allows Microsoft Backup to create "snapshots" of volumes. It is one of the many services that depend on the Remote Procedure Call (RPC) service, which is ideal to disable from a security perspective.

Disabling this service might produce one or more messages in your event log if you have services that depend on it. Typically this is used only for locally running backup software, but you should test this in your environment, especially if you are backing up users' workstations instead of just network shares and servers.

NetMeeting Remote Desktop Sharing

Installed by default (Professional)
Recommendation: Disable (manual by default)
Severity: High

Needless to say there are few things more serious than "sharing" in a Microsoft environment. This is by no means an exception. This service, while protected by permissions, is a network-based service that allows remote users to control your desktop and assume any privileges that you yourself might have. Needless to say, it gets more complex if individual users have administrative rights to their workstations.

Even if you are using NetMeeting, there can be little reason to keep this service at manual. If you want to share a desktop, build a demo workstation that can be used for this purpose and keep it turned off when not in use.

Network Connections

Installed by default
Recommendation: Manual (manual by default)
Severity: High (network abuse)

According to Microsoft, this service is responsible for managing the Network and Dialup Connections folders. It is responsible for helping the computer manage local area networking (LAN) and any remote (wide area networking) connections you might be using.

As with any service that allows remote network mapping, if you are not doing so over an encrypted link, you are asking for trouble. It is fairly easy to get around the primitive security measures found in nonencrypted links.

Network Dynamic Data Exchange (DDE)

Installed by default
Recommendation: Disable (unless you use remote ClipBook)
Severity: High (network abuse, information dispersal)

The Network DDE service seems to be a concept that had a greater purpose that is yet to materialize. Right now the only thing it connects to is the ClipBook service that we recommended that you disable.

The Microsoft description says it is a network transport and security service for DDE programs running locally and remotely. Again, test in your lab, and if you find anything besides ClipBook, let us know.

Network DDE DSDM Service

Installed by default
Recommendation: Disable (manual by default)
Severity: High (network abuse, information dispersal)

This service is the same as the Network DDE service listed. Somehow these are related, but not a whole lot of information is available about either service. Tests determine that it is related to remote use of the ClipBook service that we recommended that you disable.

Remote Registry Service

Installed by default
Recommendation: Disable
Severity: High (allows your registry to be remotely edited)

The remote registry service should be disabled unless you know and plan on using the registry changing ability of the service on a regular basis.

Server Service

Installed by default

Recommendation: Enable

Severity: Medium (deals with printing and sharing)

The server service is at the root of a lot of what Windows does, partly responsible for file, printer, and named pipe sharing. The workstation service also depends on the server service, and the workstation service is essential to the operation of Windows.

SSDP Discovery Service

Installed by default

Recommendation: Disable (manual by default)

Severity: Medium (device manipulation)

The SSDP discovery service allows the discovery of UPnP devices. UPnP is kind of the big brother of PnP; the safe devices such as scanners, printers, joysticks, and so on can be supported by UPnP, but in reality the goal of UPnP is much broader. Some hope that UPnP will one day connect your computer to your refrigerator, TV, and, of course, DVD and playback equipment. We are yet to see anything specific that is really exciting, but there are a lot of vendors (more than 30 at the time this book is published) who are working on the idea.

Task Scheduler Services

Installed by default

Recommendation: Enable

Severity: Medium (bad commands could be executed)

The task scheduler service is much like the CRON application on UNIX. It allows users or administrators to schedule jobs to be run at a later time or date. This could include running a job at a specific time on a recurring basis.

Terminal Services

Installed by default

Recommendation: Depends on security policy

Severity: High (deals with remote desktop management)

Terminal service is essentially the remote desktop service much like pcAnywhere or VNC. It is typically disabled because of the risks it presents.

Wireless Zero Configuration Service

Installed by default
Recommendation: Depends on your use of wireless services
Severity: Low

This service is discussed in Chapter 10, Wireless Configuration, in greater detail.

Service and Application Auditing

As mentioned earlier, security has many components. This chapter tackles at least two of the major components: preventive actions and auditing. In this section, we talk exclusively about auditing. With auditing, there are three challenges you need to overcome in any organization. The first is the accusatory nature of auditing. You can deal with this in two ways: by limiting the knowledge of the auditing steps you have taken, or by informing those who ask that everyone from the highest level of the company on down is audited for the overall benefit of the company.

The second challenge you need to deal with is determining the level of auditing your organization requires. Too little auditing leaves an incomplete picture, too much overwhelms the staff assigned to deal with the auditing. The processing of too much audited information and the subsequent storage of the information quickly becomes an issue.

This section of the chapter has two goals: to address in limited detail some of the above concerns, and to help you identify changes you can make in your Windows XP environment to enhance auditing and the advantages that auditing provides you. Observations are taken from personal experience along with recommendations provided by Microsoft and other reputable service providers. Your mileage may vary, and therefore you may want to do additional research on the subject.

On the first matter of the accusatory nature of auditing, it is usually a good policy to take an approach that keeps auditing somewhat secretive and also addresses concerns that everyone in the company is subjected to the auditing. You need to keep your auditing policy away from the public eye, because the more that is known about what and where you audit, the easier it is to identify the weaknesses in the auditing policy.

It is impossible to completely avoid anyone detecting auditing in place. Some of that auditing will be installed in environments where users have administrative privilege and therefore they can review that auditing policy. When that happens you must quickly let the personnel know that they must keep what they know to themselves and that they should not continue to pry. Auditing is in place to protect not only the company but to protect individuals as well, because it identifies when and who was involved when an event occurs and eliminates those not responsible.

System Auditing

The essence of system auditing involves knowing when someone logs in to or out of a system, when they changed their password, and whether their login was interactive or not. Beyond that, the only remaining issues are changes to the system by the personnel who have the necessary access to the system. These changes could range from a shutdown or restart of a system, through changes to the policies, auditing, or application preferences of a system.

Commonly, an administrator makes performance changes to a system in an attempt to streamline or speed up critical applications. He or she typically does something like starting, stopping, or changing the startup state of an application. It can be one of the most complex problems to troubleshoot when an application fails to start as you expect the next time the system is booted, not knowing that a service the application depends on has been set to "manual" when previously it was automatic and running.

Of course, the concept of "multiuser" has expanded in recent versions of Windows. In Windows 2000, it became easier to apply the multiple-user facility with Terminal Services, and now with Windows XP, direct multiuser is available natively. In most previous versions of the operating system, once one user had logged on interactively, the system was mostly unavailable to other users. Applications such as IIS and commerce components were still available, however. With versions of Windows 2000 and XP, you can have multiple interactive users logged on at the same time, so changes to the environment can be more dramatic or pronounced.

Auditing can be broken down into two components. First, changes to the environment that cover either a single computer model or a multiple domain model. Second, changes that are specific to your environment if you are applying it to one system, or if you are deploying it across a domain. Therefore, before you can begin auditing effectively, you must know whether it would be a single system or multiple systems.

The first and most basic thing we need to look at from an auditing perspective is audit policies. Audit policies define access to resources and help an administrator track success or failure to these resources. By default, auditing in general and specifically audit policies are not enabled; audit categories that can be tracked are listed here in abbreviated format:

1. **Account logon events:** Log an event each time a user attempts to log in to the system. For example, specific logged events could include login failures for unknown accounts, violations of time restriction, or accounts that have expired. You can also track users who log on locally with expired privileges and determine if an account attempt was made by a locked account.

2. **Account management:** This is a cool feature that helps you determine when a user account is managed or manipulated and helps you track user rights management.

3. **Logon events:** This tracks events occurring over the network or generated by a service startup. (Interactive logins or service startups trigger this event.)

4. **Object access:** This event triggers when a resource such as a shared folder or a printer is accessed.

5. **Policy changes:** This logs an event each time one of your security policies is successfully or unsuccessfully changed.

6. **Use of privileges:** This is for special events or special privileges such as changing the system time.

7. **Process tracking:** This provides detailed tracking of processes that a user launches while accessing the system. This might be useful for an administrator if he or she is interested in tracking activities of a specific user.

8. **System events:** This is designed to log specific system events, such as when a machine is shut down or restarted by a user.

Registry Tweaking

Let's begin by saying four things. One, registry editing is very risky; therefore, if you are not comfortable making changes to your registry, hire someone who is. Two, back up your registry at every opportunity when editing. Because it is essentially a text file with a lot of weird commands, you can have many copies. Just make sure to keep them easily identifiable. Three, respect the recovery process; have whatever process you use understood and prepared, including any disks or recovery media prepared and updated. Four, there are hundreds of registry hacks and changes that you can make, so do not get carried away.

Because there are hundreds of changes, and only a few really fit the purpose of this book, we cover just those few. Unfortunately, there is no "Registry Hacking Encyclopedia" available that covers all of the changes you can make. If you know what you want to do, and it is not covered here, search the Internet for it.

While some changes may be advantageous to tweak in a corporate environment, including those that involve restricting access to the server or workstation administrative components, some of these include limiting or eliminating the ability for users to install programs with the *.msi extension, and limit or remove user access to *.mmc or Management Console access.

The tweaking is broken down into four categories: performance, reliability, security, and helpful enhancements. But first, because of the importance of your registry, remember three things:

1. Always back up your registry before and after you make any changes, and have these changes available on removable media (we recommend a floppy disk).
2. Always have an emergency recovery disk so that you can restore the system in an emergency; however, this is no substitute for effective, tested backups or restorable systems.
3. Changing the registry can cause a system to become unstable or completely stop working. Making changes to the registry as the following disclaimer states is risky and should only be attempted by someone who is familiar with how the registry works, what components are changeable, and what components are not.

MICROSOFT DISCLAIMER: Modifying the registry can cause serious problems that could require you to reinstall your operating system. If you have not taken the necessary steps to recover from a catastrophic failure, or if you are doing this on a production system, we pity you. You should only use this information for "training" purposes and know that it was provided at your own risk.

Performance

While this is not really meant as a performance book, we include one enhancement in this chapter to improve your performance. If you increase the number of buffers that the redirector reserves for network performance, it may increase your network throughput. Each extra execution thread that you configure takes 1K of additional nonpaged pool memory, but only if your applications actually use them. To configure additional buffers and threads, create new DWORD values or modify the existing values called:

- **MaxCmds:** The range is 0–255 and the default is 15
- **MaxThreads:** Set it to the same value as MaxCmds

You may also want to increase the value of MaxCollectionCount. This value represents the buffer for character-mode named pipes writes. The default is 16 and the range is 0–65535.

Key: `HKEY_LOCAL_MACHINE\SYSTEM\CurrentControlSet\Services\`
`Lanman Workstation\Parameters`
Data Type: `REG_DWORD (DWORD VALUE)`

Reliability

Because Windows XP was designed to be an operating system that Microsoft envisioned being around much longer than previous versions, there are several interesting features that are outlined here.

Auto Update

In previous versions of Windows you had to visit a Web site to update the critical and not so critical components of your Windows system. Both good and bad news, this has changed significantly in Windows XP, where it is now a service and can be set to provide automatic updates. If you are not diligent about keeping them up-to-date, the notices can be somewhat annoying.

Dynamic Update

In previous versions of Windows, the files found on the CD were clubbed together months or years before you began your installation; therefore, you would be working with files that had scores of bugs, exploits, and things that needed to be updated that you had to do after you installed. With Windows XP, you can do a "Dynamic Update" during the install, in which after the networking component has been set up, Windows automatically updates and uses files that are outside the CD and therefore not as susceptible to bugs and exploits.

Last Known Good Configurations

In previous versions of Windows (especially Windows 2000), the last known good configuration was really meant to provide a backup and reloading capabilities of the registry. With Windows XP, the last known good configuration now also includes device drivers and therefore when you need to back up, you have more of your hardware available to you to make the recovery much easier.

Automated System Recovery

Windows XP introduces Automated System Recovery (ASR), an advanced option of the backup tool (NTBackup.exe). ASR provides the ability to save and restore applications, the system state, and critical files on the system and boot partitions. ASR replaces the Emergency Repair Disk used with Windows 2000 and Windows NT 4.0.

This feature also provides the plug-and-play mechanism required by ASR to back up plug-and-play portions of the registry and restore that information to the registry. This is useful in a variety of disaster-recovery scenarios—for example, if a hard disk fails and loses all configuration parameters and information, ASR can be applied and the backup of the system data is restored.

Error Messaging and Product Support

Windows XP now offers better, more meaningful error messages that allow you to better understand the errors that you encounter and to help you take specific, appropriate action to resolve them. The new error messages can help you resolve system problems and in less disruptive ways than restarting the system.

They also help Microsoft Product Support Services (PSS) offer better, more efficient support by providing the information support engineers need to focus on the specific problem. As a result, both users and PSS engineers save valuable time in troubleshooting. And with Windows Messenger and Remote Assistance, you can now share control of your system with Microsoft support engineers for online troubleshooting and problem resolution.

Online Crash Analysis

New to Windows XP is the Online Crash Analysis feature. With Online Crash Analysis, if you experience a system failure such as a "blue screen" crash event or Stop error, the next time you run Windows XP, you can easily use a browser to upload the system log details associated with the shutdown event to the Microsoft PSS Web site. Microsoft will analyze the report and send the results back to you by e-mail within 24 hours.

If a resolution to the error is known, you will receive a list of actions and perhaps files to resolve the problem. In cases where Microsoft cannot provide a solution for your particular Stop error, all information that you submit is used to further improve the quality and reliability of Windows. You can check the status of your reported event at any time at the Microsoft Online Crash Analysis site: *http://oca.microsoft.com/en/Welcome.asp.*

Shared DLL Support

Because many Windows-based applications perform similar functions with Windows (for example, saving files), they often share operating system components like dynamic link libraries (DLL). Sharing these components can sometimes cause problems if these applications rely on different versions of the components. To offset the negative effects of sharing, Windows XP supports the safe sharing of components, referred to as side-by-side (SxS) component sharing.

Instead of having a single version of a component that assumes backward compatibility, side-by-side component sharing enables multiple versions of a Component Object Model (COM) or Win32 application programming interface (API) component to run at the same time. With Windows XP, some of the key system components that are more likely to compromise stability are available as SxS components.

Windows XP allows Win32 components and applications to use the exact version of Microsoft components with which they are tested without being affected by other application or operating system updates. It does this by relying on XML files that contain metadata about application configuration such as COM classes, interfaces, and type libraries.

Shutdown Event Tracker

Windows XP now includes a utility called Shutdown Event Tracker, which provides a simple and standard mechanism that you can use to consistently document the reasons for shutting down or restarting your computer. You can then use this information to analyze the root causes of shutdowns and develop a more complete understanding of your system environment.

To record the reason for a shutdown or restart, you can enter it into the Shut Down Windows dialog box. The Shut Down Windows dialog box is displayed as part of the shutdown sequence or when restarting a system after a sudden shutdown. Windows provides a predefined set of reasons from which to choose. You can also stipulate your own reasons for shutting down the system. The information you provide here is recorded in the system log in Event Viewer. By default, Shutdown Event Tracker is disabled for Windows XP.

In addition to tracking reasons for shutdowns, Shutdown Event Tracker also takes a snapshot of the system state before shutdown, identifying system resource limits that are being approached or exceeded just before you initiate a system restart. It captures a number of parameters about each process running on the system, each page file on the system, each disk on the system, and overall system resource usage. You can later review the reasons for shutting down in the system log together with the corresponding system states and analyze this information.

This information is critical to understanding the root cause for system performance degradations and the performance problems that necessitate restarts. This can help improve the way you use your computer. For example, you may discover the advantage of reducing the number of applications running simultaneously and as a result, improve system uptime.

 NOTE: The Shutdown Event Tracker is not active by default.

The application window has been improved in Windows XP to allow you to easily close applications that are unresponsive. In previous versions of Windows, there was no easy way to close unresponsive applications; you were required to open Task Manager, select the application, and then click a button to close it. In Windows XP, you can still access the window of the unresponsive application. The top bar of the application window informs you that the current application is not responding, but you can now close the application by clicking the application's Close button. Clicking the Close button is equivalent to launching Task Manager and ending an unresponsive application.

Device Driver Resiliency Improvements

Installing a new device can sometimes be problematic. Windows XP has two improvements that significantly reduce the problems caused by defective device drivers: Windows Driver Protection and Driver Rollback.

Windows Driver Protection

Windows Driver Protection is a new feature that keeps you from installing and loading defective device drivers—that is, drivers that cause the system to stop functioning indefinitely (hang) or shut down unexpectedly (blue screen). A database of known defective drivers, maintained by Microsoft, is used to determine which device drivers should not be installed or loaded. An updated database is available to users through the Windows Update Web page.

If you attempt to install a new device with the Add Hardware Wizard, and the driver for that device is defective, a dialog box tells you that the driver was not installed because it causes your system to malfunction. This dialog box also contains a link to a Web page that gives you more information as well as any available driver updates.

If you use another process to install the driver—whether by using the CreateService API set or by directly writing keys into the registry—and it is later found through the use of the Windows Update Web site to be defective, the driver loading process stops the driver from being loaded.

A new icon appears in the notification area indicating that a device or application may not work due to a defective driver. When you click on the icon, the Help and Support Center displays specific details about any devices or associated drivers and any subsequent applications that were disabled.

The page in the Help and Support Center presents a list of the drivers that have been blocked since the last time the system was started. For each driver, its name, associated application, or device is displayed. It also provides a link to appropriate Help content (local or remote depending on network connectivity) that tells you how to get a newer version of the driver that works correctly.

Automated or remotely administered installations (sometimes referred to as *headless* because they usually do not have a monitor) do not receive the notifications. Also any user who is telnetted into the system does not receive the notification that drivers or applications are disabled other than there being an event log entry. Each event log entry contains a link to the Windows Update Web page to give you more information and possible updates to the driver.

Device Driver Rollback

Driver Rollback helps ensure system stability, much like the last known good configuration option first available in Windows 2000 Safe Mode. When you update a driver, a copy of the previous driver package is automatically saved in a special subdirectory of the system files (for every driver that you back up, a new value is added to the Backup keys located in the appropriate section of the registry).

If the new driver does not work properly, you can restore the previous driver by accessing the Driver tab for the device in the Device Manager and clicking Roll Back Driver. Driver Rollback permits only one level of rollback (only one prior driver version can be saved at a time); this feature is available for all device classes, except printers.

Security

In the first section, we approach the issue of the Control Panel. Often, in a larger installation base, you want to restrict modification by users as much as possible so that you limit or restrict the support calls you receive for innocent user changes. One of the best ways to approach this is to hide part of or the complete control panel applet area based on the user's level.

You may have histories on a user to help you determine the best course of action. The three "fixes" mentioned here emerged from interviews with users on the likelihood that they would make modifications.

There are multiple ways to make some of these changes; we have tried to identify at least two ways that you can make the required modification. One way is based on the registry and therefore is considerably more risky. However, all the changes listed in this section can be prohibitively damaging; therefore, attempting these changes on a virtual machine or a workstation that can easily be rebuilt should be your first course of action.

First, we cover making the necessary modifications using the Group Policy Editor, which is probably the best way to make the modification change.

We cover both how to disable it completely as well as disabling specific applets. The changes can be done per machine, on a site, domain, or organizational unit based on your specific needs. We demonstrate a local machine change.

 NOTE: These settings apply only to the Control Panel window and the Start menu. They do not prevent users from running Control Panel tools.

Hide Control Panel Tools

1. Click **Start**, click **Run**, type mmc in the Open box, and then click **OK**.
2. On the **File** menu, click **Add/Remove Snap-in**.
3. Click **Add**.
4. Click **Group Policy Object Editor**, and then click **Add**.
5. Click the target Group Policy Object (GPO). The default GPO is Local Computer. Click **Browse** to select the GPO that you want, and then click **Finish**.
6. Click **Close**, and then click **OK**.
7. Expand **User Configuration**, expand **Administrative Templates**, and then click **Control Panel**.
8. In the right pane, double-click **Hide specified Control Panel applets**.
9. Click **Enabled**. This setting removes Control Panel tools from the Control Panel window and the Start menu. To specify the Control Panel tools that you want to hide, click **Show**.
10. In the **Show Contents** dialog box, click **Add**, type the file name of the Control Panel tool that you want to hide in the **Enter the item to be added** box, and then click **OK**. Control Panel tools use the .cpl

extension and are located in the %Systemroot%\System32 folder. To find the file name of a Control Panel tool, search for .cpl files in the %Systemroot%\System32 folder. To do so:

11. Click **Start**, and then click **Search**.

12. Click **All files and folders**. In the **All or part of the file name box**, type `*.cpl`, in the **Look in** box, click **Local Disk** (drive:), where drive is the drive on which Windows is installed, and then click **Search**.

13. Repeat step 10 for each Control Panel tool that you want to hide, and then click **OK**.

14. Click **OK**, and then quit the Group Policy Object Editor snap-in.

Show Only Specific Control Panel Tools

1. Click **Start**, click **Run**, type mmc in the **Open** box, and then click **OK**.

2. On the **File** menu, click **Add/Remove Snap-in**.

3. Click **Add**.

4. Click **Group Policy Object Editor**, and then click **Add**.

5. Click the target GPO. The default GPO is Local Computer. Click **Browse** to select the GPO that you want, and then click **Finish**.

6. Click **Close**, and then click **OK**.

7. Expand **User Configuration**, expand **Administrative Templates**, and then click **Control Panel**.

8. In the right pane, double-click **Show only specified Control Panel applets**.

9. Click **Enabled**. This setting removes all Control Panel tools from the Control Panel window and the Start menu, except for the items that you specify. If you do not specify any tools or folders to display, the Control Panel window is empty. To specify the Control Panel tools that you want to display, click **Show**. Control Panel tools use the .cpl extension and are located in the %Systemroot%\System32 folder. To find the file name of a Control Panel tool, search for .cpl files in the %Systemroot%\System32 folder. To do so:

10. Click **Start**, and then click **Search**.

11. Click **All files and folders**. In the **All or part of the file name** box, type `*.cpl`, in the **Look in** box, click **Local Disk** (drive:), where drive is the drive on which Windows is installed, and then click **Search**.

12. In the **Show Contents** dialog box, click **Add**, type the file name of the Control Panel tool that you want to display in the **Enter the item to be added** box, and then click **OK**.

13. Repeat step 12 for each Control Panel tool that you want to display, and then click **OK**.

14. Click **OK**, and then quit the Group Policy Object Editor snap-in.

The following is a list of .cpl files and the corresponding Control Panel tools.

.cpl File	Control Panel Tool
Access.cpl	Accessibility
Appwiz.cpl	Add or Remove Program
Desk.cpl	Display
Hdwwiz.cpl	Add Hardware
Inetcpl.cpl	Internet Options
Intl.cpl	Regional and Language Options
Joy.cpl	Game Controllers
Keymgr.cpl	Stored User Names and Passwords
Liccpa.cpl	Licensing
Main.cpl	Mouse
Mmsys.cpl	Sound and Audio Devices
Ncpa.cpl	Network Connections
Nwc.cpl	Netware client connectivity
Odbccp32.cpl	ODBC Data Source Administrator
Powercfg.cpl	Power Options
Sysdm.cpl	System
Telephon.cpl	Phone and Modem Options
Timedate.cpl	Date and Time
Sapi.cpl	Speech

Hide Control Panel Applets (Selective Restriction)

You can hide specific Control Panel applets, which allows you to determine specifically what your users can and cannot change. This is a good step to take if you are developing a base image that needs to be fair and reasonable to a wide variety of users, yet restricts certain applets that you feel none of your users should be accessing.

It is important to note that you need to modify each and every applet that you do not want to load; it is also important to note that unlike previous and future registry changes we talk about, the data value for this hive/key is a "Yes" or "No" whereas previous and future discussion are typically around bits "0" for Off or False and "1" for On or True.

To accomplish this you need to open your registry editor and go to the following hive and key location (remember you have to do this for each applet you want to disable that is listed here):

User Key: `[HKEY_CURRENT_USER\Control Panel\don't load]`
Data Type: `REG_SZ (String Value)`
Value Data: `Yes or No`

Restrict Use of Management Console Snap-ins

Another problem that you want to prevent in a large installation base is the use of the Control Panel Management Console (MMC) snap-ins that allow modification of system values and other configuration data.

To accomplish this, you need to again open your favorite registry editor and go to the following hive and key location:

```
HKEY_CURRENT_USER\Software\Policies\Microsoft\MMC
```

You now need to create or modify a DWORD value of "RestrictToPermitted-Snapins" and set it to one of the following values:

0 = default, enable modification
1 = enable the restriction

To recap:

User Key: `[HKEY_CURRENT_USER\Software\Policies\Microsoft\MMC]`
Value Name: `RestrictToPermittedSnapins`
Data Type: `REG_DWORD (DWORD Value)`

Disable the Control Panel

This modification is slightly more restrictive than the previously mentioned change to the MMC snap-ins. You can disable the Control Panel at two levels: You can disable it on a per-user basis (which requires you to be logged on as that user), or you can disable it at the system level; the choice depends on the level of security you require.

To accomplish this at the per-user level, you need to open your registry editor and go to the following hive and key location (for the current user):

```
HKEY_CURRENT_USER\Software\Microsoft\Windows\CurrentVersion\
Policies\Explorer
```

To accomplish this at the system level, which affects all users, you need to navigate to the following hive and key location:

```
HKEY_LOCAL_MACHINE\Software\Microsoft\Windows\CurrentVersion\
Policies\Explorer
```

Regardless of which key you decide to modify, you need to edit a DWORD value of "NoControlPanel," and you need to create one if it is not already there. The value has the standard flags of 0 for disable the restriction and 1 for enable the restriction.

0 = disable restriction
1 = enable restriction

To recap:

User Key: [HKEY_CURRENT_USER\Software\Microsoft\Windows\ CurrentVersion\Policies\Explorer]

System Key: [HKEY_LOCAL_MACHINE\Software\Microsoft\Windows\ CurrentVersion\Policies\Explorer]

Value Name: NoControlPanel

Data Type: REG_DWORD (DWORD Value)

Control Panel Tweaks

- **Hide Accessibility Options in Control Panel:** Hides Accessibility Options Control Panel applet. Option affects selected user, see the status bar. Reboot your PC to activate or deactivate this option. Applicable to Windows NT/2000/XP.

- **Hide Add/Remove Programs in Control Panel:** Hides Add/Remove Programs Control Panel applet. Option affects selected user, see the status bar. Reboot your PC to activate or deactivate this option. Applicable to Windows NT/2000/XP.

- **Hide Display in Control Panel:** Hides Display Control Panel applet. Option affects selected user, see the status bar. Reboot your PC to activate or deactivate this option. Applicable to Windows NT/2000/XP.

- **Hide Add Hardware in Control Panel:** Hides Add Hardware Control Panel applet. Option affects selected user, see the status bar. Reboot your PC to activate or deactivate this option. Applicable to Windows NT/ 2000/XP.

- **Hide Internet Options in Control Panel:** Hides Internet Options Control Panel applet. Option affects selected user, see the status bar. Reboot your PC to activate or deactivate this option. Applicable to Windows NT/2000/XP.

- **Hide Regional/Language Options in Control Panel:** Hides Regional/Language Options Control Panel applet. Option affects selected user, see the status bar. Reboot your PC to activate or deactivate this option. Applicable to Windows NT/2000/XP.

- **Hide Game Controllers in Control Panel:** Hides Game Controllers Control Panel applet. Option affects selected user, see the status bar. Reboot your PC to activate or deactivate this option. Applicable to Windows NT/2000/XP.

- **Hide Mouse in Control Panel:** Hides Mouse Control Panel applet. Option affects selected user, see the status bar. Reboot your PC to activate or deactivate this option. Applicable to Windows NT/2000/XP.

- **Hide Sounds/Audio Devices in Control Panel:** Hides Sounds/Audio Devices Control Panel applet. Option affects selected user, see the status bar. Reboot your PC to activate or deactivate this option. Applicable to Windows NT/2000/XP.

- **Hide User Accounts in Control Panel:** Hides User Accounts Control Panel applet. Option affects selected user, see the status bar. Reboot your PC to activate or deactivate this option. Applicable to Windows XP.

- **Hide Power Options in Control Panel:** Hides Power Options Control Panel applet. Option affects selected user, see the status bar. Reboot your PC to activate or deactivate this option. Applicable to Windows NT/2000/XP.

- **Hide System in Control Panel:** Hides System Control Panel applet. Option affects selected user, see the status bar. Reboot your PC to activate or deactivate this option. Applicable to Windows NT/2000/XP.

- **Hide Phone/Modem Options in Control Panel:** Hides Phone/Modem Options Control Panel applet. Option affects selected user, see the status bar. Reboot your PC to activate or deactivate this option. Applicable to Windows NT/2000/XP.

- **Hide Date/Time in Control Panel:** Hides Date/Time Control Panel applet. Option affects selected user, see the status bar. Reboot your PC to activate or deactivate this option. Applicable to Windows NT/2000/XP.

- **Hide Network Connections in Control Panel:** Hides Network Connections Control Panel applet. Option affects selected user, see the status bar. Reboot your PC to activate or deactivate this option. Applicable to Windows NT/2000.

- **Hide ODBC Administration in Control Panel:** Hides ODBC Administration Control Panel applet. Option affects selected user, see the status bar. Reboot your PC to activate or deactivate this option. Applicable to Windows NT/2000/XP.

- **Hide Scanners/Cameras in Control Panel:** Hides Scanners/Cameras Control Panel applet. Option affects selected user, see the status bar. Reboot your PC to activate or deactivate this option. Applicable to Windows NT/2000.

- **Hide Faxes in Control Panel:** Hides Faxes Control Panel applet. Option affects selected user, see the status bar. Reboot your PC to activate or deactivate this option. Applicable to Windows NT/2000.

Restrict Installation of Programs from Removable Media

A lot of those reading this material are working with large installation bases where restricting configuration changes really make life easier. While it is impossible without massive modification of the operating system and making rights and group access foolproof, we offer a few tidbits that you may find useful in at least slowing down massive modification of your user's systems.

The first is to restrict installation of programs from removable media; this will include CD-ROM, floppy disks, and large capacity storage media such as external hard drives and USB devices that have storage capacity.

To accomplish this, you need to open your favorite registry editor and go to the following hive and key location:

```
HKEY_CURRENT_USER\Software\Policies\Microsoft\Windows\Installer
```

You now need to create or modify a DWORD value of "Disable Media" and set it to the following value:

0 = enable media to be installed
1 = disable media installation

To recap:

User Key: [HKEY_CURRENT_USER\Software\Policies\Microsoft\Windows\Installer]
Value Name: DisableMedia
Data Type: REG_DWORD (DWORD Value)
Value Data: (0 = default, 1 = enable restriction)

Helpful Enhancements

System Notifications

When your Windows system receives an administrative alert, does it notify all users? You can set it to notify a specific user to prevent stale notifications waiting around for other users to log on at a later time.

> *Key:* `HKEY_LOCAL_MACHINE\SYSTEM\CurrentControlSet\Services\`
> `Alerter\Parameters`
>
> *Data:* `REG_MULTI_SZ` (Multistring Value)

There is a Multistring Value called AlertNames in which you put the names of persons you want to receive administrative alerts. Place a space between names, for example: "jdoe jsmith."

Quick Launch Changes

One of the things we found most useful to our systems, but that may not be of much interest in a corporate environment, is the use of individual icons for shutdown, restart, and to lock the computer. The latter is very important in any environment. We outline all three shortcuts, but you may install the ones you find useful in your environment.

First, let's create the most important and most complex shortcut, which is the one that allows you to lock the computer.

In previous versions of Windows, you could Ctrl + Alt + Del and lock the computer. In Windows XP, Microsoft has introduced the principle of a truly multiuser system; therefore, there is no easy way to lock the computer, so we created an icon for it.

Here are the steps you need to follow to create this icon:

1. Right-click on an empty area on your desktop.
2. Select **New** and then **Shortcut** as shown in Figure 15.1.
3. In the first dialog box displayed, "Create Shortcut Wizard," type `Rundll32.exe User32.dll,LockWorkStation`. Be aware that there is no space between the comma and LockWorkStation. Then click **Next**.
4. Name the shortcut "Lock This PC" or anything else you choose, and then click on **Finish**. As before, to make it aesthetically pleasing and to distinguish the shortcut, you may want to change the displayed image. We have our own set of icons. You can use a default or if you have your own, feel free to use them.
5. To unlock the workstation or server, hold the **Windows** key (or Alt + Esc + L). This presents the login screen where you can choose the user and enter the password.

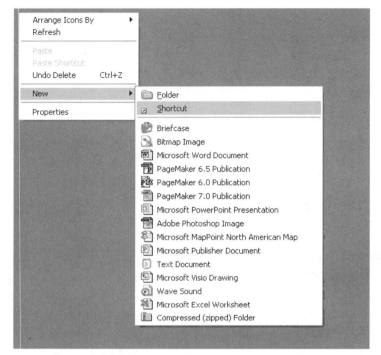

Figure 15.1   Create a shortcut on your desktop.

Now, let's create the shutdown shortcut:

1. Right-click on any empty area on your desktop. It can be anywhere, as long as there are no other icons or files located in that spot.
2. In the menu that is displayed, click on **New** and then **Shortcut**. Now a Shortcut Wizard is displayed. In the first box, type shutdown -s -t 00. This says shutdown –silent with a –time of 00 seconds.
3. Name the shortcut something that you will remember—ours is called "Shutdown This PC"—and then click on **Finish**.

As a final touch, we changed the image displayed for our new shortcut. If you want to do this, either with a default icon or with one of your own customized icons, right-click on the new icon and select **Properties**. Choose **Change Icon**, and then select the image that you want to use.

To create the restart icon, the process is the same, but to keep the confusion to a minimum, we outline the steps here:

1. Right-click on any empty area on your desktop. It can be anywhere, as long as there are no other icons or files located in that spot.

2. In the menu that is displayed, click on **New** and then **Shortcut**.

3. Now the Shortcut Wizard is displayed. In the first box, type `shutdown -r -t 00`. This says shutdown –restart with a –time of 00 seconds.

4. Name the shortcut something that you will remember—ours is called "Restart This PC"—and then click on **Finish**.

5. As a final touch, we changed the image displayed for our new shortcut. If you want to do this, either with a default icon or with one of your own customized icons, right-click the new icon and select **Properties**. Choose **Change Icon**, and then select the image that you want to use.

Performance Enhancement

Although the changes described in this section do not necessarily enhance the security of a system a great deal, they can greatly enhance the performance of your systems and therefore might be worthwhile additions.

Shutdown on Speed

By altering a few registry settings, you can dramatically decrease the amount of time it takes for Windows to shut down. To do this, first open up the registry editor and navigate to

`HKEY_CURRENT_USER\Control Panel\Desktop\`

Once there, find the value HungAppTimeout and make sure it is set to 5,000 (the default value). Now, in the same folder, look for the value WaitToKillApp-Timeout. Set this to 4,000 (the default is 20,000) as shown in Figure 15.2.

Lastly, navigate to the folder

`HKEY_LOCAL_MACHINE\System\CurrentControlSet\Control\`

and change the value WaitToKillServiceTimeout to 4,000 as well. Another thing that helps speed up shutting down is going to Control Panel, then

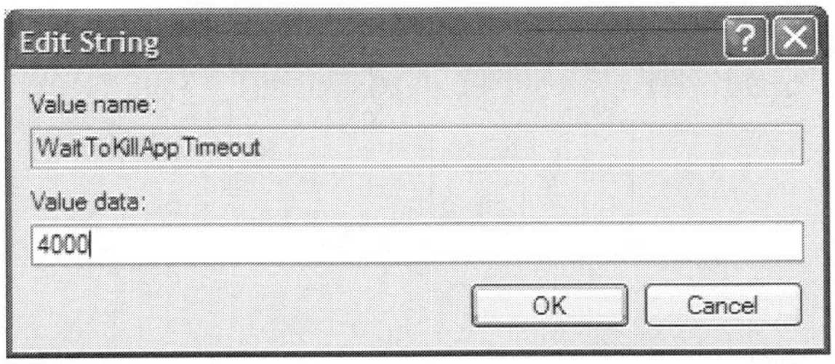

Figure 15.2   Set the shutdown interval to 4,000.

Administrative Tools, then Services, and then setting the NVidia Driver Help service to Manual.

Unloading DLLs

Another important and highly relevant security change (that also improves performance) is configuring Explorer not to cache unused DLLs. The attempt here is to cache commonly used device drivers in order to speed the loading of these for applications that might frequently use them.

Explorer often caches DLL files in memory for a period of time after they have finished being used. This can result in large amounts of memory being taken up by DLL files that are not even being used. To stop this happening, navigate to

```
HKEY_LOCAL_MACHINE\SOFTWARE\Microsoft\Windows\CurrentVersion\
Explorer
```

Now you have to create a new subkey called AlwaysUnloadDLL with a default value of 1, as shown in Figure 15.3. If you want to disable this tweak, just delete the key.

NOTE: Windows has to restart for this tweak to take effect.

Hibernation

Another really quick and easy tweak: If you are not going to use Hibernation, make sure it is disabled, because Windows reserves an amount of hard drive space equal to that of your RAM for hibernation. To disable Hibernation (Figure 15.4), go to **Control Panel**, then **Power Options**, and then **Hibernate** tab.

QoS Tweaking

Windows XP provides Quality of Service Resource Reservation Protocol (QoSRRP). Basically, programs either use QoS APIs (and are passed through QoS when trying to access information through whatever bandwidth is available), or they are passed to another API called TCI. One of the differences

Figure 15.3   Select the AlwaysUnloadDLL key.

Figure 15.4   Changing hibernation settings.

between QoS and TCI is that it is possible to reserve bandwidth for QoS applications. This is great if you use QoS applications, but if you do not use any, it means that a percentage (20 percent by default) of your bandwidth goes unused.

L2 Cache Tweakage

The L2, or second-level, cache is an integral part of your CPU. However, Windows XP is very hit-or-miss at detecting it, so setting it manually is sometimes necessary. It is easy to do: You simply have to navigate to **Run** and then **Regedit**

```
HKEY_LOCAL_MACHINE\SYSTEM\CurrentControlSet\Control\Session
Manager\Memory Management\
```

in the registry and find the value SecondLevelDataCache. You must then adjust it to the value (in kilobytes) of the L2 Cache of your processor, as shown in Figure 15.5. You should be able to find the L2 Cache value of your processor from its manufacturer.

NOTE: The L2 Cache of your processor should be entered in decimal mode.

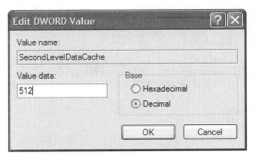

Figure 15.5   Adjusting the L2 Cache.

Brief Network Fix

This next one is a fix rather than a tweak. It is a convenience fix, but with a caveat: It fixes something that can decrease your security by making available shares to every account, including Guest. Do this *only* if you have encountered the problem and it is an issue, and certainly make sure you have the proper perimeter security. Basically, in another Windows XP quirk, it sometimes disallows network access to people, including the Guest account, meaning that most people cannot connect to your computer and access your shares, or other like items. To fix this problem, open the **Control Panel**, go to **Administrative Tools**, and open up **Local Security Settings** (Figure 15.6). Now go to **Local Policies** and then **User Rights Assignments**.

Now find the value called **Deny access to this computer from the network**. Right-click on it and go to **Properties**. Now, if the Guest account is in here, remove it by clicking it once and going to **Remove**, then close down the **Properties** dialog. While you are in the **User Rights Assignments** dialog, check the **Access this computer from the network Properties**, and make sure **Everyone** is in there (Figure 15.7).

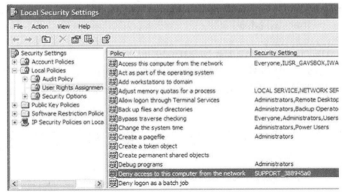

Figure 15.6   Open up Local Security Settings.

Figure 15.7 Make sure Everyone has access.

User Interface Tweaks

If you are having trouble trying to access computers over a network, hopefully these few adjustments will help.

Show File Extensions

1. In any folder that contains files click on the **Tools** menu and select **Folder Options**.
2. Then click on the **View** tab.
3. Locate where it lists **Hide extensions of known file types** and uncheck it.
4. Click **OK**.

Remove Shared Docs from My Computer

This one is really interesting. Finding the key listed would be impossible without the given information, but it is always the same. We have confirmed it on several systems.

1. Start **regedit**.
2. Navigate to `HKEY_LOCAL_MACHINESOFTWARE/Microsoft/Windows/CurrentVersion/Explorer/MyComputer/NameSpace/Delegate-Folders`.
3. Locate the key {59031a47-3f72-44a7-89c5-5595fe6b30ee}.
4. Right-click on it and select **delete**.
5. Reboot.

Turn Off Autoplay for CDs

1. Download and install **MS powertoys**, and then open **TweakUI**.
2. Click on **MyComputer**.
3. Select **Autoplay** and choose the drive by unchecking it.

Show Hidden Files

1. In any folder that contains files, click on the **Tools** menu and select **Folder Options**.
2. Click on the **View** tab.
3. Locate where it lists **Hidden files and folders** and select **Show hidden files and folders**.
4. Click **OK**.

Registry Tweak to Add Copy To and Move To to the Right-click Button

To add Copy to... and Move to... context menu options go to **Start**, then **Run**, then **Regedit**, and then create the following registry keys. In the examples below we renamed the Winzip key that we do not need in the right-click menu, changed it to "Copy To," and then added the value.

```
HKEY_CLASSES_ROOT\Directory\shellex\ContextMenuHandlers\Copy To
HKEY_CLASSES_ROOT\Directory\shellex\ContextMenuHandlers\Move To
HKEY_CLASSES_ROOT\*\shellex\ContextMenuHandlers\Copy To
HKEY_CLASSES_ROOT\*\shellex\ContextMenuHandlers\Move To
```

For all the Copy To set the default value to

```
{C2FBB630-2971-11d1-A18C-00C04FD75D13}
```

and for all the Move To set the default value to

```
{C2FBB631-2971-11d1-A18C-00C04FD75D13}.
```

Now when you right-click on a file or folder, two new options appear above the Send To option: Copy to Folder and Move to Folder. You can copy or move files or directories to other folders with this tweak.

Sort Your Start Menu

1. Open your main menu.
2. Select any program.
3. Right-click and choose **Sort by Name** and you are done.

Do Not Cache Folder Thumbnails

1. To make folders with thumbnail images start up faster, go to **Control Panel**, and then **Folder Options**.
2. Click on the **View** tab and uncheck **Do not cache thumbnails**.

Speed Up the Main Menu

1. Open **Tweak UI for WinXP** and select **Mouse**.
2. Under **Menu Speed** move the slider all the way over to **fast**.
3. Reboot.

Quick Switch User Screen

1. Press **Winkey + Q** and hold it for a second.
2. Press **Q** repeatedly to rotate to other users.

Create Your Own Pop-up Menu in the Taskbar

You can create your own pop-up window other than Start menu in the Taskbar.

1. Create a new folder and put all the shortcuts of the applications that you want to pop up in that folder.
2. Then right-click on **Taskbar**, then **Toolbars**, then **New Toolbar**, and select the folder.

System Performance Tweaks

Speed Up Diskcache

1. Open **regedit**
2. `[HKEY_LOCAL_MACHINESYSTEM/CurrentControlSet/Control-Session/Manager/MemoryManagement/IoPageLockLimit]`

3. Modify the value in Hex depending on the size of your RAM.
   RAM: modified value (Hex)
   64MB: 1,000
   128MB: 4,000
   256MB: 10,000
   512MB or more: 40,000
4. Reboot.

Disable Programs at Start-up

1. Go to **Start**, then **Run**.
2. Type `msconfig`.
3. Go to the **Startup** tab.
4. Uncheck anything you do not want to start when Windows XP boots up, but *be careful!*
5. Reboot.

Easily Disable Messenger

1. Go to **C:\Program Files\Messenger**.
2. Rename the **Messenger folder** to something like "MessengerOFF."

This does not slow down Outlook or hinder system performance.

Speed Up Network Browsing

1. Open up **regedit**.
2. Navigate to `HKEY_LOCAL_MACHINE/Software/Microsoft/Windows/Current Version/Explorer/RemoteComputer/NameSpace`
3. Find a key named {D6277990-4C6A-11CF-8D87-00AA0060F5BF}
4. Right-click on it and select **delete**.
5. Reboot.

Windows XP Memory Tweaks

The following are some Windows XP memory tweaks that are located in the Windows registry at: `HKEY_LOCAL_MACHINE/SYSTEM/CurrentControlSet/Control/SessionManager/MemoryManagement`.

DisablePagingExecutive

When enabled, this setting prevents the paging of the Win2k Executive files to the hard drive, causing the OS and most programs to be more responsive. However, it is advised that people perform this tweak *only* if they have a significant amount of RAM on their system (more than 128MB), because this setting does use a substantial portion of your system resources. By default, the value of this key is zero. To enable it, set it to 1.

LargeSystemCache

When enabled (the default on server versions of Windows 2000), this setting tells the OS to devote all but 4MB of system memory, which is left for disk caching, to the file system cache. The main effect is that it allows the computer to cache the OS kernel to memory, which makes the OS more responsive. The setting is dynamic and if for some reason more than 4MB is needed from the disk cache the space is released to it. By default, 8MB is earmarked for this purpose. At a performance hit when such changes are needed, the kernel gives up any space deemed necessary for another application. As with the previous key, change the value from zero to 1 to enable. Note that when you do this, you consume more of your system RAM than normal. While LargeSystemCache cuts back usage when other applications need more RAM, this process can impede performance in certain intensive situations. According to Microsoft, the "[zero] setting is recommended for servers running applications that do their own memory caching, such as Microsoft SQL Server, and for applications that perform best with ample memory, such as Internet Information Services."

IOPageLockLimit

This tweak is of questionable value to people who are not running some kind of server off of their computer, but we include it anyway. It boosts the Input/Output performance of your computer when it is doing a large amount of file transfers and other similar operations. This tweak does not do much of anything for a system that does not have a significant amount of RAM (128MB minimum), but systems with more than 128MB of RAM generally find a performance boost if this is set to between 8MB and 16MB. The default is 0.5MB, or 512KB. This setting requires a value in bytes, so multiply the desired number of megabytes by 1,048,576 (which is 1,024 × 1,024). Test out several settings and keep the one that seems to work best for your system.

Disable Unnecessary Services to Free System Resources

Services are programs that run when the computer starts up and continue to run because they aid the operating system's functionality. There are many services that load and are not needed that take up memory space and CPU time. Disabling these services frees up system resources that speed up your overall computer experience. We recommend that you sort through the list and read the descriptions and, depending on what you want to do with your computer, decide if you need that service. Remember, you can always turn the service back on if you find that you need it in the future.

Here is the procedure to turn off a service.

1. Click the **Start** button.
2. Select **Run** from the bottom of the right column.
3. Then type `services.msc` in the box and click **OK**.
4. Once the services window loads, you are ready to turn off unneeded services.
5. For instructional purposes, we turn off the Portable Media Serial Number service.
6. Find this service in the list and select it with the mouse.
7. Right-click and select **Properties**.
8. Once the Properties window loads, locate the **Start up type** drop-down box and select **disable**.
9. Then click **OK**. The next time the computer starts, the service will not load.

Do this with extreme care!

Internet Tweaks

Allow More Than Two Simultaneous Downloads in Internet Explorer 6

This tweak increases the number of maximum downloads to ten.

1. Start **Registry Editor**.
2. Locate the following key in the registry:
   HKEY_CURRENT_USER/Software/Microsoft/Windows/
   CurrentVersion/InternetSettings
3. On the **Edit** menu, click **Add Value**, and then add the following registry values:
   "MaxConnectionsPer1_0Server"=Dword:0000000a
   "MaxConnectionsPerServer"=Dword:0000000a
4. Quit **Registry Editor**.
5. Reboot.

Disable Schedule Task in Internet Explorer

IE 6.0 wants to run a scheduled task each time it connects to a server, which results in slower browsing.

To disable this delete the following key:

```
HKEY_LOCAL_MACHINE/Software/Microsoft/Windows/CurrentVersion/
explorer/RemoteComputer/NameSpace/{D6277990-4C6A-11CF-8D87-
00AA0060F5BF}
```

Delete Internet Browsing History

1. Launch Internet Explorer
2. Select **Tools** from the menu bar.
3. Then select **Internet Options** from the drop down menu.
4. When the Internet options load, click on the **General** tab.
5. Under the history section, change the days to keep in history to 0 (zero).
6. Click the **Clear History** button to get rid of everything else.
7. Click **OK**.
8. Clear **temp files** on close.

Clearing Temp Files on IE Close

The latest versions of Internet Explorer include some great new security improvements. For this tweak we talk about the feature that clears the temporary Internet files each time you close Internet Explorer.

1. Select **Tools** from the menu bar.
2. Then select **Internet Options** from the drop-down menu.
3. When Internet options load, click on the **Advanced** tab.
4. Under **Security** find where it says **Empty temporary Internet files folder when browser is closed** and check it.
5. Click **OK**.

Change Web Page Font Size on the Fly

If your mouse contains a wheel for scrolling, you can change font size on the fly when viewing a Web page. To do so: Press and hold the **Control** key. Scroll down (or toward yourself) to enlarge the font size. Scroll up (or away from yourself) to reduce the font size.

You also might find it useful to reduce font size when printing a Web page, so that you can fit more content on the page.

Disable or Adjust Taskbar Grouping

1. Right-click on the **Taskbar**.
2. Choose **Properties**.
3. Uncheck **Group** and similar taskbar buttons.

Automated System Recovery in Windows XP

Windows XP's Automated System Recovery (ASR) is an extension to the conventional backup-and-restore. It provides a framework for saving and recovering the Windows XP operating state in the event of a catastrophic system or hardware failure. Windows XP ASR recovers the target system in a two-step process. The first step, termed the *boot recovery process,* requires a new copy of Windows XP to be temporarily installed on the target system using the original distribution media. The second step, called the *OS restore process,* restores the files of a previously saved Windows XP installation using a backup-and-restore application (this deletes/overwrites some of the files installed by the boot recovery process).

 NOTE: Users of Windows XP Home are out of luck; ASR is not available on their system. While mention of this feature does exist in the backup utility of Windows XP Home, ASR is only functional in Windows XP Professional.

ASR Backup

The backup portion of ASR is accomplished through the ASR Wizard located in Backup. The Wizard backs up the system state, system services, and all disks associated with the operating system components. It also creates a file containing information about the backup, the disk configurations (including basic and dynamic volumes), and how to accomplish a restore.

To start the process, click **Backup** under All Programs/Accessories/System Tools. By default, Backup starts in Wizard mode. In this case it is easier to start in the Advanced Mode. To do so, just click the **Advanced Mode** link.

On the Welcome tab, click **Automated System Recovery Wizard** (Figure 15.8). This will start the Automated System Recovery Preparation Wizard, as shown in Figure 15.9. Click **Next** to continue.

The Wizard prompts you for a location and name for the media to store the backup file, as shown in Figure 15.10.

By default drive A:\ is selected, but for obvious reasons this is not a good choice. You want to change the location to another disk location. The typical backup is around 1.5–2.0GB (but could be more, depending on the amount of software installed), and because Microsoft's Backup will not "span" a backup across multiple CDs, you need to find another media to store this backup on. You can use anything from ZIP or Jazz drives to a second hard disk drive (either internal or external), which is the most recommended.

Personally we usually have two hard drives, the Master (C:\) for the system drive and the Slave (D:\ or E:\) for the most important personal files like docu-

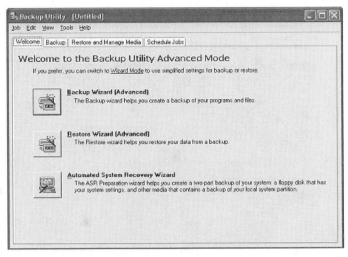

Figure 15.8 The Backup Utility

ments, pictures, artwork, e-mails, favorites, projects, Web design, software, and absolutely everything that must be kept safe. This allows us to easily reformat, clean, install, or use the Automatic System Recovery without losing any important data in the process.

NOTE: You cannot save the backup to the system drive (usually drive C:\), because this drive will be formatted when you do an ASR restore.

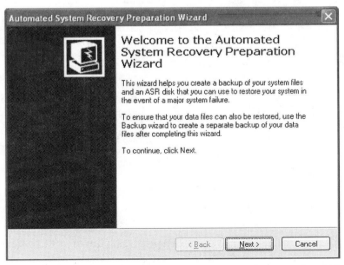

Figure 15.9 The Automated System Recovery Preparation Wizard

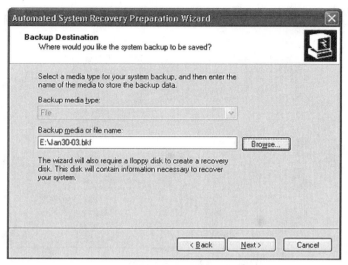

Figure 15.10 Provide the location where the backup file is to be created.

When you have selected the location and name for the backup, click **Finish** to end the Automated System Recovery Preparation Wizard, as shown in Figure 15.11.

NOTE: ASR *only* makes a backup of the files on your system drive (usually drive C:\). If you use other hard drives, you need to make a separate backup of your documents and files to make a complete "recovery" after a disaster! When you do this, Backup creates a list of all the files to back up and then continues with the backup process (Figure 15.12).

Once the disk backup is done, ASR prompts you for a blank 1.44MB formatted floppy disk to store some recovery data (Figure 15.13).

When ready, label the diskette. Pressing **OK** ends the backup portion of ASR. You need to keep your ASR backup up-to-date. If you make any changes to your OS, you need to make a new ASR backup. When installing updates from Microsoft, most prompt you to make a new ASR backup after installing the update.

ASR Restore

ASR reads the disk configurations from the file that it saved on the ASR diskette and restores all of the disk signatures, volumes, and partitions on, at a minimum, the disks required to start the computer. (It attempts to restore all of the disk configurations, but under some circumstances, it might not be able to.)

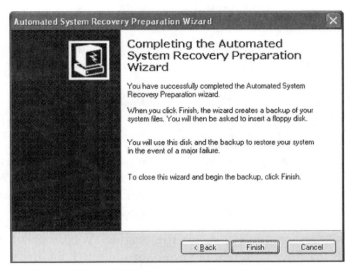

Figure 15.11 The Wizard completes.

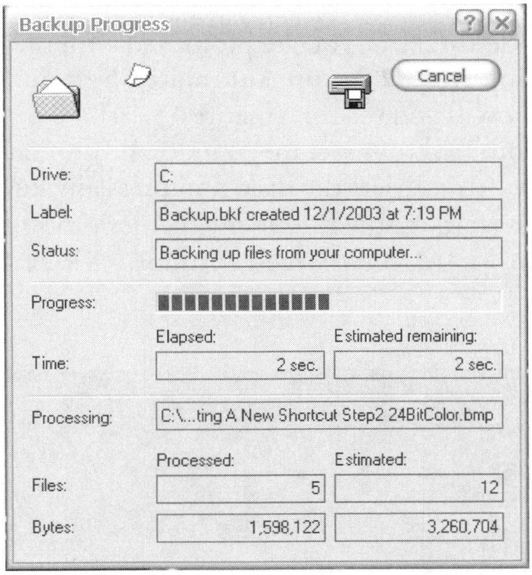

Figure 15.12 The backup process starts.

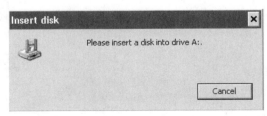

Figure 15.13 Insert a floppy disk when prompted.

To use Automated System Recovery to recover after a system failure, you need to have the following items before you begin the procedure:

- Your Automated System Recovery floppy disk
- Your previously created backup
- Your original operating system CD

NOTE: You should only use the ASR backup to restore your system if all other methods to start your Windows XP system have failed. Your system drive (usually drive C:\) will be formatted and you will lose any information that was not backed up recently.

To start the restore process, insert the original Windows XP CD in your system's CD-ROM drive, and reboot your computer. (Make sure that the option is set in your computer's BIOS to boot from CD-ROM. Check your computer or motherboard's manual on how to do this.) Usually you get the message, **Press any key to boot from CD**.

Once Windows Setup starts, you are prompted with the following text at the bottom of the screen: **Press F2 to run Automated System Recovery**, so be prepared to hit **F2** as soon as you see this (Figure 15.14).

Next you are prompted to insert the Windows Automated System Recovery Disk into the floppy drive. Insert the disk, and press any key (Figure 15.15).

The ASR process starts, and without any further prompts, your system drive is formatted (Figure 15.16), after which Windows XP examines the hard disk (Figure 15.17).

Figure 15.14 Starting Automated System Recovery.

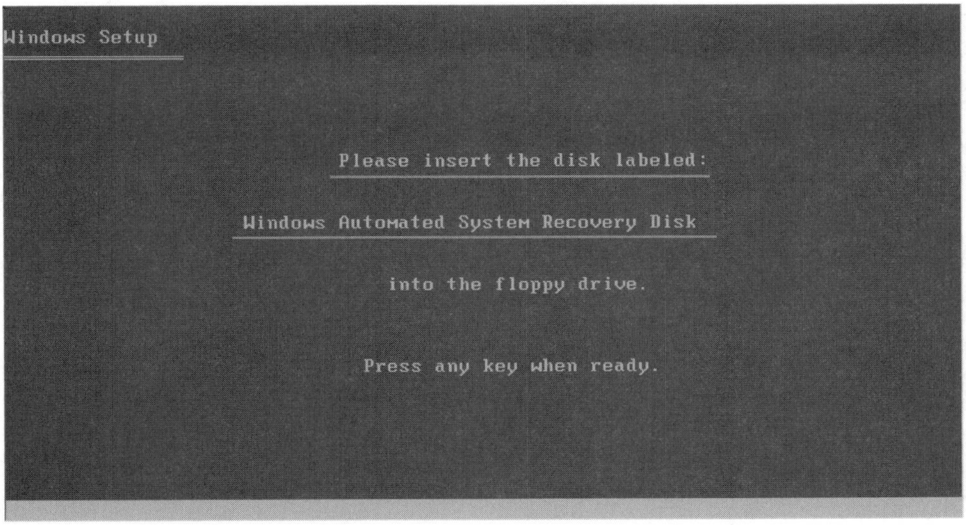

Figure 15.15   Insert the ASR floppy disk.

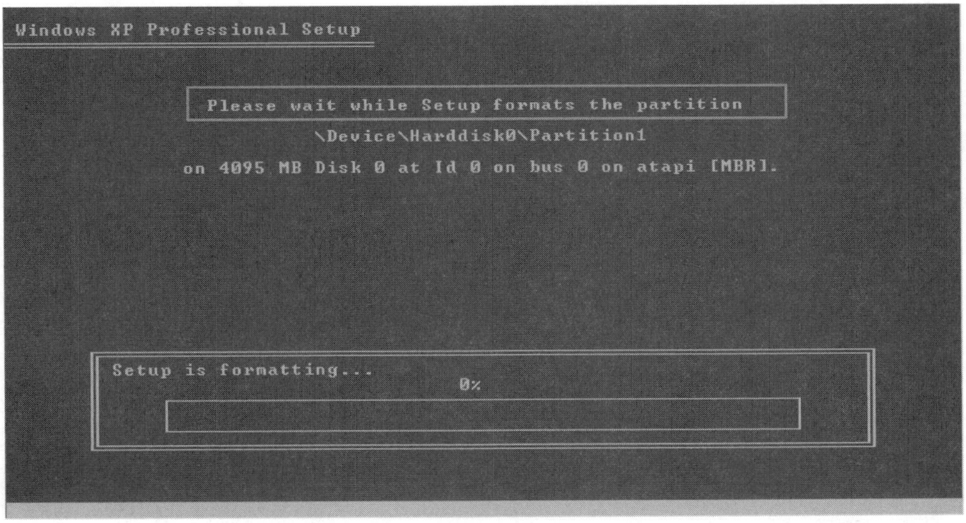

Figure 15.16   Formatting the partition.

When ready, the system prompts you to remove any floppy from the floppy drive, and reboots the system automatically. (*This time do not press any key to boot from the CD-ROM!*)

Windows Setup now continues much like a normal Windows setup would (Figure 15.18), but it does not do a complete installation.

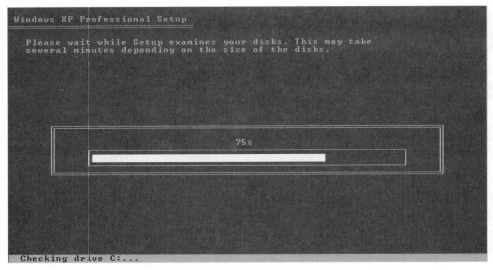

Figure 15.17   Windows XP examines the hard disk.

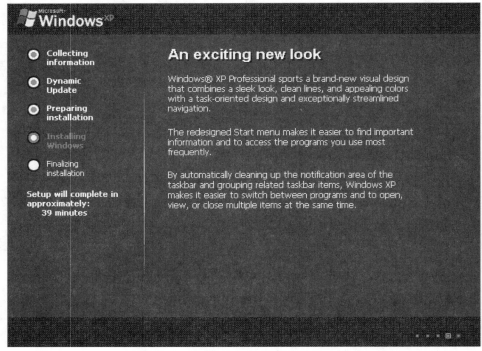

Figure 15.18   Windows XP restarts.

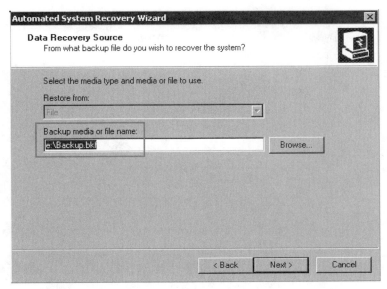

Figure 15.19   Specify the location of the backup file.

After a few minutes, the Automated System Recovery Wizard starts. After 90 seconds it automatically continues. To speed this up, just press the **Next** button.

Next the ASR Wizard asks you for the location of your backup file, as shown in Figure 15.19. By default it lists the location you saved the backup to previously, but if you moved it to a different drive, you can use the **Browse** button to point to the new location. Click **Next** to continue.

This takes you to the screen shown in Figure 15.20. Click Finish to restore your system drive. After the restore phase is completed, your system is rebooted, and you have it back in the same state as when you created the ASR backup.

Group Policy

To access Group Policy, go to **Start**, and then **Run**, and then **gpedit.msc**. There are two main branches in Group Policy: User Configuration and Computer Configuration (Figure 15.21). Changes made under User Configuration only affect the current user. Changes made under Computer Configuration apply to the machine and affect all users on that machine. The recommended setting for each is provided in parentheses.

NOTE: There is no Group Policy Editor in Windows XP Home.

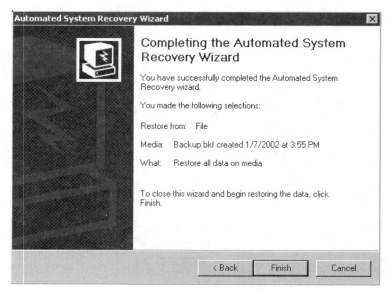

Figure 15.20   The ASR Wizard completes.

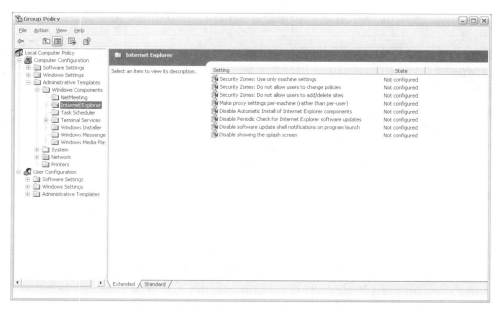

Figure 15.21   The Group Policy console

- **Turn Off System Restore Permanently:** Computer Configuration/Administrative Templates/System/**System Restore/** (Set both items under here to **Enabled**.)

- **Turn Off Built-in CD Burning:** (This still allows third-party burning software such as Nero.) User Configuration/Administrative Templates/Windows Components/Windows Explorer/**Remove CD Burning Features/** (**Enabled**)

- **Remove Shared Documents Folder:** User Configuration/Administrative Templates/Windows Components/Windows Explorer/**Remove Shared Documents from My Computer/** (**Enabled**)

- **Remove Shutdown/Logoff/Restart Message:** Computer Configuration/Administrative Templates/System/**Remove boot /Shutdown /Logon/ Logoff messages/** (**Enabled**)

- **Turn Off User Tracking:** (This also disables personalized menus.) User Configuration/Administrative Templates/Start Menu and Taskbar/**Turn off user tracking/** (**Enabled**)

- **Turn Off CD/DVD Autoplay:** Computer Configuration/Administrative Templates/System/**Turn off Autoplay/** (**Enabled**)

- **Disable IE Splash Screen:** Computer Configuration/Administrative Templates/Windows Components/Internet Explorer/**Disable Showing the Splash Screen/** (**Enabled**)

- **Disable Windows Messenger:** Computer Configuration/Administrative Templates/Windows Components/**Windows Messenger/** (Set both items to **Enabled**.) See the Registry Tweaking section earlier in this chapter on how to turn off Messenger and fix the Outlook Express "slowdown" issue.

- **Customize Internet Explorer:** (Logo, Title bar, Toolbar, icons, and text) User Configuration/Windows Settings/Internet Explorer Maintenance/**Browser User Interface/** (Leave these at default.)

- **Remove Recycle Bin Icon from Desktop:** User Configuration/Administrative Templates/Desktop/**Remove Recycle Bin Icon from Desktop/** (Leave this at default.)

- **Remove My Documents Icon from Desktop:** User Configuration/Administrative Templates/Desktop/**Remove My Documents Icon from Desktop/** (**Enabled**)

- **Remove My Computer Icon from Desktop:** User Configuration/Administrative Templates/Desktop/**Remove My Computer Icon from Desktop/** (Leave this at default.)

Registry Editor

To access Registry Editor go to **Start**, then **Run**, and then **regedit.exe** (Figure 15.22). Make sure you have a backup of the registry. Just as in the Group Editor, changes in Registry Editor affect either individual users (HKEY_CURRENT_USER) or a machine (HKEY_LOCAL_MACHINE). To edit a setting, expand the folders until you see the required entry, then double-click on it. Recommended settings are shown for each entry. Where an entry does not exist, create it.

- **Turn Off System Restore Permanently:** Computer Configuration\Administrative Templates\System**System Restore**\ (Set both items under here to **Enabled**.)

- **Turn off Built-in CD Burning:** (This still allows third-party burning software such as Nero.) User Configuration\Administrative Templates\Windows Components\Windows Explorer**Remove CD Burning Features/** (**Enabled**)

Figure 15.22   The Registry Editor

- **Remove Shared Documents Folder:** User Configuration\Administrative Templates\Windows Components\Windows Explorer**Remove Shared Documents from My Computer/** (**Enabled**)

- **Remove Shutdown/Logoff/Restart Messages:** Computer Configuration\ Administrative Templates\System**Remove boot /Shutdown /Logon/ Logoff messages** (**Enabled**)

- **Turn Off User Tracking:** (This disables personalized menus as well.) User Configuration\Administrative Templates\Start Menu and Taskbar**Turn off user tracking** (**Enabled**)

- **Turn Off CD/DVD Autoplay:** Computer Configuration\Administrative Templates\System**Turn off Autoplay** (**Enabled**)

- **Disable IE Splash Screen:** Computer Configuration\Administrative Templates\Windows Components\Internet Explorer**Disable Showing the Splash Screen** (**Enabled**)

- **Disable Windows Messenger:** Computer Configuration\Administrative Templates\Windows Components\Windows Messenger\ (Set both items found here to **Enabled**.) See the regedit section on how to turn off Messenger and fix the Outlook Express "slowdown" issue.

- **Customize Internet Explorer:** (Logo, Title bar, Toolbar icons and test) User Configuration\Windows Setting\Internet Explorer Maintenance\ Browser User Interface\ (Leave these at the default.)

- **Remove Recycle Bin Icon from Desktop:** User Configuration\Administrative Templates\Desktop**Remove Recycle Bin Icon from Desktop** (Leave at default.)

- **Remove My Documents Icon from Desktop:** User Configuration\ Administrative Templates\Desktop**Remove My Documents Icon from Desktop** (**Enabled**)

- **Remove My Computer Icon from Desktop:** User Configuration\ Administrative Templates\Desktop**Remove My Computer Icon from Desktop** (Leave at default.)

Conclusion

In this chapter we covered quite a bit of ground in areas dealing with general security. In addition to providing guidance on how to harden systems, we provided a number of tweaks intended to help the performance of your system. We also provided coverage of the Automated System Recovery tool, which can come in handy any time you need to rebuild a system, whether from a security-related intrusion and system compromise or a crash due to a faulty disk drive. Continuing on in the theme of security, in the next chapter, Chapter 16, we begin examining the authentication process used by Windows XP during logon. Following that, we discuss the concepts of authorization and access control in Chapter 17.

Chapter
16

Authentication

Sometimes it is a good idea to be absolutely certain you know who you are dealing with. Authentication is the process by which the identity of a specific entity—a person, a user, or a computer—is verified. Authentication transactions happen in many places, many times a day. Using an ATM card and PIN to withdraw cash from an ATM, providing a driver's license when making a purchase at a home improvement store with a credit card, and presenting a passport when going through customs are common types of authentication. In each of these examples some sort of authority requests proof of identification. This ID verification indicates that the person requesting the transaction is who they say they are. This process is separate from authorization, whereby it is determined that an entity is granted specific rights or permissions. Simply proving identity does not guarantee the desired outcome of the transaction. Once the authority establishes that you are who you say you are, it then attempts to authorize you to complete that transaction: the ATM ensures that you have sufficient funds to cover the requested withdrawal; the cashier contacts the credit card issuer for purchase approval; and the customs agent checks that all necessary paperwork and visas are in place for a traveler to enter or exit a country.

Windows XP Professional, like Windows 2000, provides a sophisticated authentication system, which is examined in this chapter. Specific topics covered here include the mechanics of Windows XP authentication, the log-on process, configuration and management of authentication parameters, and best practices for secure authentication. We cover authorization in detail in Chapter 17, Authorization and Access Control.

Secure Authentication Features in Windows XP

New Features

Because Windows XP is built on a Windows 2000 base, you find that there are a number of familiar secure authentication features. Windows XP, however, goes beyond Windows NT 4.0 and Windows 2000 in a number of ways. Whether you are connected to a domain, configured as a part of a workgroup, or are using a stand-alone computer, you find that authentication is even more manageable than before. Here are some of the biggest changes and additions to authentication processes, management, and configuration:

- **Everyone Group.** By default, the Everyone Group no longer includes the Anonymous Group. Previously, the Anonymous Group was granted access to any resource to which the Everyone Group was granted access, even though anonymous users are not required to supply usernames and passwords for authentication.

- **Guest Account.** By default, Windows XP workstations not joined to a domain are configured to use **Guest only** network logons. All users, *including anonymous users,* accessing resources on a computer from over a network with this default setting, are forced to use the Guest Account for authentication and are subsequently given all the same access rights and privileges as the Guest Account.

- **Service Accounts.** Two new service accounts have been added to Windows XP to enhance the granularity of service account access: LocalService for services that run locally, and NetworkService for services that run on the network. The LocalSystem account remains available as well, and is the only account that has **Act as part of the operating system** rights by default.

- **Blank Passwords.** By default, Windows XP workstations that are not part of a domain prevent users with blank passwords from logging on over the network. This is especially helpful for preventing unauthorized access to home workstations connected to the Internet. All blank password access is restricted to local logons only.

- **Password Reset Wizard.** Windows XP supplies a recovery mechanism for use in the event a user forgets his or her password. This Wizard creates a disk that can be used to reset a local account password (it cannot be used to reset a domain password). This disk is computer specific so it cannot be used on another workstation, even if the username and password are the same. Others can use this disk without proper authorization to access a local account, so it is a good idea to keep this disk in a safe location.

- **Stored User Names.** Windows XP allows a user to store frequently used username and password combinations for access to other resources, such as secured Web sites or computers in an untrusted domain. This information becomes part of the user's profile and can travel around the network with the user if roaming profiles have been enabled.

- **Fast User Switching.** Fast user switching allows multiple users of the same computer to log on without shutting down applications that may be in use by another user who is currently logged on to the system. Fast User Switching uses Terminal Services technology to provide this ability. This feature is only available on computers that are not connected to a domain.

As you see from this list, there are quite a few changes to the security and authentication strategy in previous Windows versions. However, Windows XP is interoperable with earlier versions of Windows—from Windows for Workgroups and Windows 9x on up to Windows NT 4.0 and Windows 2000. The management and configuration of secure authentication is covered later in this chapter, with attention given to interoperability issues where required. We now move into a discussion of credentials that Windows XP does support as the first step in gaining a full understanding of the Windows XP authentication process.

Authentication Services and Components

All users, groups of users, or computers that participate in a domain have accounts and are called security principals. Security principals operate within a security context. The security context defines the rights and permissions a given account has in a specific situation. For example, a user may be limited in capabilities when logging on remotely instead of locally, or be given more capabilities when logging on from Workstation A instead of Workstation B. Before these capabilities can be granted though, the account must be authenticated. How Windows actually authenticates an account is a relatively straightforward process that utilizes a number of components. This section covers the building blocks of authentication in Windows XP, for both stand-alone workstations and domain members.

Credential Types and Validation

Credentials are the pieces of evidence that substantiate a claim of identity. Business cards, drivers' licenses, passports, and so forth are all types of credentials commonly used to verify identity. Some types of credentials are considered a stronger guarantee of someone's identity: a driver's license is a stronger credential than a health club membership card.

Validation is the process by which a credential is confirmed as genuine. The body requesting the credentials verifies that the credentials are acceptable according to specific standards before granting authorization to complete a transaction. Windows verifying that the username and password combo entered by a user is analogous to a cashier verifying that the photo on a driver's license matches the person presenting it.

The strength of the credential is not just based on the credibility of the issuing body though. It is also based on the authenticity of the credential itself (for example, is it possible this credential has been tampered with?). Windows XP supports three types of credentials that offer varying levels of security for the resources that are being protected: passwords, Kerberos tickets, and smart cards. We cover configuration and management of these credential types later in this chapter.

Local Security Authority

The Local Security Authority, or LSA, is responsible for validation of credentials in Windows. The LSA is also responsible for management of local security and audit policies and the generation of tokens. Exactly how authentication occurs depends on where the account was created:

- For a user logging on to a stand-alone workstation, the authentication occurs in the local Security Accounts Manager (SAM).
- For a user logging on to a Windows NT 4.0 domain, authentication occurs in the domain SAM.
- For a user logging on to a Windows 2000 Active Directory domain, authentication occurs in the Active Directory.

The Security Accounts Manager is a protected subsystem that manages the accounts database. The SAM can be located locally or on a Windows NT 4.0 domain controller. The local SAM manages accounts used only on that computer, while the domain SAM manages accounts, both computer and user, for the domain. The Active Directory is only available in Windows 2000 and Windows 2003 domain controllers.

Regardless of where an account is authenticated, however, the LSA still handles all validation tasks at the local level. In other words, no matter where your account resides, the LSA still validates that your account is listed in an account database trusted by the LSA before passing it along to the appropriate authentication provider. Figure 16.1 illustrates the LSA and the various authentication providers.

Logon Process

Having covered the basic components of the authentication process, we now examine how all these come together and function in Windows XP logons. We first examine the log-on types supported by XP.

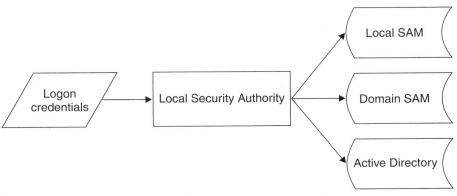

Figure 16.1   The Local Security Authority

Types of Logon

In Windows XP, just as in previous versions of Windows, users can log on over a variety of connections, including network, Internet, dial-up, and local logons. An account holder can attempt to make a connection to a resource and provide the appropriate identifying credentials, such as username and password, to a computer over any of these connection types. The four main types of OS authentication are: interactive, network, service, and batch. Dial-up authentication is covered in Chapter 12, Remote Access.

Interactive Logons

Interactive logons include log-on attempts from a user sitting at the physical workstation where the logon is occurring, users logging in via Terminal Services, and users logging in via Remote Desktop. Interactive logon credentials can be validated by a local accounts database, a domain SAM, or Active Directory.

Interactive logons utilize a number of components to pass credentials entered by the user to the appropriate account database for authentication. The first component is the Winlogon process. Winlogon.exe is a secure user mode process that launches when a user presses Control + Alt + Delete. After a user types that combination of keys, Winlogon calls the Microsoft Graphical Identification and Authentication DLL (MSGINA) to collect username name and password. The MSGINA provides the standard Windows log-on dialog box, but it can be replaced with a custom or third-party GINA.

Once the user has entered his or her username and password in the log-on dialog box and pressed enter, the MSGINA passes this information back to Winlogon, which in turn passes the credentials to the Local Security Authority, running as LSAS.exe. Finally, as discussed previously, the LSA determines whether authentication should occur locally or remotely, as demonstrated in Figure 16.2. The Winlogon process works with the MSGINA to pass user credentials to the LSA.

Network Logons

An account attempting to log on to a computer remotely (with the exception of Terminal Services, Remote Desktop, and dial-up) is said to be performing a network logon. The remote connection is attempted with the credentials you used to log on interactively. The LSA on the remote computer treats that logon as it would a local logon and uses the appropriate accounts database for authentication of the credentials it presented.

Service Logons

Users and computers are not the only entities that require authentication. Many applications require access to resources that are secured by the operating system.

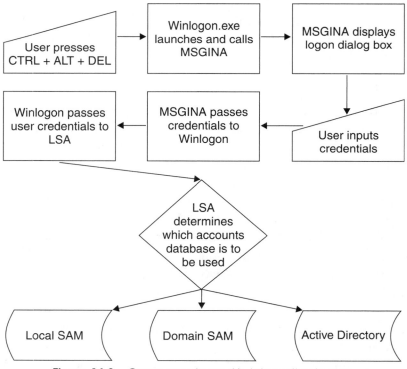

Figure 16.2 Components used in interactive logons

These resources may require the application to have an account so that the appropriate access can be given to the application. Just as a user has to have an account in the domain or on a computer where he or she is trying to print a document, an application or service also has to have the ability to log on to a computer or domain where it must access resources such as files or folders. These applications are given service accounts, which are then granted access to resources after successful authentication. As mentioned earlier in this chapter, there are three built-in service accounts in Windows XP: LocalSystem, Network Service, and LocalService; and it is also possible to create a service account manually. If you want a specific application to have access to certain protected folders or files, you may choose to create a special service account for that purpose.

 NOTE: When would you want to use a service account? Well, let's say that you have a Web site running on a Windows XP workstation that requires a specific application to always be running with it. You can add that application to the startup group to run automatically upon login, but that only works if someone is there to log in. If the computer crashes and reboots in the middle of the night and you are not there to log in after the reboot has completed, the application cannot start. However, you can configure that application (using a resource kit utility called *srvany.exe*) to run as a service and log on with a service account. It will automatically start up when the computer starts and does not require any human-user intervention.

Batch Logons

A batch logon is used by applications that run as a batch job, such as a job scheduled with the task scheduler. The job is logged on as a batch user by default in Windows XP, rather than as an interactive user.

Authentication Process

Now that you are familiar with the types of logons supported in Windows XP, as well as the basic components used to gather user credentials for logons, we look at how the actual authentication process takes place.

The Windows XP authentication process, like that of Windows 2000, supports multiple authentication protocols for use in a variety of log-on scenarios. The authentication protocol defines the process by which the supplied account credentials are verified. For the log-on types above, the protocols Windows XP uses for authentication are Windows NT LAN Manager (NTLM) and Kerberos. The default authentication protocol is Kerberos, with NTLM used as

Windows XP's second choice. Windows XP determines which protocol to use based on a simple trial and error mechanism. If Kerberos authentication fails, the backup, NTLM, attempts to authenticate.

Here is how the protocol selection process works. After the username and password passes to the LSA, the LSA passes user credentials to the Security Support Provider Interface, or SSPI. The SSPI is the boundary between the LSA and the Kerberos and NTLM authentication providers. It is a protocol-independent interface, which has the benefit of allowing developers to write applications that can function with both Windows 2000 and Windows NT 4.0 domains. The SSPI hands-off the username and password to the Kerberos server for the appropriate domain. If the Kerberos server recognizes the credentials, authentication continues, and is either deemed successful or unsuccessful. If no Kerberos server is found, however, the LSA is notified to kick off the process once again. The LSA passes the user credentials to the SSPI, which in turn passes it to the NTLM service for authentication. If no authentication provider can provide authentication of the credentials, an error message is returned to the user. Figure 16.3 illustrates this process. This flowchart demonstrates the Windows XP authentication protocol selection process.

Kerberos

The open network is full of risks. The computers connected to it may not be secured against intrusion, and the media over which network data flows can be easily tapped into. This means users can pose as someone else, computers can be fraudulently set up on the network to pose as legitimate servers, and data can easily be monitored or even modified. Both the client requesting logon and the server that provides the authentication service need to be mutually assured that they are speaking to the correct party.

Kerberos protocol is the namesake of the guardian of the gates of the underworld in Greek mythology. Kerberos, also commonly called Cerberus, was charged with preventing the living from entering and the dead from leaving the underworld. In the same way that Cerberus verified the identities of those entering and leaving the underworld, Kerberos also verifies the identity of parties communicating over a network. Kerberos is the default network authentication protocol for Windows XP and provides mutual authentication for both client and server involved in a transaction. This means that it verifies that *both* communicating parties are who they say they are. Kerberos version 5 is the version implemented within both Windows XP and Windows 2000, and is based on RFC 1510.

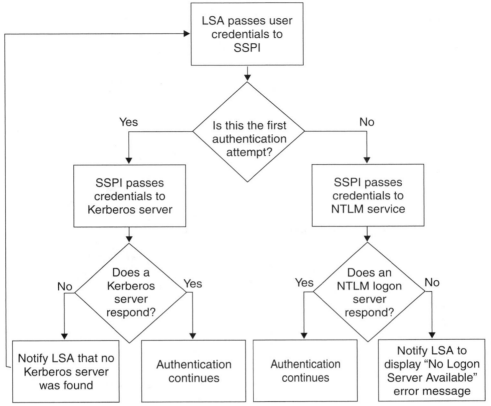

Figure 16.3   Selection of authentication protocol

Shared Secret Overview

Kerberos uses shared secrets to validate identity. A shared secret is something that is known by all parties involved in a transaction, but by no one else. Let's say two spies, Boris and Alexandra, are meeting in a park to exchange information. When they arranged the meeting, they also came up with a secret code—"73"—so they can be mutually assured that Boris is speaking to Alexandra and Alexandra is speaking to Boris. Both parties arrive at the right place and time, and Boris walks up to the woman he believes to be Alexandra and says, "By any chance do you know the current temperature in San Jose?" to which Alexandra replies, "It's 73 degrees Fahrenheit in San Jose." Boris then says "I was last in San Jose in '73. It was a lovely place." At this point both parties have shared the mutual secret with each other and the information exchange can now occur, as illustrated in Figure 16.4. Shared secrets are used to mutually validate identity of both parties in a transaction.

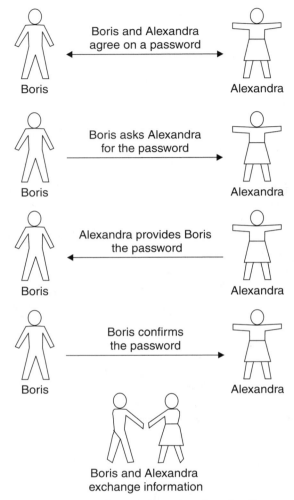

Figure 16.4 Shared secret authentication

In order for this to have qualified as mutual authentication, the secret has to be repeated by each party to ensure that both sides know the secret. By hiding the secret in the conversation, it makes it difficult for eavesdroppers to understand exactly what portion of the conversation was the secret. Kerberos handles both these tasks as well as the added feature of acting as a trusted third party, distributing the secrets to parties that wish to conduct a transaction with each other, much as a secret intelligence team would provide this service to their own agents. Let's take a look at how this works with Kerberos.

Imagine that now Alexandra and Boris want to exchange information via computer, rather than in person. In the physical world, they have all sorts of spy gadgets to protect their conversations in which they planned meetings and shared secret codes. They need to do the same thing with their computer-based communications. The first thing they have to do is determine how to share the secret code, or password, that will prove to both Boris and Alexandra that they are communicating with each other.

Because networks can be very insecure, they cannot just e-mail the password that they want to use. They need a way to ensure confidentiality. Someone could be sniffing packets as they come over the network for just such an e-mail. So how do you send a password to someone so that that person, and only that person, knows what the password is? Easy—you encrypt it and share the key to decrypt it. Kerberos does this by providing a single key that will encrypt and decrypt the password. This is known as symmetric secret key cryptography, and the "package" that contains the shared secret password is called an authenticator.

Another challenge facing Boris and Alexandra is that although they have protected the password, they need a way to be sure that someone scanning the network does not take those packets containing authenticators and reuse them to fraudulently pose as one party or the other. By using an authenticator that is different each time it is sent, it is possible to prevent these types of replay attacks. Kerberos provides this function by using a unique shared secret. It is encrypted with the secret key and decrypted by the secret key at the other end.

Now that you are familiar with the basic concepts of shared secret authentication with Kerberos, let's walk through an example of Boris and Alexandra using this protocol.

Boris and Alexandra need to send sensitive documents to each other across the network. Because this is top-secret information, Boris needs to be sure that it is actually Alexandra that he is contacting, and Alexandra likewise needs assurance that the person contacting her is actually Boris. Boris and Alexandra have decided that shared secret authentication is the way to handle this mutual identification validation, and now Boris has some information he needs to share with Alexandra. Here is the process that they use to authenticate each other:

1. As shown in Figure 16.5, Boris sends Alexandra a message that is encrypted with their secret key. The encrypted message contains the

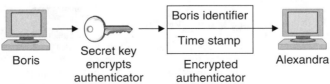

Figure 16.5 Boris makes initial contact with Alexandra.

authenticator, which in turn contains two pieces of information. One piece identifies the sender as Boris and the other is the time on Boris' computer. The time stamp acts as a unique identifier, to prevent fraudulent reuse of the authenticator.

2. Alexandra receives the message from Boris, as shown in Figure 16.6. She decrypts the authenticator with the shared key and takes a look at the time stamp from Boris' computer. The time shown must be within the acceptable range of difference from the time on Alexandra's computer. For the sake of this discussion, let's say it must be within plus or minus two minutes. If the time is within that range, Alexandra can be reasonably sure it is Boris, but if it is not, then she can refuse to communicate with the person claiming to be Boris. It is still possible for that packet to have been replayed from a previous attempt by Boris to communicate with Alexandra, but the time stamp also acts as a unique identifier. If Alexandra had previously received an authenticator from Boris with an identical time stamp, the second one could be rejected. The same holds true of any time stamp that is from a time earlier than the last time stamp received.

3. Because Alexandra is now reasonably sure that the authenticator that she received is from Boris, she responds to the message as shown in Figure 16.7. Alexandra removes just the time stamp from the message and encrypts it with the secret key. By doing so, she not only proves that she knows the secret, she also proves that she is able to decrypt and modify the message with the secret key that only Boris and Alexandra share. This assures Boris that it is actually Alexandra who is responding.

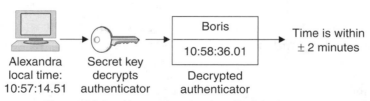

Figure 16.6   Alexandra receives Boris' message.

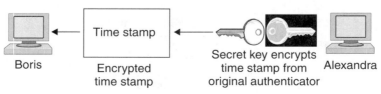

Figure 16.7   Alexandra replies to Boris' message.

Figure 16.8 Boris receives Alexandra's response.

4. Boris receives Alexandra's response (shown in Figure 16.8) and decrypts it. Once he examines the time stamp and successfully compares it with the time stamp in his original authenticator, Boris can be confident that it was from Alexandra, since only he and Alexandra share that key.

Key Distribution and Tickets

The above scenario explains how Boris and Alexandra use secret keys to authenticate each other. But there is a large piece of information missing: Exactly how and where did Boris and Alexandra get their secret keys? They would like to exchange keys with each other and only each other, prevent others from being able to use the keys, and at the same time guarantee that the sender and receiver of the keys are really Boris and Alexandra. Involving a trusted party to provide the secret key is the way this problem is solved in Kerberos.

Let's take the example of Boris and Alexandra a step further. Both of these people need to communicate with other people and exchange information over the network, as well as connect to shared resources such as databases, printers, and e-mail. Each of these resources requires a secret key to mutually authenticate both the client and server in the transaction. If each user is required to have a different secret key for each resource he or she wants to access, the total number of secret keys required for all users and resources on the network could be huge—a potential management nightmare!

Kerberos solves the two problems of key distribution and management with a Key Distribution Center, or KDC. The KDC maintains a central database of keys and the accounts that they belong to. The group of accounts that the KDC is responsible for is called a realm. You can think of a realm as being analogous to a domain. The KDC is a service running on a Windows 2000 or Windows 2003 domain controller. In fact, *all* Windows 2000 and Windows 2003 domain controllers are Key Distribution Centers. In this section, we walk through the process of key distribution.

When a client wants to talk to a server to access resources located on that server, such as files or printers, the client sends a request for authentication to the KDC. Kerberos caches account passwords as a piece of encrypted data, called a *long-term key,* on both the client and the KDC. This long-term key is used to secure communications between the KDC and clients that use Kerberos for authentication. The authentication request is composed of two parts:

1. An identifier for the client that is requesting authentication and the service or resource the client wants to access.
2. An authenticator for the KDC that contains a time stamp from the client and the client's long-tem key.

Figure 16.9 illustrates such a request from a client.

The KDC responds with a session key to be used by the client and server that wish to communicate. The session key is encrypted with the long-term key of the parties that will be communicating. The client's session key will be encrypted with the client's long-term key while the server's session key will be encrypted with the server's long-term key. The server's session key is grouped with the client's authorization level for the requested server or service. The two are encrypted together with the server's long-term key, and the resulting piece of information is called a *session ticket.* You can think of a ticket as a permit or license for accessing a server or service within a Windows 2000 domain. Tickets are required for accessing all resources in a Windows 2000 domain, including the log-on process. A session ticket is shown in Figure 16.10.

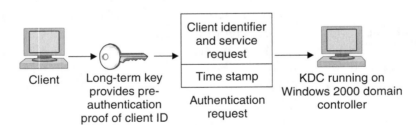

Figure 16.9 A client requests authentication assistance from the KDC.

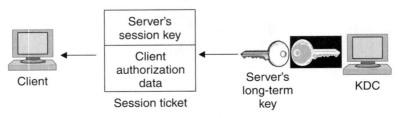

Figure 16.10 A session ticket

The first time the client contacts the KDC for authentication assistance, which occurs at logon, the KDC generates a session key for that client. In this case, the KDC is the service for which client authentication assistance is being requested. The KDC responds with a special session ticket called a TGT, shorthand for Ticket-Granting Ticket, which is to be used for further communication with the KDC itself. It contains two pieces of information:

1. A copy of the logon session key generated by the KDC
2. Client authorization data

Just as in the case of ordinary session tickets, the session key for the client is encrypted with the client's long-term key, while the TGT is encrypted in the KDC's long-term key. The TGT is illustrated in Figure 16.11.

Sending session keys to both the client and server would place a significant load on the system resources of the server where the KDC is running. Instead, the burden of session management is placed squarely upon the client. Both of these session keys are sent directly to the client that wishes to initiate communication with a server. The client is responsible for managing the ticket and all subsequent attempts to access resources with that ticket. By eliminating the need for the KDC to act as the manager of session messaging between client and server, the potential load on the memory of the server or servers running the KDC service is reduced. Making the client responsible for the session ticket management provides the additional benefit of allowing the client to directly contact the server without going through the KDC for a new session key each time it needs to access a network resource for which it has already been given session-specific information.

The session ticket is good for as long as the client remains logged on or until the ticket expires, whichever comes first. Typically, session tickets expire after eight hours. If a ticket is still valid at the time a user logs off, the ticket is destroyed to prevent unauthorized reuse of that ticket. The client can attempt to access the network resource for which it has been issued a ticket for as long as the

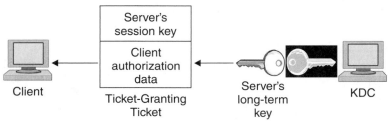

Figure 16.11   A Ticket-Granting Ticket

session-specific data it has been given is valid. The client simply presents his or her ticket for a specific resource or server each time he or she attempts to access that resource.

We now look at how the Windows XP logon process works with Kerberos.

The Kerberos Logon Process

If a workstation is not part of a Windows 2000/2003 domain, there is no Kerberos authentication, so there is not a requirement for stand-alone workstations or Windows NT 4.0 domain members to have tickets to access resources. (Kerberos is an industry standard method of authentication. Because Microsoft's Kerberos implementation is interoperable with other implementations of Kerberos, it is possible that some sort of Kerberos authentication scheme could be used in the above scenario. That is beyond the scope of this book, however.) Windows 2000 domain members must have tickets for accessing any resources or services within the domain, including logon or services running on the local computer where a user has logged on.

So how does the user get a ticket from the KDC before logging on? Recall that all Windows 2000 domain controllers are also KDCs. When a user logging on from a Windows XP workstation attempts to contact the Windows 2000 domain controller for logon, he or she needs two pieces of data:

- A TGT that allows access to the ticket-granting service
- A ticket that allows access to the workstation used for logon

Figure 16.12 illustrates this activity.

Now we walk through how this process takes place.

1. The user (Boris, for example) presses Control + ALT + Delete, also known as the Secure Attention Sequence. The MSGINA appears, Boris enters his username and password, and clicks OK. MSGINA hands the log-on credentials to Winlogon, which in turn passes them along to the LSA.

2. The LSA takes Boris' password and converts it to a preauthentication encrypted key that is stored in the workstation's credential cache and can be used by whatever authentication provider is indicated for the logon

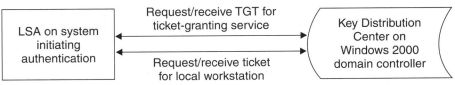

Figure 16.12   The components required for Kerberos-based logon.

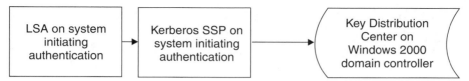

Figure 16.13   Kerberos and LSA interaction

type, which in this case is for a Windows 2000 domain. The LSA hands this information to the Kerberos SSP, which handles communication with the KDC. The LSA interfaces with the Kerberos SSP as shown in Figure 16.13.

3. The Kerberos SSP sends the preauthentication key to the authentication service on the Kerberos server. This request contains the following items:

   • An identifier for the client that it wishes to be authenticated and the service or resource the client wants to access. In this case, the client is Boris and the specific service is the authentication service.

   • An authenticator for the KDC. It contains a time stamp from Boris and his preauthentication data (Boris' password as encrypted by the LSA).

4. On receipt of this authentication request, the KDC verifys that the time stamp contained within the package is within the range of time that is permissible for that realm. If it is acceptable, the KDC sends the Kerberos SSP a ticket-granting ticket for Boris to use. The actual data structure contains the following items:

   • The session key for Boris to use.

   • A TGT for the KDC that has been encrypted with the KDC's secret key, and includes a session key for Boris and the KDC to use when communicating with each other, as well as information detailing Boris' authorization level for the KDC. Now the Kerberos SSP is in possession of one of the two items Boris needs to complete his logon.

5. The Kerberos SSP receives this message and turns its attention to the matter of obtaining access to the ticket-granting service. The ticket-granting service provides the ticket that is needed to log on to the local workstation. The Kerberos SSP sends a message to the KDC that includes these pieces of information:

   • The name of the workstation Boris is attempting to log in from and the domain the workstation belongs to.

   • Boris' TGT and authenticator that are encrypted with the session key obtained in Step 4.

6. The KDC examines the request for access to the ticket-granting service and ensures its authenticity as discussed in the previous section. If the request is deemed legitimate, the KDC returns the following items to the Kerberos SSP for use by Boris:

- A session key, encrypted with Boris' secret key, for Boris and the workstation to use when communicating with each other.
- A session ticket for accessing the local workstation, which is encrypted with the workstation's secret key.

7. Now that the Kerberos SSP has both items required for logon, it can pass this information to the LSA, which handles the task of querying the local SAM to determine what authorization levels Boris has for this workstation. On completion of that query, an access token is created. (Access tokens are discussed in Chapter 17, Authorization and Access Control.) The LSA passes this token and confirmation of Boris' identity to Winlogon, which completes the logon process and displays the Windows XP desktop.

Windows NT LAN Manager

Windows NT LAN Manager (NTLM) is the authentication protocol used for credential validation when one of the computers is running Windows NT 4.0 or when computers involved in the authentication process are configured to act as stand-alone or workgroup members, specifically:

- Windows XP authenticating to Windows XP computers in the absence of a domain
- Windows XP authenticating to a Windows NT 4.0 domain
- Windows XP authenticating to Windows for Workgroups, Windows 95, Windows 98, Windows 98 Second Edition, and Windows Me
- Windows XP authenticating to Windows NT 4.0 computers running in a Windows 2000 domain

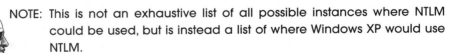 NOTE: This is not an exhaustive list of all possible instances where NTLM could be used, but is instead a list of where Windows XP would use NTLM.

NTLM Types

NTLM relies on a challenge/response method for validation of username and password. Username and password are sent across the network as a hash, rather than in clear text. It does not provide mutual authentication; that is, verification that both the user and the authentication provider are who they say they are. Instead, it only provides authentication of the account being used to log on to a server.

There are three types of NTLM supported in Windows XP. Multiple versions provide backward compatibility to older versions of Windows and provide varying levels of security. The three NTLM types are as follows

- **LAN Manager:** The oldest version of NTLM challenge/response provided by Windows XP is also the least secure. It is used when a Windows XP computer is attempting to authenticate to a computer running older versions of Windows: Windows for Workgroups, Windows 95, or Windows 98. If you are not planning to access any resources shared from workstations running these operating systems, you may wish to disable this protocol, because it is not as strong as the other versions of NTLM provided. The algorithm used to encrypt these passwords effectively limits password strength to seven characters and is not case sensitive. We cover disabling LAN Manager authentication in the next section, "Configuration and Recommended Practices."

- **NTLM version 1:** NTLM version 1 provides a more secure method of authentication than LAN Manager. It uses 56-bit encryption, allowing it to have an effective password strength of 14 characters and also allows both upper- and lowercase characters to be used. It is used on Windows NT 4.0 Service Pack 3.0 and earlier domains.

- **NTLM version 2:** With the advent of Windows NT 4.0 Service Pack 4, a newer and more secure challenge/response mechanism was made available. NTLM version 2 offers message integrity, 128-bit encryption, and session-level security. Session security is provided by the use of separate keys for message integrity and confidentiality. The RFC-compliant HMAC-MD5 algorithm used in NTLMv2 provides message integrity checking, and 128-bit encryption is used for message confidentiality.

Authentication Process

As you have learned, user authentication in Windows XP uses the LSA to pass credentials to the authentication provider. NTLM is the fallback authentication provider for Windows XP, used when Kerberos is not available. NTLM uses the MSV1_0 Authentication Package, which references the SAM database as its user accounts database.

There are two parts of MSV1_0; one that runs on the computer where the logon was initiated, and the other that runs on the computer where the account is located, as shown in Figure 16.14. If the log-on computer also houses the user

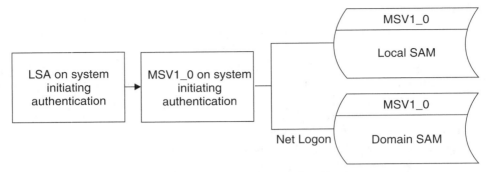

Figure 16.14 NTLM uses MSV1_0 to authenticate accounts.

account, then both portions run on the same computer. If the user account is located on a remote machine, MSV1_0 hands the request to the Netlogon service, which in turn sends the request to the remote machine.

Configuration and Recommended Practices

Part of a good security plan includes determining what rights and features will be available to a user that wishes to log on to Windows XP. Even if your Windows XP computer is not a member of a domain, it is important to ensure that it is protected from unauthorized access by other users on your network. The network to which you are connected may be just two devices using a wireless network, but if you are connected to the Internet via an "always on" connection such as DSL, you need to consider that your network now extends beyond just the boundaries of your home or office. Your username and password are the two pieces of information that you supply to get access to resources. It is important to protect these credentials, and establishing (and subsequently enforcing) a general policy on how these items will be treated in your network will go a long way toward keeping your network as safe as possible. Besides just protecting the log-on credentials, you need to devise a policy for limiting log-on access to resources on your network, to prevent unauthorized users from using "accidental backdoors" such as blank passwords or a guest account that has been given an exceptionally high level of privileges. You want to create the most restrictive local authentication policies you can for your network to prevent intruders from accessing information that you have not explicitly designated as public (such as a Web site).

This section discusses configuration and management of Windows XP credentials, authentication policies, and recommended practices. While previous sections referred to the domain log-on process, the information in this section is primarily for stand-alone Windows XP computers, because domain account management is beyond the scope of this book. Where applicable, however, specific caveats or recommendations are made in cases where domain-related issues are of particular importance.

Individual Account Settings

Some account settings affect only a single account. These settings govern certain aspects of that account's password and are configured from within the Local Users and Groups console. To access these settings:

1. Launch **Control Panel**, then select **Administrative Tools**, and then select **Computer Management**. (There are a number of other ways to reach this console besides this, but for the sake of discussion we limit it to this way for now.)
2. In the left-hand pane of the console select **Local Users and Groups** and then click on the **Users** subfolder. The users configured for this system appear in the right-hand pane of the console.
3. Right-click the user you wish to modify, and select **Properties** from the pop-up menu. The property sheet for that user appears, as shown in Figure 16.15. Click the boxes to enable or disable the settings as you desire.

The configuration options for user account passwords are as follows:

1. **User must change password at next logon:** If you reset a user's password for them and assign a generic password, it may be helpful to require the user to change the password the next time they log on. The user selects a password that is easier for them to remember and reduces the possibility of other unauthorized users attempting to guess another user's password by using the generic password that was previously assigned to the un-authorized user. If this option is selected, however, the next two options are disabled.
2. **User cannot change password:** This option is useful when used in con-junction with accounts that are used by multiple people, such as Guest Accounts. This prevents one user from changing a password, thereby locking out all users of that account. It also reduces the administrative workload from having to reset this password and disseminating the new password to all users of that account.
3. **Password never expires:** This is another option useful for multiple-user accounts, such as Guest or Administrative Accounts. If you set a maxi-mum password age in the global account policies (to be covered in the

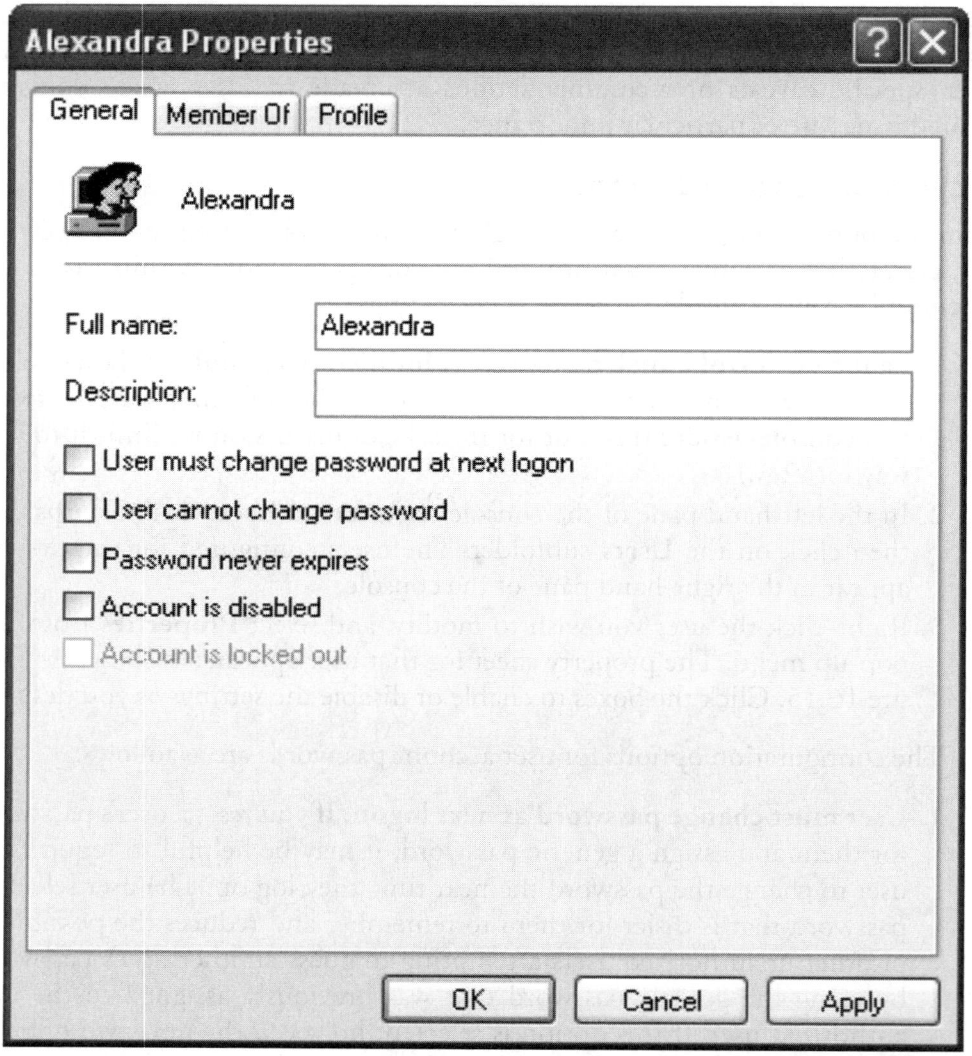

Alexandra Properties   ? X

General | Member Of | Profile

Alexandra

Full name: | Alexandra

Description: |

☐ User must change password at next logon
☐ User cannot change password
☐ Password never expires
☐ Account is disabled
☐ Account is locked out

OK   Cancel   Apply

Figure 16.15   Configure individual account settings from within Local Users and Groups.

section below), it affects all accounts except for the accounts where this has been designated.

4. **Account is disabled:** By selecting this setting, the user cannot log on. You might wish to disable an account rather than deleting it; perhaps for a user that has left, but will be replaced with someone who will need to have access to the same resources as the previous user. Disabling it prevents unauthorized access to the network by users who know the current username and password combination. Once the replacement user has

been determined, you should rename the account, change the password, and enable the account. This way the user account has the same SID and retains all previous rights and permissions.

5. **Account is locked out:** If a user has attempted to log on with incorrect credentials that exceed the maximum number of allowable attempts, this box is checked. An administrator can unlock the account by removing the check in this box. This setting cannot be selected by the administrator, only deselected. If you wish to quickly terminate user access, use the **Account is disabled** setting.

 NOTE: If a user account is locked out and auditing has been enabled, take a look at the Event Viewer to verify that the bad log-on attempts took place within acceptable parameters, such as a specific time or location. It may be that the correct user made only one or two of those bad attempts and the rest came from an unknown or un-authorized source.

Stored User Names and Passwords

Windows XP includes a new tool that helps users maintain a library of passwords for accounts they have for a variety of resources, such as Web sites (sites that require Passport or SSL logon only), network resources, and so forth. It provides the illusion of having a single set of credentials for these resources, even for resources that you do not manage directly. For example, you have an administrative account on several computers in your network, but for security reasons you do not wish to log on with an administrative account. You also have a .NET Passport for use with a variety of Web sites, as well as the credentials you need for your online brokerage. By configuring these credentials in the Stored User Names and Passwords tool, they are saved as part of your profile and automatically presented to the resource to which you request to be logged on. To configure Stored User Names and Passwords:

1. Launch **Control Panel** and open **User Accounts**.
2. Select your account name and in the Related Tasks box, click **Manage my network passwords**. However, if this computer belongs to a domain, you select the **Advanced** tab, and then click **Manage Passwords**. The Stored User Names and Passwords dialog box appears, as shown in Figure 16.16.
3. Click the button that corresponds to the action you wish to perform. If you select **Add** or **Properties**, the Logon Information Properties dialog box appears, as shown in Figure 16.17. Simply add to or change the information stored here.

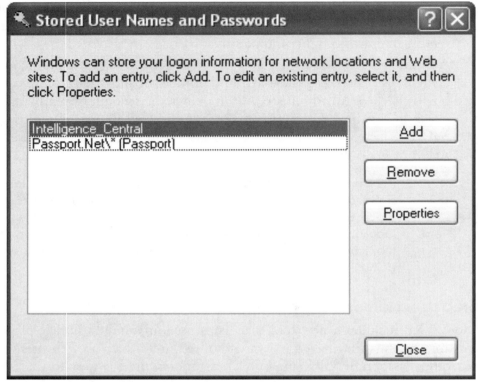

Figure 16.16 Manage Stored User Names and Passwords from within
User Accounts in Control Panel.

You can also save credentials from a command line, if you prefer to use the
command line rather than a GUI tool. The **net use** command provides the
/savecred switch, used when the user is prompted for a username and/or password. The syntax for this command is either of the following examples:

1. When prompted only for a password:

```
net use * \\computer_name\share_name /savecred
```

2. When prompted for both username and password:

```
net use * \\computer_name\share_name /u:domain_name\user_name
/savecred
```

Note that /savecred is used only in conjunction with **devicename** and is
ignored when the remote resource does not prompt the user for credential presentation automatically. /savecred, when used with password *, only caches those

Figure 16.17   Provide Server Name, User Name, and
Password in Logon Information Properties.

credentials for the duration of the logon session, rather than saving them in
Stored User Names and Passwords. Further, /savecred is only available in Windows XP Professional. It is ignored in Windows XP Home Edition.

Global Account Settings

Settings that affect all accounts are configured from within the Local Computer
Policy console. They are grouped by function, which is how they are covered
here. To open this console, launch **Control Panel**, then select **Administrative
Tools**, then select **Local Security Policy**. Alternatively, you can open the Local
Computer Policy snap-in within the Microsoft Management Console. The
groups discussed in this section are found in **Account Policies** and **Local**

Policies. Local account policies are applied in stand-alone Windows XP workstations, while domain members logging on to a Windows XP computer are subject to domain account policies.

Account Policies

Account policies include both password and account lockout–related settings. Password policy dictates password strength and lifespan, while account lockout specifies what, if anything, happens in the event that a user attempts to logon too many times with an incorrect credential set. To access these options, navigate to **Computer Configuration**, then **Windows Settings**, then **Security Settings**, then **Account Policies**, in the left-hand pane.

Let's look at Password Policy first. Clicking the **Password Policy** folder under **Account Policy** displays the configuration options, as shown in Figure 16.18.

All of the options here are configured in accordance with a well thought out password policy that you must devise for your network. In addition to keeping passwords secret and safe, they should also be difficult to guess. You can accomplish this by requiring them to be strong, unique, and changed frequently.

- **Maximum password age:** Requiring users to change their passwords frequently helps prevent fraudulent use of passwords. The shorter the duration you set, the more often a user has to create a new one. This can be difficult for users when initially implemented, especially when this imple-

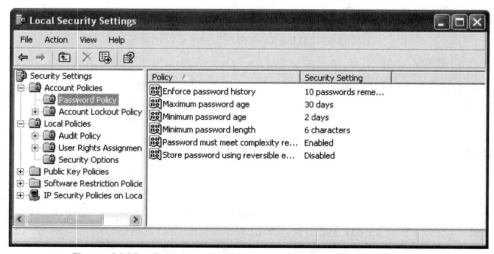

Figure 16.18   Password Policies are managed from within the Local Security Policy console.

mentation is in conjunction with other settings. It also means an additional level of work for you, the administrator, who may have to assist with the reset of their passwords (although the Password Reset Wizard can provide some relief). You need to balance the aging requirement with the actual level of security requirements in your network.

- **Enforce password history:** This is a great one to set to keep users from defeating the requirement to change their password every so many days. Some crafty users will try to change their password to the exact same password, which really does not do much in the way of keeping things secure. By setting a history, users have to create a unique password each time they are forced to change their password.

- **Minimum password age:** This is another way to defeat the users who want to reuse the same password. This prevents him or her from changing the password *n* times, where *n* represents the number of unique passwords required in a single day, and reverting back to their original password.

- **Minimum password length:** By specifying a specific length of a password, you are doing two things—making passwords difficult to guess and preventing the use of blank passwords. Six characters is a recommended minimum, while 14 characters is the maximum permitted. By default, Windows XP workstations that are not part of a domain prevent users with blank passwords from logging on over the network. This is especially helpful for preventing unauthorized access to home workstations connected to the Internet. All blank password access is restricted to local logons only.

- **Passwords must meet complexity requirements:** In addition to requiring passwords of a minimum length, you can also require that they consist of both alphanumeric and special characters and use both upper- and lowercase letters. In addition, by enabling this policy, Windows XP prohibits users from including their username or their "friendly name" as configured in their account properties sheet as part of their password.

NOTE: To make it easier for users to remember long and seemingly random combinations of letters, symbols, and numbers, encourage them to create "passphrases." A good strong passphrase can be a nonsensical expression such as "Bob is your uncle" or "The White Sox won the pennant!" but with a twist—substitute numbers and symbols for letters and spaces. "Bob is your uncle" becomes B0b_1s_y0ur_uncle, and "The White Sox won the pennant!" becomes The_Wh1te_S@x_W0n_the_pennant! Voila! Instant, difficult to guess (and type), but easy to remember password.

- **Store passwords using reversible encryption for all users in the domain:** This option should be selected only when CHAP authentication is required for Remote Access Service or Internet Authentication Service. Enabling this is equivalent to storing passwords in plain text, which is a definite security no-no! Enable only when absolutely required.

Now that you have made it difficult for fraudulent users to guess passwords, you need to limit their opportunity of trying to crack those passwords with dictionaries or manual attempts. The account lockout options are designed to do just that. These options are found in the same Account Policy area as Password Policy, shown in Figure 16.19.

- **Account lockout threshold:** The first option you need to configure is the number of bad log-on attempts permitted before the account is administratively disabled. By default, this is set at zero or disabled. No other account lockout options can be set until the threshold is set to some number above zero. The maximum number of attempts allowed is 999. The more secure the network, the lower this number should be. Three to five attempts should be adequate for most networks.

- **Account lockout duration:** This setting sets the amount of time that an account will be locked out. In other words, how many minutes will elapse from the time the account is locked out to the time that the account is unlocked and log-on attempts can begin again. A setting of zero means

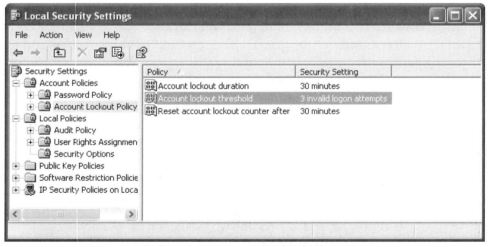

Figure 16.19 Account Lockout Policy dictates when and how user accounts are disabled after too many bad attempts to log on.

that the administrator must manually unlock the account. Setting the duration to 25 minutes strikes a nice balance between making a dictionary attack difficult and letting the administrator have enough time to get out of the office for lunch without having to return to unlock someone's account.

- **Reset account lockout counter after:** This setting provides yet another way to cut down on some of the administrative work of unlocking accounts. Windows XP tracks the number of bad log-on attempts in preparation to locking out an account. Specifying a span of time between a number of bad log-on attempts that are not sufficient to lock out the account and the point at which the bad log-on attempt counter is set not only slows down an intruder guessing passwords, but also provides an additional bit of room for error for a user who may have repeatedly fat-fingered a recently changed password.

When setting an account lockout policy, it is important to set up auditing and check the logs any time a user account is locked out and you are made aware of it. This way you can become aware of any suspicious log-on activity as soon as possible.

Changing the Way Users Log On

There are a number of ways the log-on experience for users can be modified, from requiring smart cards to automation of the log-on process to policies that limit time and location of logons. This section reviews these log-on process modifications.

Smart Cards

Smart cards are an excellent way to physically and logically secure access to your computer's resources. A smart card is very similar to an ATM card: In order to complete a transaction, both the card and a PIN are required. The card is read in a reader attached to the computer, and the user is prompted to enter his or her PIN. When smart cards are used, this credential combination is used in place of the account password stored within the operating system.

Smart cards use public and private key cryptography and can only be used for domain account authentication; local account authentication is not supported on Windows XP. Kerberos version 5 protocol is used with smart cards to authenticate to Windows 2000 domains, while Kerberos with x.509 v3 certificates are used with non–Windows 2000 domains. Unlike passwords, smart card PINs are not sent over the network. Like Windows accounts, smart cards can be set to lock after too many bad log-on attempts. An administrator must unlock any locked cards.

Automating Logon

Going in the opposite direction from the security provided by smart cards is the ability to automate user logons. When automated logon is configured, users do not have to use the Control + Alt + Delete command to initiate logon, nor do they enter a username or password. Instead, user credentials are stored in the registry, which is then parsed for this information when required for loading a specific user's operating system environment.

It is highly recommended that any computer configured with automatic logon be physically secure and protected from unauthorized network access. While automatic logon offers a great deal of convenience to users, because they can boot up and get right to work on their Windows XP computer, it also leaves a gaping hole where a certain level of security would have been provided by entering user credentials. All users of that system have access to all network resources that are granted to the account that was logged on automatically. As you can imagine, this is a dangerous situation. Even weak passwords can provide a higher level of local logon deterrence to unauthorized users. The log-on screen works in much the same way a sign alerting intruders to the presence of a burglar alarm works. A trespasser is not sure if there really is an alarm system, and may not be willing to risk finding out one is truly installed. An unauthorized user may not be willing to take the 10 or 15 extra seconds to figure out what the weak password is before he or she is caught with the proverbial hand in the cookie jar. Another danger point with automated logons is that user passwords are stored in plain text in the registry. Any remote user that is a member of the Authenticated Users group by default has access to the key where this is stored. This makes it an easy target for users looking for unauthorized access to the files of another user.

To set up automated logon you must edit the registry. As always, use extreme caution when making modifications to the registry and be sure you have a good backup before you start. Any registry change can have unexpected and unpleasant results. When you are ready to proceed, you perform the following steps:

1. Open a registry editor, such as **regedit.exe**.
2. Locate HKEY_LOCAL_MACHINE\SOFTWARE\Microsoft\Windows NT\CurrentVersion\Winlogon.
3. Double-click **DefaultUserName**.
4. In the Value data box, type the username, and then click **OK**.
5. Double-click **DefaultPassword**.
6. In the Value data field, type the password and click **OK**.

7. Double-click **AutoAdminLogon**.

8. Enter **1** in the Value data box and click **OK**.

Changes take effect on the next reboot.

Disabling the Welcome Screen

The Windows XP Welcome screen provides the usernames of all users with local accounts on a computer. Users viewing this screen can attempt to log on with the username of another user by guessing the password. If this is an unacceptable risk in your network and you are not in a domain, you can use the traditional Control + Alt + Delete screen instead. To do so, perform these steps:

1. Open **Control Panel**, click **User Accounts**.

2. Click **Change the way users log on or off**.

3. Remove the check in the **Use the Welcome screen** check box.

Authentication Policies

A number of specific settings can be applied through policies defined either locally, across a number of computers, or domainwide. Local policies on a single computer are configured with the Local Security Policy tool. Settings that are to be applied to a number of computers are configured with the Group Policy tool, and templates can be used to make configuration of a number of options easier. Domain account policies are defined in the Domain Group Policy. Account policies were discussed earlier in this chapter, so this section provides an overview of the authentication policy options that are available for the Windows XP network administrator in a nondomain environment. To modify any of these policies:

1. Launch **Control Panel**, then select **Administrative Tools**, then select **Local Security Policy**.

2. In the left-hand pane of the console select **Local Policies**, and then select the appropriate folder for the option you wish to modify.

3. In the right-hand pane, right-click the policy you wish to modify and select **Properties** from the pop-up menu. The property sheet for that policy appears. Make changes as appropriate for the policy you are configuring.

User Rights Assignment

User rights pertain to the specific activities that users may perform, such as loading or unloading device drivers, limiting access to specific computers, or changing the system time. These rights can be assigned to a user or a group; Microsoft's stance is and always has been that it is better to set permissions and rights by group, rather than by individual users. If you only have a handful of users in your network, management by group may be more difficult than administering each user independently. However, if you have more than 10 to15 users, group management is usually easier in the long run. Regardless of whether you manage by users or groups, assigning rights uses the same process: Double-click the policy option under the **User Rights assignment** folder, click the **Add User or Group** button, and supply the appropriate user or group name(s).

The following user rights deal with authentication-related issues.

- **Access this computer from the network:** Permits a user to connect to a specific computer via network.
- **Deny access to this computer from the network:** Prohibits a remote user or group from accessing a specific computer from the network. Useful for securing servers with large numbers of directories that should not be accessed by anyone other than a specific group or user.
- **Allow logon through Terminal Services:** Users are permitted to connect to the computer via terminal services.
- **Deny logon through Terminal Services:** Disables terminal service access to specific users or groups, while still allowing those with "Allow logon through Terminal Services" rights to continue doing so.
- **Log on as a batch job:** Allows a user, such as a service account, to log on by means of a batch job.
- **Deny logon as a batch job:** Prevents specific users and groups from logging on as a batch.
- **Log on as a service:** Enables accounts to log on as a service, in order to access resources on behalf of an application.
- **Deny logon as a service:** Prevents specific users and groups from logging on as a service.
- **Log on locally:** Permits users to use this computer locally.
- **Deny logon locally:** Prohibits specific users or groups from using the computer locally. Useful in instances where a computer is in a public area but you want to limit the use to a specific user or two.

Security Options

Security Options govern specific configuration options that are used to increase or decrease security on a given computer. These options are assigned to the computer, not users or groups, unlike User Rights Assignment. All users of this computer are subject to these policies. The following Security Options deal with authentication-related issues and are located in the Security Options folder under Local Security Policy. To modify a policy, double-click it and make the necessary changes.

- **Do not display last user name:** Hides the last username in the Control + Alt + Delete log-on screen. This makes it difficult for fraudulent users to access your network by guessing passwords based on known usernames.
- **Do not require CTRL+ALT+DEL:** Eliminates the need to press Control + Alt + Delete to log on. This puts the user credentials at risk, as the MSGINA is no longer able to use a secure channel to transmit credentials, and a fraudulent user can capture the password, even without sending data over a network.
- **Message text for users attempting to log on:** You can specify a legal warning or disclaimer that appears before users are permitted to log on.
- **Message title for users attempting to log on:** This controls the title of the window where pre-log-on messages appear. Title suggestions include Warning, Notice, and Attention.
- **Number of previous logons to cache** (in case a domain controller is not available)**:** Sets the number of log-on attempts to be stored by a domain account. This is helpful for remote computers where an Internet connection must be made before a domain controller can be contacted. If the ISP has unreliable service, a domain user can be locked out if the connection cannot be made. The downside of this is that a fraudulent user can disconnect a computer from the network and use recently changed credentials to log in to the network without being blocked by a domain controller. Zero disables caching.
- **Prompt user to change password before expiration:** Gives users a warning that they will be required to change account passwords in the near future.
- **Require domain controller authentication to unlock:** Prevents a user from using cached credentials to log on to a computer that has been locked.

- **Smart card removal behavior:** If smart cards are used, you can determine what will happen if a card is removed while the computer is in use. The choices are Lock workstation, Force Log off, and No action.

- **Allow anonymous SID/Name translation:** Enables anonymous users to translate SIDs into usernames and vice versa.

- **Do not allow anonymous enumeration of SAM accounts:** Prohibits anonymous users from enumerating the SAM.

- **Do not allow Stored User Names and Passwords to save passports or credentials for domain authentication:** Prevents passport or domain authentication credentials from being saved after user has logged off, if Saved Passwords has been configured.

- **Sharing and security model for local accounts:** Guest only requires all network logons to use the Guest account. Classic allows network users to use their own credentials.

- **Let Everyone permissions apply to Anonymous users:** Grants Everyone group permissions to anonymous users.

- **Do not store LAN Manager hash value on next password change:** LAN Manager hash is deleted after a password change.

- **Force log off when log-on time expires:** Requires a user to be forcefully logged off the computer if a time constraint has been placed on his or her account. The account equivalent of Cinderella's carriage becoming a pumpkin at midnight.

- **LAN Manager Authentication Level:** Sets LAN Manager authentication requirements for networks with down-level Windows hosts.

- **Minimum session security for NTLM SSP based (including secure RPC) clients:** Permits configuration of the following options:
  - Require message integrity
  - Require message confidentiality
  - Require NTLMv2 session security
  - Require 128-bit encryption

- **Allow system to be shut down without having to log on:** Permits or prohibits a computer from being shut down without the user being logged on.

Conclusion

In this chapter we covered authentication, the process of verifying the identity of the user attempting to access a computer or other network resource. Once a user's identity has been proven to a reasonable level, authorization can occur. Windows XP Professional can provide total authentication services or it can interoperate with Windows NT, Windows 2000, and Windows 2003. The specific procedures of Windows XP authentication were covered including Kerberos and NTLM and how the log-on process works with each of these authentication types. Also covered in this chapter were new authentication features within Windows XP and best practices for configuration and management of Windows XP authentication. From here we move to the next step for a user to access a network resource or computer. Authorization, or determining that a verified user has been granted permission to access a specific resource or given the right to perform a specific task, is covered in the next chapter.

Chapter

17

Authorization and Access Control

In Chapter 16, we discussed authentication, the process of verifying the identity of the party requesting access to a computer, file, folder, or other resource. This chapter picks up from there to discuss what happens once the identification of the user is authenticated, starting with the example presented at the beginning of Chapter 16: an ATM transaction.

To use an ATM, you are required to present an ATM card and the correct PIN for that ATM card. Once the ATM has verified that the credentials match the account designated on the card, it asks you what type of transaction you want to perform. For example, if you want to withdraw cash, you must meet a number of criteria for approval or authorization, such as:

- You have not exceeded your daily withdrawal limit.
- You have that amount of cash in your account.

If you meet all of the qualifications, your request is approved or authorized. If you do not meet all of the qualifications, your request will be denied.

The same holds true for Windows XP and many other operating systems as well. After being authenticated, you must then be approved or authorized to use the resources or perform the task you are attempting. In this chapter we talk about permissions, the authorization process, policies, and authorization strategy planning. Configuration guides are provided where appropriate for these topics. It is important to understand these topics so that you can adequately secure the network resources for which you are responsible.

Permissions

In this section we cover permissions and how to set them.

Overview of Permissions

Let's begin with a look at what permissions and rights are and the differences between the two. Permissions are used to sanction a user to act upon on object. An object is a resource such as a file, folder, or printer that can be controlled by an operating system process. Permissions explicitly grant or deny access to a particular object and sets limits on what level of access is provided. A sign in a store window that says "Come in, we're open" is analogous to a permission to use a specific printer. Similarly, a "No trespassing" sign is analogous to an access-denied message when an unauthorized user attempts to use the same printer.

Rights allow users to perform certain tasks on the computer or operating system, such as backing up files or folders, loading device drivers, or changing the system time. Rights apply to the whole system, not just a single object, and may supercede a specific permission in some cases. An example of this is performing system backups and restores. A user that is granted rights to perform backups and restores needs to have access to all files and folders to successfully back them up. For example, a specific user may not be granted permissions to the human resources department files for privacy reasons. However, this same user is given the right to perform backups and restores on the server where these files reside, which gives him or her the ability to perform these actions on those files and folders. Granted, the user still does not have access to these resources at the file level, but you can see how the right overrides the permission to a certain extent.

Access Control Lists

The creator of an object has full control over the object, including the right to give or deny others access to the object. The list of entities that have been given or denied access is called an access control list (ACL). The entities listed on an ACL have accounts, are called access control entries or ACEs (also known as security principals), and can be users, groups, computers, or services.

Each security principal is known to the operating system by its SID, or Security Identification. The user-friendly name of the account, such as BobF or Joan's Team, is simply a property of the account. The SID is the actual identifier of the account—if an account is deleted, the SID is destroyed and all permissions and rights associated with that SID also are destroyed. Recreating the account with the same user name will not restore the permissions or rights.

In addition to enumerating specific entities granted or denied permission, ACLs also catalog the level of access allowed or denied, as well as any audit-related settings. These functions are split between two different types of ACLs:

- **Discretionary Access Control List (DACL):** This list contains ACEs and their respective permission levels.
- **System Access Control List (SACL):** This list contains audit-related data.

File and Folder Permissions

Permissions are granted to users, groups, computers, or services in a very granular manner. This allows access to be tailored to the level most appropriate for the security of the data or resource involved. Permissions granted to a single user apply only to that user. Permissions granted to a group apply to all members of that group.

Permissions available for assignment are based on the file system in use on the partition where the file is located. NTFS (NT file system) is the recommended file system; it offers greater scalability than FAT or FAT32, including support for disks over 32GB and greater granularity of permissions for files and folders. This chapter focuses on the richer permissions available with NTFS, which are more complex than those available for FAT or FAT 32.

Folder Permissions

The following permissions are available for folders that reside on NTFS partitions:

- **Read:** Permits users to view the files and folders within a folder as well as the folder's attributes, ownership, and permissions.
- **Write:** Permits users to create new files and folders within the folder, change the folder's attributes, and view the folder's ownership properties and permissions.
- **List Folder Contents:** Permits users to view only the names of files and folders within the folders.
- **Read and Execute:** Grants the user both Read permission and List Folder Contents permissions.
- **Modify:** Permits a user to delete the folder plus provides all abilities associated with Write and Read and Execute permissions.
- **Full Control:** Grants a level of permission that is an accumulation of all the above levels of permissions, as well as granting the ability to assign permissions to that folder.

File Permissions

The following basic permissions are available for files that reside on NTFS partitions:

- **Read:** Permits a user to read the file and view file attributes, ownership, and permissions.
- **Write:** Permits a user to overwrite the file, change the file's attributes, and view file ownership and permissions.
- **Read and Execute:** Permits a user to run applications and grants Read permission.
- **Modify:** Permits a user to modify and delete the file and grants Write and Read and Execute permissions.
- **Full Control:** Grants a level of permission that is an accumulation of all the above levels of permissions, as well as granting the ability to assign permissions to that file.

Advanced File and Folder Permissions

Further levels of permission beyond the basic file and folder permissions explained previously are available on NTFS partitions. These provide greater levels of granularity than the aforementioned combinations.

- **Traverse Folder/Execute File:** Permits or prohibits navigating through folders to reach other files or folders.
- **List Folder/Read Data:** Permits or prohibits viewing the names of files and folders within the folder.
- **Read Attributes:** Permits or prohibits viewing the attributes of a file or folder.
- **Read Extended Attributes:** Permits or prohibits viewing the extended attributes of a file or folder.
- **Create Files/Write Data:** Permits or prohibits creation of files within the folder, making changes to specified files, and overwriting existing content.
- **Create Folders/Append Data:** Permits or prohibits creation of folders within the folder and adding data to the end of the file without changing, deleting, or overwriting existing data.
- **Write Attributes:** Permits or prohibits changing the attributes of a file or folder.
- **Write Extended Attributes:** Permits or prohibits changing the extended attributes of a file or folder.

- **Delete Subfolders and Files:** Permits or prohibits deletion of folders and files within the folder.
- **Delete:** Permits or prohibits deletion of the file or folder.
- **Read Permissions:** Permits or prohibits reading the permissions of a file or folder.
- **Change Permissions:** Permits or prohibits changing the permissions of the file or folder.
- **Take Ownership:** This allows or denies taking ownership of a file or folder.

These advanced permissions are combinations of the basic permissions for very specific purposes. Table 17.1 shows how the basic permissions combine to provide these special permissions for folders.

Table 17.2 shows how the basic permissions are combined to provide these special permissions for files.

Table 17.1   Effective Special Permissions for Folders

Advanced Permission	Full Control	Modify	Read and Execute	List Folder Contents	Read	Write
Traverse Folder/ Execute File	Yes	Yes	Yes	Yes	No	No
List Folder/ Read Data	Yes	Yes	Yes	Yes	Yes	No
Read Attributes	Yes	Yes	Yes	Yes	Yes	No
Read Extended Attributes	Yes	Yes	Yes	Yes	Yes	No
Create Files/ Write Data	Yes	Yes	No	No	No	Yes
Create Folders/ Append Data	Yes	Yes	No	No	No	Yes
Write Attributes	Yes	Yes	No	No	No	Yes
Write Extended Attributes	Yes	Yes	No	No	No	Yes
Delete Subfolders and Files	Yes	No	No	No	No	No

Table 17.2 Effective Special Permissions for Files

Advanced Permissions	Full Control	Modify	Read and Execute	Read	Write
Traverse Folder/Execute File	Yes	Yes	Yes	No	No
List Folder/Read Data	Yes	Yes	Yes	Yes	No
Read Attributes	Yes	Yes	Yes	Yes	No
Read Extended Attributes	Yes	Yes	Yes	Yes	No
Create Files/Write Data	Yes	Yes	No	No	Yes
Create Folders/Append Data	Yes	Yes	No	No	Yes
Write Attributes	Yes	Yes	No	No	Yes
Write Extended Attributes	Yes	Yes	No	No	Yes
Delete	Yes	Yes	No	No	No
Read Permissions	Yes	Yes	Yes	Yes	No
Change Permissions	Yes	No	No	No	No
Take Ownership	Yes	No	No	No	No

Setting Permissions

Permissions are set on the Security tab of the Properties page of the object. This Security tab is visible only to users with the appropriate permissions, as noted in Read Permissions listed in Table 17.2. The ACL, ACEs, and specific permissions are displayed here, as well as the effective permissions of each user, bringing into play the advanced permissions previously noted. On some OEM versions of Windows XP Professional, you may notice differences from what is presented here.

 NOTE: The Security tab only appears on NTFS partitions on Windows XP Professional.

Setting Basic Permissions

To modify the list of accounts or ACEs with permissions to an object:

1. Right-click an object such as a file, folder, or printer, and select **Properties** from the context menu, then click the **Security** tab (Figure 17.1).
2. To add a new ACE, click the **Add** button. The Select User or Group dialog box appears, as shown in Figure 17.2.

Figure 17.1 File and folder permissions are set on the Security tab of the Properties sheet.

3. Type the name of the account that you wish to give permission in the **Enter the object name to select** field. Windows XP automatically verifies the name that you entered as being valid. An underlined name means that the verification is successful.

4. Click **OK** when done.

5. If you wish to delete an ACE, simply select the name of the account on the Security tab and click **Remove**.

To modify the basic permissions for an ACE:

1. Select the account name from the **Group or user names** field in the top half of the **Security** tab page of the **Properties** sheet.

2. In the lower half of the page in the **Permissions** field, click the check boxes to add or remove permissions for the account.

3. Click **OK** to complete the task.

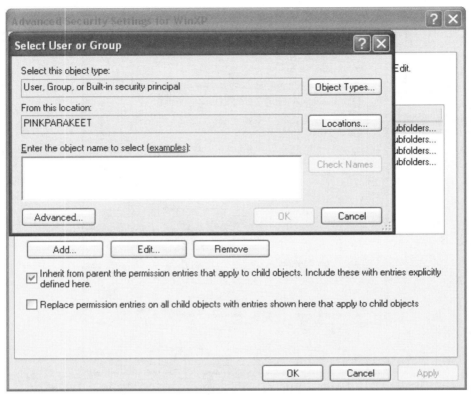

Figure 17.2 Adding a new ACE

Setting Advanced Permissions

The Properties sheet Security page provides additional information about the advanced permissions for an object, including these items:

- Special permissions
- Access inheritance options
- Ownership information
- Effective permissions

To add or modify the advanced permissions of an object:

1. Right-click an object such as a file, folder, or printer, and select **Properties** from the context menu, then click the **Security** tab.
2. Click the **Advanced** button. The Advanced Security Settings page appears, as shown in Figure 17.3.

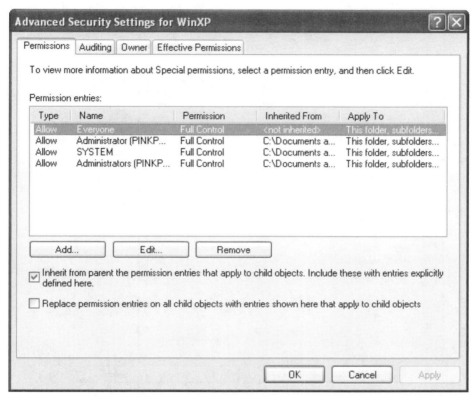

Figure 17.3   Advanced Security Settings

3. Select the account to manage, then click **Edit**.
4. Click to add or remove the specific permissions for an account, as shown in Figure 17.4.

Viewing Effective Permissions

Once you have set all your permissions, you may wish to view the effective permissions for that user or group to ensure that they match what you had intended. This is especially helpful when troubleshooting a user's access problems. The Effective Permissions tab is shown in Figure 17.5. This page lists all the permissions that apply to a security principal for a file or folder.

To reach the Effective Permissions page:

1. Right-click the object and select **Properties** from the context menu, then click the **Security** tab.
2. Click the **Advanced** button. The Advanced Security Settings page appears.

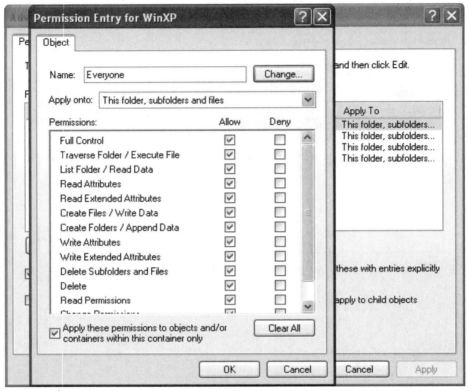

Figure 17.4 Modifying advanced permissions

3. Select the **Effective Permissions** tab.
4. Click the **Select** button to open the Select User or Group dialog box.
5. In the **Name** box, type the name of the built-in security principal, group, or user for which you would like to view Effective Permissions.

Inheritance of Permissions

By default, the permissions applied to a folder propagate to the files and folders located within it. This is called inheritance. You can modify or block this inheritance to increase security if so desired. For example, a specific directory called Finance houses critical financial information for your company. This location contains a number of files and two subdirectories, one called Board of Directors, the other called Department Documentation. The entire finance department may need access to the files and the Department Documentation folder, while the Board of Directors folder is only accessible to certain departmental members. You may find it easier to block inheritance to the Board of Directors folder

Figure 17.5 The effective permissions for a specific account

than to apply permissions to each item individually, especially if the permissions on the Finance folder change frequently. Blocking inheritance means changes made to parent folders do not affect child folders and files.

To block permission changes made to parent folders from affecting child folders and files:

1. Open the **Advanced Security Settings** page for the file or folder.
2. Click the **Permissions** tab.
3. In the lower half of the page, clear the **Inherit from parent the permission entries that apply to child objects** check box.
4. Click **OK**.

How to Manage Ownership Permissions

By default the creator of an object is the owner. The owner has full control over the object, including the ability to change permissions on the object.

Occasionally, it may be necessary for another user to take ownership of an object, such as when users are on vacation or have left their job permanently. Users can be given permissions to change permissions on a folder, but the ultimate solution to folder administration is to give a user Take Ownership permission. Members of the Administrators group have this ability automatically. Alternatively a new user can be delegated to have this permission. Ownership is not automatically switched when Take Ownership permission is granted. Once the user has authorization to take ownership, the user must actively take this ownership.

To view the ownership information:

1. Right-click the file or folder and select **Properties** from the secondary menu.
2. On the **Security** tab, click the **Advanced** button to view the **Advanced Security Settings** of the resource. The Advanced Security Settings sheet appears.
3. Click the **Owner** tab, as shown in Figure 17.6. Users who have been assigned permission to take ownership are displayed in this pane.

To take ownership of an object:

1. Select the appropriate name from the list on the **owner** tab
2. Indicate if the change in ownership will apply to subcontainers and objects.
3. Click **OK**.

While a member of the Administrators group can take ownership of any object, this may be a time-consuming process if ownership of a number of objects must be taken, such as in the case of a change in administrative staff. You can opt to have all administrators be the owner of all objects created by any other member of the administrators group by default if you so desire. To do so:

1. Open **Control Panel** and select **Performance and Maintenance**.
2. Click **Administrative Tools** then double-click **Local Security Policy**.
3. Under Security Settings, double-click **Local Policies**, and then click **Security Options**.
4. Double-click the policy **System objects: Default owner for objects created by members of the Administrators group**.
5. In the drop-down list box, select **Administrators group** as shown in Figure 17.7 and click **OK**.

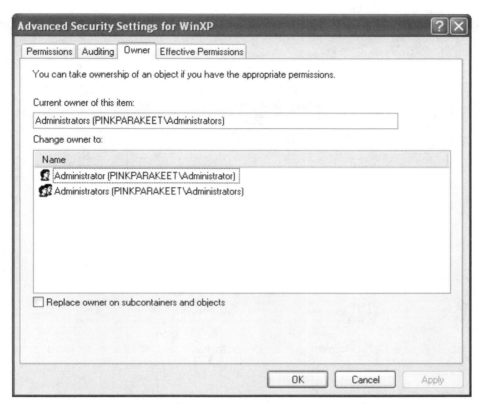

Figure 17.6 Displaying ownership permissions

Windows XP ACL Defaults

You may find it helpful to know the default settings for Windows XP Discretionary Access Control Lists. Recall that DACLs are the ACLs that contain user-specific permissions assignments and levels of access. Knowing and understanding these defaults can be helpful when troubleshooting user-access problems.

All newly created objects are given a DACL. All inheritable ACEs from the parent object are incorporated into the new DACL. This means that if you create a new folder and assign the Legal group access to it, not only does the Legal group have access, but any other groups or users specified in the parent folder that were not specifically blocked can, too. If the creator specifies no DACL, and there are no inheritable users or groups in the parent object, the object is given the default ACL. The same holds true for specific permission levels assigned to a user or group for that object.

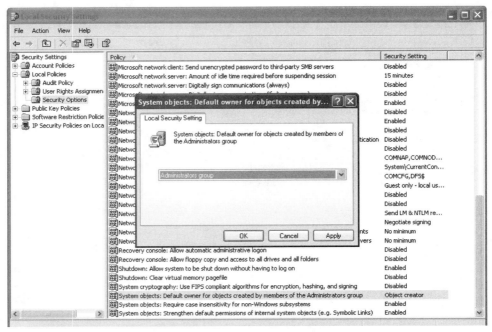

Figure 17.7 Permitting the Administrators group to own all objects created by any member of that group.

Authorization Process

The Windows XP authorization process is fairly straightforward. When a user account is created, it is given a Security Identification. The SID is the principal identifier for the account. In addition to storing the user's name as part of the account properties, Windows XP also stores all the rights and permissions assigned to a user. The SID is used by Windows XP to reference the account. At the time a user logs on, Windows XP creates a security access token. The token contains the Security Identification for the user account, the SIDs for any groups that account may be a member of, and the user-friendly names for the user group accounts. Every process that is running on behalf of this user has a copy of the access token. In much the same way that a doorman checks the guest list in an apartment building, Windows NT checks the security IDs within the token when a user tries to access an object. The SIDs are checked against the list of access permissions for the object to ensure that the user has sufficient permission to access the object. If sufficient permission exists, the user is granted access. Alternatively, if the user has been specifically denied permission or has no explicitly granted permission for his or her account or any other group he or she is a member of, the user is blocked from accessing the resource.

Creating an Access Control Strategy

In order to effectively manage access controls such as permissions, we recommend that you create a written plan covering the use and policies surrounding access controls. It is much easier to manage access controls (and subsequently troubleshoot problems) if you have a known baseline from which to work. If you know what should be deployed, it is a much faster job to identify the variations from the plan and allow exceptions according to a set of rules known and agreed to by all. Naturally, any access control plan should be part and parcel of a larger general security plan and the policy set for the network as a whole.

Planning

Planning is the most important element in building your strategy. You need to have a clear idea of what you are trying to do before you go about implementing your strategy. Without good planning, deploying and subsequently enforcing any security policies will be very difficult. Haphazardly applying security controls can result in your users being unable to access resources they should be able to reach, while leaving other areas exposed to unauthorized users. Further, troubleshooting these problems can take much longer than if they had been applied in an organized manner. The result: unnecessary service outages. Delays in repairing access problems, whether due to a denial of service attack or a user simply being unable to open a file containing critical and time-sensitive data that he or she should have had access to, can and should be avoided. This section leads you through the general planning process, and provides you with a list of questions designed to prompt you to consider all aspects of an access control plan before you start configuring ACLs.

Requirements Gathering and Analysis

Start by gathering the requirements for the project. The requirements include both the goals and the constraints of the final plan. Goals are what you want to accomplish. Constraints are the limits placed on the manner in which the goals can be accomplished. Be sure to interview all stakeholders, including management and users, to include all requirements. Ask stakeholders what they want to accomplish. A common mistake made by administrators is to develop an access control plan that meets all their security requirements, but limits or prevents users from accessing resources they need to reach. This is not a good situation and can lead to bad feelings between users and IT staff if not resolved to the benefit of everyone. Remember, keeping resources secure is absolutely vital, but if no one can use the resources after they have been secured, there is no point in even having them. However, meeting with or interviewing stakeholders before you implement a plan gives you the ability to determine how to compromise or work out alternate access methods for those resources, and keeps all parties happy in the end.

As part of this process, identify specific risks that you may have in your network. Visiting vendors, temps, contractors, special client requirements, or budgetary issues may create special circumstances that need to be accommodated. You may find it helpful to categorize and prioritize these risks. This helps when resolving conflicts between risks and user-access requirements. This information can be used to demonstrate the tradeoffs needed and allows executing management to determine what risks and consequences they can expect from certain actions.

Managing requirements over time is important. New security risks are continually identified, corporate requirements for access change, and technology changes. It is important to review changing requirements over time. How often this is done and the process by which is it done should be part of the overall strategy.

Security Methods to Be Used

How you meet the requirements gathered in the first phase of this process is the next question to answer. You need to develop and design a security specification plan. This plan must include all the items to be secured, the users and groups that need to be given access, the types of access needed, and how it is to be implemented. It is wise to create verification and validation plans as well. Verification plans detail how you test to ensure that the requirements are met. Validation plans measure how well the implementation method is performed in this regard. Are users able to reach specific resources as planned? Are users denied access to resources as desired? Testing these items in a lab or in a limited pilot environment, before overall deployment, is definitely helpful and can identify sticky issues before they are put into production. If you have ever spent the weekend trying to figure out why, after changing the inheritance settings on a couple of folders, the vice president of marketing can no longer access the sales forecasts for the next six months, you understand the value of testing early and often!

Policies and Processes

This often-overlooked step involves creating a document for use by all parties affected by the access control plan. A document for general distribution should be created that outlines what is specifically allowed and denied, how it shall be enforced, as well as how to go about getting an exception to the policy. Another document should be created for the administrative team that spells out the specific processes and policies, including auditing (covered in the next section), associated with access control as well as the circumstances under which exceptions can be made.

Configuring Auditing

Auditing is another important area to include in the access control plan. Auditing allows you to monitor specific objects for access attempts and determine if these attempts indicate potentially unauthorized access or a user that needs a bit more training. Auditing plans should include a list of items to be audited and what they will be audited for. Once that is determined, you need to determine how often the logs are to be reviewed, by whom, and the archive policy. In addition, an escalation path for dealing with problems revealed by audits should be developed and documented. Auditing can really slow down your computer, so you do not want to set auditing for everything. Selectively choose what you really need. Typically, auditing is used to find users doing things they *should not* be doing, so it makes sense to only audit the failures at first, assuming that you have fully secured all network resources. If you determine a pattern that needs further investigation, you can modify what you are auditing at that time.

Once you have determined what you will audit, you can go about the business of setting up auditing. While covering the details of audit configuration, we also discuss the types of things that can be audited.

Account Log-on Events

If you would like to track users logging on and logging off locally, you should enable auditing of account log-on events. This particular audit is helpful to determine if someone is attempting to use a dictionary or brute force attack to gain access to your network. A series of repeated log-on failures at an unusual time is a clue that this activity may not be legitimate. For example, a user named Dillon may only work from 8 A.M. to 5 P.M., Monday through Friday. A review of the audit log, however, shows that Dillon makes five attempts to log on every night between 12:30 A.M. and 2:30 A.M. Your account policy settings require a lockout after five incorrect log-on attempts, but the account lockout expires after four hours. Because the "real" Dillon has never been locked out of his computer and requested that you reset his password, you determine that this is most likely an unauthorized user and begin to investigate this issue.

This option is set through the Audit Policy object within Local Security Settings. It is reached by the following method:

1. Click **Start**, then **Settings**, then **Control Panel**, then **Local Security Policy**.
2. Click on **Audit Policy** in the left-hand column, as shown in Figure 17.8.

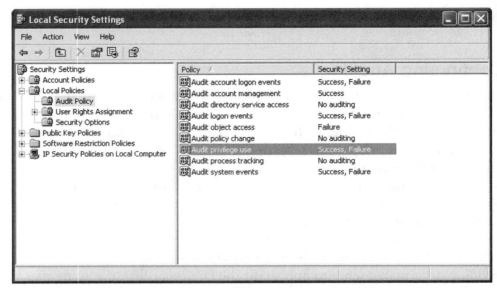

Figure 17.8 Audit Policy is configured within Local Security Settings.

3. Double-click **Audit account log-on events** in the right-hand pane to reach the screen shown in Figure 17.9.
4. When defining this setting, you can specify Windows XP audits successes, audits failures, or to not audit the event type at all. Success audits generate an audit entry in the audit logs when an account log-on attempt succeeds. Failure audits also generate an audit entry in the audit logs when an account log-on attempt fails. Simply check Success and/or Failure. To stop auditing log-on events, clear both the Success and Failure check boxes.

Account Management

If you are interested in tracking when user account changes are being made or attempted, you should enable this option. When an attempt is made to modify a user or group account, such as unlocking an account, changing a password, creating a new account, and so on, it is tracked in the audit logs. Keeping track of who is making changes in user accounts, when, and why is helpful in a network where a number of people have the ability to create or change user accounts.

This option is also set within Local Security Settings\Local Policies\Audit Policies. The parameters permit you to audit successes, audit failures, or not audit the event type at all. Success audits generate an audit log entry when any

Figure 17.9 Configuring auditing of log-on events.

account management event succeeds. Failure audits generate an audit log entry when any account management event fails. To set this value, check Success and/or Failure. To stop auditing account management events, clear both the Success and Failure check boxes.

Directory Service Access

If your Windows XP computer is a member of a Windows 2000 domain, you can see this option to audit directory service access, but it has no value on Windows XP, even if configured. This setting controls whether or not to enable auditing of a user accessing an Active Directory object that has its own system access control list specified.

Log-on Events

This option controls whether or not network log-on activity is audited for success or failure. Unlike account log-on events, this only deals with log-on attempts being attempted from a remote computer. However, it is useful to monitor network log-on attempts for the same reasons as local attempts. If you determine that particularly disturbing patterns in log-on attempts are beginning to develop, you can take precautionary measures in advance.

This option is also set within Local Security Settings\Local Policies\Audit Policies. The parameters permit you to audit successes, audit failures, or not audit the event type at all. Success audits generate an audit log entry when any network log-on attempt succeeds. Failure audits generate an audit log entry when any network log-on attempt fails. To set this value, check Success and/or Failure. To stop auditing log-on events, clear both the Success and Failure check boxes.

Object Access

Object access auditing tracks attempts to use specific objects such as files, folders, registry keys, printers, processes, or the like. This setting is only valid on objects that have been configured for auditing and only for objects residing on an NTFS partition.

 NOTE: If you do not enable editing for *both* the object access parameter in Local Security Settings\Local Policies\Audit Policies *and* the SACL on the property sheet for the objects (registry keys, files, folders, processes, etc.) that you want to monitor, auditing will not function. Be sure that you enable both auditing components!

This option is set within Local Security Settings\Local Policies\Audit Policies. Success audits generate an audit entry when a user successfully accesses an object that has a SACL specified. Failure audits generate an audit entry when a user unsuccessfully attempts to access an object that has a SACL specified. To disable auditing, remove the check mark from both Success and Failure.

To Audit Files, Folders, and Printers

After you enable auditing in Local Policies\Audit Policies, you can specify the files, folders, and printers that you want audited. To do so:

1. Locate the file, folder, or printer you want to audit.
2. Right-click the object to be audited, and then click **Properties**.
3. Click the **Security** tab, and then click **Advanced**.
4. Click the **Auditing** tab, and then click **Add**. The Auditing Entry dialog box will appear as shown in Figure 17.10.
5. In the Object Name box, type the name of the user or group whose access you want to audit. You can browse the computer for names by clicking **Advanced**, and then clicking **Find Now** in the Select User or Group dialog box.
6. Click **OK**.
7. Select the **Successful** or **Failed** check boxes for the actions you want to audit and then click **OK.** Each of the actions you select appears in the audit log if the criteria for success or failure are met.
8. Click **OK**, and then click **OK** again to close the object's property sheet.

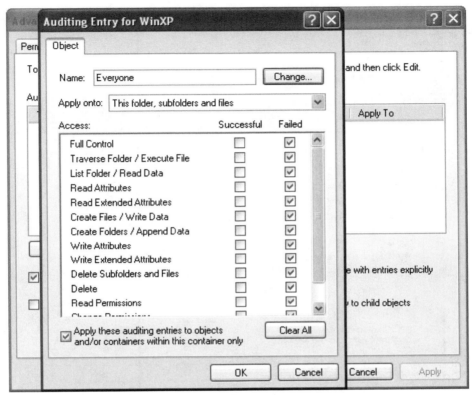

Figure 17.10   Enabling auditing on a folder.

To Audit Activity on a Registry Key

You can also audit registry key modifications. This is helpful for troubleshooting—for one thing you can determine which key was modified, and for another, you can determine who did it so you can follow up with additional questions about the configuration changes (as well as a quick reminder of the dangers of editing the registry without a full backup at the ready).

1. To open Registry Editor, click **Start**, then **Run**, then type `regedit.exe`, and then click **OK**.
2. Click the key you want to audit.
3. On the Edit menu, click **Permissions**.
4. Click **Advanced**, and then click the **Auditing** tab.
5. Double-click the name of a group or user.
6. Under Access, select or clear the **Successful** and **Failed** check boxes for the activities that you want to audit or to stop auditing (again refer to Figure 17.10).

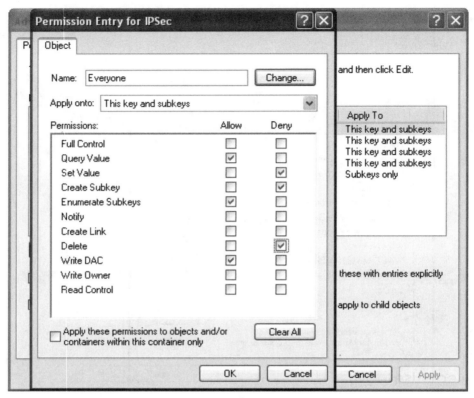

Figure 17.11 Setting a SACL on a registry key.

The options for success and failure auditing on registry key permissions, shown in Figure 17.11, are as follows:

- **Query Value:** An attempt to read a registry key entry
- **Set Value:** An attempt to set entries in a registry key
- **Create Subkey:** An attempt to create subkeys of a selected registry key
- **Enumerate Subkeys:** An attempt to identify the subkeys of a registry key
- **Notify:** A notification event from a key in the registry
- **Create Link:** An attempt to create a symbolic link in a particular key
- **Delete:** An attempt to delete a registry object
- **Write DAC:** An attempt to write a discretionary access control list on the key
- **Write Owner:** An attempt to change the owner of the selected key
- **Read Control:** An attempt to open the discretionary access control list on a key

To Audit Access of Global System Objects

This audit policy option allows the auditing of system objects such as DOS devices, mutexes, and semaphores. Once enabled, system objects can be created with a default system access control list.

This option is configured from within Computer Configuration\Windows Settings\Security Settings\Local Policies\Security Options. To set it, simply click **Enable** or **Disable** as appropriate, then reboot.

Policy Changes

This option permits you to audit changes to the user rights assignment policies, audit policies, or trust policies. If you have a number of administrators, you may find it helpful to know who is making what changes, when, and why.

Like the previous audit options, policy change auditing is enabled within Computer Configuration\Windows Settings\Security Settings\Local Policies\ Audit Policy. You can audit successes and/or failures. Success audits generate an audit log entry when a change to user rights assignment policies, audit policies, or trust policies is successful. Failure audits generate an audit log entry when a change to user rights assignment policies, audit policies, or trust policies fails. To stop auditing, remove checks from both the Success and Failure check boxes.

Privilege Use

Earlier in this chapter the difference between a right and permission were defined. Rights, as you recall, are the special privileges assigned to users for various functions. If you want to monitor if your users are using their powers for good or evil, this is the way to do it. It is also a good way to see who is changing the system time on a computer, if you note that scripts and batch jobs are not executing as intended. Auditing system time change can also give you a clue as to who is running demo software beyond the legal limits specified in that application's license agreement. If a user suddenly shifts the time and date on his or her computer to show a date 30 or 60 days past, it could be because the demo copy they are running is about to expire. This can help keep you in compliance with licensing agreements.

Like the previous audit options, policy change auditing is enabled within Computer Configuration\Windows Settings\Security Settings\Local Policies\ Audit Policy. You can audit both successes and failures. Success audits generate an audit log entry when the exercise of a user right succeeds. Failure audits generate an audit log entry when the exercise of a user right fails. To disable auditing of this option, simply remove the checks from both Success and Failure check boxes.

Not all user rights are audited however. Windows XP does not audit the following user rights, even if you have chosen to audit user rights:

- Bypass traverse checking
- Debug programs
- Create a token object
- Replace process level token
- Generate security audits

Auditing Backups and Restores

If you want to audit the back up and restoring of files, you must enable a second policy. This is a quick and easy way to determine when and who performed a backup or restore. An IT manager may use this to be sure his administrators are doing backups according to schedule. However, an audit log entry is generated for each and every file that is backed up and restored, so if you are backing up hundreds of files, you may not want to do this, or you may only want to enable it on the local system being backed up by another server over the network.

To enable or disable this feature, locate **Audit the use of Backup and Restore privilege** within Computer Configuration\Windows Settings\Security Settings\Local Policies\Security Options and select **Enable** or **Disable**.

Process Tracking

To track the application usage habits of a specific user or group of users, enable process tracking. This generates a log entry every time a designated user or group launches or attempts to launch a given application or process. If an application is licensed by user, rather than by seat, and a single Windows XP computer is shared by two or more users, you may be out of compliance if you have not obtained enough licenses for this application. With process tracking, however, you can monitor how many users are using this application and compare it to the number of licenses you have on hand. This audit feature provides information for process exit, handle duplication, and indirect object access in addition to simple application launch.

Process tracking auditing is enabled within Computer Configuration\ Windows Settings\Security Settings\Local Policies\Audit Policy. You can audit both successes and failures. Success audits generate an audit log entry when an audited process use succeeds. Failure audits generate an audit log entry when the audited process use fails. To disable auditing of this option, simply remove the checks from both Success and Failure check boxes.

System Events

To track events such as a purge of the security log (where audit log entries are stored), or monitor system reboots, enable system event logging. This is a great way to track the last time a system was rebooted.

System event auditing is enabled within Computer Configuration\Windows Settings\Security Settings\Local Policies\Audit Policy. You can audit both successes and failures. Success audits generate an audit log entry when a system event is executed successfully. Failure audits generate an audit log entry when a system event is attempted unsuccessfully. To disable auditing of this option, simply remove the checks from both Success and Failure check boxes.

Event Viewer

The Event Viewer is the tool used to view the logs generated by Windows XP. These logs are

- **Application logs:** Present application-specific information such as application hangs, installation completion notifications, or file system checks.
- **Security logs:** Present security-elated information such as password expirations, bad log-on attempts, or other audit-related information as configured by the administrator.
- **System log:** Presents system-level information such as expired DHCP addresses or master browser election updates.

The Event Viewer presents this information in the context of the Microsoft Management Console and is shown in Figure 17.12.

The Event Viewer groups the events that it presents into the following categories:

- **Error:** Signifies that a major problem has occurred. These problems could include such things as an application crash, a failed certificate enrollment, or a domain controller that could not be contacted.
- **Warning:** Indicates that something is wrong, but it is not a major problem at this time. Examples include corrupt system objects, a required resource such as a network drive does not exist, or memory used by an application is not free.
- **Information:** Communicates general information such as that a service has started successfully, an application error has occurred, or application configuration has completed successfully.

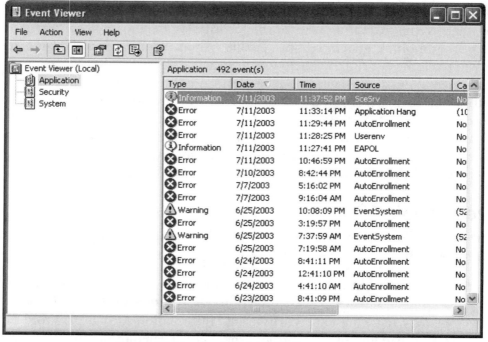

Figure 17.12   The Windows XP Event Viewer

- **Success Audit:** Indicates that a specific audited event was completed successfully.
- **Failed Audit:** Indicates failure of a specific audited event.

These logs should be reviewed periodically, or at least as often as indicated in your security plan. Once reviewed, they can be purged or saved for future examination. They can give you many clues to things going on, such as a flaky network card, a potential intrusion, or the general health and status of a computer. If you do not review them periodically, you could be missing the first indication of a big problem that is about to happen.

Using Event Viewer

This section covers how to view, interpret, and manage event logs.

Viewing Event Logs

To open Event Viewer you have two options. The easiest way is to go directly to it by clicking **Start**, **Settings**, **Control Panel**, then **Administrative Tools**, and finally **Event Viewer**. Alternatively, you can reach it through the Computer

Management Console. Some administrators find this more useful, as a number of other systems-related settings are also reachable in this console. To open it:

1. Click **Start**, **Settings**, **Control Panel**, then **Administrative Tools and Computer Management**.
2. In the console tree under System Tools, click **Event Viewer**.
3. The Application, Security, and System logs are displayed in the Event Viewer window, as shown in Figure 17.13.

To view the details of an event recorded in one of the Event Viewer logs just double-click the event that you want to view. The Event Properties dialog box appears as shown in Figure 17.14.

Reviewing an Event

The Event Properties dialog box displays header information and a description of the event, which can be used to clarify the event. The top portion of the Event Properties dialog box presents the following information, as appropriate to the type of event:

- Date the event occurred
- Time the event occurred

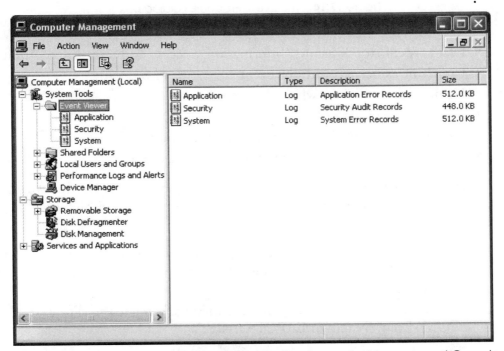

Figure 17.13   Reaching the Event Viewer within the Computer Management Console.

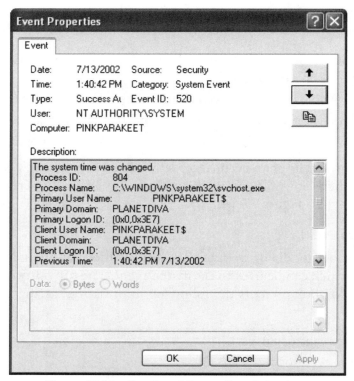

Figure 17.14 The Event Properties dialog box

- Event type: Error, Warning, Information, Success Audit, or Failure Audit
- Username associated with the event
- Name of the computer where the event occurred
- Source of the event
- Category: Classification of the event by the type of event
- Event ID: A number that identifies the specific event

The main portion of the Event Properties dialog box is the description. The information presented here varies by the type of event, but typically it includes such information as:

- The text of the error message as it appeared in any pop-up message. For example, "Windows cannot obtain the domain controller name for your computer network."
- The name of the component that the message is related to. For example, "COM+Event System or EAPOL service."

- An explanation of the circumstances that might generate the message and, if appropriate, a recommended user action. For example, "A socket operation was attempted to an unreachable host."

If you have reviewed the information presented here and would like to know more, you can search online for the specific event ID or error message. There are several ways to do this. One way is to visit *www.technet.com*. TechNet contains the Microsoft KnowledgeBase and documentation for Microsoft products. Another way is to manually navigate to this URL: *http://www.microsoft.com/windowsxp/pro/support/ee.asp*. The Windows XP Events and Errors search page provides a simple form you can use to input the event information, as shown in Figure 17.15.

Securing the Audit Logs

There are two techniques for securing the audit logs. These prevent loss of data and viewing of the data by unauthorized personnel.

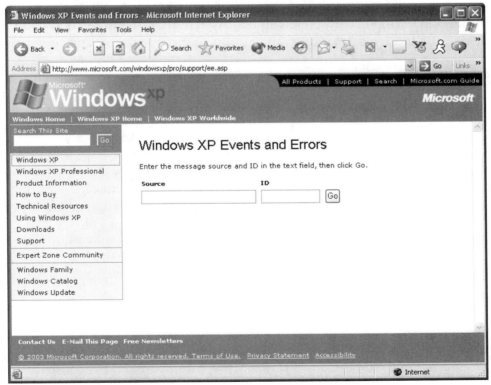

Figure 17.15   The Windows XP Events and Errors search page

System Shutdown

This is one dramatic, but useful, tool to prevent loss of potential security audit information. If Windows XP is unable to log security events, it shuts down. This prevents unaudited activities by users in the event that the security log is unusable for any reason. The most common reason for the security log to be unusable is that it is full, and the settings for retaining or overwriting existing logs are set to prevent loss of existing log data.

To configure this option, open the Security Options in the Local Policies console (Computer Configuration\Windows Settings\Security Settings\Local Policies\Security Options). Select **Enable** or **Disable** as appropriate. Once this policy is set, and the security log is unusable, the following Stop error is displayed, and the system will shut down.

```
STOP: C0000244 {Audit Failed}
An attempt to generate a security audit failed.
```

To make the system usable again, an administrator must log on and either archive or purge the security log to make room for new audit data. If you find that you are performing this step often, revisit the amount of data that you are auditing. In addition to experiencing poor system performance issues, you may be gathering more information than you can reasonably review and respond to.

Limit Access to Auditing and Security Logs

You can also limit the users that can configure auditing and review and purge the security logs. By assigning the right to manage auditing and security logs to a smaller group than the entire Administrator's group (the default), you limit the number of people who can set and view logs. This security setting also determines which users can specify object access auditing options for individual resources, but does not allow a user to enable file and object access auditing in general, unless audit object access is also configured in Computer Configuration\Windows Settings\Security Settings\Local Policies\Audit Policies.

To configure this option, navigate to the User Rights Assignment area of the Local Policies console located in Computer Configuration\Windows Settings\Security Settings\Local Policies\User Rights Assignment\. Enable or disable as desired.

Conclusion

Recall that authorization occurs after a user has already been authenticated as a user with a valid account for access to the system to which access is desired. Authorization provides the level of access that will be granted to that user. Windows XP provides a range of access levels to files and folders on a host. These access levels range from no access to full control over an object. The various permissions that can be assigned may be applied singly or in combination with each other. They may also be inherited from the parent folder or the folder where the specific object in question is located.

Securing your resources with a strong level of access control is important. It is not enough, however, to simply lock down files and folders to protect them. Haphazardly applying strict permissions to all files can cause a loss of productivity for network users who are unable to access needed resources in a timely manner. It can also add additional workload to administrative staff that reset permissions on a regular basis to accommodate user needs. To avoid these issues while still protecting your network resources, you should devise a security policy that takes into consideration both security requirements and user access requirements. The policy should indicate who needs access to what, under what circumstances exceptions should be made, and the process for granting exceptions. In addition to setting guidelines for access control, implement an auditing policy as well. Set up auditing to track access to resources and then review audit logs to monitor for suspicious access patterns, such as numerous failed attempts to access a resource.

From here we move into Chapter 18, Virtual Private Networks, where you learn to set up secure network access for your remote users using tunneled, encrypted, and encapsulated data packets.

Chapter

18

Virtual Private Networks

The Internet is a diverse place; there are hundreds of thousands of networks, millions of computers, and an incomprehensible number of users. These networks, computers, and users are mostly benign and are just like you and your organization; trying to use the Internet as a tool, something to improve your business. There are those out there, however, who lurk in the shadows, who seek to cause harm, take advantage of or damage your property, your investments, and your company, clients, and customers.

There are as many reasons why these people do this as there are things they do. It could be as simple as a fun way to entertain themselves, or they could be into corporate espionage and trying to steal important data from your company. This data could be e-mail addresses for spam or credit card information for theft. They could be looking for places to store data (mp3s or movies that they then share out), or finally they could just be doing it to prove a point.

As we talked about in other chapters, there are a number of security threats that you can mitigate using firewalls and hardening systems—active blockers that help you minimize the threats. Beyond mitigation there is also a need for integrity, confidentiality, and privacy, and none of these previous tools and services can really do anything to help you in this area.

We found in our examination of common practices in corporations that either the corporation is very familiar with and actively uses Virtual Private Networks (VPNs) or is unfamiliar with them and does not use them. Those who do use them or are familiar with them patronize several leading vendors. In this chapter we talk about the Windows XP functionality that is included and briefly about the popular vendor versions.

Virtual Private Networking software is a lot like firewall software in that there are many vendors who provide applications, hardware, and tools to plan, build, and maintain these virtual connections. There is little interoperability, however, between these vendors, because each knows that following a specific path that is unique might give them a competitive edge.

With previous versions of Microsoft Windows there was little choice when it came to encrypting, providing for integrity, and keeping your data safe and confidential. However, in the latest version of the popular operating system a very robust client has been built in and therefore should be utilized at its fullest potential. In this chapter we talk about the included Virtual Private Networking client, as well as troubleshooting and supporting VPN connections to your host computers.

The world of VPN clients is diverse, but in most cases extremely lacking in functionality, support, and basic features. Clients exist from Checkpoint, Cisco, NetScreen, Symantec, and others, but are typically only useful with a specific vendor's product. You may have a few different firewalls, which means you may have several different clients.

Within this scenario you are going to need something neutral that can provide services to multiple products in varying versions. While we cannot realistically provide the necessary interoperability information for each vendor, we do provide the inner workings of the included client, as well as configurations by the four largest. At the time of this book's publication, the four largest vendors are Cisco, Checkpoint, Symantec, and NetScreen.

What a VPN Is

A Virtual Private Network is essentially a couple of hosts or a couple of networks that are connected over a larger Wide Area Network (WAN) that travels across a public networking backbone. A VPN, for our purposes, is one that at a minimum provides some level of integrity, and at other times provides encryption and therefore, confidentiality.

The terms associated with a Virtual Private Network are over-utilized in many different areas of computing, but only really fit here and in some networking circles. We need to talk about how trust relationships work, and how a VPN must maintain a confidential, proprietary, sensitive, and economical approach to data security.

Let's diagram what we are working with. The first diagram, Figure 18.1, shows a non-tunneled network-to-host connection and the second diagram shows a tunneled network-to-host connection. We then use those same diagrams to overlay a VPN connection so that it is easy to understand.

The network diagram in Figure 18.1 shows a home user talking to a corporate network with no integrity or encryption. Common problems in this situation include "man-in-the-middle" attacks and eavesdropping.

In the diagram shown in Figure 18.2, the exposed section of the network—basically, anything that is outside of the local LAN all the way to the home

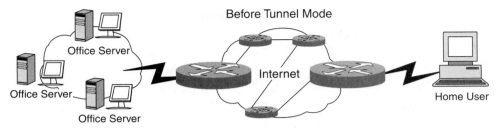

Figure 18.1   Connecting over the Internet without a VPN

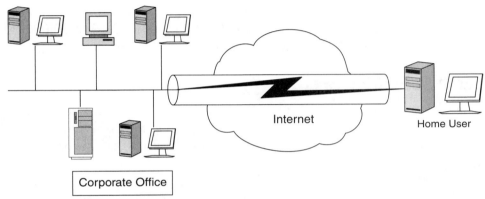

Figure 18.2   A connection over the internet with a VPN

user—is encrypted to prevent the problems revealed in Figure 18.1. Also, the addition of the VPN adds integrity to the communications channel, and thus allows you to have a verifiable source and destination for the data.

Encryption

Encryption is a great way to provide confidentiality to your organization, and most encryption done through VPNs should provide integrity using some form of hashing. But, a host is only as secure as its weakest link. Therefore, you need to patch, and you also need to run a firewall on all machines either at the network layer or at the host layer.

Some terminology around encryption:

- **DES:** Data Encryption Standard is an encryption algorithm that uses a 56-bit symmetric key to encrypt the data. There are roughly 72,000,000,000,000,000 possible combinations, which is a huge amount to crack. A typical desktop computer would take nearly 15 years at current processor and memory levels to crack them, but well-funded groups have supercomputers and some of the smaller groups have cobbled together a few computers that can crack iterations of this kind in under a few minutes or hours.

- **3DES:** Also referred to as Triple-DES, it uses the same method as DES, but in Triple-DES the data is encrypted with the 56-bit key, then decrypted with a second 56-bit key, and finally reencrypted with a third 56-bit key. This combination of keys equals a 168-bit cipher text. The 168-bit key poses a considerable challenge because possible combinations come close to being impossible to break. Although nothing is impossible, in this case there are nearly 375,000,000,000,000,000,000,000,000,000, 000,000,000,000,000,000,000 possible combinations.

How IP Security Works

Internet Protocol Security (IPSec) can be initiated by either the source or the destination because it is a form of public key cryptography. Either side can begin the negotiation, and that is part of IPSec's (and public key cryptography's) charm.

Internet Key Exchange (IKE), the key management protocol used with IPSec, has two modes of operation: main mode and quick (or aggressive) mode. Also, IKE has two major functions: Security Authority management and maintenance of the authentication keys to secure the information.

Main Mode

Main mode is the standard and slower mode for IKE authentication. With main mode there is identity protection, because working at the slower process the computers can wait for encryption to be completed before submitting identity information.

The parameters that must be satisfied in main mode are:

- **Encryption Algorithm:** In Windows XP, this is either DES or 3DES.
- **Hash Algorithm:** In Windows XP, this is either HMAC MD5 or SHA1.
- **Authentication Method:** Certificate, preshared key, or Kerberos.
- **Diffie-Hellman Group (DH):** This is the group that determines the base keyring material.
- **Diffie-Hellman Exchange:** The public exchange of some basic key information values. The actual keys are not exchanged (that is fairly insecure), because they would travel across the network in a format that is capable of being intercepted in some cases.

Quick (Aggressive) Mode

Quick/aggressive mode transfers the same amount of information as in main mode, but whereas in main mode the information is transferred in roughly six packets, with quick/aggressive mode this is done in four packets.

Virtual Private Networks, XP, and You

The following are some Windows XP Virtual Private Network technologies, and then we discuss configurations.

- **PPTP:** Point-to-Point Tunneling Protocol is an open industry standard (see IETF's Web site, RFC 2637) that supports tunneling of Point-to-Point Protocol (PPP) frames. Point-to-Point frames can include IP and other protocols. There are two tunneling protocols in use within Windows XP that support PPTP and L2TP, of which PPTP is easier to set up and configure. PPTP encapsulates, encrypts, and compresses the data so that it is hidden from would-be hackers.
- **L2TP:** Layer 2 Tunneling Protocol, also called the *Data Link Layer,* is a quasi-physical layer that provides similar functionality to PPTP. In Windows XP, L2TP was designed to function natively over most IP networks. L2TP, just like PPTP, encapsulates packets; however, L2TP can encapsulate the frames/packets of other protocols. As a result, L2P2 is much more robust than PPTP.

These two very common protocols are bound together by Internet Protocol Security, which acts like a glue. IPSec, much like PPTP and L2TP, is an open standard (see IETF's Web site, RFC 2661) that was developed to support a wide variety of vendors and protocols for interoperability.

IPSec implements at the lower layers of the OSI Model, unlike Secure Socket Layer (SSL) or Transport Layer Security (TLS). The good news with IPSec is because it operates at the lower layers, it is obscured from the application layer and therefore can be made invisible to the user.

The OSI Model travels down the OSI stack and across the network to the other side where it does the reverse. Because of this, the application need not be aware of the underlying protocol changes such as encapsulation and encryption by IPSec.

There are three things that you need to work out with IPSec before you can implement it. You need to identify which protocols you are going to use, which mode you are going to use it in (transport versus tunnel), and what authentication method you are going to use. IP Security is made up of two protocols: AH and ESP. Let's take a look at Figure 18.3.

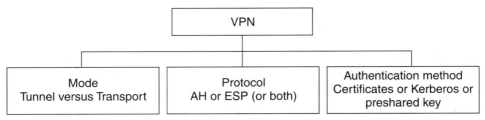

Figure 18.3 Relationship of the VPN components

Protocols

Authentication Header (AH) provides for integrity and validation and Encapsulating Security Payload (ESP) provides for encryption and data security. AH does a lot more than that, including the antireplay protection, authentication, and all forms of integrity (but not confidentiality). It is helpful to know the protocol numbers for the most popular protocols along with the protocol numbers for those associated with IPSec. TCP is 6, UDP is 13, AH is 51, and ESP is 50. If you want to know more about protocol numbers navigate to *http://www.iana.org/assignments/protocol-numbers.*

Authentication Header

AH is performed on the IP packet header, not the data inside. However, because the packet header encapsulates the data to some extent, this integrity is partially provided to the entire packet. This separation allows for AH and ESP to work together seamlessly, whereas if they did the same job it would be harder and more complex.

The components of the authentication header protocol, as shown in Figure 18.4, have five fields that are described here:

1. **Next Header:** This is the section where the next protocol is described so that when AH is stripped off there is some indication what protocol will follow. This is typically 6 for TCP.
2. **Length:** This field indicates the total length of the authentication header.
3. **Security Parameter Index (SPI):** The SPI holds the negotiation information from the agreement that was negotiated during the communication between two computers. This is done during the IKE handshake phase in which each computer indicates what protocol, method, and mode it intends to accept.
4. **Sequence Number:** The sequence number tracks the number of packets in a specific conversation. The sequence number is important with regard to replay protection because this is the field that is tracked to provide this functionality.

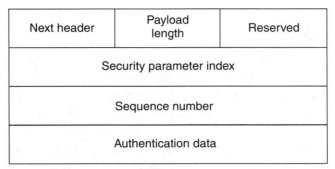

Figure 18.4 The authentication header

5. **Authentication Data:** The authentication data field contains the Integrity Check Value, or ICV, which is the signed portion of the authentication header. The signature function is provided by either SHA1, or HMAC MD5.

Encapsulating Security Payload

ESP provides some of the same services found in AH to the data payload of a packet including antireplay protection, authentication, and integrity. But unlike AH, ESP is capable of providing encryption and therefore confidentiality of the payload. The definitions of DES and 3DES, the two available forms of encryption in Windows XP, were covered earlier in this chapter.

ESP is two sections of the larger packet: the ESP header and the ESP trailer. In the ESP header (Figure 18.5), you find an SPI and a sequence number. In the ESP trailer, you find padding, padding length, and finally the next header information. The reason you find the SPI, sequence number, and next header information in ESP is because it can be used without AH and vice versa.

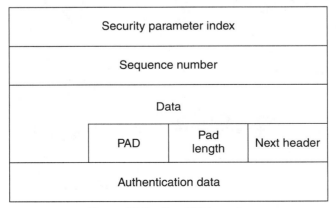

Figure 18.5 The ESP header

Modes

Transport Mode

IPSec transport mode is fully routable, except when intersecting with a network where NAT is in use. NAT becomes a problem because the Integrity Check Value has been changed as part of the packet repackaging. Transport mode only works if IPSec is supported on both hosts and the same authentication methods are used on both machines. This is the typical method employed for host-to-host VPN tunnels (Figure 18.6). Transport mode, however, only protects the message content, so it is still possible to detect the full route of the conversation.

Tunnel Mode

Tunnel mode typically is used only in network-to-network and network-to-host communications. With tunneling, both the data and the IP packet are encapsulated and protected. With tunnel mode, it is possible to project a route across a tunnel. If you are familiar with it, this is what happens when you tracert and see only two or three hops, whereas under normal circumstances, you would see ten or twelve hops.

In Figure 18.7, we see how the typical network exists—where your router connects to another router, which connects to still another router, and so on.

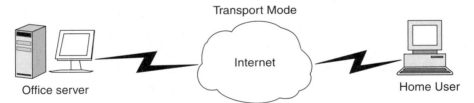

Figure 18.6 A host-to-host VPN tunnel uses transport mode.

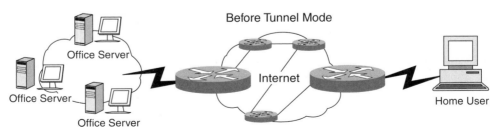

Figure 18.7 The standard routed network

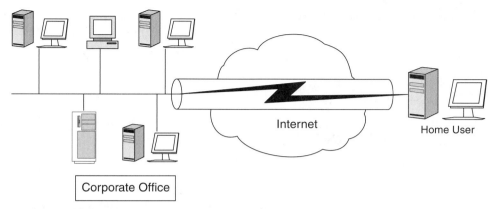

Figure 18.8   The source and destination routers are hidden in tunnel mode.

In Figure 18.8, we see that with the introduction of a VPN tunnel, only the source and destination routers (where the tunnel is actually built) are seen by the VPN traffic and the users who use the tunnel. This is because the tunnel encapsulates the original IP packets into another protocol and makes the original path partly obscured. The same path exists, however, but it is hidden "inside" the VPN tunnel.

Authentication Modes

Kerberos

Kerberos is a symmetric key authentication protocol that originally was developed by the bright folks at Massachusetts Institute of Technology (MIT). The original (and current available purpose) of the protocol is to authenticate or verify the identity of devices and users. The origin of the name Kerberos is the three-headed dog that guarded the gates of Hades.

Symmetric key is the use of a single key in encryption; the opposite or alternate form is public key which involves more than one key, typically a public key and a private key.

X.509 Certificates

X.509 certificates are both a symmetric and asymmetric key authentication protocol (among other things). X.509 is a substandard of the X.500 standard, which encompasses a great deal of the cryptographic and authentication technology in use today.

The X.500 standard is a collection of named entities used primarily in databases (for hierarchy data structures see Chapter 4 on Active Directory).

Think of a structure that maintains information on people, computers, and other devices.

In the latest standard there are 11 key fields available: The most notable ones are:

- Issuing authority
- Signing algorithms
- Length of certificate validity
- Information about the owner of the certificate

One of the most important aspects of certificates is their portability, which has made them very appealing to many organizations. If your organization has or is considering certificates, a popular deployment is Public Key Cryptography (PKI). This book will not effectively cover PKI, but it should be evaluated by your organization.

Preshared Key

Of all the authentication methods available, the preshared key is the simplest; it's a simple pass phrase. Basically the preshared key authentication method works on the principle that you enter the key on both sides of the equation and they are compared during the handshake and set-up phase of the Virtual Private Network.

Understanding IP Security and Policies

You now have the process to create your first Virtual Private Network. To configure IP Security, we use the Microsoft Management Console Snap-in (MMC), but before we do that, we need to talk about some of the things to configure in the MMC. This is a quick overview.

Thus far we talked about encryption and about modes (tunnel versus transport). With that information, we go to the next step, which is setting up the IP Security Policy. We first describe how to set up a policy on an individual workstation. Next, we show you how you can do this on a larger, global scale for a bigger organization.

First, you have to add the MMC Snap-in to edit IP Security Policies. You do that by going to **Start**, and then **Run**, and in the command line presented type MMC.exe.

Doing the above presents the screen shown in Figure 18.9.

You now add the IP Security Policy Snap-ins as shown in Figure 18.10.

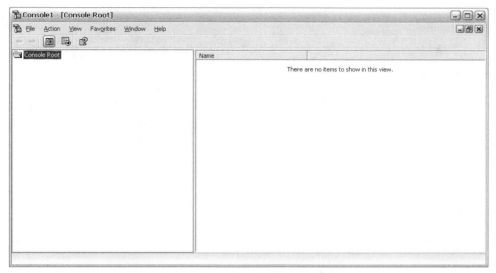

Figure 18.9   The MMC Console

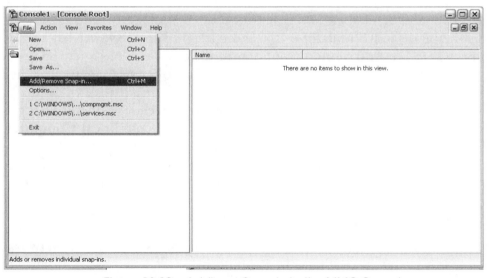

Figure 18.10   Adding a Snap-in to the MMC Console.

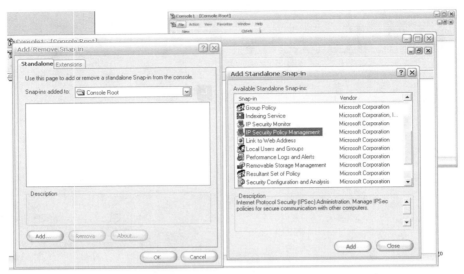

Figure 18.11 Select IP Security Management.

To speed up this process, select **Add/Remove Snap-in** from under the **File** menu, which brings up a new dialog box as shown in Figure 18.11. This dialog box has two tabs: Standalone and Extensions.

Select the default **Standalone** tab, and click **Add** in the lower left corner. This brings up the **Add Standalone Snap-in** dialog, which has a few Snap-ins that you can add. Now scroll down to **IP Security Policy Management**. Click on the **Add** button.

When you click on Add, you get the opportunity to choose exactly what you intend to manage with this Snap-in. As an exercise, choose **Local Computer**, which should be the default, as shown in Figure 18.12, and click **Finish**.

This returns you to the diagram in Figure 18.11 and you need to choose **Close**, because at this time you are not going to add any more Snap-ins.

Configuring a Virtual Private Network

Now that you have a fairly complete understanding of Virtual Private Networking, you learn how to configure it. Keeping in mind what you have already learned, let's start to configure your first VPN. The best way to do that is to click on the **Start** menu, then **Settings**, and finally **Network Connections**. (See Figure 18.13.)

Clicking on **Local Area Connection** presents the menu shown in Figure 18.14. Click on the upper left-hand area under **Network Tasks** and choose **Create a new connection**.

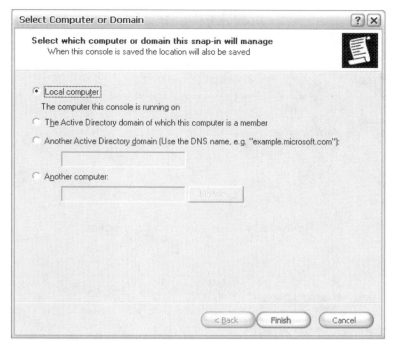

Figure 18.12   Select Local computer.

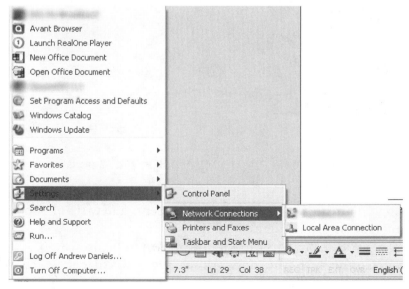

Figure 18.13   Open the Network Connections applet.

Figure 18.14   Create a new connection.

Figure 18.15   The New Connection Wizard starts.

Clicking on **Create a new connection** presents a new set of windows, starting with the one shown in Figure 18.15.

Clicking on **Next** presents the window shown in Figure 18.16.

Choose **Connect to the network at my workplace**, which takes you through to the VPN configuration.

As you can see in Figure 18.17, you must choose **Virtual Private Network connection** to set up your VPN.

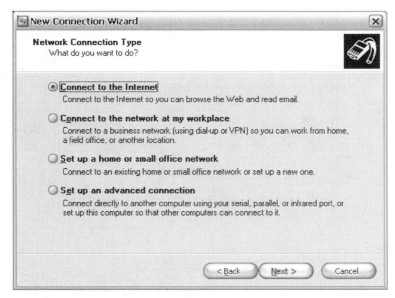

Figure 18.16   Select Connect to the network at my workplace.

Figure 18.17   Select Virtual Private Network connection.

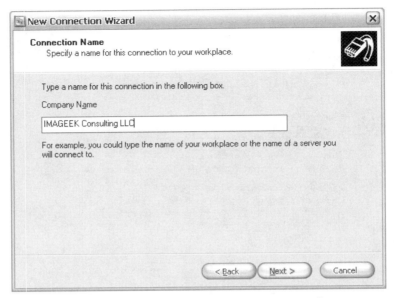

Figure 18.18 Specify a name for this connection.

In Figure 18.18, you need to put something descriptive in the Company Name field. While it seems to indicate one would only use this for company connectivity, nothing prevents you from using it any way you choose.

In Figure 18.19, you need to indicate whether or not you should dial a connection before trying to establish a VPN connection. This is important if you are working on a dial-up user or for someone who connects mostly through a modem.

You need to identify the remote VPN server to establish the tunnel. This remote server is either a home-built solution or one of the popular vendors such as Cisco, Checkpoint, Symantec, or NetScreen, among others. Figure 18.20 shows how the screen appears.

If desired, you can select the box to create a shortcut to this connection on your desktop. Click on **Finish** as shown in Figure 18.21.

To launch this new connection, simply double-click the shortcut on the desktop. The screen shown in Figure 18.22 appears.

NOTE: You have the ability to save the username and password and also make them available to all users, both of which are certainly more convenient. But doing so significantly reduces the effectiveness of your security posture and therefore might cause you much grief later on.

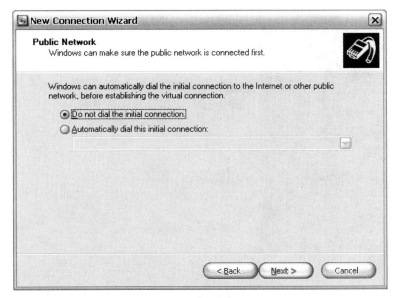

Figure 18.19 Select the option appropriate for your network.

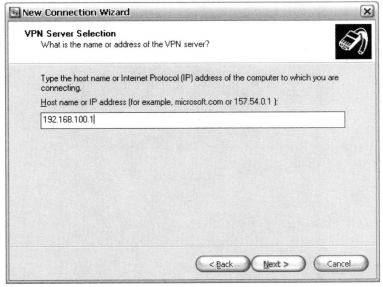

Figure 18.20 Provide the name of the VPN server to which you want to connect.

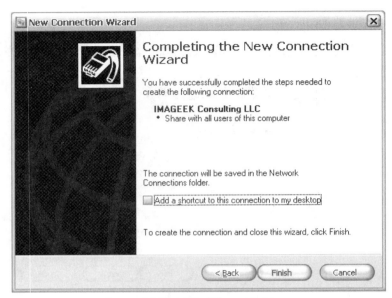

Figure 18.21 The Wizard finishes.

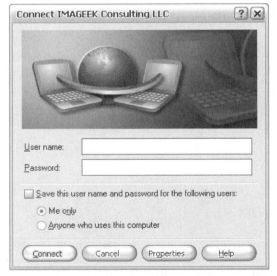

Figure 18.22 Launching the VPN connection.

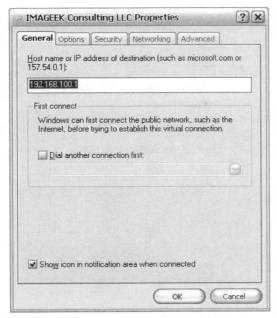

Figure 18.23 The VPN connection Properties sheet

To verify or edit the configuration parameters for this connection, click on the **Properties** link. The properties sheet shown in Figure 18.23 appears.

Almost all the settings on the various tabs are configured in the set-up phase, except the Security tab, which allows you to configure the IPSec settings as shown in Figure 18.24.

With the Windows XP VPN client, it is left up to the VPN server at the corporate office which encryption type to use, though only DES and 3DES are available.

Setting Up and Maintaining Multiple VPN Connections

You can create multiple VPN connections on each workstation by following the same steps as you did for the first connection. For this to work, the networks presented by the remote VPN must not overlap or all kinds of problems occur.

This means that if you have one VPN to 12.87.42.0/24 (a class C network) and you also want to set up a VPN to 12.87.41.0/22, then you have an overlapping network because 12.87.42.0/24 is a part of 12.87.41.0/22 and that causes problems.

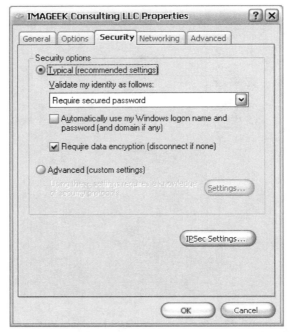

Figure 18.24 Configuring IPSec settings

At this point we need to discuss the types of basic policies and what we can do with advanced policy editing. There are three default IPSec policies that are explained here:

1. **Client (Respond Only):** With the Client (Respond Only) policy the computer only uses IPSec if the other host or server it is communicating with requests it. Kerberos is the default authentication method.

2. **Server (Request Security):** With this policy the client always attempts to negotiate IPSec, but permits unencrypted communication if that is all the server allows. This policy also permits unsecured ICMP traffic.

3. **Secure Server (Require Security):** In this policy, IP Security is requested for all inbound and outbound connections. The client accepts unencrypted messages, but always responds using IP Security. Just like the Server (Request Security) policy, this policy allows for unencrypted ICMP traffic.

Because default policies are fairly rudimentary and crude, we discuss how to create new policies. To do that, click on **Action** in the IPSec Policy Management console, and then **Create IP Security Policy**, which allows you to build a new policy.

Now let's go through this in the following figures.

Figure 18.25 shows the IP Security Policy Wizard that starts after we select **Create IPSec Policy** from the **Action** menu. This creates a policy with some of the same options as the three defaults discussed earlier. This also lets you be more specific in your IP Security configuration, which might be required by your organization.

The next window is where you name the policy. You need to note that only one security policy can be enforced at one time; therefore, you can create as many as you want, but there is no sharing allowed.

We need to choose the authentication method to be used in this IP Security policy. Figure 18.26 demonstrates enabling the default rule that will be used when no other rule is applicable. Our choices are Kerberos, certificate, and finally a preshared key, as shown in Figure 18.27.

For the example shown in Figure 18.28, we use preshared key because it is the simplest. Select the box for **Edit Properties**, then click on **Finish**, as shown in Figure 18.29.

In Figure 18.30, we have one security rule and two tabs at the top: **Rules** and **General**. We start by looking at the fields within the rule.

There are five fields and they are:

1. IP Filter List
2. Tunnel Settings
3. Filter Actions

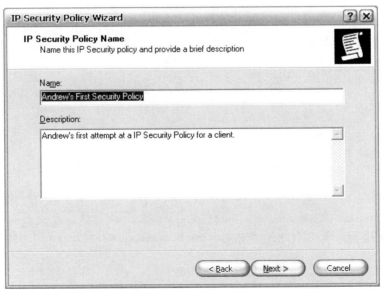

Figure 18.25   IPSec Policy Wizard

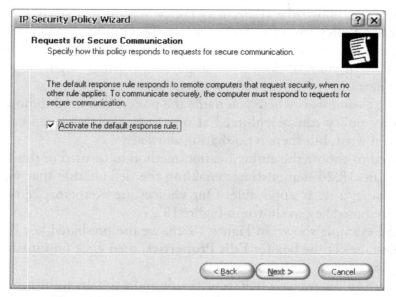

Figure 18.26 Activating the default response rule.

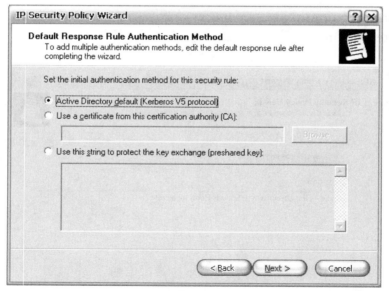

Figure 18.27 Specify the initial authentication method to be used for this rule.

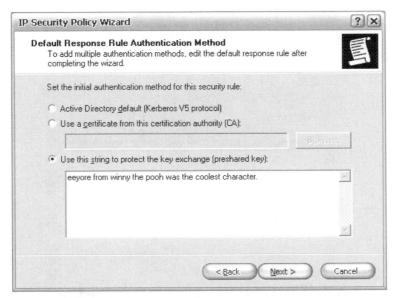

Figure 18.28   Entering the key to be shared.

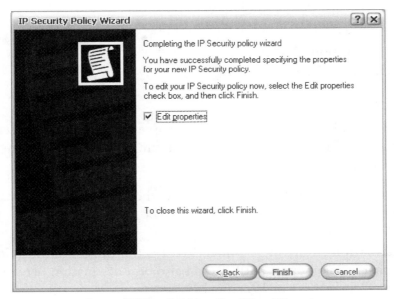

Figure 18.29   Finishing the IPSec Wizard.

Figure 18.30 Examining the IPSec rules.

4. Authentication Methods
5. Connection Types

IP Filter List

In a manner similar to that discussed in Chapter 7, Internet Connection Firewall, you can configure some common and familiar settings with the IP Filter List, including:

- **Source Address:** The address where the communications channel is being opened from; this could also be a source network. Example: 192.168.100.1 or 192.168.100.*.

- **Destination Address:** The intended target of the communications channel that is being opened; this could also be a destination network. Example: 192.168.101.1 or 192.168.101.*.

- **Protocol:** This is the protocol ID, or the transport protocol used by the protocol. Point-to-Point Tunneling Protocol uses Generic Routing Encapsulation (GRE) packets. GRE packets are identified by their protocol identification. For example, HTTP is an application protocol and it uses TCP as the transport protocol.

- **Source Port:** This is the port (usually randomly chosen by the application) above 1,024 and below 65,535.
- **Destination Port:** If the protocol is TCP or UDP, then this is a number between 1 and 1,024; some common examples include Telnet = 23, SSH = 22, FTP = 20 (data), 21 (control), HTTP = 80, HTTPS = 443.

Tunnel Settings

In this section, you'll choose either transport or tunnel, which were discussed in the Mode section earlier in this chapter. Select one of these modes based on the VPN architecture in your network.

Filter Actions

The filter action setting is what determines how the traffic is handled. There are three filter actions that we discuss here:

1. **Permit:** Allow the packets to be transmitted without IP Security protection. IP Security means encryption and encryption means overhead because some math has to be done, and compression is being performed. Therefore it may not be advantageous for you to encrypt and verify SNMP monitoring traps or simple troubleshooting commands like ping and traceroute.
2. **Block:** Drop the packet.
3. **Negotiate Security:** Allows the administrator to define the desired encryption and integrity algorithms to secure the data.

Authentication Methods

This is where we define the method of the authentication to use for the rule. Each rule can have multiple authentication methods, and you can determine the order in which each method is executed. Previously in this chapter, we discussed Kerberos, certificates, and preshared keys. Additionally, Chapter 16 covers Kerberos in greater detail.

Connection Types

This is where you need to identify what specific interfaces or types of interfaces a particular filter applies to. You can have the rule apply to any of the following:

- All Network connections
- Local Area Network (LAN) connections
- Remote Access connections

Troubleshooting VPN Issues

Connection Fails to Initiate

The only real way to gain valuable data for this specific problem is to examine the firewall or virtual private network device on the other end, either through logs or debugging information.

High Latency and Packet Loss

This could be caused by any number of things, but the biggest issues are usually processing power, failures at your networking layer (for example, your ISP is having problems), or an insufficient amount of available memory on the host computer.

Conclusion

This chapter provided an overview of the IPSec VPN client that is included in Windows XP. Although the technology and functionality of the VPN are complex, Microsoft has provided a very simple interface to use for configuring the client. It is important to be sure that your client configuration settings match the VPN host setting, however. Misconfiguring the client can result in hours of troubleshooting, so in the event of a failed connection, always double-check the client configuration. For additional details on VPN technology, visit *www.microsoft.com* for the latest white papers and knowledge base articles.

Appendix

Tools

This appendix covers a number of tools and utilities that provide value for Windows XP management. Some of these tools are built-in, while others are found on the Windows XP installation media. Here we also cover Service Packs; specifically, what they are, where to get them, and how to install them.

Tools and Utilities

This section provides instructions for use on a variety of tools and utilities arranged in the following five categories:

- Memory
- Disk
- CPU
- Network
- General Management

The rationale for the division is simple. Tools are typically used to optimize system performance or to manage the utilization of some portion of the system, whether hardware, software, operating system, or data. The main areas of performance concern and the main areas where performance bottlenecks occur are memory, disk, CPU, and network throughput. Tools and utilities that address a single area explicitly are covered in that category. Tools and utilities that do not fit neatly into a single category or address general issues such as account management or task automation are included in the general management category.

Memory
Memory Profiling Tool

This command-line tool creates a text file with memory utilization information similar in nature to what you find on the Task Manager Processes tab. Memsnap.exe is included with the Windows XP Support Tools. To install the

Support Tools, run Setup.exe from the Support\Tools folder on the Windows XP CD-ROM.

Usage: memsnap [-t] [-g] [-?] [<logfile>]

Options: `<logfile>` textfile for mesnap output, memsnap.log by default

- **-t**   Add tagging information (time (GMT), date, machinename)
- **-g**   Add GDI and USER resource counts
- **-?**   Help

Output of memsnap is shown in Table A.1

Memsnap is useful for determining what applications or processes are hogging memory. Memsnap can be scheduled to run at specific times with the AT tool, which gives you the option to see how things are running at various times during the day.

Disk

Defragmenting a Drive

Defrag.exe is a built-in command-line utility that lets you perform disk defragmentation tasks from a command line. Defragmentation is the process of moving data chunks on a disk into a more space-efficient arrangement. Running defrag is analogous to repacking a messy suitcase: by rearranging the contents of the disk it may be possible to free up additional space that would otherwise be unusable for new data.

Usage: defrag <volume> [-a] [-f] [-v] [-?]

Options: `<volume>` drive letter or mount point (d: or d:\vol\mountpoint)

- **-a**   Analyze only
- **-f**   Force defragmentation even if free space is low
- **-v**   Verbose output
- **-?**   Display this help text

Disk Partioning

Diskpart.exe is a built-in command-line utility that lets you manage partitions from a text-based console. If you are moving to the world of Windows from the world of UNIX, you may find this tool to be helpful as you learn to use GUI disk administration tools.

Table A.1 Memsnap

Process ID	Proc.Name	Wrkng.Set	PagedPool	NonPgdP1	Pagefile	Commit	Handles	Threads
00000000	(null)	20480	0	0	0	0	0	1
00000004	System	221184	0	0	0	32768	441	52
00000318	smss.exe	450560	5208	640	180224	180224	21	3
0000036C	csrss.exe	3235840	57152	6888	1818624	1818624	592	11
00000384	winlogon.exe	2105344	46480	45544	5517312	5517312	432	17
000003B4	services.exe	3506176	28396	10560	1597440	1597440	315	18
000003C0	lsass.exe	1589248	36112	8512	3551232	3551232	336	21
0000047C	svchost.exe	4407296	26204	10208	1617920	1617920	391	10
00000508	svchost.exe	26693632	155432	147580	17326080	17326080	1928	100
00000618	svchost.exe	2433024	14868	4504	897024	897024	79	6
00000638	svchost.exe	4870144	32160	8992	2142208	2142208	193	17
00000710	spoolsv.exe	4698112	24532	4112	2813952	2813952	160	11
00000180	PackethSvc.exe	1687552	13404	1680	425984	425984	49	3
000001BC	alg.exe	4370432	33268	5408	1097728	1097728	116	5
000001D8	HPConfig.exe	3756032	32600	3040	888832	888832	122	4
000001F4	mdm.exe	4562944	30936	2840	1105920	1105920	183	6
0000021C	NAVAPSVC.EXE	5414912	21352	21426560	4321280	4321280	105	9
0000044C	explorer.exe	13287424	109228	23320	2607616	2607616	722	22

Usage: DISKPART launches the console. Enter the commands below as desired.

active: Activates the current basic partition.

add: Add a mirror to a simple volume.

assign: Assign a drive letter or mount point to the selected volume.

break: Break a mirror set.

clean: Clear the configuration information, or all information, off the disk.

convert: Converts between different disk formats.

create: Create a volume or partition.

delete: Delete an object.

detail: Provide details about an object.

exit: Exit DiskPart.

extend: Extend a volume.

help: Prints a list of commands.

import: Imports a disk group.

list: Prints out a list of objects.

online: Online a disk that is currently marked as offline.

rem: Does nothing. Used to comment scripts.

remove: Remove a drive letter or mount point assignment.

rescan: Rescan the computer looking for disks and volumes.

retain: Place a retainer partition under a simple volume.

select: Move the focus to an object.

File System Utility

Fsutil.exe is a built-in command-line utility for performing file system maintenance on your Windows XP workstation. Again, if you are a UNIX administrator, this tool may be more to your liking than the GUI tools provided for disk and file system management in Windows XP.

Usage: fsutil [desired switch] [subcommand]

behavior: Control file system behavior. Subcommands are:

  • **query:**   Query the file system behavior parameters

  • **set:**   Change the file system behavior parameters

file: File specific commands

fsinfo: File system information. fsinfo commands include:
- **drives:**   List all drives
- **drivetype:**   Query drive type for a drive
- **ntfsinfo:**   Query NTFS-specific volume information
- **statistics:**   Query file system statistics
- **volumeinfo:**   Query volume information

hardlink: Hardlink management

objected: Object ID management

quota: Quota management

reparsepoint: Reparse point management

sparse: Sparse file control

usn: USN management

volume: Volume management

Sample output from a request to display NTFS information is as follows:

```
C:\Documents and Settings\Owner>fsutil fsinfo ntfsinfo c:
NTFS Volume Serial Number :        0x04e42552e42546f0
Version :                          3.1
Number Sectors :                   0x00000000037c86f8
Total Clusters :                   0x00000000006f90df
Free Clusters  :                   0x0000000000448ade
Total Reserved :                   0x0000000000000000
Bytes Per Sector  :                512
Bytes Per Cluster :                4096
Bytes Per FileRecord Segment    :  1024
Clusters Per FileRecord Segment :  0
Mft Valid Data Length :            0x0000000005387c00
Mft Start Lcn  :                   0x000000000004494d
Mft2 Start Lcn :                   0x000000000001c698
Mft Zone Start :                   0x000000000011ea80
Mft Zone End   :                   0x00000000001bc7a0
```

Disk Manager Diagnostics

Dmdiag.exe is a command-line tool that allows you to view detailed disk information about a computer. It is included with the Windows XP Support Tools. To install the Support Tools, run Setup.exe from the Support\Tools folder on the Windows XP CD-ROM.

Usage: dmdiag [-v || -f file]

Options:

-f file   Specifies the filename for the output file, defaults to dmdiag.txt

-v   Prints a verbose version

-?   Prints help

Below is an example of the data output by diskdiag:

```
C:\WINDOWS\system32>dmdiag -v

---------- Computer Name and OS Version ----------

        Computer name: KACKIEC
             NT build: 2600
             CPU Type: x86
        DMDIAG Version: 5.1.2600.0 shp

---------- LDM File Versions ----------

        2600.0.503.0 shp - C:\WINDOWS\System32\dmadmin.exe
        2600.0.503.0 shp - C:\WINDOWS\System32\dmconfig.dll
        2600.0.503.0 shp - C:\WINDOWS\System32\dmdlgs.dll
        2600.0.503.0 shp - C:\WINDOWS\System32\dmdskmgr.dll
        2600.0.503.0 shp - C:\WINDOWS\System32\dmdskres.dll
        2600.0.503.0 shp - C:\WINDOWS\System32\dmintf.dll
        2600.0.503.0 shp - C:\WINDOWS\System32\dmremote.exe
        2600.0.503.0 shp - C:\WINDOWS\System32\dmserver.dll
        2600.0.503.0 shp - C:\WINDOWS\System32\dmutil.dll
        2600.0.503.0 shp - C:\WINDOWS\System32\dmview.ocx
        2600.0.503.0 shp - C:\WINDOWS\System32\drivers\dmboot.sys
        2600.0.503.0 shp - C:\WINDOWS\System32\drivers\dmio.sys
        2600.0.503.0 shp - C:\WINDOWS\System32\drivers\dmload.sys

---------- Mount Points ----------


---------- Drive Letter Usage, Drive Type ----------

C: = \Device\HarddiskVolume2 [Fixed]
D: = \Device\CdRom0 [CDRom]

---------- Consolidated LDM Configuration Data ----------

ERROR: scan operation failed:
        A format error was found in the private region of the disk
```

```
ERROR: scan operation failed:
        A format error was found in the private region of the disk

---------- \Device\Harddisk0 ----------

\Device\Harddisk0\DP(1)0x7d8200-0x2f10c00+1 (Device)
\Device\Harddisk0\DP(2)0x36e8e00-0x6f90df200+2 (Device)
\Device\Harddisk0\DR0                (Device)
\Device\Harddisk0\Partition0         (SymbolicLink) ->
\Device\Harddisk0\DR0
\Device\Harddisk0\Partition1         (SymbolicLink) ->
\Device\HarddiskVolume1
\Device\Harddisk0\Partition2         (SymbolicLink) ->
\Device\HarddiskVolume2


---------- Partition Table Info Disk 0 ----------


            3,648 Cylinders
              255 Tracks/Cylinder
               63 Sectors/Track
              512 Bytes/Sector
               12 MediaType
       58,605,120 Sectors (total)
   30,005,821,440 Bytes (total)
       29,302,560 KB
           28,616 MB
             27.9 GB


                0 StartingOffset
   30,005,821,440 PartitionLength
                0 HiddenSectors
                0 PartitionNumber
                0 PartitionType
                0 BootIndicator
                0 RecognizedPartition
                0 RewritePartition


              MBR PartitionStyle
                4 PartitionCount
         f34ff34f Signature


        Starting          Partition       Hidden        Total
Partition      Partition
        Boot Recognized      Rewrite
  Offset (bytes)   Length (bytes)     Sectors      Sectors
Number    Type (HEX)
    Indicator  Partition  Partition
```

```
        8,225,280         49,351,680       16,065       96,390
0         0x84
          0           1           0
        57,576,960    29,948,244,480    112,455    58,492,665
1         0x07
          1           1           0
                    0           0           0           0
2         0x00
          0           0           0
                    0           0           0           0
3         0x00
          0           0           0
```

```
  30,005,821,440 Bytes (58605120 sectors) Geometric size
  30,005,821,440 Bytes (58605120 sectors) True size (measured)
  30,005,821,440 Bytes (58605120 sectors) Reported size
(Partition0)
               0 Bytes (        0 sectors) missing/wasted


---------- DMIO Kernel List ----------

dmdiag: GET_VOLINFO ioctl failed: The handle is invalid.

---------- LDM Disk Header Harddisk0 ----------

ERROR: scan operation failed:
      A format error was found in the private region of the disk

---------- LDM Disk Config Harddisk0 ----------

ERROR: scan operation failed:
      A format error was found in the private region of the disk

---------- LDM Disk KLOG Harddisk0 ----------

ERROR: scan operation failed:
      A format error was found in the private region of the disk

---------- DMAdmin Simple Query ----------

dmdiag: ERROR: No disk groups loaded

---------- DMAdmin Verbose Query ----------

dmdiag: ERROR: No disk groups loaded
```

CPU

Process Resource Monitor

Use this utility to determine which process is hogging all the CPU time or memory on your computer. Pmon.exe is a command-line tool that works just like the Processes tab on Task Manager, but within a command interface. It is included with the Windows XP Support Tools. To install the Support Tools, run Setup.exe from the Support\Tools folder on the Windows XP CD-ROM.

Usage: pmon

To update on demand, press any key. To quit pmon, press CTRL+C.

Sample output from pmon is as follows:

```
Memory:   507376K Avail: 175572K  PageFlts:    181
InRam Kernel: 2564K P:29596K
 Commit: 263344K/ 200396K Limit:1186332K Peak: 316104K
Pool N: 9136K P:30024K


                Mem   Mem    Page    Flts Commit   Usage    Pri
Hnd Thd  Image
CPU  CpuTime  Usage Diff    Faults Diff Charge  NonP Page
Cnt Cnt  Name

                100720 128  1803038   32
File Cache
89  15:45:29     20    0        1    0        0    0
0  0    0  1 Idle Process
 0   0:05:05    220    0     8010    0       32    0
0  8  300 49 System
 0   0:00:00    464    0      232    0      172    0
5 11   21  3 smss.exe
 0   0:02:08   4496    0     5833    0     1816    6
53 13  543 13 csrss.exe
 0   0:00:07   2376    0    22385    0     6624   44
55 13  516 19 winlogon.exe
 0   0:00:09   3036    0     2565    0     1440    9
28  9  317 17 services.exe
 0   0:00:07    796    0    32416    0     3340    7
35  9  318 19 lsass.exe
 0   0:00:03   3248    0     1185    0     1344    6
22  8  364 10 svchost.exe
 0   0:01:15  24056    0   198677    0    16604   67
115  8 1540 84 svchost.exe
 0   0:00:01   2192    0     2255    0      896    4
14  8   75  6 svchost.exe
 0   0:00:05   4212    0     1301    0     2000    7
30  8  187 17 svchost.exe
```

```
 0     0:00:01    3932    0      1949    0    2672    4
23  8   165 12 spoolsv.exe
 0     0:00:00    1484    0       368    0     416    1
13  8    49  3 ethSvc.exe
 0     0:00:00    1172    0       290    0     288    1
12  8    30  4 CDAC11BA.EXE
 0     0:00:00    1144    0       283    0     236    1
12  8    26  2 gearsec.exe
 0     0:00:00    3232    0       835    0     872    3
32  8   122  4 HPConfig.exe
 0     0:00:00    2044    0       517    0     528    2
17  8    83  4 imapi.exe
 0     0:00:05    3288    0      5739    0     992    2
30  8   117  5 mdm.exe
 0     0:00:02    5548    0     10896    0    4740    3
21  8   104  9 NAVAPSVC.EXE
 1     0:13:10   17520    0    248633   17   18748   20
113 8   680 22 explorer.exe
 0     0:00:00     736    0       180    0     184    0
 7  8     8  1 carpserv.exe
 0     0:00:00    2712    0      1153    0     648    1
27  8    33  1 S3Tray2.exe
 0     0:00:02    2264    0       639    0     548    1
25  8    28  1 hpdisply.exe
 0     0:00:12    3208    0      1035    0    1172    2
28  8    56  2 ONETOUCH.EXE
 0     0:00:00    1544    0       411    0     388    1
15  8    21  1 hpsysdrv.exe
 0     0:00:13   12452    0     29164    0    3536   10
70  8   353 11 NAVAPW32.EXE
 0     0:00:00    3636    0       977    0     824    3
31  8    94  3 tfswctrl.exe
 0     0:00:00    3848    0       984    0     908    3
26  8   105  4 lper.exe
 0     0:00:00    2192    0       567    0     528    2
27  8    45  2 qttask.exe
 0     0:00:13    8748    0      7393    0   14112   14
74  8   387 16 msmsgs.exe
 0     0:04:16    6028    0     27792    0    8136   14
83  8   309  9 aim.exe
 0     0:00:22    3716    0     30067    0     592    7
35  8   184  1 ctfmon.exe
 0     0:00:03   16212    0      5123    0    6484   10
75  8   319 13 YPager.exe
 0     0:00:00    2824    0       719    0     656    1
27  8    51  1 Config.exe
 0     0:00:04    3236    0   1290844  107    1000    3
22  8   109  7 rvice.exe
```

```
 0    0:04:24    9024    92    123868    25    11828    16
156   8    593 16  OUTLOOK.EXE
 0    0:00:00    2856     0       730     0      676     2
30    8     77  3  mostat.exe
 0    0:02:09   16272     0     33962     0    15460    18
95    8    690 13  iexplore.exe
 7    0:47:15   12636     0    286744     0    42632    40
217   8   1587 18  iTunes.exe
 0    0:00:22    7588     0     17142     0    14340    17
91    8    742 11  iexplore.exe
 0    0:01:00   29116     0     26076     0    10216    11
114   8    291  5  WINWORD.EXE
 0    0:00:00    1424     0       367     0     1424     1
15    8     20  1  cmd.exe
 0    0:00:00     908     0       223     0      344     1
 7 13      7  1  pmon.exe
```

Network

DHCP Locator Utility

The dhcploc.exe command-line tool displays the DHCP servers active on the local subnet. It is helpful for troubleshooting DHCP problems and also for determining if unauthorized DHCP servers have been placed on your network. Dhcploc.exe is included with the Windows XP Support Tools. To install the Support Tools, run Setup.exe from the Support\Tools folder on the Windows XP CD-ROM.

> *Usage:* dhcploc [-p] [-a:"list-of-alertnames"] [-i:alertinterval] machine-ip-address
> [list of valid dhcp servers ip addresses]

Netdiag

Netdiag is a command-line diagnostic tool that is used to test network connectivity and displays a range of helpful information including patch levels. A series of tests is run to discover information about the network client installed. Netdiag requires that TCP/IP is installed and bound to at least one adapter on the computer where it is to be run. Netdiag is included with the Windows XP Support Tools. To install the Support Tools, run Setup.exe from the Support\Tools folder on the Windows XP CD-ROM.

> *Usage:* netdiag [/Options]>
> *Options:*
> **/q**   Quiet output (errors only).

/v Verbose output.

/l Log output to NetDiag.log.

/debug Even more verbose.

/d:<DomainName> Find a DC in the specified domain.

/fix Fix trivial problems.

/DcAccountEnum Enumerate DC machine accounts.

/test:<TestName> Tests only this test. Nonskippable tests will still be run. Valid tests are:

- **Ndis** Netcard queries test
- **IpConfig** IP config test
- **Member** Domain membership test
- **NetBTTransports** NetBT transports test
- **Autonet** Autonet address test
- **IpLoopBk** IP loopback ping test
- **DefGw** Default gateway test
- **NbtNm** NetBT name test
- **WINS** WINS service test
- **Winsock** Winsock test
- **DNS** DNS test
- **Browser** Redir and Browser test
- **DsGetDc** DC discovery test
- **DcList** DC list test
- **Trust** Trust relationship test
- **Kerberos** Kerberos test
- **Ldap** LDAP test
- **Route** Routing table test
- **Netstat** Netstat information test
- **Bindings** Bindings test
- **WAN** WAN configuration test
- **Modem** Modem diagnostics test
- **Netware** Netware test
- **IPX** IPX test
- **IPSec** IP Security test

/skip:<TestName> Skip the named test. Valid tests are:

- **IpConfig** IP config test

- **Autonet** Autonet address test
- **IpLoopBk** IP loopback ping test
- **DefGw** Default gateway test
- **NbtNm** NetBT name test
- **WINS** WINS service test
- **Winsock** Winsock test
- **DNS** DNS test
- **Browser** Redir and Browser Test
- **DsGetDc** DC discovery test
- **DcList** DC list test
- **Trust** Trust relationship test
- **Kerberos** Kerberos test
- **Ldap** LDAP test
- **Route** Routing table test
- **Netstat** Netstat information test
- **Bindings** Bindings test
- **WAN** WAN configuration test
- **Modem** Modem diagnostics test
- **Netware** Netware test
- **IPX** IPX test
- **IPSec** IP Security test

Below is an example of the output from netdiag.

```
C:\Documents and Settings\Owner>netdiag
. . . . . . . . . . . . . . . . . . . . . . . . . . . . . . .
    Computer Name: KACKIEC
    DNS Host Name: KackieC
    System info : Windows 2000 Professional (Build 2600)
    Processor : x86 Family 6 Model 8 Stepping 0, AuthenticAMD
    List of installed hotfixes :
        KB821557
        KB823559
        KB823980
        Q147222
        Q322011
        Q323255
        Q327979
        Q328310
        Q329048
        Q329115
```

```
                    Q329170
                    Q329390
                    Q329441
                    Q329834
                    Q331953
                    Q810243
                    Q810565
                    Q810577
                    Q810833
                    Q811493
                    Q811630
                    Q814033
                    Q814995
                    Q815021
                    Q815485
                    Q817287
                    Q817606


Netcard queries test . . . . . . . : Passed
    [WARNING] The net card 'RAS Async Adapter' may
not be working because it has not received any packets.
    [WARNING] The net card 'WAN Network Driver' may
not be working because it has not received any packets.
    [WARNING] The net card 'WAN Network Driver - Packet
Scheduler Miniport' may not be working because it has not received
any packets.
    [WARNING] The net card 'VIA Compatable Fast Ethernet
Adapter - Packet Scheduler Miniport' may not be working.
    [WARNING] The net card 'VIA Compatable Fast Ethernet
Adapter' may not be working.
    [WARNING] The net card '1394 Net Adapter' may not
be working because it has not received any packets.


Per interface results:

    Adapter : Local Area Connection 2

        Netcard queries test . . . : Passed

        Host Name. . . . . . . . . : KackieC
        Autoconfiguration IP Address : 169.254.101.152
        Subnet Mask. . . . . . . . : 255.255.0.0
        Default Gateway. . . . . . :
        Dns Servers. . . . . . . . :
        IpConfig results . . . . . : Failed
            Pinging DHCP server  - not reachable
            WARNING: DHCP server may be down.
```

```
            AutoConfiguration results. . . . . . : Failed
                 [WARNING] AutoConfiguration is in use.
DHCP not available.
            Default gateway test . . . : Skipped
                 [WARNING] No gateways defined for this adapter.

            NetBT name test. . . . . . : Passed
                 No remote names have been found.

            WINS service test. . . . . : Skipped
                 There are no WINS servers configured for this
interface.

            Ipx configuration
                 Network Number . . . . : 00000000
                 Node . . . . . . . . . : 00038a000011
                 Frame type . . . . . . : 802.2

    Adapter : Wireless Network Connection 2

            Netcard queries test . . . : Passed

            Host Name. . . . . . . . . : KackieC.attbi.com
            IP Address . . . . . . . . : 192.168.1.106
            Subnet Mask. . . . . . . . : 255.255.255.0
            Default Gateway. . . . . . : 192.168.1.1
            Dns Servers. . . . . . . . : 216.148.227.68
                                         204.127.202.4
            AutoConfiguration results. . . . . . : Passed

            Default gateway test . . . : Passed

            NetBT name test. . . . . . : Passed
                 [WARNING] At least one of the <00>
'WorkStation Service', <03> 'Messenger Service', <20>
'WINS' names is missing.

            WINS service test. . . . . : Skipped
                 There are no WINS servers configured for this
interface.

            Ipx configuration
                 Network Number . . . . : 00000000
                 Node . . . . . . . . . : 00032f02cd4f
                 Frame type . . . . . . : 802.2

    Adapter : Local Area Connection
```

```
                  Netcard queries test . . . : Failed
                  NetCard Status:          DISCONNECTED
                      Some tests will be skipped on this interface.

                  Host Name. . . . . . . . . : KackieC
                  IP Address . . . . . . . . : 0.0.0.0
                  Subnet Mask. . . . . . . . : 0.0.0.0
                  Default Gateway. . . . . . :
                  Dns Servers. . . . . . . . :

                  Ipx configration
                      Network Number . . . . : 00000000
                      Node . . . . . . . . . : 00c09f0b4f4d
                      Frame type . . . . . . : 802.2

           Adapter : IPX Internal Interface

                  Netcard queries test . . . : Passed

                  Ipx configration
                      Network Number . . . . : fd202b1a
                      Node . . . . . . . . . : 000000000001
                      Frame type . . . . . . : Ethernet II

           Adapter : IpxLoopbackAdapter

                  Netcard queries test . . . : Passed

                  Ipx configration
                      Network Number . . . . : fd202b1a
                      Node . . . . . . . . . : 000000000002
                      Frame type . . . . . . : 802.2

           Adapter : NDISWANIPX

                  Netcard queries test . . . : Passed

                  Ipx configration
                      Network Number . . . . : 00000000
                      Node . . . . . . . . . : b23720524153
                      Frame type . . . . . . : Ethernet II

    Global results:

    Domain membership test . . . . . . : Passed
        Dns domain name is not specified.
        Dns forest name is not specified.
```

```
NetBT transports test. . . . . . . : Passed
    List of NetBt transports currently configured:
        NetBT_Tcpip_{F23068E8-B56F-455A-B2C5-817C88DD0321}
        NetBT_Tcpip_{EF710793-E9C7-4C9F-B9F3-D9149BFAB92B}
    2 NetBt transports currently configured.

Autonet address test . . . . . . . : Passed

IP loopback ping test. . . . . . . : Passed

Default gateway test . . . . . . . : Passed

NetBT name test. . . . . . . . . . : Passed

Winsock test . . . . . . . . . . . : Passed

DNS test . . . . . . . . . . . . . : Passed

Redir and Browser test . . . . . . : Passed
    List of NetBt transports currently bound to the Redir
        NetBT_Tcpip_{F23068E8-B56F-455A-B2C5-817C88DD0321}
        NetBT_Tcpip_{EF710793-E9C7-4C9F-B9F3-D9149BFAB92B}
    The redir is bound to 2 NetBt transports.

    List of NetBt transports currently bound to the browser
        NetBT_Tcpip_{F23068E8-B56F-455A-B2C5-817C88DD0321}
        NetBT_Tcpip_{EF710793-E9C7-4C9F-B9F3-D9149BFAB92B}
    The browser is bound to 2 NetBt transports.

DC discovery test. . . . . . . . . : Skipped
DC list test . . . . . . . . . . . : Skipped
Trust relationship test. . . . . . : Skipped
Kerberos test. . . . . . . . . . . : Skipped
LDAP test. . . . . . . . . . . . . : Skipped
Bindings test. . . . . . . . . . . : Passed
WAN configuration test . . . . . . : Skipped
    No active remote access connections.

Modem diagnostics test . . . . . . : Passed
Netware configuration
    You are not logged in to your preferred server .
    Netware User Name. . . . . . . :
    Netware Server Name. . . . . . :
    Netware Tree Name. . . . . . . :
    Netware Workstation Context. . :

IP Security test . . . . . . . . . : Passed
    Service status is: Started
```

```
    Service startup is: Automatic
    IPSec service is available, but no policy is assigned or
active
    Note: run "ipseccmd /?" for more detailed information
The command completed successfully
```

As you can see this provides an extensive amount of configuration detail that can be useful for troubleshooting purposes.

Netsh

Netsh is a built-in text-based console tool that can be used to configure various aspects of Windows XP networking, such as interfaces, protocols, filters, routes, and remote access service. It can even be used to script networking functions and scheduled to run at a specific time with the AT command or the Scheduled Task Wizard. Netsh also lets you save networking configuration information in a text file for backup purposes or for use when configuring other workstations with similar requirements.

Netsh is a command-line interface with a number of different contexts. You'll notice the command prompt changes to netsh plus the current context when you run it. Each context has a variety of commands available within it. The top-level commands are:

..   Goes up one context level.

?   Displays a list of commands.

abort   Discards changes made while in offline mode.

add   Adds a configuration entry to a list of entries.

alias   Adds an alias.

bridge   Changes to the "netsh bridge" context.

bye   Exits the program.

commit   Commits changes made while in offline mode.

delete   Deletes a configuration entry from a list of entries.

diag   Changes to the "netsh diag" context.

dump   Displays a configuration script.

exec   Runs a script file.

exit   Exits the program.

help   Displays a list of commands.

interface   Changes to the "netsh interface" context.

offline   Sets the current mode to offline.

online   Sets the current mode to online.

popd Pops a context from the stack.

pushd Pushes current context on stack.

quit Exits the program.

ras Changes to the "netsh ras" context.

routing Changes to the "netsh routing" context.

set Updates configuration settings.

show Displays information.

unalias Deletes an alias.

The following subcontexts are available:

- bridge
- diag
- interface
- ras
- routing

Netsh allows you to abbreviate the commands—just type the first few characters of the command and press **Enter**. There is no set number of characters that must be typed. You just need to type enough that it is apparent which command you intended, and to distinguish between similar commands.

Below is the output from netsh showing the IP configuration for an adapter.

```
netsh interface ip>show config

Configuration for interface "Wireless Network Connection 2"
    DHCP enabled:                        Yes
    InterfaceMetric:                     0
    DNS servers configured through DHCP: 216.148.227.68
                                         204.127.202.4
    WINS servers configured through DHCP: None
    Register with which suffix:          Primary only

Configuration for interface "Local Area Connection 2"
    DHCP enabled:                        Yes
    InterfaceMetric:                     0
    DNS servers configured through DHCP: None
    WINS servers configured through DHCP: None
    Register with which suffix:          Primary only

Configuration for interface "Local Area Connection"
    DHCP enabled:                        Yes
    InterfaceMetric:                     0
    DNS servers configured through DHCP: None
```

```
        WINS servers configured through DHCP: None
        Register with which suffix:           Primary only


netsh interface ip>show interface


MIB-II Interface Information
--------------------------------------------------------
Index:                               1
User-friendly Name:                  Loopback
GUID Name:                           Loopback
Type:                                Loopback
MTU:                                 32768
Speed:                               10000000
Physical Address:
Admin Status:                        Up
Operational Status:                  Operational
Last Change:                         0
In Octets:                           0
In Unicast Packets:                  0
In Non-unicast Packets:              0
In Packets Discarded:                0
In Erroneous Packets:                0
In Unknown Protocol Packets:         0
Out Octets:                          0
Out Unicast Packets:                 0
Out Non-unicast Packets:             0
Out Packets Discarded:               0
Out Erroneous Packets:               0
Output Queue Length:                 0
Description:                         Internal loopback
                                     interface for 127.0.0 network


Index:                               2
User-friendly Name:                  Wireless Network Connection 2
GUID Name:                           {EF710793-E9C7-4C9F-B9F3-
                                       D9149BFAB92B}
Type:                                Ethernet
MTU:                                 1500
Speed:                               11000000
Physical Address:                    00-03-2F-02-CD-4F
Admin Status:                        Up
Operational Status:                  Operational
Last Change:                         3384798204
In Octets:                           43104480
In Unicast Packets:                  62065
In Non-unicast Packets:              17851
In Packets Discarded:                0
In Erroneous Packets:                0
```

```
In Unknown Protocol Packets:        922
Out Octets:                         11318417
Out Unicast Packets:                57495
Out Non-unicast Packets:            899
Out Packets Discarded:              0
Out Erroneous Packets:              12
Output Queue Length:                0
Description:                        Linksys WPC11 Instant
                                    Wireless Network PC Card -
                                    Packet Scheduler Miniport


Index:                              3
User-friendly Name:                 Local Area Connection 2
GUID Name:                          {F23068E8-B56F-455A-B2C5-
                                    817C88DD0321}
Type:                               Ethernet
MTU:                                1000
Speed:                              10000000
Physical Address:                   00-03-8A-00-00-11
Admin Status:                       Up
Operational Status:                 Operational
Last Change:                        3381668925
In Octets:                          433359
In Unicast Packets:                 0
In Non-unicast Packets:             3312
In Packets Discarded:               0
In Erroneous Packets:               0
In Unknown Protocol Packets:        63
Out Octets:                         476309
Out Unicast Packets:                0
Out Non-unicast Packets:            3332
Out Packets Discarded:              0
Out Erroneous Packets:              0
Output Queue Length:                0
Description:                        WAN Network Driver -
                                    Packet Scheduler Miniport


Index:                              4
User-friendly Name:                 Local Area Connection
GUID Name:                          {C5C326A6-5FF7-449C-83FA-
                                    FDEDD1492B87}
Type:                               Ethernet
MTU:                                1500
Speed:                              10000000
Physical Address:                   00-C0-9F-0B-4F-4D
Admin Status:                       Up
Operational Status:                 Non Operational
Last Change:                        3381668926
In Octets:                          3532
```

```
In Unicast Packets:                    0
In Non-unicast Packets:                0
In Packets Discarded:                  0
In Erroneous Packets:                  0
In Unknown Protocol Packets:           46
Out Octets:                            0
Out Unicast Packets:                   0
Out Non-unicast Packets:               0
Out Packets Discarded:                 0
Out Erroneous Packets:                 0
Output Queue Length:                   0
Description:                           VIA Compatable Fast Ethernet
                                       Adapter - Packet Scheduler Miniport
```

Pathping

Pathing ping combines components of ping and tracert and adds additional functionality to create a single tool for troubleshooting routing or networking problems. It works by sending packets to each router between the source and destination computers over a period of time. It displays the level of packet loss at each router, which can then be used for troubleshooting or isolating a connectivity problem.

Usage: pathping [-g host-list] [-h maximum_hops] [-i address] [-n] [-p period] [-q num_queries] [-w timeout] [-P] [-R] [-T] [-4] [-6] target_name

Options:

-g host-list   Loose source route along host-list.

-h maximum_hops   Maximum number of hops to search for target.

-i address   Use the specified source address.

-n   Do not resolve addresses to hostnames.

-p period   Wait period milliseconds between pings.

-q num_queries   Number of queries per hop.

-w timeout   Wait timeout milliseconds for each reply.

-P   Test for RSVP PATH connectivity.

-R   Test if each hop is RSVP aware.

-T   Test connectivity to each hop with Layer-2 priority tags.

-4   Force using IPv4.

-6   Force using IPv6.

Below is an example of a pathping to yahoo.com:

```
C:\Documents and Settings\Owner>pathping yahoo.com

Tracing route to yahoo.com [66.218.71.198]
over a maximum of 30 hops:
  0  KackieC.attbi.com [192.168.1.106]
  1  10.150.128.1
  2  12.244.98.209
  3  12.244.67.17
  4  12.244.72.206
  5  gbr1-p70.sffca.ip.att.net [12.123.13.58]
  6  tbr1-p012402.sffca.ip.att.net [12.122.11.65]
  7  ggr2-p300.sffca.ip.att.net [12.123.13.190]
  8  so-1-1-0.edge1.SanJose1.Level3.net [209.0.227.29]
  9  so-5-0-0.gar1.SanJose1.level3.net [209.244.3.137]
 10  gige9-1.ipcolo3.SanJose1.Level3.net [64.159.2.73]
 11  unknown.Level3.net [64.152.69.30]
 12  w1.rc.vip.scd.yahoo.com [66.218.71.198]

Computing statistics for 300 seconds...
                Source to Here   This Node/Link
Hop  RTT    Lost/Sent = Pct    Lost/Sent = Pct  Address
  0      KackieC.attbi.com [192.168.1.106]
                                 0/ 100 =   0%   |
  1   16ms     0/ 100 =   0%     0/ 100 =   0%   10.150.128.1
                                 0/ 100 =   0%   |
  2   18ms     0/ 100 =   0%     0/ 100 =   0%   12.244.98.209
                                 0/ 100 =   0%   |
  3   18ms     0/ 100 =   0%     0/ 100 =   0%   12.244.67.17
                                 0/ 100 =   0%   |
  4   28ms     0/ 100 =   0%     0/ 100 =   0%   12.244.72.206
                                 0/ 100 =   0%   |
  5   ---    100/ 100 =100%    100/ 100 =100%
gbr1-p70.sffca.ip.att.net [12.123.13.58]
                                 0/ 100 =   0%   |
  6   ---    100/ 100 =100%    100/ 100 =100%
tbr1-p012402.sffca.ip.att.net [12.122.11.65]
                                 0/ 100 =   0%   |
  7   ---    100/ 100 =100%    100/ 100 =100%
ggr2-p300.sffca.ip.att.net [12.123.13.190]
                                 0/ 100 =   0%   |
  8   30ms     0/ 100 =   0%     0/ 100 =   0%
so-1-1-0.edge1.SanJose1.Level3.net [209.0.227.29]
                                 0/ 100 =   0%   |
  9   25ms     0/ 100 =   0%     0/ 100 =   0%
so-5-0-0.gar1.SanJose1.level3.net [209.244.3.137]
                                 1/ 100 =   1%   |
```

```
   10    27ms       1/ 100 =   1%       0/ 100 =   0%
gige9-1.ipcolo3.SanJose1.Level3.net [64.159.2.73]
                                       0/ 100 =   0%    |
   11    34ms       1/ 100 =   1%       0/ 100 =   0%
unknown.Level3.net [64.152.69.30]
                                       0/ 100 =   0%    |
   12    31ms       1/ 100 =   1%       0/ 100 =   0%
w1.rc.vip.scd.yahoo.com [66.218.71.198]

Trace complete.
```

By determining where packet loss and latency is greatest, you can narrow down the focus of your troubleshooting.

General Management

ACL Diagnostics

The AclDiag tool alerts you to discrepancies in the Access Control Lists (ACLs) of objects in Active Directory. With AclDiag, you can display, compare, and reapply if necessary, inheritance, audit, and permissions settings of an object when the Active Directory is used. It is included with the Windows XP Support Tools. To install the Support Tools, run Setup.exe from the Support\Tools folder on the Windows XP CD-ROM.

> *Usage:* acldiag <Object DN> [/schema] [/chkdeleg] [/geteffective:<User/Group>] [/fixdeleg] [/cdo]
>
> *Options:*
>
> **/schema**   Checks if the security on the object includes schema defaults.
>
> **/chkdeleg**   Checks if the security on the object includes any of the delegation templates currently in use by the Delegation Wizard.
>
> **/geteffective:<User/Group>**   Prints out various permissions of specified user/group in a readable format. You can specify a \"*\" for <User/Group>. It will print the effective rights of all users and groups that show up in the ACL.
>
> **/cdo**   Output a comma-delimited output instead of readable format. This is useful when loading the information into databases or spreadsheets.
>
> **/skip**   Do not display the security description.
>
> **/fixdeleg**   Fix any delegations that have been applied to the object by the Delegation of Control wizard.

Application Deployment Diagnosis

Addiag.exe displays information about software installed or available for installation on a computer managed by IntelliMirror, such as current user, logon credentials, and SID, if Terminal Server and Windows installer information are running.

Usage: addiag [/verbose:[TRUE|FALSE]][/user:[TRUE|FALSE]] [/trace:<string>][/test:<string_list>][/debug:<ulong>] [/?:[TRUE|FALSE]]

Options:

/verbose   Flag specifying if diagnostics are to be run in verbose mode (Extra Info). It defaults to FALSE.

/user   Flag specifying if diagnostics are to be run for user (TRUE)/computer (FALSE). It defaults to TRUE.

/trace   Takes a string specifying what system tracing should be turned on or off. The value must be between 1 and 260 characters in length and can be one of the following:

- AppMgmtOn
- AppMgmtOff
- CStoreOn
- CStoreOff
- MSIOn
- MSIOff
- UserEnvOn
- UserEnvOff

/test   Takes a list of strings specifying the list of diagnostics to be run. Legal values are a combination of:

- **<Info>**   Dumps general information
- **<TS>**   Dumps TS information
- **<LocalApps>**   Dumps local managed applications list
- **<ServerApps>**   Dumps server deployed applications list
- **<MSIApps>**   Dumps local MSI applications list
- **<GPOList>**   Dumps local GPO list
- **<ScriptList>**   Dumps local script application list
- **<ADHistory>**   Dumps local AD policy history
- **<MSIFeatures>**   Dumps local MSI features list
- **<MSILnks>**   Dumps MSI shortcuts in the profile
- **<EventDump>**   Dumps application log-related events
- **<Check>**   Performs AD integrity check

/debug   Takes an unsigned long specifying the trace level (debug only).

/?   Flag specifying command line usage. It defaults to FALSE.

Dependency Walker

Depends.exe is useful for discovering dependencies within applications. This can significantly ease the pain associated with trying to figure out why an application does not start up properly. It displays the minimum set of required files along with detailed information about each file including a full path to the file, base address, version numbers, computer type, debug information, and so on as shown in Figure A.1.

Depends.exe is included with the Windows XP Support Tools. To install the Support Tools, run Setup.exe from the Support\Tools folder on the Windows XP CD-ROM.

Distributed File System Utility

Dfsutil.exe enables administrators to perform maintenance of the Microsoft Distributed File System (DFS) from the command prompt. It is included with the Windows XP Support Tools. To install the Support Tools, run Setup.exe from the Support\Tools folder on the Windows XP CD-ROM.

Usage: dfsutil [/OPTIONS]

/?   Usage information

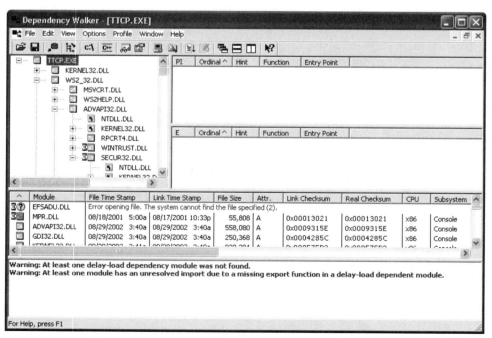

Figure A.1   Output of the dependency walker utility.

/ADDSTDROOT:<DfsName> /SERVER:<ServerName>
/SHARE:<ShareName>
/ADDDOMROOT:<DfsName> /SERVER:<ServerName>
/SHARE:<ShareName>
/REMROOT:<DfsName> /SERVER:<ServerName> /SHARE:<Share-Name>

Client-side switches:

- **/PKTFLUSH**   Flush the local DFS cached information.
- **/SPCFLUSH**   Flush the local DFS cached information.
- **/PKTINFO [/LEVEL:<Level>]**   Show DFS internal information.
- **/SPCINFO**   Show DFS internal information.

Console Utilities

Tired of scrambling around trying to build MMC consoles with all the right tools on one workstation, only to have to build them again on another workstation? Annoyed that you have to jump through hoops to find administrative tools that were much more easily accessible in Windows NT 4.0? Here is a list of commonly used console utilities and the command line you type in to access each one. No more trying to find the right plug-in for the right task that you want to perform! Just go to **Start**, then **Run**, and enter the appropriate command. Alternatively, you can type these in at a command prompt. (See Table A.2)

Registry Editor

Regedit.exe is the GUI registry editor, but reg.exe allows you to edit the registry from the command line. Editing the registry is a dangerous thing and doing it at a command line is even riskier. Another drawback is that you need to know specifically which key you want to access, because there is no way to browse to it at the command line, and using the query command to display keys is really time-consuming. However, this could come in handy if you need to script a number of changes for a large group of computers. It is also useful for checking, comparing, or copying registry information.

Usage: REG operation [Parameter List]
Options: [QUERY | ADD | DELETE | COPY | SAVE |
LOAD | UNLOAD | :RESTORE | COMPARE | EXPORT | IMPORT]

Table A.2 Console Utilities

Console Name	Description	Command
Certificates console	The Certificates console allows you to browse the contents of the certificate stores for yourself, a service, or a computer.	`certmgr.msc`
Computer Management console	The Computer Management console provides an integrated console window for a number of management functions related to the local system.	`compmgmt.msc`
Device Management console	Device Manager displays a list of hardware devices installed on the local computer. You can view and/or set properties for each device in this console.	`devmgmt.msc`
Disk Defragmenter console	Use the Disk Defragmenter to optimize disk space utilization.	`dfrg.msc`
Disk Management console	Disk Management is used to manage the logical disks and partitions on a Windows XP system.	`diskmgmt.msc`
Event Viewer console	Event Viewer displays a variety of system logs, including security, system, and application logs.	`eventvwr.msc`
Group Policy console	The Group Policy console enables management of group policies.	`Gpedit.msc`
Indexing console	The Indexing console provides fast and flexible searching on file contents and properties.	`ciadv.msc`
Local Users and Groups console	Enables management of local users and group accounts. Only available on Windows XP Professional.	`lusrmgr.msc`
Performance Monitor console	Performance Monitor enables tracking, graphing, and reporting of various system performance counters within Windows XP.	`perfmon.msc`
Removable Storage console	Catalogs removable media and manages automated libraries.	`ntmsmgr.msc`
Removable Storage Operator Requests console	Provides a frameless view for catalogs of removable media and management of automated libraries.	`ntmsoprq.msc`
Services console	Permits viewing and management of Windows XP services.	`services.msc`
Shared Folders console	The Shared Folders console enables management of shared folders, sessions, and open files.	`fsmgmt.msc`
Windows Management Infrastructure console	Configures and controls the Windows Management Instrumentation service.	`wmimgmt.msc`

Sample output from a query of a registry key is below.

```
C:\Documents and Settings\Owner>reg query hklm\system
\currentcontrolset\services
\tcpip\parameters

! REG.EXE VERSION 3.0

HKEY_LOCAL_MACHINE\system\currentcontrolset\services\
tcpip\parameters
    NV Hostname REG_SZ   KackieC
    DataBasePath         REG_EXPAND_SZ
%SystemRoot%\System32\drivers\etc
    NameServer  REG_SZ
    ForwardBroadcasts   REG_DWORD        0x0
    IPEnableRouter      REG_DWORD        0x0
    Domain       REG_SZ
    Hostname     REG_SZ  KackieC
    SearchList   REG_SZ
    UseDomainNameDevolution   REG_DWORD        0x1
    EnableICMPRedirect  REG_DWORD        0x1
    DeadGWDetectDefault REG_DWORD        0x1
    DontAddDefaultGatewayDefault   REG_DWORD       0x0
    EnableSecurityFilters   REG_DWORD        0x0
    TcpWindowSize   REG_DWORD        0x6270
    DhcpDomain   REG_SZ  attbi.com
    DhcpNameServer       REG_SZ  216.148.227.68 204.127.202.4

HKEY_LOCAL_MACHINE\system\currentcontrolset\services\
tcpip\parameters\Adapters

HKEY_LOCAL_MACHINE\system\currentcontrolset\services\
tcpip\parameters\DNSRegisteredAdapters

HKEY_LOCAL_MACHINE\system\currentcontrolset\services\
tcpip\parameters\Interfaces

HKEY_LOCAL_MACHINE\system\currentcontrolset\services\
tcpip\parameters\PersistentRoutes

HKEY_LOCAL_MACHINE\system\currentcontrolset\services\
tcpip\parameters\Winsock
```

Service Pack 1a

At the time this book was written the most current service pack for Windows XP was Service Pack 1a (SP1a). This service pack offers a rollup of hotfixes previously available, as well as updates Windows XP functionality above and beyond what was available in Service Pack 1. For a complete list of fixes included in SP1, see *http://support.microsoft.com/support/ServicePacks/Windows/ XP/SP1FixList.asp.* To obtain SP1a, visit *http://www.microsoft.com/windowsxp/ pro/downloads/servicepacks/sp1/default.asp* to download it.

Service packs are notorious for breaking things that worked just fine prior to the installation. For that reason it is important to test thoroughly before applying any service packs to a machine that is mission critical. Some administrators prefer to apply hotfixes as they are released, so that they can determine what specifically "broke" something on a computer. However, if you have users that have Windows Update running and you do not have policies in place to prevent them from doing these updates themselves, you may be unable to control how and when hotfixes are installed.

Service packs are not all bad, however. They often provide new functionality that is not otherwise available for a given operating system. Additionally, if you load a fresh copy of an OS on a computer, it is much easier to install the latest and greatest service pack plus a few patches than to download 50 or more hotfixes all at once and install them one at a time. It is possible to install multiple hotfixes with a single reboot, but each executable file must still be kicked off. Not a lot of fun when you have over 50 to install!

Index

inform**IT**

www.informit.com

YOUR GUIDE TO IT REFERENCE

Articles

Keep your edge with thousands of free articles, in-depth features, interviews, and IT reference recommendations – all written by experts you know and trust.

Online Books

Answers in an instant from **InformIT Online Book's** 600+ fully searchable on line books. For a limited time, you can get your first 14 days **free**.

POWERED BY
Safari®
TECH BOOKS ONLINE®

Catalog

Review online sample chapters, author biographies and customer rankings and choose exactly the right book from a selection of over 5,000 titles.